Resolving Mass Disputes

Resolving Mass Disputes

ADR and Settlement of Mass Claims

Edited by

Christopher Hodges

Centre for Socio-Legal Studies, Oxford, UK; Erasmus University Rotterdam, the Netherlands

Astrid Stadler

University of Konstanz, Germany; Erasmus University Rotterdam, the Netherlands

Edward Elgar

Cheltenham, UK • Northampton, MA, USA

Published by
Edward Elgar Publishing Limited
The Lypiatts
15 Lansdown Road
Cheltenham
Glos GL50 2JA
UK

Edward Elgar Publishing, Inc.
William Pratt House
9 Dewey Court
Northampton
Massachusetts 01060
USA

A catalogue record for this book
is available from the British Library

Library of Congress Control Number: 2013943236

This book is available electronically in the ElgarOnline.com
Law Subject Collection, E-ISBN 978 1 78254 691 7

MIX
Paper from responsible sources
FSC® C013056

ISBN 978 1 78254 690 0

Typeset by Servis Filmsetting Ltd, Stockport, Cheshire
Printed and bound in Great Britain by T.J. International Ltd, Padstow

Contents

Figures, tables and boxes

FIGURE

TABLES

BOX

Contributors

Iris Benöhr, PhD, British Academy Postdoctoral Fellow, Centre for Socio-Legal Studies, University of Oxford Law Faculty, University of Oxford, UK.

Naomi Creutzfeldt, PhD, ESRC Research Fellow, Centre for Socio-Legal Studies, University of Oxford, UK.

Michael Faure, PhD, Professor of Comparative Private Law and Economics, Erasmus University, Rotterdam; Professor of Comparative and International Environmental Law, Maastricht University, The Netherlands.

Liao Haiqing, Graduate student majoring in civil procedure law, Fudan University Shanghai, PR China.

Deborah R. Hensler, PhD, Judge John W. Ford Professor of Dispute Resolution, Stanford University, California; former Director of RAND Corporation Institute for Civil Justice, USA.

Christopher Hodges, PhD, Head of the CMS/Swiss Research Programme on Civil Justice Systems, Centre for Socio-Legal Studies, University of Oxford, UK; Erasmus Professor of the Fundamentals of Private Law, Erasmus University, Rotterdam, The Netherlands; Solicitor of the Senior Courts of England and Wales.

Julia Hörnle, PhD, Professor in Internet Law, Queen Mary, University of London, UK.

Jasminka Kalajdzic, LLB, LLM (Toronto), Associate Professor of Law, University of Windsor, Canada.

Xandra E. Kramer, Professor of Law, PhD, Chair in European Civil Procedure, Erasmus University, Rotterdam; Deputy Judge District Court Rotterdam, The Netherlands.

Michael Legg, LLB (UNSW), LLM (UC Berkeley), Associate Professor, Faculty of Law, University of New South Wales, Australia.

Richard Marcus, Distinguished Professor of Law, Horace O. Coil ('57) Chair in Litigation, University of California, Hastings, USA.

Astrid Stadler, PhD, Professor of Law, Chair in Private Law, Civil Procedure Law, Comparative Law and Private International Law, University of Konstanz, Germany; Chair in Comparative Mass Litigation, Erasmus University, Rotterdam, The Netherlands.

Ianika Tzankova, PhD, Chair on Mass Claim Dispute Resolution, Tilburg University; Partner of BarentsKrans, Den Haag, The Netherlands.

Stefaan Voet, PhD, Doctoral Research and Teaching Assistant at the Institute for Procedural Law, Ghent University, and Attorney at the Bar of Bruges. JD, Ghent University Law School, Belgium.

Zhang Wusheng, PhD, Professor of Law, Fudan University Shanghai, PR China.

Table of cases

UNITED KINGDOM

EUROPEAN

European Court of Justice

INTERNATIONAL

Australia

Canada

1. Introduction

Christopher Hodges and Astrid Stadler

I. GENERAL SCOPE OF THE CONTRIBUTIONS

Mass litigation is on the reform agenda across Europe and the legislative landscape has changed impressively in recent years. Many aspects of collective redress litigation, particularly the comparative and international perspective, have been highlighted in various publications recently.[1] Most of them have a focus on the political context such as whether to strengthen private or public enforcement of consumer and/or competition law or on questions raised in the context of contentious litigation, such as how to design procedural instruments effectively, or how to handle cross-border multiparty cases. The focal point of the contributions in this book is a different one. We take as a starting-point the observation that mass claims are a "nuisance" for both parties and courts. Preventing contentious litigation and encouraging parties to settle disputes is particularly important for mass claims. Therefore the contributions are about new ways of settling mass disputes.

Whereas there is vast experience and plenty of case law on settlements

[1] The number of articles in legal periodicals has become almost uncountable. For books on mass litigation see, for example, Duncan Fairgrieve and Eva Lein, *Extraterritoriality and Collective Redress* (Oxford University Press 2012); *Procesos Colectivos – Class actions, I Conferencia Internacional y XXIII Jornadas Iberoamericanas de Derecho Procesal*, IAPL et al (Buenos Aires 2012); Jenny Steele and Willem van Boom (eds), *Mass Justice – Challenges of Representation and Distribution* (Edward Elgar 2011); Christopher Hodges, Stefan Vogenauer and Magdalena Tulibacka, *The Costs and Funding of Civil Litigation – A Comparative Perspective* (Oxford 2010); Fabrizzio Cafaggi and Hans-W Micklitz, *New Frontiers of Consumer Protection – The Interplay between Private and Public Enforcement* (Intersentia 2009); Matthias Casper, Nils Janssen, Petra Pohlmann and Reiner Schulze (eds), *Auf dem Weg zu einer europäischen Sammelklage* (Sellier 2009); Rachael Mulheron, *Reform of Collective Redress in England and Wales*, Research Paper, 97 <www.civijusticecouncil.gov.uk>; Christopher Hodges, *The Reform of Class and Representative Actions in European Legal Systems: A New Framework for Collective Redress in Europe* (Hart 2008).

in the classic class action countries like the USA, Canada and Australia, for many courts in Europe mass disputes and settlement approval are a completely new terrain. Notably the US class action system has repeatedly refined its rules, enhanced the court's managerial role and made considerable efforts to minimize the risks typical of class actions.[2] Within Europe, the Dutch Mass Settlement Act of 2005 (Wet collectieve afwikkeling massaschade, WCAM) is unique and very interesting. It is an excellent example of how courts struggle to find standards and instruments to improve settlement proceedings. But people also look for alternatives to court pathways. One of the most significant alternatives that has been identified in the EU is the "new world" of consumer dispute resolution. This has been developing quietly in some Member States for 40 years, but has only recently come into the full glare of the EU policy spotlight. The mechanisms and implications need urgently to be examined.

It is well known that the majority of mass claims in whichever mechanism you look at, whether courts or Consumer Alternative Dispute Resolution (CDR), are settled – a need which has confronted people and courts, partly as a result of the cost of litigation. This has long been understood in the context of litigation – certainly in common law jurisdictions, although less so traditionally in more efficient civil procedure systems like Germany, but now given increased momentum in Europe through the implementation of the EU Mediation Directive into all Member States' civil procedures.[3] In the new world of CDR, research has recently shown how important settlement through mediation etc. is in that context also, where it applies to the majority of claims in many CDR systems. ADR/CDR systems and settlements both help to unburden the court system and are arguably the best way of satisfying the parties.

With respect to the US class action system, experience shows that once a mass litigation has got off the ground (e.g. beyond the certification stage) there is a high probability of it being settled before trial.[4] The contributions in this book demonstrate that there is not only a very similar tendency in

---

[2] Hannah Buxbaum, *Class Actions, Conflict and Global Economy, Liber amicorum Rolf Stürner* (Tübingen 2013) vol 2, 1443, 1450, who strongly argues that European legislatures and scholars should be more open-minded and learn from the US class action system instead of rejecting it completely.

[3] Directive 2008/52/EC of 21 May 2008 on certain aspects of mediation in civil and commercial matters.

[4] For Canada, Jasminka Kalajdzic indicates in her contribution (p. 134) a settlement rate of 96 per cent in (certified) class actions although approximately one-quarter of all proposed class actions are not certified. There is, however, a diversity of opinions with respect to the blackmailing effect of class action in the US and Canada, Kalajdzic Chapter 6, p. 134.

the other major class action jurisdictions of Australia and Canada, but that one can also see similar issues arising all around the globe. So we are delighted that colleagues from Europe, the USA, Canada, Australia and China have agreed to contribute to this book. Their contributions all point towards an international convergence of the importance of settlements, mediation and ADR. It is a global observation that if court claims, especially mass or collective procedures, present a problem in a jurisdiction, it will start to look at promoting settlement.

We have also decided to include a chapter on the development in China, since it illustrates clearly how the same ideas of ADR and settlement prosper in what is – at first glance – a completely different system. The Chinese legal system has undergone an impressive reform process since the 1990s and we can observe that new regulations have adopted elements from both the 19th-century roots of Chinese civil law in continental Europe[5] and from modern US law. Based on a combination of these elements with traditional and new Chinese approaches a completely new autonomous civil law system is emerging. With respect to mass claims, the PRC Code of Civil Procedure has more or less adopted the US class action idea (Sec. 54[6]), but civil courts are very much afraid to use these instruments and to admit mass claims.[7] As the contribution of Zhang Wusheng explains, courts have found ways to evade the rules on representative proceedings but, owing to the political influence of defendants there is not always an independent exercise of judicial powers. In academic circles, the question whether China should rely on the US class action system is a highly controversial one. Some scholars fear a litigation culture and favour European approaches like reducing the potential of group disputes by a comprehensive social security system, and by redirecting mass claims

---

5 A draft for a Chinese Civil Code prepared in the late Qing Dynasty (1644–1911) closely followed the Roman Pandects and adopted more or less the German Civil Code (enacted in 1900), but the draft never came into force. The first modern Chinese Civil Code to be enacted at least for some years was based on this draft. It was developed from 1929 to 1931 and was also strongly influenced by Japanese, German and Swiss law. However, the laws enacted in the Republic of China were abrogated by the People's Republic of China from 1949.

6 A recent revision of China's Civil Procedure Code (originally enacted in 1991) came into force on 1 January 2013. The two provisions dealing with mass claims (now Articles 53 and 54, formerly Articles 54 and 55) were already implemented with a first revision in 2007. Because of a new article on "public interest litigation" added by the 2013 reform the number of the articles changed.

7 Wusheng Zhang, 'Analysis and Introduction of the US Class Action in China' (2009) 14 *Zeitschrift für Zivilprozess* 371.

to alternative dispute resolution mechanisms.[8] Last but not least, based on a revival of Confucian ethical values, the government emphasizes the role of courts and authorities (which are formally separated but still not strictly independent of each other) as arbitrators.[9] Court-based mediation has always been a key principle of the Chinese civil justice system, but was pushed aside in favour of adjudication during the 1980s.[10] Since the early 2000s, however, there has been growing pressure on judges to settle disputes[11] and their careers depend very much on their success in settling cases. In China, preventing contentious litigation is particularly important for mass disputes. Since the government fears that allowing mass claims before civil courts might seriously endanger social harmony and stability, it has a strong interest in either mediation[12] or settlements.[13] As a consequence they are also starting to look very closely at ADR systems based on the EU model,[14] and also at how public regulators and criminal courts can be used to deliver restoration and compensation.

Unsurprisingly all these aspects intertwine. CDR and Online Dispute Resolution (ODR) have obvious attractions as the way out of the political dilemma over collective redress at the European level. Since the Commission is not able to come forward with a proposal for a harmonized model of collective redress mechanisms, other than general principles, the focus has shifted to ADR, CDR and mediation. The 2012 resolution of the European Parliament on the Commission's consultation paper emphasized

---

8 Yu Fan, *Group Litigation: About its Problems of System and Practice* (Peking University Press 2005), 428.

9 Gao Xujun, 'Konfuzianisums und die Rechtsordnung Chinas' in Uwe Kischel and Christian Kirchner (eds), *Ideologie und Weltanschauung im Recht* (Mohr Siebeck 2012) 23, 43.

10 Fu Hualing and Richard Cullen, 'From Mediatory to Adjudicatory Justice: The Limits of Civil Justice Reform in China' in Margaret Woo and Mary E Gallagher, *Chinese Justice – Civil Dispute Resolution in Contemporary China* (Cambridge University Press 2011), 33.

11 Margaret Woo and Mary E Gallagher, 'Introduction' in Margaret Woo and Mary E Gallagher (supra note 10), 8; Fu Hualing and Richard Cullen (supra note 10), 48–53; Astrid Stadler and Zhang Dahai, 'Kollektiver Rechtsschutz und Klagen im öffentlichen Interesse in China nach der Zivilprozessrechtsreform 2012' (2013) *Recht der Internationalen Wirtschaft* (forthcoming April/May).

12 Fu Hualing and Richard Cullen (supra note 10), 25.

13 Yuanshi Bu, 'Gestalten, Schlichten, Richten oder Abweisen, Gegenwärtige Reformströmungen im Lichte der anstehenden Novelle des Zivilprozessrechts in China' (2010) 15 *Zeitschrift für Zivilprozess International* 359.

14 For a similar tendency in Japan cf Motoko Yoshida, 'Promoting the Use of Mediation: Approach from the Legal and Economic Perspective' (2010) 15 *Zeitschrift für Zivilprozess International* 415.

that ADR and ODR are necessary, but they are an even more attractive option for the business sector if consumers can eventually resort to collective court proceedings.[15] In this respect the Netherlands is a very good example of a "mixed approach". The Dutch WCAM is quite successful and helps consumers and investors to obtain compensation without burdening the court system with lengthy proceedings, whilst the *Geschillencommissie* system quietly processes many individual and collective claims.

Since litigation cannot be prevented by ADR or mediation in all cases, it becomes extremely important to look at the possibility of mass settlements. If we consider both mechanisms (ADR and settlements) with respect to their effects of unburdening the judicial system from mass claims, it seems necessary to scrutinize the existing experience in the US, Canada and other countries with mass settlements. Although the process of negotiating mass settlements would also be extremely interesting to analyse in detail, the chapters in the first part of the book have a different focus. They will look at the role of courts with respect to settlements and their approval. As courts – for very good reasons – have the obligation to approve mass settlements[16] it is worth taking into account how they cope with that task and how meticulously they look at the merits of the claims.

The second part of the book looks at one of the major alternatives to courts that have emerged onto the European scene for the resolution of consumer disputes, and in which settlement plays an important and intrinsic role. The phenomenon of CDR is clearly a highly significant development, both in its own right and in relation to its impact on pre-existing concepts, structures and practice, i.e. on justice, access to justice, and the need for courts and lawyers. The issues with CDR are summarized further at the end of this chapter. Both parts of the book are preceded by Michael Faure's chapter providing an observation of CDR and mass settlements from an economic perspective. It analyses risk aversion and rational apathy of consumers, but also points out that utility-maximizing attorneys and judges may jeopardize efficient mass settlements and resolution of consumer claims.

It is significant that the European Commission's 2013 Recommendation on collective redress puts forward common principles for *both* judicial and

---

[15] European Parliament (P7 TA [2012] 0021, 2 February 2012 <www.europarl.europa.eu/sides/getDoc.do?pubRef=-//EP//TEXT+TA+P7-TA-2012-0021+0+DOC+XML+V0//EN)>.

[16] For example, Rule 23 (e) (3) Federal Rules of Civil Procedure (FRCP); Sec 33 V Federal Court of Australia Act 1976 (Cth); Art 7:907 Dutch Civil Code.

out-of-court procedures, and applicable equally to each method.[17] It also specifies that "Member States should ensure that the parties to a dispute in a mass harm situation are encouraged to settle the dispute consensually or out-of-court, both at the pre-trial stage and during civil trial".[18] This policy decision confirms not only the equally importance attached to ADR as to judicial dispute resolution procedures, but also the importance of settlement whichever procedure may be used.

We mentioned above that ADR/CDR/ODR is not the only technique to which governments are turning to resolve disputes. We may see innovation appearing in various forms and, indeed, in various combinations of techniques. In this volume, Stefaan Voet outlines developments in Belgium in the separate but related areas not just of the "piggyback" technique by which individual claimants may become civil parties to criminal proceedings and be awarded compensation for their losses at the end of the criminal process, but also the exciting Belmed CDR portal. Voet notes that the criminal-piggyback technique is available in various European jurisdictions, but it is only when (as in Belgium and the UK) it is mandatory for courts to address "private" compensation that it appears to have been used. The examples cited certainly appear to have been effective, and relatively efficient. The criminal-piggyback approach is similar in function to the approach found in Denmark and the UK where consumer or sectoral regulators have been given powers to facilitate, seek a court order for, or themselves order, companies to pay compensation to those whom they have harmed, as part of standard enforcement activity.[19]

Another important example of effective combining of techniques is the developing relationship between ombudsmen and regulators, exemplified in the UK. A new trend in disputes, or conduct that is illegal or at least questionable, might be picked up by either an ombudsman or a regulator from the data that comes to them. Any issue of legality can then be resolved (by the regulator or the courts) and implemented in resolution of disputes by the ombudsmen or courts, or voluntarily by the sector's traders, perhaps under the influence or compulsion of regulatory powers.

---

17 Commission Recommendation of 11 June 2013 on common principles for injunctive and compensatory collective redress mechanisms in the Member States concerning violations of rights granted under Union Law, C(2013) 3539/3, recital 13 and paras 25–28.

18 Ibid para 25.

19 See Christopher Hodges, *The Reform of Class and Representative Actions in European Legal Systems: A New Framework for Collective Redress in Europe* (Hart 2008).

II. SETTLEMENT OF MASS DISPUTES

1. Mass Settlements – Two Sides of the Coin

Implementing new instruments of collective redress is a great challenge for legislatures since it requires finding a balance between the efficient administration of the "mass" and the protection of fundamental individual rights. This becomes particularly difficult if the instruments are not only designed to provide a remedy against trivial, albeit widespread (consumer) damages, but also for the enforcement of "regular" damages of consumers or investors. Procedural efficiency will often not allow courts to scrutinize each individual claim, even if the cases are brought together in whatever type of collective instrument. Claimants in mass disputes therefore regularly face the risk that both their procedural rights in participating in the litigation and their claims under substantive law will be curtailed in order to handle the case in due time. Furthermore, in many "big" cases of product or pharmaceutical liability, at least in the USA[20], defendants face bankruptcy in view of the aggregate amount of damages. As a consequence claimants in mass litigation must often be aware that even in case of a judgment in favour of the class or group they will probably not receive the full amount of damages they could claim from a strict perspective of substantive law. Therefore for a number of good reasons parties to a mass litigation often prefer to settle the dispute. Tort victims, consumers and investors may benefit from a settlement. Even though accepting a reduction of their claims they can expect at least compensation in part, but in the foreseeable future, and without lengthy execution proceedings against the defendant. Settlement also offers the chance of avoiding the risk of being left behind as unsecured insolvency creditors of the defendant company. Individual lawsuits will rarely offer better chances.

Corporate defendants also often prefer settlements to long-lasting court proceedings albeit for slightly different reasons. The usual advantages, such as the avoidance of litigation costs and the uncertainty of the outcome of litigation, apply for them as well. Furthermore, the prospective damage to their company's image by media coverage of the litigation is very often a strong argument in favour of an early settlement. If the lawsuit is not frivolous they also prefer to meet as many claims as possible at a single blow and on a calculable economic basis in order to remove the liability from their books (sometimes even thus avoiding bankruptcy).

---

[20] See for example Linda S Mullenix, *Mass Tort Litigation* (2nd edn West 2008), Ch 2 D, 478 et seq.

The downside of mass settlement is, however, that the class or group members can never be sure that their representative made the most of the situation. Collective settlements involve the risk of collusion and rather "cheap" settlements. The history of the US class action is full of examples of suspicious settlements with the group members left behind with dubious "discount coupons" instead of money damage awards or cy-près solutions granting only indirect benefit to the class or consumers in general. In product liability cases, conflicts of interest within the group or class – e.g. those having already suffered damage and the group of future victims – implicate difficult settlement negotiations and require judicious solutions.[21]

2. Principals, Agents, Adequate Representation and the Role of Judges in Mass Litigation

One of the key issues raised in any jurisdiction is: Is not any settlement better than expensive and complex proceedings which have unpredictable results and block judicial capacity? There is certainly no uniform answer to this question. Economists would generally favour settlement as a low-cost solution, but rightly emphasize the importance of the quality of the settlement.[22] From a strictly rule-of-law concept "the idea of a lawsuit is to get a decision from a court about whether the defendant is liable to the plaintiff".[23] In a traditional two-party litigation, settlements depend on party autonomy and the question of whether a settlement should be preferred over (ongoing) litigation has to be answered by the parties themselves. Mass disputes are different. For the reasons mentioned above, both sides may have strong incentives to settle the case, but the absent group or class members are not involved in the settlement negotiations. Mass settlements are not only difficult and complex for attorneys to negotiate, they also involve a number of principal-agent conflicts and court approval of settlements is an easy way out only at first sight. If we assume that any settlement may not necessarily be a good settlement, what are the standards to be applied by courts? How can courts find out whether a settlement

---

[21] For examples see John Coffee, 'Class Wars: The Dilemma of the Mass Tort Class Action' (1995) 95 *Columbia L Rev* 1344, 1368.

[22] Michael Faure in this volume, Chapter 2, sub VII.

[23] Richard Marcus in this volume, Chapter 7, p. 154. According to Jasminka Kalajdzic in this volume, Chapter 6, sub IV a, p. 140), in Canada, public policy is said generally to favour the compromise, and courts assume that there is a "strong" presumption that proposed settlements are fair and reasonable – both are facts she finds "troubling".

proposed by the parties is fair and adequate with respect to the absent group or class member?

Mass settlements must therefore be considered in the broader context of representation and it becomes clear that the traditional role of judges changes in mass litigation.[24] The European Commission's lengthy debate before coming forward with a "coherent approach" on collective redress mechanism in 2013 has a lot do with these questions. Existing proposals and drafts ran into the opposition of politicians and of the business sector for various reasons. One major argument is that the US class actions model – and anything that looks like it – constitutes a foreign element in the political, social and judicial systems in Europe.[25] Indeed, most European countries have a tradition of public enforcement in many fields of law, particularly in consumer and competition law. They have only gradually become used to the idea that private actions can positively complement current public enforcement or can step in where such enforcement does not exist. However, most private instruments of enforcing mass claims or of collective redress are ultimately based on the rationale that the interests of "the mass" are being represented by a group or class plaintiff, be it a member of the class, a representative body like a non-profit organization, or even a public entity. Collective actions thus do not fit readily into the European "individualistic" civil justice systems, which are almost entirely based on the enforcement of individual claims in two-party litigation.[26] There is a wide consensus today that Europe should not simply copy the US class actions system with all the factors that are responsible for a "litigation culture" or "lawyer-driven" litigation.

Nevertheless, the implementation of any collective redress regime will

---

24 Particularly, if the collective redress mechanism is based on an opt-out system with settlements which purport to bind absent class or group members, Rebecca Money-Kyrle and Christopher Hodges, 'European Collective Action: Towards Coherence?' (2012) 19 *MJ* (4), 477, 495.

25 For example Alexander Bruns, 'Einheitlicher Kollektiver Rechtsschutz in Europa?' (2012) 4 *Zeitschrift für Zivilprozess* 399–419; Franz Jürgen Säcker, *Die Einordnung der Verbandsklage in das System des Privatrechts* (CH Beck 2006); for a critical assessment of the ineffectiveness of repressive damage awards cf Rolf Stürner, 'Privatautonomie und Wettbewerb unter der Hegemonie angloamerikanischer Rechtskultur' (2010) 210 *Archiv für die civilistische Praxis* 106, 125.

26 Only representative actions by consumer associations or public interest groups have been established and widely used since the 1970s, but the legal standing given to these groups has often been restricted to suing for injunctive relief; for a comparative overview, see Rolf Stürner, in IAPL et al (eds) *Procesos Colectivos – Class actions, I Conferencia Internacional y XXIII Jornadas Iberoamericanas de Derecho Procesal* (Buenos Aires 2012) 74.

impose greater responsibility on the courts compared with traditional civil proceedings. The 2013 Commission Recommendation on collective redress emphasizes throughout the importance of maintaining traditional approaches towards a balanced mechanism, respecting the rights of claimants and defendants.[27] The detailed proposals comprise a series of safeguards intended to maintain that balance and to guard against abuse, such as maintaining the 'loser pays' principle, banning punitive damages, only giving standing to designated representatives who satisfy clearly defined conditions of eligibility, initial verification that cases have merit – and, importantly for this analysis, judicial verification of the legality of collective settlements.

In the US[28] and in the UK[29] the prevailing notion for a long time was that a judge should be an impartial umpire in the proceedings between adversaries, interfering in the parties' activity only in order to make sure that the lawyers played the game.[30] As a consequence, any active court management does not easily mesh with the traditional role of judges in an adversarial system. Over the years US judges have developed a kind of case management in order to cope with an increasing workload and owing to the growing importance of pretrial discovery which made it more and more necessary for judges to intervene with parties' disputes over their obligations under discovery rules.[31] While US civil procedure nevertheless generally maintained a more passive role for judges, it was always accepted that class actions required a completely different approach. The need for private enforcement by means of class actions has thus obviously fundamentally changed the role of judges. They certify classes and sub-classes,

---

[27] Commission Recommendation (supra note 17).

[28] Cf Judith Resnik, 'Managerial Judges' (1982) 96 *Harvard L Rev* 376; for the involvement of magistrate judges see Linda Silberman, 'Masters and Magistrates' (1975) 50 *NYU L Rev* 1297; Haimo Schack, *Einführung in das US-amerikanische Zivilprozessrecht* (4th edn, München 2011) para 149.

[29] Neil Andrews, *English Civil Procedure* (Oxford University Press 2003), para 13.12; Neil Andrews, 'Development in English Civil Procedure: How Far Can the English Courts Reform their Own Procedure?' (1997) 2 *Zeitschrift für Zivilprozess International* 14.

[30] In the US, this traditional juridical role was partly based on the idea of the drafters of the US Constitution that courts should be independent from the executive. They also wanted to ensure the vesting of substantial adjudicatory power in the people by creating the jury system (US Constitution Amendment VII); Resnik (supra note 28) 381.

[31] Resnik (supra note 28) 378; Collin Wallace, 'Working Paper – Future of the Judiciary' (1982) 94 *FRD* 225, 228; John Anthony Jolowicz, 'The Active Role of the Court in Civil Litigation', *General Report to the 9th International Congress of Comparative Law* (Teheran 1974), 239.

they appoint lead plaintiffs, they identify "common issues" and issues for individual adjudication, and, finally, they scrutinize and approve settlements. It is particularly the individualistic approach of class actions and the focus on competitiveness and financial incentives for lawyers in the US that requires powerful judges as a strong counterweight.[32] For England and Wales, the implementation of the new Civil Procedure Rules in 1999 led to a paradigm shift.[33] Judges were generally assigned a more active role than before. This trend has been supported and extended as a result of the introduction of costs management under the 2010 Jackson reforms.[34] In particular, the English Group Litigation Order (GLO) system confers significant powers on the court that include the identification of issues to proceed as a test case, the appointment of the lead solicitor, and details to be included in the pleadings.

On the continent, the adversarial system was always less distinct. Common law scholars have often described the different assignment of roles among judges and counsel as "inquisitorial"[35] or as "judicial activism".[36] Judges have always taken a more active part in handling cases, in the preparation of preliminary hearings and trials and in the taking of evidence.[37] This role model seems to be more suitable for the handling

---

32 Stürner (supra note 25), 67, 88 describes this as an "overkill effect": too much individual freedom produces conflicts that need the "strong man"; for a similar analysis Peter Gottwald, 'Aktive Richter – Managerial Judges' in *Law in East and West – Waseda Festschrift*, Institute of Comparative Law, Waseda University (Tokyo 1988), 705, 706.

33 Neil Andrews, 'Contracts and English Dispute Resolution', Nagoya University Comparative Study of Civil Justice, vol 5, 188: "English procedure had previously avoided judicial management . . . English civil procedure has moved from an antagonistic style to a more co-operative ethos". See also Adrian Zuckerman, *Zuckerman on Civil Procedure: Principles and Practice* (3rd edn, Thomson, Sweet & Maxwell 2011) and Deirdre Dwyer (ed) *The Civil Procedure Rules Ten Years On* (Oxford University Press 2009).

34 Rupert Jackson, *Review of Civil Litigation Costs: Final Report* (The Stationery Office 2010) ('Final Report') <http://www.judiciary.gov.uk/about_judiciary/cost-review/jan2010/final-report-140110.pdf>; the principal implementation is in the Legal Aid, Sentencing and Punishment of Offenders Act 2012.

35 Resnik (supra note 28) 380: "Our system was 'adversarial' rather than 'inquisitorial'"; Benjamin Kaplan, Arthur T von Mehren and Rudolf Schaefer, 'Phases of German Civil Procedure' (1958) 71 *Harvard L Rev* 1193, 1443.

36 For a description of the shift in judicial role towards more court management as "judicial activism", see Donald Horowitz, *The Courts and Social Policy* (Brookings Institution Press 1977).

37 In the 1970s and 1980s some academics in Germany argued that judges should not act as umpires between plaintiffs and defendants, but as "social engineers" assisting the "weaker party": Rudolf Wassermann, *Der soziale Zivilprozess*

of mass disputes than the idea of the judge as an umpire. In 1985, John Langbein in comparing US and German civil procedure emphasized the growing manifestations of judicial control in the US multiparty "Big Case" and already observed a convergence of the two systems: "In principle, managerial judging is more compatible with the theory of German procedure than with our own".[38] However, there seems to be a reverse of the positions now: today the idea of an even more active and protective role for the court in collective proceedings sparks suspicion in Germany and Europe and is deemed to endanger one of the basic pillars of the civil justice system, particularly the impartiality of the judge.

Apart from the rather technical problems of case management, it is the representative character of collective actions that inevitably implies a greater responsibility for judges. Some US courts have even gone so far as to term the judge a fiduciary of the absent class members.[39] It is a main feature of group actions that the group members are not formally parties to the litigation and do not have the right to participate actively in the proceedings. Instead, the group or lead plaintiff acts on their behalf, and this is probably the only way to make mass claims and really big cases manageable. As a consequence, principal-agent problems[40] can occur and there must be a number of safeguards to protect the interests of absent group members. The contributions in the first part of this book will primarily address one: the challenging task for courts of approving mass settlements.

If a group or class action finally results in a proposed settlement of the case, the representative role of the lead plaintiff becomes extremely

(Luchterhand 1978); Rudolf Wassermann, *Der politische Richter* (Pieper 1982) 56; Theo Rasehorn, Helmut Ostermeyer, Diether Huhn and Fritz Hasse, *Im Namen des Volkes* (Luchterhand 1968) – an approach that did not become generally accepted. Perhaps unsurprisingly, modern Chinese civil justice also assigns the function of social engineers to civil judges, Yuanshi Bu, 'Gestalten, Schlichten, Richten oder Abweisen – Gegenwärtige Reformströmungen' (2010) 15 *Zeitschrift für Zivilprozess International* 366, 368.

38 John Langbein, 'The German Advantage in Civil Procedure' (1985) 52 *Univ of Chicago L Rev* 823, 825.

39 *Reynolds* v *Beneficial Nat Bank*, 288 F3d 277, 280 (7th Cir 2002); Barbara J Rothstein and Thomas E Willging, *Managing Class Action Litigation, A Pocket Guide for Judges* (Federal Judicial Center 2005), 8. This is indeed in contrast to the traditional juridical role of the adversarial system which was based on the guideline that "disengagement and dispassion supposedly enable judges to decide cases fairly and impartially" (Resnik (supra note 28), 376).

40 For details of agency issues in enforcing consumer interests, Franziska Weber, *Towards an Optimal Mix of Public and Private Enforcement in Consumer Law* (Rotterdam 2012) 87 et passim. See also Michael Faure in this volume, Chapter 2.

important. Therefore group or class action regulations often require judicial review of the fairness, reasonableness and adequacy of the settlement as a special safeguard for the interests of the group members.[41] For many jurisdictions in Europe, it is a completely new challenge. In the traditional bipolar lawsuit, settlements achieved by the parties are not often subject to judicial review because negotiating an adequate settlement can be left to party autonomy. Collective actions, however, are more vulnerable to collusion, and they require special safeguards to protect the absent group members who do not participate in the settlement process and typically lack the knowledge, resources and motivation to object to a proposed settlement. Therefore judicial review and approval for the settlement is necessary. In some jurisdictions courts are even granted the power to make additional orders, e.g. with respect to the distribution of any money paid under the settlement.[42]

Concern about the potential for conflicts of interest and abuse between agent-intermediaries and principals becomes more acute in jurisdictions when the intermediaries seek levels of remuneration that are either intrinsically substantial and/or significant in proportion to the size of individuals' claims and of the total claim value. Such issues underpin concern over contingency or success fees for lawyers and large fees for the new breed of independent "third party" litigation funders.[43]

3. Can Conflicts of Interest be Avoided From the Very Beginning?

Mass settlements may raise the suspicions of judges for various reasons. There might be collusion between the representative of the group and the defendant, resulting in a low settlement amount for the whole group or a much too generous compensation for the group representative and her counsel. The settlement may not treat all group members equally although it should do so, or it may – on the contrary – fail to treat particular groups of the class differently where the facts of the case indicate it would be appropriate to do so. Thus, unfair settlements may result from a conflict of interest between the representative and the represented group, or from conflicts within the group or class. Class action regulations can minimize

---

41 See Rebecca Money-Kyrle and Christopher Hodges (supra note 24), 495: "The issue is thus one of democratic representation as much as of judicial fairness."

42 Eg Federal Court of Australia Act (Clth) s 33V (2).

43 Christopher Hodges, John Peysner and Angus Nurse, *Litigation Funding: Status and Issues* (Centre for Socio-Legal Studies, University of Oxford, and Lincoln University Law School 2011) found that commercial funders typically charge 30 per cent or more of the sum recovered, after costs and expenses.

the potential for conflict in several ways. One key issue is the selection of the group representative, which is, however, beyond the scope of this book.[44] Another safeguard operates through certification requirements.[45] Generally a group or class action will only be certified if the plaintiff's claim is typical of the whole class. Thus, in many situations, the interests of the group representative or lead plaintiff and those of the class or group members will not be in conflict. In the US, courts now tend to emphasize scrutiny of the common features and to take into consideration the merits of the plaintiffs' claims before certifying a class – issues that were subject to two US Supreme Court cases in 2012–13.[46] In order to minimize the potential for conflicts within the class courts should be given a broad discretion with respect to the certification and the formation of sub-classes.[47]

The European system offers another chance of avoiding potential conflicts. Non-profit associations and public authorities have traditionally played an important role in representing group or public interests with respect to injunctive and declaratory relief. Consumer associations and private interest groups are bound to their statutory interests, they are often controlled by public institutions and their primary incentive is not to gain profit.[48] If they are granted legal standing to initiate group actions in

---

[44] For the various options of how to select a group representative cf Astrid Stadler, 'Collective Redress Litigation – A New Challenge for Courts in Europe' in Alexander Bruns et al (eds) *Liber Amicorum Rolf Stürner* (Tübingen 2013).

[45] For a discussion on safeguards in class actions and the "catch 22" problem that barriers to abuse also operate as barriers to litigation, and may render collective actions toothless, largely by increasing cost and delay to an extent that makes actions unviable, see Rebecca Money-Kyrle and Christopher Hodges, 'Safeguards in Collective Actions' (2012) 19.4 *Maastricht Journal of International and Comparative Law* 477–504.

[46] See Richard Marcus in this volume, Chapter 7, p. 161.

[47] Mass torts, in particular, often raise issues of individual causation and damages which are better adjudicated upon individually. In these circumstances, a group or class action should be certified only to try certain common issues (not whole cases) at a preliminary stage, and cases might proceed through individual proceedings at a later stage. In the US, there are examples of judges certifying a class action notwithstanding that the class was likely to be decertified at a later stage of the proceedings for adjudication of individual issues; see, for example, the certification of the asbestos class action (*Jenkins* v *Raymark Indus,* 19 FRD 269, 282, [ED Tex 1985], affirmed 782 F2d 468 [5th Cir 1986]) and the certification of the nationwide class action "Agent Orange". For details see Peter H Schuck, *Agent Orange on Trial: Mass Toxic Disasters in the Courts* (Bellknap Press 1986); Myriam Gilles, 'Opting Out of Liability: The Forthcoming, Near Total Demise of the Modern Class Action' (2005) 104 *Michigan L Rev* 373, 383.

[48] Stürner (supra note 26) 74, 88.

appropriate cases, they will not be a member of the class themselves and there can be a presumption of adequate representation.[49] The same is true for public authorities acting as representatives in group or class actions.[50] Thus, principal-agent issues become less important and even information asymmetries can be mitigated because consumer associations or authorities will regularly be better informed than individual consumers.[51]

Admittedly, an active role of these institutions in collective redress litigation will raise other controversial issues, particularly with respect to adequate financial resources and accountability. Legal standing should be given only to those institutions showing credibility and a strong commitment to acting in the collective interest of their members or consumers.[52] They will need a democratic structure or should probably be controlled in the same way as public agencies.[53] In implementing the EC Injunctive Directive some Member States have already defined criteria for the legal standing of representative organizations, but these are definitely issues that require further deliberation. Furthermore Michael Faure in his contribution[54] expresses worries that if consumer organizations have a monopoly there might be a divergence of interests between the organization and the consumer. Competition between several associations may avoid that problem. In any case, one has to concede that not all types of mass damages are suitable for class representation by associations and non-profit organizations.

The importance that European justice systems attach to avoiding conflicts of interest can be seen from the inclusion in the European

---

[49] Of course in some cases one may have doubts about the goals of these organizations, Richard Marcus (in this volume) Chapter 7, p. 163.

[50] Group litigation regulations in Sweden (Sec 5 and 6 Group Litigation Act 2003), Denmark (§ 254c Administration of Justice Act), and Norway (Sec 35-3 Dispute Act) give legal standing to private associations and public bodies like the consumer ombudsman; in Finland (§ 4 Class Action Act 444/2007) and Poland (Art 4 8 [2] Group Litigation Act) only ombudsmen have the right to bring group actions (in Poland in addition to individual members of the group). Consumer organizations also have legal standing for group actions, for example in Bulgaria (Ch 3 Civil Procedure Code), Italy (Art 140 *bis* Consumer Code), and Portugal (Art 17 7 Law 24/96).

[51] Franziska Weber (supra note 40) 150 et seq.; for restrictions on legal standing see also Rebecca Money-Kyrle and Christopher Hodges (supra note 24), 487–9.

[52] Roger Van den Bergh and Louis Visscher, 'The Preventive Function of Collective Actions for Damages in Consumer Law' (2008) 1 *Erasmus L Rev* 5, 28.

[53] Franziska Weber (supra note 40), 153; Christopher Hodges, *Collectivism: Evaluating the Effectiveness of Public and Private Models for Regulating Consumer Protection*, 207, 217.

[54] In this volume, Chapter 2, V 2.

Commission's 2013 Recommendation on collective redress of a power for courts to stay proceedings where funding is provided by a third party if there is a conflict of interest between the third party and the claimant party and its members.[55]

4. "Opt-out" as a Safeguard Against Unfair Settlements?

Group or class members may have the right to opt out of the proposed settlement and thus escape its binding effect. In the US, the 2003 reform of class actions rules provides the court with the discretion to grant the chance for a second opt-out once a settlement has been reached (Rule 23 [e] [3] Federal Rules of Civil Procedure (FRCP)). The Dutch WCAM proceedings are based on the court approval for an out-of-court settlement of mass torts and provide an opt-out mechanism for those tort victims who do not want to participate in the settlement. This is a very strong weapon against unfair settlements if at least three conditions are met: the claimants must receive adequate notice of the settlement terms; they must be in a position to assess the pros and cons of the settlement; and they must have real alternatives to enforce their claims. With respect to the first requirement, class or group proceedings involving a large number of unidentified victims present a particular challenge in terms of submitting the settlement to their attention.[56] In the Netherlands, the Amsterdam court's efforts to inform the tort victims who will be bound by the approved settlement (often residing in countries all over the world) seem to be guided by US class actions practice.[57] The court's instructions with respect to the notification of the injured parties became more precise step by step and case by case.[58] Nevertheless, its notification practice raises concern and might turn out to be an obstacle to the Europe-wide recognition of the court's decisions under the Brussels I Regulation.[59] In big international cases, even the

---

[55] Commission Recommendation (supra note 17), para 15(a).

[56] For the form of notice used in Australia cf Michael Legg (this volume), Chapter 8, p. 179–181.

[57] Art 1013 (5) Dutch Code of Civil Procedure (CPC). For a general discussion on the effects of the opt-out mechanism, see Christopher Hodges (supra note 1), 118–30; Astrid Stadler, 'Group Actions as a Remedy to Enforce Consumer Interests' in Fabrizzio Cafaggi and Hans-W Micklitz (supra note 1), 305, 317.

[58] For a detailed analysis of the notification practice, see Hélène van Lith, *The Dutch Collective Settlements Act and Private International Law: Aspecten van Internationaal Privaatrecht in de WCAM* (Maklu 2011), Chapter 3.3; Karen Jelsma and Manon Cordewener, 'The Settlement of Mass Claims, A Hot Topic in The Netherlands' (2011) *Intl L Q* 13, 17.

[59] Xandra Kramer, in this volume, Chapter 3 sub V, p. 82 et seq.

most careful and vigilant attempts to reach all group members by public announcements apparently accept that not all of them will definitely receive the information. The Dutch Parliament has recently enacted legislation improving the WCAM proceedings.[60] In Australia, adequate notice is even more important than in other class action systems since a final settlement requires a "closed class" and therefore the action converts into an opt-in proceeding requiring affirmative steps by those class members who want to benefit from the settlement.[61]

When implementing group or class actions to enforce trivial damages, one should bear in mind that group members will have no incentive to opt-out and will tend to accept any settlement since individual litigation is not an option. Defendants may thus get off lightly unless courts intervene. But also with respect to "regular" damages court approval plays an important role because it sends a signal that the settlement is fair and adequate and thus influences the decision of group members to accept it. In the US, the "second opt-out" (Rule 23 [e] [4] FRCP) is a controversial provision. In practice, defendants reserve the right to withdraw from the settlement if more than a certain number of claimants opt-out[62] – a solution provided by law now in the German Capital Market Model Case Act (s 17 [1]). One may also be concerned about evidence from the Netherlands and UK of the arrival on the scene of independent claims' intermediaries who seek to attract class members to opt-out of settlements with the lure of gaining higher damages. Classic economic analysis might support such activity if it results in higher recoveries, but there is some evidence that the result may not be achieved for the enticed claimants whereas significant fees may be gained by the enticers.[63]

5. Criteria and Standards to be Applied in Evaluating Proposed Settlements

Regulations on the judicial review of proposed settlements are sometimes very vague and do not provide detailed criteria to be applied by the courts. In the US, Rule 23 (e) FRCP requires only that the settlement be "fair,

---

60 Ianika Tzankova and Deborah Hensler, in this volume, Chapter 4, sub IV, p. 98 et seq. The amendments came into force on 1 July 2013.

61 Those class members who do not come forward are not only excluded from the settlement, they also face the risk that their claims are extinguished unless the court excludes them from the class, for details Michael Legg in this volume, Chapter 8.

62 Richard Marcus in this volume, Chapter 7, p. 157.

63 For details see Christopher Hodges in this volume, Chapter 5.

reasonable and adequate".[64] The Dutch WCAM is a little bit more specific.[65] In reviewing settlements courts must often assess the adequacy of attorney's fees, the administration and distribution of funds, and last but not least the recovery of class members. In this last respect judicial review can be understood to require comparison of the relief granted in the settlement to what group or class members might have obtained by a court judgment. Nevertheless, the review has to take into account that "compromise is the essence of a settlement"[66]. In practice, it will always be a question of how meticulously courts will and can consider the alternatives to the proposed settlement without litigating the merits of the case.[67] There seems to be a widespread consensus that courts should not ignore the legal situation of the group or class member completely, and that they must resist the temptation to rubber-stamp proposed settlements solely in order to bring the litigation to an end. From an economic perspective, based on empirical studies on judges' incentives, Michael Faure also doubts whether judges will fulfill the sometimes high expectations in their monitoring tasks.[68] In the US, legal scholars emphasize that a summary assessment based on the facts and evidence presented so far is necessary, but also sufficient. This will always leave a broad range of acceptable settlements. Courts in the US[69] and in Australia have also developed catalogues listing criteria to be applied (the "nine-factor test"[70]) when looking over class action

---

[64] The provisions in Australia (Michael Legg in this volume, Chapter 8, p. 177) do not provide any criteria for approving settlements.

[65] Court approval may be refused if "the amount of the compensation is not reasonable having regard, inter alia, to the extent of the damage, the ease and speed with which the compensation can be obtained and the possible causes of the damage" (Article 907 III lit b Dutch Civil Code). Approval may also be denied if "the interests of the persons on whose behalf the agreement was concluded are otherwise not adequately safeguarded". The Swedish Group Litigation Act 2003 s 26 provides that, a settlement shall be confirmed by the court "provided that it is not discriminatory against particular members of the group or in another way manifestly unfair".

[66] *Milstein* v *Werner*, 57 FRD 515, 524-525 (SDNY 1972).

[67] Timothy E Eble (1999) *Federal Class Action Practice Manual*, Chapter 9, § 49 <www.classactionlitigation.com/fcapmanual/chapter9.html>; Janet Walker, 'Class Action Settlement Approval; Res Judicata; Claims Administration and Cy-Près Awards', in IAPL et al (eds) *Procesos Colectivos – Class actions, I Conferencia Internacional y XXIII Jornadas Iberoamericanas de Derecho Procesal* (Buenos Aires 2012) 535, 538; Christopher Hodges (supra note 1) 120.

[68] Michael Faure in this volume, Chapter 2 p. 59.

[69] David F Herr, *Manual for Complex Litigation*, Federal Judical Center (4th edn, West 2008), 22.923.

[70] Michael Legg in this volume, Chapter 8, p. 188; Practice Note CM 17 2010 based on Part IVA of the Federal Court of Australia Act 1976. In Canada, courts

settlements. They are meant to alleviate the tightrope walk between accepting the negotiated compromise in the light of the complexity and risks of further litigation, on the one side, and taking into consideration the legal position of the parties, on the other side.

Whereas all the jurisdictions we are considering seem to give courts a broad (and necessary) discretion when approving settlements, there are few legal provisions which are explicitly restrictive on the court's standards of approval. In Germany, for example, a recent reform of the only instrument of collective redress, the Capital Market Model Case Act (Kapitalanleger-Musterverfahrensgesetz, CMMCA), generated such a new standard of court approval. The proceedings under this law, which was enacted in 2005 as a reaction to the big Deutsche Telekom securities litigation, are not exactly like a group action. They are closer to the English Group Litigation Order, however with a very limited scope of application which is restricted to securities cases. Once investors who have suffered damages due to false or misleading capital market information have sued the defendant(s), the CMMCA offers the chance of having factual and legal issues that are common to all claims decided by the Court of Appeals with a legally binding effect for all claimants. The Court of Appeals selects a test case for that purpose and all other pending cases are suspended and will be resumed once the Court of Appeals has decided on all issues selected for the test case before it. Different from traditional group actions, the test case plaintiff is not deemed to be a representative of the other claimants. These are allowed to participate in the test case proceedings as "interested parties". In practice, however, it turns out that the vast majority of them do not interfere. The original version of the CMMCA allowed a settlement of all disputes during the test case proceedings only if all claimants of the suspended proceedings would consent to it explicitly. Section 18, which became effective in November 2012, now gives the test case plaintiff a mandate to negotiate a settlement for all claimants. A proposed settlement will become legally binding on all "interested parties" based on an opt-out mechanism if less than 70 per cent of them opt-out. The settlement requires the approval of the Court of Appeals and its decision will be based on the situation of the test case proceedings. The court will not take into consideration the merits of each claim. Given that the Court of Appeals is not familiar with the details of the other pending actions and has only very limited information with respect to these cases this seems logical. The issues listed for the test case proceedings will regularly not include all the

---

have developed more or less the same factors, see Jasminka Kalajdzic in this volume, Chapter 6 sub IV, p. 138 et seq.

conditions of entitlement of the individual claims.[71] But how can the Court of Appeals decide whether the settlement is fair and adequate if it is not getting the full picture of the cases? The legislature obviously believed that the parties to the test case will not allow unmeritorious claims to benefit from the settlement. Maybe the rights of "interested parties" to comment on the settlement and to opt-out are sufficient safeguards against unfair settlement terms. The rationale behind the new regulation is simple (but probably also wrong): As the Court of Appeals does not even possess the complete files of the individual lawsuits there was a deep concern that it would be too time-consuming and too complex to take the merits of all claims into consideration. Once again, the legislature faced the challenge of balancing the public interest in bringing mass litigation to an end without overloading the courts against the protection of the "interested parties" who are not able to overlook the situation and fairness of the settlement. The reform of the German CMMCA is another piece of evidence that even parliaments tend to prefer a quick settlement of mass disputes and to reduce judicial control to a minimum.[72]

6. Settlements in International Mass Disputes

The court's task becomes even more complicated if the case involves an international dimension. The Dutch settlement cases provide excellent examples, and are explained below by Ianika Tzankova and Deborah Hensler, and also by Xandra Kramer. Since its coming into force in 2005 the WCAM has attracted big international cases, particularly securities cases where non-US shareholders were excluded from US class actions.

The *Royal Shell* and *Converium* collective settlements approved by the Amsterdam Court[73] involved thousands of shareholders domiciled in different countries all over the world. Without a settlement of such cases, the courts would have faced complex conflict-of-laws problems and might

---

[71] Thus, even if the test case plaintiff wins the test case with respect to all issues listed, some of the other claimants may still lose their case despite the binding effect of the test case decision, if they cannot successfully prove other elements of their alleged claims.

[72] For the particular situation of the German test case proceedings it would have been a much better solution to ask at least the courts of first instance trying the individual cases to comment on the settlement. Since they are familiar with the details of each claim they are in a much better position to estimate whether each plaintiff could win his or her case, and hence should be allowed to benefit from the settlement.

[73] Court of Appeal Amsterdam 29 May 2009, *LJN*: BI5744 (Shell); Court of Appeal Amsterdam 17 January 2012, *LJN*: BV1026 (Converium).

have had to apply a multiplicity of substantive laws to the claims of the group members. Is a settlement a good chance to release the court from the conflict-of-laws problem? In both cases the Amsterdam Court approved the settlement without even mentioning the conflict-of-laws question. Given that national liability rules and tort law can differ considerably this approach appears to be taking the easy way out.[74] Without a settlement these differences have to be taken into account, for example by forming sub-classes or sub-groups.[75] Given a limited settlement amount to be distributed among the group or class members, including unmeritorious claims in the settlement contract is done at the expense of those injured persons with sound claims, and cannot be accepted as an adequate representation of the interests of the whole group.[76] Ignoring the conflict-of-laws issue completely with respect to the approval of a settlement thus seems difficult to accept.[77] Even if the settlement agreement includes a choice-of-law clause, this clause itself must be subject to a reasonableness test. Therefore a comparative analysis of the treatment of the group members which includes weighing the merits of their claims is necessary and often recommended.[78] Otherwise group members may take benefit from a settlement even though they are not entitled to compensation under the applicable law.

In its *Converium* decision of January 2012,[79] the Amsterdam Court simply relied on one main argument for assuming the reasonableness of the compensation awarded to the non-US-exchange purchasers excluded

---

74 Liability rules may differ considerably, for example, with respect to statutes of limitation, the allocation of the burden of proof, the requirements of default or contributory negligence, and the entitlement to compensation for pain and suffering in case of bereavement of the next of kin.

75 Many group or class action regulations allow for the formation of subgroups in order to cope with differences within the group of class members: Rule 23 (c) (4) FRCP; Section 20 Swedish Group Litigation Act 2003; § 14 Finish Class Action Act 444/2007; Section 35-10 Norwegian Dispute Act; Article 6 Polish Group Litigation Act 2009.

76 For the approval of (domestic) class action settlements in Canada Jasminka Kalajdzic reports that the settlement need not "be reasonable vis-à-vis particular class members" (Chapter 6 sub IV). However, arguably a preferential treatment of only one or even a small number of class members is always at the expense of the others.

77 Rob Polak and V Hermans, 'International Class Action Settlements in the Netherlands after the Morrison and Ahold Decisions' (2011) *Class & Group Actions* <www.iclg.co.uk>, 33.

78 David F Herr, *Manual for Complex Litigation*, Federal Judical Center (4th edn, West 2008), 21.62 with respect to Rule 23 (e) (1) (C) FRCP.

79 Court of Appeal Amsterdam 17 January 2012, *LJN*: BV1026

from the US class action. As none of them had made any attempt to sue the defendant for damages outside the US[80] the court concluded that they obviously faced real obstacles to pursuing their claims and were in a worse position than the US-exchange purchasers. As a consequence, the much lower settlement amount in the settlement in Europe was deemed to be appropriate. It seems rather questionable whether this is an acceptable application of the reasonableness test. Certainly, the apathy of the aggrieved parties can be taken into account, but it may have many reasons. Particularly with respect to on-going settlement negotiations, group members may have refrained from filing a lawsuit. Should this argument be used to avoid considering whether some group members should be treated differently from others with respect to the potential strength of their claims? Some academics rightly point out that the Amsterdam Court should test the "reasonableness" by considering foreign laws.[81] This will not always require a very detailed comparison, but fundamental differences in substantive laws should indeed be reflected in the terms of the settlement. Admittedly, this approach will add some complexity to the process of negotiating a settlement in international cases, and to the effort of the courts reviewing the settlement. However, if we are serious about accepting only reasonably balanced settlements, coping with that task will be inevitable.

7. How Can Courts Obtain the Necessary Information to Evaluate the Position of the Group Members?

The adversarial nature of the litigation is lost once the parties have successfully negotiated a settlement, and it is up to the court to detect flaws or abuses. Therefore courts must anticipate a number of recurring potential abuses, and compensate for the lack of significant opposition to the settlement. According to the contributions in this book, almost everywhere courts are obliged to give notice of the settlement to the class members and grant the chance of submitting objections to the proposed settlement.[82] In the US and Canada, a fairness hearing must be held,[83] in other jurisdictions

---

80 Court of Appeal Amsterdam 17 January 2012, *LJN*: BV1026, sub 6.4.2.

81 Rob Polak and V Hermans (supra note 77), 33.

82 USA: Rule 23 (e) (5) FRCP and Securities Act s 27 (a) (5), Securities Exchange Act s 21 D (a) (5); Federal Court of Australia Act (Clth) Australia s 33 X; in Canada notice of the proposed settlement to the class member is not always mandatory, but common practice, see Jasminka Kalajdzic in this volume, Chapter 6, sub 3.

83 Rule 23 (e) (2) FRCP; Article 1013 (5), (6) Dutch CPC. See for example Ontario's Class Proceedings Act, 1992, SO 1992, c.6, s. 29.

it is at least common practice to do so.[84] One should not be too optimistic, however, that a large number of group members will object to the proposed settlement. Inertia of class members may indicate consent or acquiescence, but sometimes they are simply not in a position to judge the fairness of the settlement and are not inclined to seek expensive legal advice in order to detect collusion or misuse. Silence on behalf of the class members probably weighs differently from case to case depending – inter alia – on their qualifications[85] and the stake class members have in the action.[86] The main responsibility often lies with the court. Those who do come forward and raise objections – at least in the US – often have in mind only to retain the right to appeal approval of the settlement over their objections, thus delaying the whole proceedings and getting leverage to extract concessions for their own benefit.[87] Therefore the argument that a neutral "guardian" should be appointed to represent the interests of the group members during the negotiation and approval process carries some weight.[88]

Some national rules also allow the consulting of experts, particularly with respect to the economic aspects of settlements (e.g. coupon settlements).[89] Other instruments include giving notice of the settlement terms to public institutions, state officials or associations who might comment on or object to the settlement based on their knowledge of the dispute.[90] Provisions like Rule 23 (e) (3) FRCP require that the parties reveal

---

84 For Australia see Michael Legg in this volume, Chapter 8, p. 182. See also Antonio Gidi, 'The Class Action Code: A Model for Civil Law Countries', (2005) 23 *Arizona J. of Internat. & Comp. L.* 37, 45 (Art 14.6).

85 Business owners or institutional investors are regularly in a better position to assess the benefits of a settlement than are consumers or small investors, but they may prefer the anonymity as an absent class member for various reasons to having a prominent role in a public fairness hearing.

86 Michael Legg in this volume, Chapter 8, p. 187 et seq.

87 Richard Marcus in this volume, Chapter 7, p. 156.

88 Michael Legg in this volume, Chapter 8, p. 197, 198; Eduard Brunet, 'Class Action Objectors: Extortionist Free Riders or Fairness Guarantors' (2003) *The University of Chicago Legal Forum* 403; Sylvia Lazos, 'Abuse in Plaintiff Class Action Settlements: The Need for a Guardian During Pretrial Settlement Negotiations' (1985) 84 *Michigan L Rev* 308.

89 Cf for the Netherlands Article 1016 CPC; for US class actions David F Herr, *Manual for Complex Litigation* (4th ed. West Publishing 2008), 22.925 and 28 USC § 1712 (d) as amended by the Class Action Fairness Act 2005; for the situation in Israel see Magen Amichai and Segal Peretz, 'National Report Israel, Globalization of Class Actions', 2007, <http://www.law.standford.edu/calender/details/1066/> (2007), 37–8; Class Action Law Israel (2006), Sec 19; for general observations see Rebecca Money-Kyrle and Christopher Hodges (supra note 24), 496.

90 US: 28 USC § 1715; Sec 25 of the Israeli Group Action Law 2006.

any agreements made in connection with the proposed the settlement. In Australia, the plaintiff's counsel must also submit to the court a statement explaining the settlement terms and why the plaintiff's side decided to accept the settlement in view of the further prospects of the litigation.[91] As a matter of course this kind of statement is privileged and must not be revealed to the defendant, but it might help the court understand the settlement terms.

From the contributions in this book it becomes clear that the established class actions systems in the US, Canada and Australia provide the courts generously with instruments for getting as much information as possible in order to decide upon the adequacy and fairness of a proposed settlement. European jurisdictions seem to be more reluctant to give judges "inquisitorial" powers which might be in conflict with the traditional party autonomy in civil proceedings. The feeling that courts should not interfere with settlements negotiated by the parties still prevails over understanding the risks of representation in mass litigation and the disadvantages of mass settlements.

III. THE NEW WORLD OF CDR

1. Explaining CDR

Consumer Alternative Dispute Resolution (CDR) is the resolution of disputes that arise out of trading between consumers and traders (C2B disputes).[92] Such disputes can, of course, be raised directly between them, and/or through lawyers through court processes, and/or in other ways, such as by public regulators. However, the CDR group of systems that has emerged is specifically designed to handle C2B claims. CDR can now be seen to exist in its own distinct universe and operates independently of the courts (and lawyers). CDR systems are designed to process individual claims, but almost all of them can inherently also process multiple similar disputes. Thus, CDR is a means of providing collective redress.[93] CDR systems exist in parallel with courts and sometimes compete with them.

---

91 Michael Legg in this volume, Chapter 8, p. 186.

92 What follows draws heavily on the findings of an ongoing research project on CDR, much of which is published in Christopher Hodges, Iris Benöhr and Naomi Creutzfeldt-Banda, *Consumer ADR in Europe* (Hart 2012).

93 Discussions on "collective redress" frequently overlook the fact that the mechanism that speakers have in mind is a court-based mechanism of a "collective action", on the incorrect assumption that that is the only option. In fact, "collective redress" is the functional objective, and a "collective action" is only one option, alongside others such as CDR and regulatory mechanisms.

Most CDR schemes operate on the basis of "traditional" settlement techniques, namely mediation/conciliation and (subsequently) a decision, whether technically binding or not, reached through a quasi-judicial procedure akin to, or formally involving, arbitration. Historically, many CDR systems adopted an arbitration model, involving three or one arbitrators, to whom the parties could agree to submit a dispute, and who would make a determination on the legal merits, which would be either binding between them or not. More recent CDR schemes have evolved away from the quasi-adversarial model of arbitration to a more inquisitorial model involving expert ombudsmen, or their case-handling staff. Some CDR schemes have emerged as intrinsic parts of new regulatory systems, notably under EU sectoral legislation for major market sectors like financial services, communications, energy and utilities. Others have arisen as part of self-regulatory arrangements based on codes of business practice in specific sectors, such as for travel companies or motor vehicles.

CDR has long been familiar in the Nordic states, the Netherlands (*Geschillencommissie* and KiFiD), and the UK, all of which have good systems, even if they could all be improved further. In those countries, CDR has grown over 40 years and occupies a distinct and increasingly well-used place in the landscape. In Sweden, for example, virtually *no* consumer sues a trader in court, except where the decision of the CDR body (the ARN or a sectoral ADR body) is not implemented by the trader. This post-CDR legal enforcement stage is necessary because CDR decisions in Sweden are not legally binding on traders, and compliance is voluntary, but compliance is generally high and is significantly enhanced by an effective "name and shame" procedure and culture. CDR decisions in some other countries are legally binding (for example where a dispute is agreed to be submitted to binding arbitration, or where a CDR scheme is made binding on the trader by statute, such as the UK's Financial Ombudsman Service (FOS)). The Netherlands' *Geschillencommissie* CDR system has gone one better, and guarantees payment by the traders' association, although the current challenge there is how to ensure coverage for traders who are not members of trade associations.

Naomi Creutzfeldt examines the multiple origins of CDR schemes in Chapter 10 of this volume identifying a series of different origins, forces and developments that have collectively contributed to the growth of CDR. One influence may be the failure of court-based civil procedure systems to deliver accessibility to justice for C2B disputes, and the development of ADR techniques within civil procedure systems, but there are additional external forces such as cultural aspects that favour resolution of problems through collaborative rather than adversarial means, the impact of increasing regulation of the EU market and the importance of consumers in that market, the advent of new technology for both selling and dispute resolution (and the integration of these two modes), the impact of choice for consumers and especially businesses in relation to pathways for dispute resolution, and the ability of CDR systems to resolve mass problems better – and more cheaply – than court-based systems.

Even the most efficient court systems can be overtaken by swifter, cheaper and more user-friendly alternative solutions. The development of DR has been significantly encouraged by being included – almost unnoticed by many people – in EU legislation that has created and harmonized regulatory systems for many major sectors. A decade ago, EU regulatory legislation *encouraged* firms to use ADR, but from around 2005 regulatory legislation *required* them to have it. Requirements for CADR systems have been established by EU Recommendations as long ago as 1998[94] and 2001.[95]

These points are taken up by Iris Benöhr, who focuses on the important financial services sector. She shows the close links between CDR and regulation (and therefore between ombudsmen and regulators) and that the legal regimes and organizations of both are undergoing significant development. Focusing on the insurance sector, she demonstrates that sophisticated ombudsmen schemes have existed for some years in Germany, France and the UK. Although their structures differ, which would make either voluntary or imposed harmonization challenging, they use the same techniques in practice, namely a conciliation stage followed by a decision stage. One major difference lies in whether (and how) the decision is legally binding. But the insurance sector does see the need for CDR decisions to be accepted by its undertakings in the vast majority of individual cases, if general confidence in the CDR system is to be maintained. It is striking that in all three of the countries studied, the original stimulus for the creation of a national CDR scheme lay with the business sector, even if (especially in the UK) the CDR arrangements were later put into legislation as part of a wider construction of the regulatory system. This shows that there are sectors where business can see the advantages of having CDR schemes and of making them work. Crucial elements in achieving this are providing sufficient resources, and independent governance and transparency.

---

94 Commission Recommendation of 30 March 1998 on the principles applicable to the bodies responsible for out-of-court settlement of consumer disputes (98/257/EC), available at http://eur-lex.europa.eu/LexUriServ/LexUriServ.do?uri=OJ:L:1998:115:0031:0034:EN:PDF

95 Commission Recommendation of 4 April 2001 on the principles for out-of-court bodies involved in the consensual resolution of consumer disputes (2001/310/EC), available at http://ec.europa.eu/consumers/redress/out_of_court/adr/acce_just12_en.pdf

CDR is shortly to take a major further step of integration within the European dispute resolution architecture as a result of its formalization and expansion under the EU's new regime, set out in 2011 proposals[96] that were passed in early 2013, and will be in force in 2015.[97]

A specific manifestation of ADR has developed to support online trading. Julia Hörnle examines online dispute resolution (ODR), which has become firmly embedded in online trading, and is set to be enhanced by the EU ODR Regulation (establishing a Belmed-like portal at EU level) and by an UNCITRAL agreement. Having effective support for ODR in place is regarded as being essential for the development of digital and cross-border trading. The whole process, from filing to adjudication, can be done without paper documents or physical meetings. ODR can be extremely swift and cheap. It also offers an exciting vision of spreading access to justice to millions of people in less developed countries, if handled carefully. A great deal of ODR already exists – it is a basic requirement for major online traders, such as eBay, Amazon and Paypal. eBay's ODR platform handles over 60 million e-commerce disputes annually: most of them very simple types, such as non-delivery, or delivery of a damaged or wrong item. ODR is considered to be essential in supporting trade: When Paypal introduced its ODR facility, buyers' claims decreased by 50 per cent and seller losses under chargebacks fell by 20 per cent.

2. CDR and Settlement

A major feature of CDR systems that is of interest to this book is the fact that almost all CDR systems are designed to facilitate settlement of disputes. They do this not only as an inherent part of their function and procedure, but also as a preliminary stage in the process *before* ending in a stage in which a decision on the merits is reached by an independent third party. Indeed, most CDR schemes involve a succession of distinct stages: first, discussion of the dispute directly between consumer and trader (and this is often a mandatory first stage); secondly, assessment of the issue by

---

[96] See Communication by the European Commission on "Alternative Dispute Resolution for consumer disputes in the Single Market", COM(2011) 791/2.

[97] Directive 2013/11/EU of the European Parliament and of the Council of 21 May 2013 on alternative dispute resolution for consumer disputes and amending Regulation (EC) No 2006/2004 and Directive 2009/22/EC (Directive on consumer ADR), OJ L 165/63, 18.6.2013, and Regulation (EU) No 524/2013 of the European Parliament and of the Council of 21 May 2013 on online dispute resolution for consumer disputes and amending Regulation (EC) No 2006/2004 and Directive 2009/22/EC (Regulation on consumer ODR), OJ L 165/1, 18.6.2012.

the independent third party (triage), in which one or other party might be quickly advised to drop or settle the case immediately; third, a more detailed stage of mediation or conciliation between the parties, seeking to achieve mutual agreement between them; and only finally a stage where the third party (or a fresh third party) makes a determination on the legal merits of the dispute, which may or may not be legally binding between the parties.

Research has shown that in many CDR schemes, the incidence of cases that are resolved at these various stages equates to a broadly based pyramid. In other words, most cases are resolved, or 'fall out' of the process, at the initial more informal stages, and only a small percentage reach the final determination stage.

Societies clearly benefit from the availability of quick and cheap dispute resolution processes for a major body of disputes that are typically small in value and relatively straightforward in relation to their facts and applicable law. Claims handled by CDR schemes are typically about relatively minor problems and small amounts of money,[98] although some financial services or insurance disputes can be larger (the UK Financial Ombudsman Scheme (FOS) has raised its upper limit to £150,000).

CDR schemes can also be designed – as many are – to process mass disputes far more quickly and more efficiently than a private collective action. In this context, mass claims can simply be lodged with the CDR body, who will process them. It is often the CDR body that first recognizes that a "mass problem" is arising, and that there is a need for a consistent approach towards multiple similar cases. The UK FOS applies various

---

[98] Data found in the Oxford study for 2010 included:

- In France, many cases handled by the FFSA *médiateur* were around €100, and some as low as €5. The average award of the national energy *médiateur* was €373, the average amount in dispute in the cases of the médiateur of EDF was €1,120 (with 23 per cent of cases over €2,000).
- In Germany, 86 per cent of claims made to the Insurance Ombudsman involved under €5,000, and over 90 per cent were under €10,000. A normal claim made to the transport ombudsman (Söp) is between €10 and €200.
- In the Netherlands, the average claim value for *Geschillencommissie* cases varies between sectors, from €206 for taxis and an average of €5,980 for housing guarantees. In 2009, 9 per cent of the *Geschillencommissie* claims were less than €250, there was no claim involving a value of more than €10,000, and the largest segment of claims (24 per cent) were for €1,001–2,000.
- The average value of an award in the arbitration system in Spain was €366.
- The average amount claimed in cases before the UK's Ombudsman Service: Communications was £587 and the average award was £198.

techniques to ensure that "collective issues" are resolved in a consistent manner, either by itself selecting test cases or by referring issues to the regulatory authority or to the courts for decisions on the law, after which it can apply the rules to all similar cases that it receives. The process of issue identification and test or representative cases is similar to how many courts would manage a collective action, so the CDR process is unsurprising in managerial terms. However, the CDR bodies do not operate under "class action rules" of procedure, so appear to have greater flexibility in selecting a procedure that would fit the particular circumstances. Perhaps an issue is raised here of uncertainty over whether "due process rights" are threatened: this is an area that would repay further empirical research before theorists reach for their book of principles.

3. Issues with CDR and ODR

CDR and ODR systems dispose of individuals' legal rights. Hence, it is important that CDR bodies satisfy requirements of democratic accountability and other principles of justice, which also apply to courts. As noted above, the EU promulgated criteria for ADR over a decade ago: Commission Recommendation of 30 March 1998 on the principles applicable to the bodies responsible for out-of-court settlement of consumer disputes (98/257/EC)[99] and Commission Recommendation of 4 April 2001 on the principles for out-of-court bodies involved in the consensual resolution of consumer disputes (2001/310/EC).[100] These two sets of criteria are not absolutely identical, but neither are they particularly intrinsically inconsistent. The 1998 criteria are:

I. Independence: guaranteeing the impartiality of the decision-making body.
II. Transparency: appropriate measures must be taken, including:
III. Adversarial: allowing all the parties to present their viewpoint and to hear the arguments and facts put forward by the other party, and any experts' statements.
IV. Effectiveness.
V. Legality.

---

99 Available at http://eur-lex.europa.eu/LexUriServ/LexUriServ.do?uri=OJ:L:1998:115:0031:0034:EN:PDF

100 Available at http://ec.europa.eu/consumers/redress/out_of_court/adr/acce_just12_en.pdf

VI. Liberty: The decision taken by the body concerned may be binding on the parties only if they were informed of its binding nature in advance and specifically accepted this.

VII. Representation: the procedure does not deprive the parties of the right to be represented or assisted by a third party at all stages of the procedure.

The 2001 criteria are:

A. Impartiality.
B. Transparency.
C. Effectiveness.
D. Fairness.

The 2013 EU legislation has not introduced new criteria, but has introduced the above criteria into law to form essential quality requirements for the various diverse forms of CDR that exist across Member States at national level and are beginning to be established at pan-EU level. Particularly important issues can be predicted to give rise to ongoing debate as the relevance of CDR systems gains wider recognition. In particular, debates are likely to focus on the relevance of:

- whether the constitutional/justice/due process requirements are, or can be, satisfied by CDR systems, and
- whether individual CDR schemes satisfy the requirements of independence and impartiality, and to what extent problems can be satisfactorily overcome through governance and transparency.

In Western democracies, courts have been valued on the basis of their adherence to principles of justice, due process and fair procedures. But orderly and fair procedures have been allowed to escape the scrutiny of what process evaluators call KPIs – Key Performance Indicators – especially cost and duration. The most important development that has taken place in dispute resolution in the first decade of the 21st century is that individuals and consumers with disputes, who have hitherto had few options other than the traditional court pathways for channelling their disputes, have been presented with new options and have voted silently with their feet by using the new pathways and not using the court options. The simple attractions of these new pathways are speed, low cost, and perhaps above all their user-friendliness. In other words, users of small claim dispute resolution procedures have made their choices based on the KPIs. User power has not only introduced KPIs as criteria for assessment of dispute resolution procedures, now that it has some real options, it has even elevated KPIs over the traditional legal standards as being the most important criteria in selection among the options.

This is an application of the simple principles of competition: the availability of pathways have traditionally been controlled by suppliers, and have been monopolized and restricted, with rent-gaining behaviour. The introduction of more options has introduced competition, and users have turned their backs on the traditional court processes in favour of new pathways and providers. As a result, CDR systems have become mainstream dispute resolution pathways.

The key point is that CDRs are not only faster and cheaper than courts, but, above all, they are usually (more) *user-friendly*. Busy people cannot afford the time to deal with lawyers and courts. People have become used to the speed of modern communications and do not want to have to put up with slow dispute resolution systems. Many CDR and ODR systems have the huge practical advantage that all people have to do is send simple online details of a complaint and the responsibility for dealing with it becomes the responsibility of the ombudsman or other CDR body, acting impartially but in effect as the consumer's friend. In many cases, consumers just want advice and a second opinion: if they are told by a reliable expert third party that they have no cause for complaint, they will trust that opinion if it is made by a respected body. One feature that will increase respect will be where the intermediary has no financial incentive to institute further proceedings – here an ombudsman is *unlike* a lawyer.

People who might choose litigation have voted with their feet, and have deserted courts, or are deserting them. In addition, CDRs are capturing C2B claims that people would never bring in courts. As a single illustrative example, one can see this from UK data. County Court claims in England and Wales for *all* non-family cases have fallen from 2 million in 2008 to 1.5 million in 2011 (of which only 163,905 were defended and allocated to a track). In contrast, contacts to the UK FOS have risen over the past decade from nothing to 1.2 million in 2011 (which that year turned into 264,375 cases for determination). These figures show not only a growth in the dispute resolution function of CDR schemes compared with courts but also a growth in consumers seeking advice or triage from CDR bodies compared with lawyers or other sources.

CDR schemes can weed out unmeritorious claims at an early stage, and support claims that would otherwise not be brought. Four out of five contacts received by the UK FOS do not turn into complaints. Many of these are requests for information, or for an independent opinion of whether there may be anything to complain about. Thus, many CDR schemes provide a valuable information service. The importance of reliable, independent information pre-sale can be illustrated in Sweden, where there is a strong national network of information bodies. It is difficult to prove this empirically, but I suspect that the number of disputes that arise in Sweden (around 11,000 annually in the ARN) is low compared with many other similar non-Nordic countries, and this is attributable to good pre-sale and post-sale sources of advice. It is also notable that good CDR schemes have high levels of public trust. A survey found that 70 per cent of people asked said they had faith in the UK FOS.[101]

Two points can be observed here. First, consumers may be accepting a certain lowering of standards in terms of essential requirements, provided the standards achieve a certain minimum level, as opposed to the highest level, which should be demonstrated by courts. Undoubtedly, some CDR systems achieve the same level of accuracy, fairness, independence, and so on as can many courts. But who would guarantee that every court decision absolutely achieves all of these standards? Secondly, consumers accept less than the highest level of protection because they value high performance of the KPIs more than they value achievement of the highest level of the legal principles.

There are two consequences of this situation. First, a debate is needed about what minimum level of essential requirements and KPIs are acceptable, and what the balance between them should be. Secondly, there need to be effective mechanisms to ensure that *all* dispute resolution providers achieve the required standards. In some countries, it has traditionally been very rare for judges to be accused of bias. Control or response mechanisms have therefore been almost non-existent. Even in countries where confidence in the judiciary is low, control or response mechanisms have been difficult to devise or apply. It is fundamentally important that high standards are achieved by courts, and seen to be maintained. But in the world of CDR and similar mechanisms, regulatory systems must be imposed from the start on CDR providers and they must be effective. If they are not effective, confidence in these pathways will evaporate and the pathways will collapse. Lawyers might welcome that, but state courts would not be able to cope, and there would be a major risk of collapse in civil society.[102]

---

[101] *Annual Review of Consumer Complaints about Insurance, Credit, Banking, Savings, Investments. Financial Year 2011–2012* (Financial Ombudsman Service, 2012). The survey also found 76 per cent supporting the local Trading Standards Authorities.

[102] These issues are explored further in the following chapters of this book.

4. Overcoming Funding and Costs Barriers

Many CDR systems offer the considerable attraction to governments that they are financed largely or wholly by the private sector, saving public funds. In civil procedure systems, by contrast, litigants usually pay their own costs but courts are usually heavily subsidized by the state.[103] The picture on who funds CDR systems is not uniform, but may well be evolving as a result of the global financial crisis towards more privatized funding. In some states, major business sectors have seen commercial advantages in funding specialist CDR schemes covering their sector (note the points here in Benöhr's analysis of the insurance sector). Intelligent governments will be able to maximize such advantages so as to entice more sectors to fund sectoral CDR schemes. Or governments may simply impose a funding requirement by law. The issue of funding is inter-linked with the issue of whether decisions by a CDR body should be binding on traders (or on consumers). But there may remain a need in some or all states for public funding of a residual CDR body to handle cases that do not fall under privately funded arrangements. The picture across Europe is far from uniform and has some way to evolve. But the development of 'privatized justice' highlights the importance of ensuring that CDR bodies satisfy the constitutional criteria of independence, impartiality, and so on, referred to above.

5. CDR as Part of the Regulatory System

CDR systems also offer the invaluable benefit that they can deliver cheap and effective regulatory data, and hence make a substantial contribution to having behavioural impact and to maintaining and raising standards of business practice in the marketplace. The source of this benefit lies in the ability of CDR bodies to record *every* contact in their IT systems, and then aggregate them all so as to see a complete picture of what is going on in the marketplace. Even if a contact is merely an inquiry rather than a complaint, and even if a complaint is rejected as being unfounded, the fact that it has been made can be recorded, and every single contact, when aggregated, contributes to a complete picture of what is happening in the market.

Holistic quality systems that operate on the basis of post-marketing data have spread across many regulatory systems. For example, the effectiveness

---

[103] Christopher Hodges, Stefan Vogenauer and Magdalena Tulibacka, *The Costs and Funding of Civil Litigation – A Comparative Perspective* (Oxford 2010).

of the EU regulatory system for identifying unsuspectedly unsafe medicines rests on the pharmacovigilance system, into which all adverse drug reaction[104] reports are entered and scrutinized for unexpected signals. Similar post-marketing vigilance systems have been introduced in many other sectors – medical devices, general product safety, etc. These systems all depend on capturing as many adverse event reports as possible, in a single database, and then looking for trends and signals. The information is then re-cycled to firms, regulators, the market and purchasers. That is what private enforcement based ultimately on courts cannot do, but one based on CDR systems can do – and already does.

A fundamental feature of such post-marketing vigilance systems is that the data should not just be collected but should be fed back – to the traders involved but also to customers, market commentators and regulators. Leading CDR schemes, such as the FOS and the telecoms regulator OFCOM, now publish statistics on the number and type of claims received, naming the firms involved. The results have been striking. The introduction of such public transparency revealed that almost all of the then 200,000 complaints against financial institutions in 2010 were only against the four large retail banks. For the first time, consumer complaints, consumer complaint systems, and the activities revealed that gave rise to such complaints, became items for scrutiny by the main Boards of the banks. Customers reacted: trading behaviour improved.

IV. GENERAL CONCLUSIONS

A culture of settlement is spreading across Europe, from the introduction of mediation in the courts to the development of new CDR systems that are built on facilitating settlement in most disputes,[105] and the inclusion of restorative justice into the duties of some public enforcement bodies. Does the spread of a culture of settlement signify a philosophical desire or trend in some societies for less confrontation? If so, is this a feature of particular societies (and legal systems) and not others? What are the reasons for such a trend, what prerequisites must exist for the culture of settlement to flourish, and what consequential changes occur or are necessary in legal systems? Does a settlement culture in fact signify a deep philosophical

---

[104] Confusingly, the acronym is also ADR!

[105] Pablo Cortés, 'A Comparative Review of Offers to Settle – Would an Emerging Settlement Culture Pave the Way for their Adoption in Continental Europe?' (2012) 32.1 *Civil Justice Quarterly* 42.

state within a civil society, or does it merely manifest a desire for greater speed and efficiency in dispute resolution? To what extent may increased computerization by courts "claw back" disputes from CDR?

This book raises a whole series of questions. It is a challenge, at this stage, for legal scientists to provide answers, since the underlying changes seem to be both cultural and market-led, and the direction and speed of change largely now depend on political decisions. These are our thoughts about the future, at least on the important questions that arise and that call for political debate and decision.

We are already seeing the development of new forms and architectures within European legal systems, as CDR systems grow with their own architectures and courts wither. It will be important to debate what criteria are necessary for all or any dispute resolution pathway to satisfy. To what extent, if at all, should we accept exceptions to general principles? How can we ensure that ombudsmen and regulators satisfy the essential constitutional requirements that we demand from courts, such as independence, integrity, openness and fairness.

A series of key challenges exist for the developing CDR system: In Europe, governments will have to address the requirements for implementation of the ADR/ODR legislation. Will they adopt minimal implementation or be more imaginative? Will the CDR and ODR systems, and wider ADR systems, develop further? The main issues that need to be addressed are: funding, what is binding on whom, and extending to full coverage. Will the courts and lawyers see the development of CDR and regulatory oversight of redress as a challenge? If so, how will they respond? Will they be capable of responding by improving their performance criteria by reducing cost, improving speed, and providing effective outcomes? Or has the combined voice of business and consumers in fact already made clear their choice in favour of new forms of dispute resolution that are more responsive?

One fundamentally important question is whether CADR or courts should decide the law. A number of commentators regard it as unconstitutional and/or unacceptable that law is declared or clarified anywhere other than by judges in courts. One objection raised relates to whether a phenomenon of "disappearing judgments" (akin to the phenomenon of "disappearing trials" in USA and elsewhere) will lead to perpetuation of uncertainty because rules are not clarified (which may be highly undesirable in unclear or controversial situations such as commercial or civil rights law), or may lead to a collapse in respect for the rule of law itself if courts are not seen to apply law reasonably regularly. Some responses to those points are made. First, arbitration is extensively used, especially in commercial disputes, and that takes much "business" away from courts in a non-transparent fashion. Secondly, law can be clarified by means other than courts, such as by regulators, codes or guidance, and by parliaments and increased use of law commission reviews and restatement-type approaches. Thirdly, Hodges et al have suggested that consumer ADR bodies should not decide points of law, but they should be able to refer them to courts and regulators as necessary for decision, so that the results can then be applied by the CDR body. It may well be that these arguments and counter-arguments will not be resolved soon, and so are likely to continue as sources of irritation and even hostility.

The contributions in this book tackle thorny issues. In China, the omnipresent political trend to court-based mediation and settlement strongly nourishes the suspicion that not all settlements are based on the free will of the parties. While this can mostly be ascribed to the lack of judicial independence in China, in Western countries the constraints of litigation costs may have more subtle effects on the parties but often lead to similar results. The UK provides an excellent but alarming example of where settlements have already become a standard practice in individual civil litigation – irrespective of the even greater pressure to settle mass disputes which clog courts for years and require considerable creativity to find new ways of funding. Although any tendency to accept ADR, mediation and settlement as *standard instruments* to handle civil disputes comes into conflict with the idea of the rule of law and the pivotal role of courts in a constitutional state, with respect to mass disputes there is obviously no way out of this dilemma once the the regulatory systems have failed to prevent infringements.

Thus a task for the future will be to find at least a balance between *ex ante* and *ex post* control by both public and private actors. We must create a legal architecture in Europe which offers several ways and options in order to address diverse situations.[106] Although negotiations and settlements save on many social costs and must therefore be an important part of the system, they cannot be the only pillar. Self-regulation, ADR and CDR systems offer an excellent chance of filtering out a number of disputes, but they are not suited for cases which involve complicated fact-finding and highly controversial legal issues. For the latter category of cases, public authorities, special arrangements, or court-based private actions are necessary to assist in the enforcement of damages claims.[107] For many mass dis-

---

[106] In any case, in order to evaluate exiting models further empirical research will be necessary, Rebecca Money-Kyrle and Christopher Hodges (supra note 24), 504.

[107] For a three-pillar system see Christopher Hodges in Jenny Steele and Willem van Boom (supra note 1), 101–7; see also Christopher Hodges (supra note 1), 235 et seq.

putes a settlement will be the best solution. However, the lesson to be learnt from the settlement part of the book is that we need independent judges acting with responsibility. If settlements are seen to be unfair or collusive, it will quickly undermine trust in the judicial system. Some contributors report that courts rely on a rather strong presumption that the proposed settlements are fair and they can list only a few cases where a proposed settlement was rejected.[108] Does that indicate that "utility-maximizing judges"[109] fail to apply standards for approval strictly or does this provide evidence that settlements apart from some outliers are very often indeed "fair and reasonable"? Being aware of the incentives for lawyers and judges monitoring settlements is only a first step in developing an efficient system of mass justice, albeit a very important one. We suggest that robust mechanisms are needed to ensure that settlements are fair. Judges cannot be expected to have the tools or experience to evaluate an arrangement that is being put forward by all, or the principal, parties. Merely including a right for some to object will not be enough. Some independent scrutiny, or mechanism for a "devil's advocate" challenge, will be required.

We will not only have to watch the developments described in this book closely, it will also be necessary to compare the results of self-regulation and mass settlements with the efficiency of public enforcement proceedings in order to establish a well-balanced system.

---

108 See Jasminka Kalajdzic, in this volume, Chapter 6, p. 141.
109 Michael Faure, in this volume, Chapter 2, p. 58.

2. CADR and settlement of claims – a few economic observations

Michael Faure

I. INTRODUCTION

Enforcement of consumer law is a topic that has received a fair amount of attention in law and economics scholarship. However, it is probably fair to state that generally the topic of consumer alternative dispute resolution in consumer cases (abbreviated as CADR) and mass settlement of claims are not topics that have been studied in a great deal of detail in law and economics scholarship. For the purposes of this chapter I will attempt to apply general notions following from the law and economics methodology to some of the issues that are central to this volume. The goal of my contribution is certainly not to describe or criticize legal rules, since other contributors will undoubtedly do so and, moreover, to an important extent I will in that respect build upon earlier scholarship such as the studies by Van Boom and Loos on collective enforcement of consumer law[1] and by Steele and Van Boom on mass disputes[2] and the recent interesting comparative study by Hodges and Benöhr and Creutzfeldt-Banda on CADR[3]. When thinking about potential problems of consumer ADR and settlement of claims from an economic perspective one tends to think of situations where a consumer would suffer a loss but would, for a variety of reasons, not be able to seek a remedy via the traditional civil justice system. The reasons for particular failures in the private litigation system in case of consumer losses have certainly been identified in law and economics literature. A recent overview of the state of the art in that respect is *inter*

[1] See Willem van Boom and Marco Loos (eds), *Collective Enforcement of Consumer Law: Securing Compliance in Europe Through Private Group Action and Public Authority Intervention* (Europa Law Publishing 2007).

[2] Jenny Steele and Willem van Boom (eds), *Mass Justice, Challenges of Representation and Distribution* (Edward Elgar 2011).

[3] Christopher Hodges, Iris Benöhr and Naomi Creutzfeldt-Banda (eds), *Consumer ADR in Europe. Civil Justice Systems* (Hart 2012).

alia provided in Tuil/Visscher (2010) where problems facing consumers (but also victims more generally) in the civil justice system are identified and potential solutions are discussed from both a legal as well as from an economic perspective[4]. To an important extent this contribution will rely on the findings in that volume.

This contribution will be structured as follows: in order to ease the discussion I will start with a hypothetical case of a loss suffered by a consumer and see which potential problems could arise (II); next I will illustrate that the starting-point for an economic analysis would be that a market failure may arise which may justify some intervention (III). A first question that arises is how the aversion against potentially high litigation costs could be remedied (IV); the other problem that arises is that rational apathy may arise because of dispersed losses; potential remedies for that issue will be addressed as well (V). Then the question will be addressed how CADR may change the picture which until then will have mostly been focusing on the civil justice system (VI), turning next to the second central theme of this volume, the settlement of mass claims. In that respect the question arises which problems play a note in settlement of mass claims as far as the incentives of lawyers are concerned (VII) as well as concerning the potential incentives of judges (VIII). Section IX will conclude.

II. A HYPOTHETICAL CASE

Assume a hypothetical case of a Belgian citizen inheriting an amount of €125,000 in 2008 (after paying taxes) which he wants to invest safely. He visits his bank and the bank gives him the following advice:

- Invest €80,000 at risk (basically in stock with potentially high revenues).
- Put €20,000 in a savings account (relatively low interest, but low risk and immediately available).
- Invest €25,000 in a bond of the KBC (equally safe and providing a steady interest rate of 5 per cent, repayable after five years).

In 2012 the customer receives a letter from his bank telling him that unfortunately the bond of €25,000 of the bank has lost most of its value

---

[4] Mark Tuil and Louis Visscher (eds), *New Trends in Financing Civil Litigation in Europe – A Legal, Empirical and Economic Analysis* (Edward Elgar 2010).

because it was invested in Greek sovereign debt. This was totally unforeseeable; the bond will hence not be repaid in 2013 but now in 2012 and the consumer will only receive approximately €21,000 hence leading to a loss of €4,000. Let us assume for sake of simplicity that the bank violated a variety of legal rules, probably some Belgian statutes implementing European directives concerning the mandatory disclosure of information as well as Belgian rules of private law[5].

The interesting point from the perspective of this volume is whether the consumer in this hypothetical case can effectively seek any redress. How should this problem be viewed from an economic perspective?

III. STARTING-POINT: MARKET FAILURE

In theory the customer in the case under discussion could use a variety of remedies.

- A first possibility is for example to report the presumed violation to public authorities and ask for public law enforcement[6]. This may certainly be an option, but probably not very attractive to the consumer since public law enforcement will not necessarily guarantee him repayment of his losses[7].
- A second option would be to use a mediation system like CADR[8]. In fact, in the particular case at hand the customer had written to the

[5] Belgium constitutes an interesting case in consumer law since for a long time it has been falling behind as far as the enforcement of CADR is concerned; but is now leapfrogging with the introduction of a variety of new CADR models. For details see Stefaan Voet, 'Belgium' in Hodges, Benöhr and Creutzfeldt-Banda (supra note 3), 25–36.

[6] This option also exists in many OECD jurisdictions. For a comparative overview see Michael Faure, Anthony Ogus and Niels Philipsen, 'Enforcement Practices for Breaches of Consumer Protection Legislation', (2008) 20 *CLR* 361–401.

[7] There are, however, possible regimes where public law enforcement is mixed with private law enforcement or at least with compensation of losses. See in this respect the contribution by Julia Hörnle, Chapter 13, this volume and see Franziska Weber, *Towards an Optimal Mix of Public and Private Enforcement in Consumer Law. A Comparative Law and Economics Analysis of European Consumer Law Enforcement (Package travel vs. misleading advertising)* (dissertation, Rotterdam, 28 June 2012), who equally discusses mixes of public enforcement and compensation of consumers.

[8] For an earlier study on institutions for the cheap resolutions of disputes with consumers see Jules Stuyck, Evelyne Terryn, Veerle Colaert, Tom Van Dyck, Neil Peretz, Nele Hoekx and Piotr Tereszkiewicz, *An Analysis and Evaluation of*

bank to express his disappointment concerning his losses and had asked for relief, but the bank had replied that this was not possible. Of course in many legal systems CADR is now available, especially for financial losses. For example in the UK a consumer could turn to a financial ombudsman and also in Belgium a mediation service for banks is available through Belmed[9]. However, CADR may not always be an adequate remedy. Even though in this particular case (of Belgium) it may be that as in other countries like Sweden a value limit would apply[10]. Moreover, it is also indicated that consumers often still lack awareness of available CADR systems, also because the financial institutions may not point the customer at the option of seeking relief via CADR[11].

Assuming hence that the customer lacks awareness of the CADR or that he tried the Belmed mediation system but that it did not provide him with relief the only option left is:

- Civil litigation[12]. However, given the possibly uncertain outcome and the high-risk aversion of the consumer (especially concerning potential high lawyer's fees), a problem of rational apathy (also referred to as rational disinterest) may arise: the risk-averse consumer may find the investments in the suit (more particularly the lawyer's fees, assuming he cannot call on legal aid) too high, compared to the potential benefit (of €4,000)[13]. The result is that a potentially meritorious suit is not brought and that, as a result of this failure, the bank is not sufficiently deterred from their behavior through a liability suit. From an economic perspective a market failure therefore arises

---

Alternative Means of Consumer Redress Other than Redress Through Ordinary Judicial Proceedings, A Study for *The European Commission* (Leuven: The Study Center for Consumer Law – Centre for European Economic Law, 2007, available at <http://ec.europa.eu/consumers/redress/reports_studies/comparative_report_en.pdf>).

9 For details see Voet (supra note 5), 25–36.

10 Yolanda Girzl, at the conference at Erasmus University on 27 June 2012, indicated that in Sweden a value limit of €2.000 applies which would exclude our case from CADR.

11 See Iris Benöhr, Chapter 11, this volume.

12 For an overview as to possibilities of private enforcement and their weaknesses see Katalin J Cseres, 'Enforcement of Collective Consumer Interests: A Competition Law Perspective' in Van Boom and Loos (supra note 1), 125–72.

13 I disregard for a moment that the consumer would, in case of litigation, also run the risk of having to pay (a part of) the legal fees of the bank if he lost the case.

because a socially desirable suit is not brought[14]. This, hence, merits an analysis of potential ways to remedy this market failure. One obvious option is to improve the working of CADR, which is the central topic of this volume. However, as indicated, CADR may not always work (given information deficiencies, financial limitations or the simple fact that the mediation does not lead to the result desired by the customer). Hence the second option is to remedy the rational apathy in civil litigation by finding solutions in the funding of civil litigation that reduce the risk aversion of the customer (IV). However, in addition, a second problem may arise. For the individual customer the losses (in this case €4,000) may still be bearable or at least too high to bring a private law suit. He is, however, not the only customer suffering a loss from the particular bank and hence the total social losses may be substantially larger. This also justifies the question whether a remedy for dispersed losses can be found. I will first address potential remedies for high-cost aversion (IV) and then turn to potential solutions for dispersed losses (V).

IV. REMEDYING HIGH-COST AVERSION

Turning first to the primary problem of the risk-averse customer (aversion to high legal fees) several alternatives can of course be presented that could potentially remedy the problem the customer is facing[15]. The question of how to finance civil litigation and thus remedy risk aversion is of course widely studied in the law and economics literature and as such is not new. However, the fact that none of those remedies is completely satisfactory[16] also underscores the need to develop systems of CADR, as clearly discussed in this volume. One could think of the following alternative remedies to relieve the risk aversion of the hypothetical customer in our case.

---

14 There may be many reasons why a private right might not be enforced by consumers. See Michael Faure, Anthony Ogus and Niels Philipsen, 'Curbing Consumer Financial Losses: The Economics of Regulatory Enforcement' (2009) 31 *Law & Policy* 181–2.

15 Many of those remedies have been discussed in Tuil and Visscher (supra note 4) as a result of which I will largely draw on that volume. However, see on the costs of civil litigation in Europe also the interesting study by Christopher Hodges, Stefan Vogenauer and Magdalena Tulibacka (eds), *The Costs and Funding of Civil Litigation: A Comparative Perspective* (Hart 2010).

16 Not so much because they could theoretically not work, but mostly because they simply do not exist in many legal systems.

1. Conditional Fee Arrangements

With a conditional fee arrangement in this particular case I simply refer to a method of paying the lawyer on the basis of the result obtained by the lawyer[17].

Conditional fees have a strong economic appeal for the simple reason that they align the incentives of the clients and the lawyer[18]. From the perspective of the consumer the main advantage would be that it reduces his risk aversion, certainly if the result-based fee is constructed like a "no cure, no pay" model. Earlier research has indicated that some form of result-based remuneration exists in many legal systems, although the precise shape may differ[19]. Economic literature moreover indicates that, although many forms of result-based fees are applied on both sides of the Atlantic, this apparently happens without alleged problems as a result[20]. An advantage of a result-based remuneration system is, moreover, that it provides strong incentives for lawyers to *ex ante* monitor the quality of cases and that thus excessive or frivolous litigation would be avoided, since lawyers would only have an incentive to accept meritorious cases. This seems to be confirmed in empirical research by Helland and Tabarrok, indicating that contingency fees discourage the filing of low quality suits and hence increase the legal quality of cases[21].

2. Legal Expenses Insurance

Another way to solve the risk aversion of the consumer and hence to give potential plaintiffs incentives to bring meritorious claims is to use insurance techniques. The principle is relatively simple: the insurer takes over the risk of having to pay legal expenses from the plaintiff with risk aversion and can in that way stimulate that meritorious claims would be brought. The classic legal expenses insurance is a before the event insurance (also abbreviated as BTE) whereby a risk-averse individual *ex ante*

---

[17] For a more nuanced approach to the different categories of result-based remuneration of lawyers see Michael Faure, Fokke Fernhout and Niels Philipsen, 'No Cure, No Pay and Contingency Fees' in Tuil and Visscher (supra note 4), 33–56.

[18] Which in some legal literature is precisely why they are considered as problematic since lawyers are not supposed to have a stake in the outcome of the case.

[19] See Faure, Fernhout and Philipsen (supra note 17), 33–56.

[20] So Tuil and Visscher (supra note 4), 175–90.

[21] See Eric Helland and Alex Tabarrok, 'Contingencies Fees, Settlement Delay and Low-quality Litigation: Empirical Evidence from Two Data Sets' (2003) 19 *J L Econ & Org* 517–42.

seeks coverage against the risk of being engaged in a trial and incurring legal expenses[22]. The basic model is that the procedural risk (and hence the expenses) are shifted to the insurance company. The insurer will of course function as a gatekeeper and screen the case on the merits. As a result, in principle only meritorious claims will be brought[23]. A surprising empirical fact is, however, that notwithstanding the theoretical advantages of legal aid insurance very few individuals in fact conclude those insurance policies. Even in legal systems where the insurability of legal expenses would be high (*inter alia* given fixed fee systems like in Germany) the coverage is on average not very high[24]. The only European system with high coverage for legal expenses insurance is a country like Sweden where legal expenses insurance is mandatorily added on to health care insurance[25]. Hence, in practice many individuals do not possess BTE insurance, as a result of which it may not always help the consumers.

Another possibility is to conclude insurance after the event on an *ex post* basis, referred to as after the event insurance or ATE. Van Boom rightly argues that ATE insurance is probably no longer an insurance contract since the premium in fact amounts to a contingency (a proportion of the proceeds) that the winning insured would have to receive from his injurer once winning the case after the event[26]. So far ATE is limited to the UK but in that country the system is used relatively frequently[27].

In sum, insurance solutions may theoretically be available in many legal systems, but many individuals simply do not purchase them. In the absence of a mandatory system, insurance may hence not help the consumer.

---

22 For details see Willem van Boom, 'Financing Civil Litigation by the European Insurance Industry' in Tuil and Visscher (supra note 4), 92–108.

23 See Tuil and Visscher (supra note 4) and Louis Visscher and Tom Schepens, 'A Law and Economics Approach to Cost Shifting, Fee Arrangements and Legal Expense Insurance' in Tuil and Visscher (supra note 4), 7–32.

24 For an overview see Matthias Kilian, 'Alternatives to Public Provision: The Role of Legal Expenses Insurance in Broadening Access to Justice: The German Experience' (2003) 30 *Journal of Law and Society* 36 and see Francis Regan, 'Whatever Happened to Legal Expenses Insurance?' (2001) 26 *Alt LJ* 293–7 and see also Matthias Kilian and Francis Regan, 'Legal Expenses Insurance and Legal Aid – Two Sides of the Same Coin? The Experience from Germany and Sweden' (2004) 11 *Int'l J Legal Prof* 238.

25 See on the Swedish model Francis Regan, 'The Swedish Legal Services Policy Remix: The Shift from Public Legal Aid to Private Legal Expenses Insurance', (2003) 30 *Journal of Law and Society* 49–65.

26 Van Boom (supra note 22).

27 See Paul Fenn and Neil Rickman, 'The Empirical Analysis of Litigation Funding' in Tuil and Visscher (supra note 4), 142.

3. Transfer of Claim

A third alternative prefers transferring a claim to a third party. The model assumes that a customer (like presumably the one from our case) may have a meritorious claim but has neither the money nor the time to bring the lawsuit. A transfer supposes that he sells his claim to a third party who purchases the claim and of course pays a lower price than the total value of the claim[28]. The advantage of such a transfer for the consumer can be obvious: he may have a possibility of receiving compensation quickly of a certain amount without costs and risks. Of course, the victim will not receive full compensation since the buyer will reduce the value of the claim with a risk premium given the uncertainty of recovery[29].

It seems an interesting and attractive model, but is not that often used in practice. First of all many legal systems do not allow such a transfer of a (liability) claim[30]. Another problem is that even in legal systems that do allow a transfer of claim, coordination and information difficulties may arise during litigation[31]; the purchaser of the claim may still depend on the seller for example to obtain information to make his claim successful. The incentives of the victim, who sold the claim and hence has already cashed it in, to actually cooperate during litigation may be limited, which could jeopardize the attractiveness of the system altogether.

4. Third-party Funding

A fourth model which looks like a transfer of a claim, but is actually different, is a system whereby a third party simply finances litigation (third-party funding or abbreviated TPF), against a payment which can consist in a part of the proceeds in case of success[32]. The way it usually works is that a private company offers a plaintiff cash in exchange for a property interest in an unresolved law suit. The enterprise will usually offer cash in the form of an advance on the settlement amount. Third-party funding

---

28 For the mechanics of this see Andrea Pinna, 'Financing Civil Litigation: The Case for the Assignment and Securitization of Liability Claims' in Tuil and Visscher (supra note 4), 109–30.

29 See Tuil and Visscher (supra note 4), 187–8.

30 For details on the attitudes of the legal system, see Pinna (supra note 28).

31 See also Tuil and Visscher (supra note 4), 188.

32 See on the economics of third-party funding Keith Hylton, *The Economics of Third-party Finance Litigation*, Boston University School of Law Working Paper, number 11-57 (2011), <http://www.bu.edu/law/faculty/scholarschip/workingpaper/2011.html> or at <http://ssrn.com/abstract=1971229>.

has become very popular in the US[33], but so far has not really taken off in Europe[34].

5. Public-private Partnerships

Another alternative would be to use public funding of legal expenses. However, in such a private-public partnership it would not amount to traditional legal aid which is provided to the less wealthy free of charge. The idea with a public-private partnership is that the government would intervene to finance meritorious claims precisely because bringing these claims would increase social welfare. A variety of those contingency legal aid funds (CLAF) exists for example in Quebec and Ontario (both in Canada)[35]. An interesting example is also provided by the supplementary legal aid scheme (SLAS) from Hong Kong. In this system lawyers are still paid on an hourly basis by the public fund. Clients on the other hand pay a contribution to the fund on a "no cure, no pay" basis: if they lose their case, they do not owe anything to the fund and if they win, a fixed percentage of their claim will be paid to SLAS to cover the expenses of the lawyer. The fund itself (SLAS) monitors the quality of the performance by the lawyer. The system would be particularly attractive for individuals seeking access to justice who earn too much for the (public) legal aid scheme and too little to be able to pay the expensive hourly fees themselves[36]. It has, however, been argued that this kind of contingency style public fund usually only works as a complement to other measures such as contingency fees and mostly for areas in which litigation is uncertain and costly[37].

6. Summary

Of course, using a bit of imagination, still many more arrangements could be thought of to provide incentives to potential plaintiffs to bring meritorious claims. One model not yet discussed would be to pay attention to

---

33 For details see Deborah R. Hensler, 'Financing Civil Litigation: The US Perspective' in Tuil and Visscher (supra note 4), 153. She refers for example to websites like <www.fundmysuit.com> where enterprises offer funding for litigation.

34 For experiences with third-party funding in Europe see Maya Steinitz, 'Whose Claim is it Anyway? Third Party Litigation Funding' (2011) 95 *Minn L Rev* 1268–338.

35 See Sonja Keske, Andrea Renda and Roger Van den Bergh, 'Financing and Group Litigation' in Tuil and Visscher (supra note 4), 84–5.

36 For details see Faure, Fernhout and Philipsen (supra note 17), 48–9.

37 See Keske, Renda and Van den Bergh (supra note 35), 85.

fee shifting. The law and economics literature has discussed in detail the different merits of the so-called American rule (whereby each party bears its own litigation costs) versus the English rule (whereby the loser pays all the costs). The literature argues that the English rule has the effect that the stakes become higher, which would more particularly incentivize plaintiffs with high value claims to bring a law suit. One method not discussed yet would thus be to use an English fee shifting rule in order to provide incentives to potential plaintiffs with high quality claims to actually sue[38].

This overview is presented just to show that, at least on paper, various arrangements exist that could deal with the first problem we identified as a cause of the market failure, being the aversion of the consumer against the risk of high litigation costs. Any of the arrangements discussed above could remedy that risk aversion and hence make sure that the meritorious suit is nevertheless brought. The mere fact that so many alternatives are, at least in theory, available should also be welcomed from an economic perspective. After all, as one of the editors of this book often reminded me, law and economics scholars should like competition and hence should welcome a large variety of options being available to consumers.

However, in practice one will often notice that in the EU the theoretically possible options are in many legal systems simply not available. Sometimes legal rules may prohibit particular solutions (like a transfer of claim or third-party funding). In other cases problems may arise on the supply side of legal services (for example many European legal systems still prohibit particular forms of result-based remuneration for lawyers[39]); in other cases a theoretically available option is simply not used because of problems on the demand side (like legal expenses insurance which is in many legal systems only purchased to a very limited extent).

In sum, since especially in European legal systems the many theoretically possible alternatives to remedy the risk aversion following from high litigation costs will not be available in practice, the meritorious suit may after all often not be brought and the market failure may continue.

V. REMEDYING DISPERSED LOSSES/ RATIONAL APATHY

A second cause of the market failure, identified above, is that the loss of the individual consumer may be relatively limited, but that many other

[38] Ibid, 73–82, see also Visscher and Schepens (supra note 23), 11–16.
[39] For details see Faure, Fernhout and Philipsen (supra note 17).

consumers may be in a similar situation. The fact that losses are scattered over a wide number of consumers may lead to a relatively small loss for each of them[40] or at least an individual loss which is too low to bring a claim[41]. The aggregate loss of all consumers can, however, be so substantial that bringing a suit would certainly be beneficial for society. This brings me to the second aspect central to this volume, the potential solutions for so-called mass claims. Again, it is an issue that has been addressed in law and economics literature from various angles.

1. Collective Action/Group Litigation

The starting point is that granting the right to a group to act on behalf of all individuals that suffered a loss may reduce the rational apathy[42] because costs can now be shared collectively and hence spread to all individuals. Bundling of the claims allows a lower cost per individual. This, so the theory predicts, will lead to more claims being filed and hence to increased deterrence[43]. There is also empirical evidence supporting that claim: Eisenberg and Miller found that the costs of individual litigation and legal counseling decreased with the increasing number of participants in a class action[44].

However, collective action, for example via a class action, does not only have benefits. One of the problems is that someone has to act on behalf of the class. Usually it is an attorney who acts as an entrepreneur and will represent the class. His interest is that he, after judging the merits of the case, makes a substantial upfront investment, hoping to collect a substantial fee out of a positive judgment or a settlement. In those situations the classic principal-agent problem always arises, that the interests of the agent (the attorney in this case) may not always collide with the interests of the prin-

---

40 See also Stefaan Voet, Chapter 12 in this volume.

41 This is referred to as the well-known rational apathy problem see Hans-Bernd Schäfer, 'The Bundling of Similar Interests on Litigation. The Incentives for Class Actions and Legal Actions Taken by Associations' (2000) 9 *Eur J Law Econ* 183.

42 See Keske, Renda and Van den Bergh (supra note 35), 59.

43 See *inter alia* Hans-W Micklitz and Astrid Stadler, 'The Development of Collective Legal Action in Europe, Especially in Germany' (2006) 17 *EBLR* 1473–503.

44 Theodore Eisenberg and Geoffrey Miller, *The Role of Opt-outs and Objectors in Class Action Litigation: Theoretical and Empirical Issues*, NYU Law and Economics Research Paper, No. 04-004, SSRN: <www.ssrn.com/abstract 528147>.

cipals (the victims he represents)[45]. A related issue is that a way of financing the claim still has to be found. Often attorneys representing a class will pre-finance the claim on the basis of a conditional fee arrangement.

Questions also arise concerning the formation of the class. The traditional choice is between, on the one hand, freedom for individuals to join the group (a so-called opt-in model) versus, on the other hand, a model whereby in principle all are presumed to join the class unless they have shown themselves not to be interested (an opt-out model)[46]. Economists strongly favor opt-out systems for the reason that since there was a rational apathy problem anyway it allows much better deterrence; only a small number of victims would actually use the opt-out[47]. Lawyers, on the other hand, do not like the mandatory aspect of the opt-out and hence would prefer a system where the victims can voluntary choose to join[48]. This again is criticized since "in many instances the problem of rational apathy would avoid most individuals from bringing a claim anyway"[49] as a result of which the argument that an opt-out model would frustrate the access to individual justice is in fact often an empty shell.

Benefits of a collective action system (like a class action) are therefore large since the system allows remedying rational apathy in case of scattered losses and could thus add to deterrence. However, an important counter-argument against class actions is that they would be substantially more costly than individual litigation since class actions would take considerably longer than other trials and would require more attention by the judge[50]. The empirical evidence on whether class actions are really more expensive than individual litigation seems to be inconclusive[51] as a result of which it was proposed to conduct a cost benefit analysis of class actions[52].

---

45 See Keske, Renda and Van den Bergh (supra note 35), 64 and Mark Tuil and Louis Visscher, 'New Trends in Financing Civil Litigation in Europe: Lessons to be Learned' in Tuil and Visscher (supra note 4), 175, 177 and 185.

46 See on the differences Keske, Renda and Van den Bergh (supra note 35), 60–1.

47 Ibid, 61.

48 See on the opt-in system also the inaugural address of Astrid Stadler 'Group Actions as a Remedy to Enforce Consumer Interests' in Fabrizzio Cafaggi and Hans-W. Micklitz (eds), *New Frontiers of Consumer Protection – The Interplay between Private and Public Enforcement* (Intersentia 2009) 305, 317.

49 See Tuil and Visscher (supra note 4), 185.

50 Keske, Renda and Van den Bergh (supra note 35), 63.

51 See on the US perspective Hensler (supra note 33), 155–63.

52 See Deborah R. Hensler, *Class Action Dilemmas: Pursuing Public Goals for Private Gain* (Rand Corporation 2000).

2. Representative Suit: Consumer Organizations

Another way to solve the collective action problem in cases of scattered harm is not to start a collective action, but to grant a right to a representative organization such as an NGO or consumer organization to file suit on behalf of the victims[53]. One of the problems that could equally arise in this situation is again the principal-agent problem. Questions can in some cases be asked on whether the association really acts to represent the interests of the victims in an adequate way[54]. This possible problem of a divergence of interests between the representative organization and the consumer may be especially large in the situation (as is often the case in European Member States) that the consumer organization is in fact a monopoly. Competition could better guarantee that the organization acts to represent the victims in an adequate way. In addition to the possible divergence of interests[55] also a consumer organization may face financing problems. Again, some of the techniques discussed before, like conditional fees, could be used to guarantee that only meritorious suits are brought. If the organization has to finance the suit just with the budget collected from memberships fees adequate funding cannot be raised[56].

3. Summary

If one were to summarize the lessons from law and economics theory one could hold that there is a preference for a collective action, for the reason that this is presumed to solve the principal-agent problem in a better way than a representative suit. The collective action would then preferably be financed via a result-based remuneration scheme to guarantee sufficient funding and a focus on meritorious suits[57]. At EU level there is today

---

53 See all those representative actions by consumer organizations, Keske, Renda and Van den Bergh (supra note 35), 67–72.

54 Ibid, 70 and see also Tuil and Visscher (supra note 4), 186.

55 Which is also signaled as a potential problem by Tzankova, Chapter 4 in this book.

56 Law and economics scholars indeed warn that consumer associations may misuse their enforcement powers for opportunistic reasons. See in that respect especially Roger Van den Bergh, 'Should Consumer Protection Law be Publically Enforced? An Economics Perspective on EC Regulation 2006/2004 and its Implementation in the Consumer Protection Laws of the Member States' in Van Boom and Loos (eds), (supra note 1). But see also Schäfer (supra note 41), 183–223.

57 See Keske, Renda and Van den Bergh (supra note 35), 72.

apparently not a fixed choice made between either collective actions or representative suits for consumer losses[58].

VI. WHAT MAKES CADR DIFFERENT?

I have so far analyzed the potential difficulties the consumer would face in bringing a (potentially meritorious) suit and the potential solutions the legal system could give to solve either risk aversion or rational apathy of the consumer. It is now time to turn to the central topic of this volume, being the question to what extent CADR could solve some of the problems that have been discussed earlier. The potential advantages of a CADR system could be addressed either from the perspective of the consumer (VI.1) or from society's perspective (VI.2).

1. The Consumer Perspective

From the consumer perspective we can be brief since the potential advantages of an ADR system have been well described in the extensive literature promoting CADR[59]. One obvious advantage for the consumer is that the barriers to access to justice are usually substantially lower and that the costs involved for the consumer to bring his claim to a CADR board are usually substantially lower as well. A long-existing model is for example the Dutch *Geschillencommissies* which are reported to function well in solving consumer claims[60]. One reason for the lower costs of CADR is not only that the costs for reaching a CADR board are usually trivial, but also that there is no need for a representation by a lawyer[61].

Although CADR could therefore in principle be welcomed, at least from the consumer perspective, some problems may remain. First, not all legal systems or all types of services may have CADR systems in place; second, even if those systems exist there may still be some rational apathy (or ignorance) as a result of which the consumer does not reach the system. Problems could still exist in cases of scattered losses, as a result of which collective action may still be needed in combination with CADR.

---

58 See in this respect the Introduction of Christopher Hodges and Astrid Stadler, in this volume, who refer to the fact that the debate at EU level was currently (in 2012) in an impasse.

59 See *inter alia* Hodges, Benöhr and Creutzfeldt-Banda (eds) (supra note 3).

60 See also Introduction by Christopher Hodges and Astrid Stadler, this volume.

61 See for example the description of the Belgian Belmed model by Stefaan Voet, Chapter 12, this volume.

2. Society's Perspective

From society's perspective the goal is simple: if CADR is able to reach speedy decisions at low costs and of high quality it should of course be welcomed, especially if it could be held that the total social costs of a CADR system would be lower than the costs of handling a similar claim through the court system[62]. Generally, the costs of solving cases via a CADR system are, because of flexible and simple rules of evidence and procedure, presumed to be substantially lower than the costs of the civil court system[63]. CADR systems are usually also part of self-regulation by industry. The presumed advantages of self-regulation are that it generates better information (since traders and consumers are likely to be better informed than bureaucrats). Thus a self-regulatory system would, given the information advantage, be able to solve cases at lower costs than a court system that fails this informational advantage[64]. Moreover, given the self-regulatory nature of CADR the system is often privately financed (by industry)[65], which has substantial advantages in providing incentives for cost reduction. Hence, it can be assumed that the CADR system will be designed in such a way that it will be able to solve cases at lower costs than the (presumably government financed) court system.

Given the lower evidentiary threshold and easier procedure (without the involvement of professional lawyers) one can also expect the CADR system to reach superior decisions[66]. There are, however, from society's perspective, a few potential downsides as well. A first point is that it has to be remembered that the involvement of lawyers and the evidentiary and procedural rules in the civil court system are not of course pointless. They are meant to contribute to better fact-finding and a correct application of legal rules and hence to increase the quality of the decisions. But the

---

[62] It is held in the literature that self-regulatory mechanisms like CADR may be able to achieve compliance at significantly lower administrative costs than through public enforcement processes. Moreover, it is equally held that consumers and consumer associations may be motivated to pursue the case in an efficient way, whereas public enforcement agencies may lack the same motivation. See Faure, Ogus and Philipsen (supra note 14), 161–91.

[63] Faure, Fernhout and Philipsen (supra note 17).

[64] See on the advantages of self-regulation *inter alia* Anthony Ogus, 'Rethinking Self-regulation' (1995) 15 *OJLS* 97–108.

[65] Although this is apparently not always the case. Jolanda Girzl, at the conference at Erasmus University, on 27 June 2012, reported that the ECC-net system in Sweden is government financed.

[66] Naomi Creutzfeldt-Banda reported that CADR systems are indeed able to reach speedier decisions than the court system. See Chapter 10 in this book.

speedier, lower cost decisions without involvement of professional lawyers in the CADR system could potentially lead to more erroneous decisions or, in economic terms, increase error costs. Economists would generally hold that there is a trade off in the sense that the advantages of CADR (in term of lower costs) would have to be compared to the potential dangers (in terms of increased error costs). In cases where these advantages outweigh the costs CADR remains in society's interest. This can obviously be the case when the issues at stake, for example, only concern a material loss (and not, for example, personal injury), when the amounts are relatively limited and where the facts of the case are relatively simple as a result of which the professionals within the CADR board can be assumed to reach correct decisions and thus reduce error costs.

A second danger with any system involving low costs and low thresholds is that it could attract frivolous suits[67]. This can certainly be a potential danger, but CADR systems can also build in controls to avoid wasting time on frivolous suits and this should not constitute an insurmountable problem.

A third potential problem is related to the danger of capture. A CADR body instituted by industry could constitute a monopoly and not be sufficiently independent; especially if the system is also financed by traders the simple question can be asked: can you trust them? Again, this is a point that merits attention, but is not insurmountable either. Guarantees could be built into the system, for example, involving traders as well as consumers or independent experts to guarantee an objective decision-making of high quality[68].

A final point is that CADR systems are usually concluded on a voluntary basis and only bind traders that are members of a particular trade organization. This always raises the question what to do with the so-called "rogue" traders that do not wish to be a member of the trade association and do not wish to join the CADR system. On the one hand one could expect a kind of branding advantage of joining the CADR system: it could lead to a reputational reward for the trader[69]. However, there is always a

---

67 A point that is also stressed by Weber (supra note 7).

68 Interestingly, during the conference preceeding this book, Lewis Shand Smith, Ombudsman of the Ombudsman Service in the UK reported that introducing competition between various CADR models may also have its dangers since traders could exercise pressure on the CADR body for favorable decisions, threatening otherwise to bring cases to a competing CADR body. Shand Smith rightly warned that this could create an undesirable race to the bottom which could lower quality and threaten independence.

69 See Introduction by Christopher Hodges and Astrid Stadler, this volume.

danger that consumers do not recognize the branding or are not aware whether or not a particular trader joined the voluntary system. In that case rogue traders could effectively free ride on the collective efforts of the sector without having to pay for it. Involving the rogue traders or clearly signaling to consumers which traders joined the CADR system and which not hence remains an important point of attention.

VII. SETTLEMENT OF MASS CLAIMS: LAWYERS' INCENTIVES

Let me now turn to the second aspect, central to this volume, the settlement of mass claims. Again there is substantial law and economics literature on the benefits of settlements compared to decisions by the court. Given the high costs, both for the parties involved (not only lawyer fees but also opportunity costs of the parties) as well as the high administrative costs, economists would generally favor settlements compared to long and costly court procedures. In a seminal paper Priest and Klein[70] held that in principle, when parties are well informed on their chances in a lawsuit, they would always try to settle. Only the cases where plaintiffs and defendants had a 50-50 chance of winning would go to court. Another obvious reason for court cases would be those where (one of the) parties have misperceptions on their likelihood of winning.

From an economic perspective a settlement could generally be preferred as a low-cost solution saving on many social costs, especially when the quality of the outcome of the settlement would be the same as that of a court decision. Problems could only arise, for example, in cases of unequal bargaining power where the settlement would, for example, favor one of the parties (in a consumer conflict presumably the trader), as a result of which insufficient deterrence would occur. Hence, generally one would, as was mentioned before comparing ADR with court cases, prefer a settlement when the gains of the settlement (in the saving on costs) would be higher than the error costs resulting from the settlement. This is therefore a trade off to be made which in many cases may favor the settlement. However, there is economic literature explaining why efficient settlements do not always occur, related both to the incentives of the lawyer involved (VII) as well as to the incentives of judges monitoring the settlement (VIII).

---

70 G.L. Piest and B. Klein, 'The Selection of Disputes for Litigation' (1984) 13 *Journal of Legal Studies* 1.

1. Timing of Settlement

There is law and economics literature indicating how, in theory, different remuneration systems for lawyers also affect the timing of a settlement. Generally, one can hold that a lawyer who bears his own costs under a contingency fee system would accept a settlement offer sooner (and probably for lower amounts) than under an hourly fee system. By accepting settlement of the case, the lawyer could (under conditional fees) save on costs and would thus have incentives to settle for low amounts and relatively quickly[71]. In that case conditional fees would create a potential conflict of interests between the lawyer and his client[72]. However, one should realize that a conflict of interest also arises under an hourly system, albeit in the opposite direction. In that case the self-interested lawyer will have an incentive to refuse the settlement in order to increase the hours he can spend on the case.

The empirics with respect to this issue seem to be somewhat divided: Rickman (1999) argues that in repeat periods of bargaining lawyers under a contingency fee system could also reject early settlement offers as "hard bargaining" in order to increase the final offer[73]. However, in another study Fenn and Rickman argue that lawyers who bear some risk (through contingent payment) appear indeed to settle their cases sooner[74]. Interestingly, they also found that legally aided cases were associated with longer delays to case closure, thus arguing that legal aid would reduce the incentives for case monitoring[75]. Helland and Tabarrok analyzed the effects of fee limits on contingencies fees and found that in Florida fee limits led to a 21 per cent increase in settlement duration[76]. The argument hence runs that limits on contingency fees reduced the lawyers' incentives to monitor the cases carefully, as a result of which they take longer to settle. The fee limits that thus were meant to protect clients apparently had the adverse effect of increasing settlement duration[77].

---

[71] See Hugh Gravelle and Michael Waterson, 'No Win No Fee: Some Economics of Contingent Legal Fees' (1993) 103 *The Economic Journal* 1205–20.

[72] See Faure, Fernhout and Philipsen (supra note 17), 37.

[73] Neil Rickman, 'Contingent Fees and Litigation Settlement' (1999) 19 *Int'l Rev L & Econ* 295–317.

[74] See Fenn and Rickman (supra note 27), 145.

[75] Paul Fenn and Neil Rickman, 'Delay and Settlement in Litigation' (1999) 109 *The Economic Journal* 476–491.

[76] Helland and Tabarrok (supra note 21), 517–42.

[77] See Fenn and Rickman (supra note 27), 143–4.

2. Influence of Payment on the Incentives to Settle

We have just analyzed the influence of different payment systems for lawyers on a delay in settlement, but the literature obviously equally indicates that the payment system can also generally have an influence on the incentives of a lawyer to accept a settlement. It can generally be held that a shift to a result-based compensation system provides better incentives for a lawyer to accept a settlement. Under a result-based compensation system lawyers may have a greater propensity to settle since they will only continue to negotiate (or decide to litigate) when it is cost effective[78]. In theory a system whereby the lawyer is paid on an hourly basis has the reverse (undesirable) effect: lawyers may have incentives not to accept a reasonable settlement and hence to litigate too many cases, although the latter could be controlled through legal ethics or through reputational sanctions. These reputational effects may, however, mostly work in cases of repeat players such as, for example, commercial clients rather than with individuals (like consumers) who are so-called "one-shooters".

There is ample empirical evidence of how the payment systems of lawyers influence incentives to settle, especially in cases of collective actions (like class actions).

Various studies of Hensler have shown dangers of so-called collusive settlements. These collusive settlements would be mainly beneficial for the attorney (receiving high fee awards) but not for the consumers[79]. Well-known cases are those whereby the settlement provided victims with low-value coupons for price reductions on further purchases instead of damage payments, whereas the attorney's fee was calculated on the basis of the total value of the coupons[80]. To some extent principal-agent problems may arise that could endanger the efficiency of a settlement in collective action cases. However, as Hensler makes clear[81] some of the horror stories of abuses by (US) attorneys involved in class actions are more myths than reality, arguing that such abuses would be more the exception than the rule.

Other potential problems that emerge from the literature are the danger of unmeritorious suits being brought in order to extract an early settlement[82]. Plaintiffs would bring (unmeritorious) class actions, exercising

---

78 Faure, Fernhout and Philipsen (supra note 17), 37.

79 Hensler (supra note 33), 157–8.

80 See Keske, Renda and Van den Bergh (supra note 35), 65 and Deborah R Hensler, *Class Action Dilemmas: Pursuing Public Goals for Private Gain* (Rand Corporation 2000).

81 Chapter 4 in this book.

82 Keske, Renda and Van den Bergh (supra note 35), 66.

pressures to settle (in order to avoid legal fees and reputational losses) as a result of which defendants would settle (even for high amounts) although the case may have no merits at all. Even though this type of "legal blackmail"[83] may certainly occur, Hensler also stresses that these horror stories should not be overstated, as there is no strong empirical evidence that this would actually often occur in the legal practice of class actions[84].

The result is that in theory the payment system (more particularly conditional fees) could either give incentives for too early or too many settlements (in case of legal blackmail), although the empirical evidence on both issues is inconclusive.

3. Arguments for Monitoring

Given the potential problems resulting from the principal-agent relationship between the class and the lawyer representing the class, there are some arguments for including safeguards[85]. In principle various types of remedies for this principal-agent problem could be worked out, varying from (1) restoring control by the class members to (2) judicial review of the merits of the case, the terms of the settlement and the amount of the contingency fee and (3) auctions determining the lawyer to represent the class[86]. The most popular type of safeguard, at least in the US, is the second one, a judicial review which can be found in Rule 23 (e) of the Federal Rules of Civil Procedure which requires the judge to review (after a public hearing) and then approve a proposed settlement only if he finds that the settlement is "fair, reasonable and adequate"[87]. Federal judges also used this rule to extend their authority for reviewing and approving (or disapproving) fee requests in class actions[88]. This shows that in collective actions there is an important task for the judge not only to review the terms of the settlement but also to review the fee requested in such a class action. This review by the judge could hence provide an important remedy against collusive settlements[89]. However, this lays an important task on the shoulders of the judge to protect consumers against collusive settlements. This obviously raises the important question[90], what type of judges we need to deal

83 Introduction by Christopher Hodges and Astrid Stadler (supra footnote 2).
84 See Ianika Tzankova and Deborah R. Hensler Chapter 4 in this book.
85 See also Introduction by Christopher Hodges and Astrid Stadler.
86 See Keske, Renda and Van den Bergh (supra note 35), 67.
87 See Hensler (supra note 33), 156.
88 Ibid, 157.
89 Tuil and Visscher (supra note 4), 185.
90 Raised by Astrid Stadler during her inaugural address, cf 'Collective Redress

with this important task. This question merits a brief look at the economic literature addressing the incentives of judges.

VIII. SETTLEMENT OF MASS CLAIMS: JUDGES' INCENTIVES

1. Theory: What do Judges Maximize?

There is an interesting law and economics literature starting with a paper by Robert Cooter[91] and followed by a paper by Posner[92], which argued that judges in fact maximize for the same reasons as everybody else: utility. Posner focuses on the situation of federal judges in the US where income is fixed and where judges hence cannot increase their income through more efforts. Posner argues that the judges' utility is a function of income, leisure and reputation. Given that the income of the judges is fixed, maximizing leisure and reputation becomes quite important[93]. Judges therefore balance leisure and judging without endangering other components of their utility function, like reputation[94]. Posner holds that especially judges who have reached a high-income level will prefer to maximize leisure. He argues "the opportunities for a leisured judicial life, especially at the appellate level, are abundant"[95].

According to this view, utility-maximizing judges would hence maximize leisure and reputation. The question arises how that would affect their incentives to judge settlements in mass claims. After all, as was just mentioned, it is expected that judges seriously review settlements as far as the content and the fee structure is concerned and certainly not to rubber stamp settlements. What does the empirical evidence indicate in that respect?

Litigation – A New Challenge for Courts in Europe' in Alexander Bruns et al (eds) *Liber Amicorum Rolf Stürner* (Tübingen 2013, forthcoming).

[91] Robert D. Cooter, 'The Objectives of Private and Public Judges' (1983) 41 *Public Choice* 101–37.

[92] Richard A. Posner, 'What Do Judges and Justices Maximize? (The Same Thing Everybody Else Does)' (1993) 3 *Sup Ct Econ Rev* 1–41.

[93] Ibid, 13–15 and David Stras, 'The Incentives Approach to Judicial Retirement' (2006) 90 *Minn L Rev* 1417–46.

[94] Richard A. Posner, *How Judges Think* (Harvard University Press 2008) 77.

[95] Ibid, 61.

2. Empirics

The reputation of judges definitely seems to be important. A study by Beenstock and Haitovsky[96] shows that judges will try to avoid court congestion and a backlog of cases since this could harm their reputation. Beenstock and Haitovsky show that judges tend to work harder under pressure in order to avoid congestion. The productivity even goes down if the number of judges increases. Interestingly, this research shows that when the caseload increases judges tend to terminate cases more rapidly.

Helland and Klick have examined the behavior of judges in class action cases and found that judges more easily grant the attorney's fee request in order to terminate cases rapidly, thus avoiding court congestion (which may damage their reputation)[97]. The rationale behind the behavior of judges is that a failure to grant a fee request would delay the termination of the case and hence increase court congestion. Helland and Klick showed that when the caseload increased, judges exercised less control on settlements and on average higher fees where authorized. These empirical studies therefore cast some doubt on whether the high expectations some have from the judiciary as far as their monitoring task is concerned, may be fully justified. Especially in cases of court congestion the monitoring function by the judge may be reduced.

IX. CONCLUDING REMARKS

This brief overview of the law and economics literature with respect to CADR and settlement of mass claims shows that (as is often the case) there are no easy and optimal solutions to provide incentives for the consumer from the case we took as a starting-point to sue that would cure risk aversion and the rational apathy problem. Not only is it theoretically in some cases difficult to predict how parties may behave; also the empirical studies we discussed are not one directional as far as the results are concerned.

Interestingly, behavioral studies addressing the incentives of attorneys, but also decision-makers (like judges) show that utility maximizing attorneys or judges may jeopardize an efficient resolution of consumer claims.

---

[96] Michael Beenstock and Yoel Haitovsky, 'Does the Appointment of Judges Increase the Output of the Judiciary?' (2004) 24 *Int'l Rev L & Econ* 351–69.

[97] Eric Helland and Jonathan Klick, 'The Effect of Judicial Experience on Attorney Fees in Class Actions' (2007) 36 *J Legal Stud* 171–87.

From an economic perspective there are quite a few good arguments in favor of CADR, especially for smaller cases of scattered (economic) losses where CADR could provide a low-cost solution and decisions of at least similar quality to the court system. It is in that respect striking that CADR is still a relatively limited phenomenon that only exists in a few legal systems and for particular branches of industry[98]. In that respect it has been mentioned that self-voluntary regulation (like a CADR system) might only emerge in particular industries when it is in the interests of members of that industry to have them[99].

This raises the question why there may be so much opposition to the creation of CADR bodies. Public choice analysis teaches that when this is the case there is probably a resistance by interest groups who can gain from keeping inefficient solutions in place or who resist the creation of efficient solutions[100]. This shows that an efficient solution to CADR and the settlement of mass claims needs an integrative study combining neo-classic approaches with behavioral law and economics and public choice in order to examine incentives of the interest groups involved as well. Probably in that way the poor consumer that was central to our case could obtain an adequate remedy for his losses.

---

98 Although, as the study by Christopher Hodges, Iris Benöhr and Naomi Creutzfeldt-Banda (supra note 3) indicates, there is certainly a trend in many legal systems to increase CADR.

99 Anil K Gupta and Lawrence J Lad, 'Industry Self-regulation: An Economic, Organizational and Political Analysis' (1983) 8 *Academy of Management Review* 416–25 and Faure, Ogus and Philipsen (supra note 14), 172.

100 See Chris Hodges in his inaugural address.

PART A

Settlements of mass claims

3. Enforcing mass settlements in the European Judicial Area: EU policy and the strange case of Dutch collective settlements (WCAM)*

Xandra E. Kramer

I. INTRODUCTION

Enhancing the enforcement of rights and judicial decisions has been one of the priorities on the Brussels civil justice agenda since the Amsterdam Treaty. Mutual recognition is regarded as the cornerstone of judicial cooperation in civil matters, and this cooperation in its turn is the engine of a genuine area of justice.[1] The focus of attention has been primarily on facilitating classical cross-border proceedings usually involving two parties, and on the enforcement of resulting court judgments. General policy aims are directed at furthering judicial cooperation in order to facilitate access to justice and to support the pan-European enforcement of rights.

At the same time, the landscape of both domestic and cross-border litigation is changing in Europe. First, classical two-party court litigation is supplemented by what is now in the EU context referred to as collective redress mechanisms. These mechanisms exist in different variations in most of the Member States and outside the EU, and go by different names (*e.g.* collective or representative actions, class actions, group litigation, mass settlements).[2] These mechanisms aim to increase access to justice and

* This contribution has been made possible with the support of the Netherlands Organisation for Scientific Research (NWO) within its Innovational Research Incentives Scheme (VIDI).

1 See Art 67(4) TFEU. See further Section II.

2 See for a concise introduction Diego Corapi, 'Class Actions and Collective Actions', in Duncan Fairgrieve and Eva Lein (eds), *Extraterritoriality and Collective Redress* (Oxford University Press 2012) 3, and for a comparative overview in the same book Duncan Fairgrieve and Geraint Howells, 'Collective Redress Procedures: European Debates' 15.

efficiency by allowing the bundling of claims for the purpose of acquiring injunctive relief and/or compensation. Another regulatory aim generally attributed to collective redress is that of deterrence. Secondly, in policy and in practice there is a shift to out-of-court dispute-settlement mechanisms or alternative dispute resolution. The mass settlement, including the Dutch 'WCAM settlement agreement', is a specific type of collective redress, bearing elements of both mass litigation and alternative or 'out-of-court' dispute resolution.

Although, as part of the area of judicial cooperation, the EU is active in all three indicated areas – cross-border enforcement, collective redress, and alternative dispute resolution – there is as yet no match. For example, the Dutch WCAM settlement procedure is often viewed with suspicion, and this two-headed 'strange case' does not seem to fit into the current legislative framework, particularly the Brussels I Regulation. In addition, during the recast of the Regulation that was completed at the end of 2012,[3] it became clear that the future of collective redress has not yet been settled. Since 2010, after initiatives to regulate collective redress at the sectoral level in the area of consumer and competition law, joint efforts have concentrated on a 'coherent approach'. What makes the debate complex is that it blends collective (court) action with collective relief, procedural law with regulation, and public enforcement with private enforcement. The fear of importing a US-style class action associated with abusive litigation as a 'nightmare scenario' (leaving aside whether this fear is justified) does not make it any easier. In June 2013, the European Commission released its long-awaited Recommendations on collective redress.[4] This marks an important and – for the moment – last step in the EU policy and legislative activities.

The academic debate on collective actions and redress is intensive. In relation to recognition and enforcement, most attention has been paid

---

[3] The (amended) Recast proposal was adopted in December 2012 and the new Regulation (Brussels I*bis*) will apply as of 10 January 2015: Regulation (EU) No 1215/2012 of the European Parliament and of the Council of 12 December 2012 on jurisdiction and the recognition and enforcement of judgments in civil and commercial matters (recast), OJ 20 December 2012, L 351/1.

[4] Communication from the Commission to the European Parliament, the Council, the European Economic and Social Committee and the Committee of the Regions, 'Towards a European Horizontal Framework for Collective Redress', COM(2013) 401/2 and Commission Recommendation on common principles for injunctive and compensatory collective redress mechanisms in the Member States concerning violations of rights granted under Union Law, C(2013) 3539/3. This recommendation was published after submitting this paper for publication and will not be discussed extensively.

to US class actions.[5] In the last couple of years, the issue of recognition and enforcement of European class actions has been added to the discussion. This chapter aims to explore and evaluate the EU area of judicial cooperation in civil matters with a view to enforcement and collective redress, and particularly mass settlements. The question is whether, and to what extent, mass settlements are or should be enforceable within the EU. The discussion will centre on the Dutch WCAM settlement as the most important example. Though this Dutch mass settlement mechanism has not yet resulted in numerous cases, it has involved a few prominent international cases (notably *Shell* and *Converium*) that have attracted attention worldwide.

II. JUDICIAL COOPERATION AND ENFORCEMENT IN THE EUROPEAN JUDICIAL AREA

1. Recognition and Enforcement as Cornerstone

The free movement of judgments is sometimes regarded as an independent – and fifth – freedom along with the traditional four freedoms that promote the functioning of the internal market. The founding Treaty had already called for Member States to enter into negotiations with each other, with a view to securing for the benefit of their nationals the simplification of formalities governing the reciprocal recognition and enforcement of judgments.[6] A note to the Member States of 1959 stated: 'A true

---

[5] See inter alia Andrea Pinna, 'The Recognition and Res Judicata of US Class Action Judgments in European Legal Systems' (2008) *Erasmus Law Review* 31; Leandro Perucchi, *Anerkennung und Vollstreckung von US class action-Urteilen und-Vergleichen in der Schweiz, Schweizer Studien zum internationalen Recht* (Schulthess 2008); Mark Stiggelbout, 'The Recognition in England and Wales of United States Judgments in Class Actions' (2011) *Harvard International Law Journal*, 433; Rachael Mulheron, 'The Recognition, and Res Judicata Effect of a United States Class Actions Judgment in England: A Rebuttal of Vivendi' (2012) *Modern Law Review*, 180; Stefania Bariatti, 'Recognition and Enforcement in the EU of Judicial Decisions Rendered upon Class Actions: The Case of U.S. and Dutch Judgments and Settlements', in Fausto Pocar, Ilaria Viarengo and Francesa Clara Villata (eds), *Recasting Brussels I* (CEDAM 2012) 319; Antonio Gidi, 'The Recognition of US Class Action Judgments Abroad: The Case of Latin America' (2012) *Brooklyn Journal of International Law* 893.

[6] This was laid down in Art 220 EEC Treaty, and later the provision was included in Art 293 EC Treaty.

internal market between the six States will be achieved only if adequate legal protection can be secured'.[7] It was added that economic life would be disturbed if it were not ensured that various rights arising out of a multiplicity of relationships could be recognised and enforced. Thus, the establishment of rules on recognition and enforcement was regarded initially as a derivative of economic objectives. At the time, the focus was on establishing a legislative framework for the cross-border enforcement of judgments in civil and commercial matters through a simple harmonised intermediate procedure: namely, that of exequatur.

After substantial extension of the competence in the civil judicial area pursuant to the Treaty of Amsterdam, attention shifted from purely economic motives to the objective of creating an area of freedom, security, and justice. This objective was articulated in Article 61 within Title IV of the EC Treaty, in which the judicial cooperation was embedded. Article 67 of Title V of the Treaty on the Functioning of the European Union (TFEU) no longer speaks about 'to progressively establish' such an area, but simply states that the Union shall constitute an area of freedom, security, and justice. Since the Tampere Council conclusions of 1999, mutual recognition has clearly been pinpointed as the cornerstone of judicial cooperation.[8] This is also expressed in Article 67 (4) TFEU, which states that the Union shall facilitate access to justice, in particular through the principle of mutual recognition of judicial and extrajudicial decisions in civil matters. This is reiterated in Article 81 TFEU, which provides that judicial cooperation in civil matters is based on the principle of mutual recognition.

The objective to establish a genuine area of justice and, to this end, to enhance judicial cooperation in civil matters has been firmly backed up by policy initiatives.[9] In the Hague programme,[10] and even more markedly in the Stockholm programme,[11] the needs of European citizens are at the forefront, and the rights of access to justice and effective enforcement (*effet*

---

[7] Quoted by Paul Jenard, Report on the Convention on Jurisdiction and the Enforcement of Judgments in Civil and Commercial Matters (Signed at Brussels, 27 September 1968), OJ 1979, C 59/2.

[8] Tampere European Council, 15 and 16 October 1999, Presidency conclusions, no 33.

[9] See in particular the Programme of measures for implementation of the principle of mutual recognition of decisions in civil and commercial matters, OJ 2001, C12/1.

[10] The Hague Programme: strengthening freedom, security and justice in the European Union, 13 December 2004, OJ 2005, C 53/1.

[11] The Stockholm Programme – An open and secure Europe serving and protecting the citizen, 11 December 2009, OJ 2010, C 115/01.

utile) are viewed within the context of fundamental rights.[12] More importantly, policy has been translated into impressive legislative activities. This has resulted in 15 instruments focusing on different aspects of cross-border litigation and the applicable law, but with an emphasis on facilitating effective access to justice and on recognition and enforcement.

2. Horizontal Judicial Cooperation versus Vertical (Sector-Specific) Harmonisation

It must be noted that competence in the area of judicial cooperation is limited to cases having 'cross-border implications', as specified by Article 81 TFEU. The Commission attempted but failed to establish instruments on the basis of this competence that extended to domestic cases, arguing that these may also have cross-border effects and distort the internal market.[13] This restraint limits the practical effects of the wide range of instruments established on this basis, since an estimate of only 1 to 3 per cent of the civil law cases are cross-border.[14] However, in view of the large number of parties involved, mass litigations or settlements are more likely to have cross-border implications than individual litigation. The Intellectual Property Enforcement Directive[15] and recent instruments in the area of consumer ADR[16] are not based on Article 81, but on Article 114 TFEU. This competence for in principle sector-specific instruments evidently does not include the limitation to cross-border cases. The initiatives regarding collective redress do not only aim at judicial cooperation

---

[12] See also in this regard Magdalena Tulibacka, 'Europeanization of Civil Procedures: In Search of a Coherent Approach' (2009) *Common Market Law Review* 1527, 1533–5.

[13] These concerned the proposals regarding orders for payment, small claims and mediation. See Xandra E Kramer, 'A Major Step in the Harmonization of Procedural Law in Europe: The European Small Claims Procedure Accomplishments, New Features and Some Fundamental Questions of European Harmonization', in Anthonie Willem Jongbloed (ed), *The XIIIth World Congress of Procedural Law: The Belgian and Dutch Reports* (Intersentia 2008) 353, 279–82.

[14] See also Burkard Hess, 'Procedural Harmonisation in a European Context', in Xandra E Kramer and CH (Remco) van Rhee (eds), *Civil Litigation in a Globalising World* (TMC (TMC Asser Press)/Springer 2012) 159, 162–3. The percentage is based on the Heidelberg-report evaluation the application of the Brussels I Regulation, see Burkard Hess, Thomas Pfeiffer and Peter Schlosser, *The Brussels I Regulation 44/2001.The Heidelberg Report on the Application of Regulation Brussels I in 25 Member States (Study JLS/C4/2005/03)* (CH Beck 2008) 39 ff.

[15] Directive 2004/48/EC on the enforcement of intellectual property rights, OJ 2003, L 157/45.

[16] See section II 3.

within Article 81 but also concentrate on Article 114 TFEU as a possible basis.

3. Mass Settlements: Where Do They Fit In?

The question is where do mass settlements fit into the policy and the legislative scheme of judicial cooperation in civil matters? There are three aspects to consider: the phenomenon of collective procedures and redress as such; the specific form of the mass settlement; and the recognition and enforcement of these settlements.

First, from the outset, collective redress mechanisms aim at increasing effective access to justice within the meaning of Article 81(2) sub (e) TFEU. In 1975, *Cappelletti* was already referring to the 'massification' of society in this context.[17] He and Garth designated the representation of group and collective interests as the second wave of the famous 'three waves of access to justice'.[18] The variety of national collective litigation procedures that have been put into place in many countries around the globe all aim to respond to the phenomenon of massification. The often relatively small damages and/or procedural and substantive burdens in these cases will, as a result of rational apathy, keep victims from enforcing their rights. As a matter of procedural economy, and sometimes public policy, collective or representative proceedings can enhance effective access to justice.

Secondly, mass settlements do not necessarily involve litigation. For example, in the Dutch WCAM scheme, settlements are not connected with litigation. Within the judicial cooperation area, settlements can be placed under the umbrella of alternative dispute resolution within the meaning of Article 81(2) sub (g) TFEU. Since the end of the 1990s, the development of ADR mechanisms has been an important aspect of the European civil justice agenda, particularly consumer ADR.[19] The Mediation Directive

---

[17] Mauro Cappelletti, 'Vindicating the Public Interest through the Courts: A Comparativist's Contribution' (1975–76) *Buffalo Law Review* 643 at 645.

[18] The first being the emergence of legal aid and the third a fully developed approach to access to justice encompassing all dispute processing institutions and procedures. See Mauro Cappelletti and Bryant Garth, 'Access to Justice. The Worldwide Movement to Make Rights Effective: General Report', in Mauro Cappelletti and Bryant Garth (eds), *Access to Justice: A World Survey* (Sijthoff and Noordhoff 1978), 21 ff.

[19] See inter alia Commission Recommendation 98/257/EC of 30 March 1998 on the principles applicable to the bodies responsible for out-of-court settlement of consumer disputes, OJ 1998, L 115/31 and Recommendation 2001/310/EC of 4 April 2001 on the principles for out-of-court bodies involved in the consensual resolution of consumer disputes, OJ 2001, L 109/56.

of 2008 provides requirements on quality, recourse, enforceability and limitation periods, and confidentiality for both commercial and consumer mediation.[20] Extensive ADR studies[21] in the area of consumer law were followed by a Directive on consumer ADR and a Regulation on consumer on-line dispute resolution (ODR), adopted in 2013.[22] These two instruments are technically not part of the area of judicial cooperation, since they are based on Article 114 and not on article 81 TFEU. The overarching idea is that ADR is used too little, whereas it can have great advantages over court litigation. Similarly, the mass settlement may also have advantages in view of costs, time, and voluntary compliance.

Thirdly, there is the aspect of the recognition and enforcement of such settlements. The mutual recognition and enforcement of judgments and of decisions in extrajudicial cases is ensured by Article 81(2) sub (a) TFEU. In a practical sense, this question can arise when an interested party seeks recognition or enforcement of the settlement in another Member State. This will occur only in the unlikely event that the responsible party does not live up to its obligations under the settlement. More important is the situation in which a victim initiates an individual action against the responsible party in another Member State, claiming that he is not bound by the settlement. This raises the question concerning recognition of the settlement and preclusive effect of a court approval of such a settlement. Clearly, as elaborated above, recognition and enforcement of both judgments and extrajudicial decisions are considered crucial for the European judicial area.[23] Collective redress mechanisms are also an important tool to support the enforcement of substantive EU law. In this regard, the full recognition and enforcement of mass settlements should be the starting-point.

---

[20] Directive 2008/52/EC of the European Parliament and of the Council of 21 May 2008 on certain aspects of mediation in civil and commercial matters, OJ 2008, L 136/3.

[21] See inter alia Study on the use of Alternative Dispute Resolution in the European Union, Civic Consulting of the Consumer Policy Evaluation Consortium (CPEC), 2009, available at http://ec.europa.eu/consumers/redress_cons/adr_study.pdf; Leuven Study, An analysis and evaluation of alternative means of consumer redress, 2007, available at http://ec.europa.eu/consumers/redress/reports_studies/comparative_report_en.pdf.

[22] Directive 2013/11/EU on alternative dispute resolution for consumer disputes and amending Regulation (EC) No 2006/2004 and Directive 2009/22/EC (Directive on consumer ADR), OJ 2013, L 165/63 and Regulation (EU) No 524/2013 on online dispute resolution for consumer disputes and amending Regulation (EC) No 2006/2004 and Directive 2009/22/EC (Regulation on consumer ODR), OJ 2013, L 165/1.

[23] See Section II 1.

Article 81 (2) (g) TFEU provides competence for measures to eliminate obstacles to the proper functioning of civil proceedings and, where necessary, to promote the approximation of the rules of civil procedure in the Member States. On the basis of this provision, harmonised European procedures have already been established.[24] The provision may also be used to create a European procedure for collective redress. However, at the moment the prospects of reaching an acceptable compromise for such a uniform procedure are extremely low.

III. EU POLICY AND COLLECTIVE REDRESS

The EU has been particularly active in the area of collective redress. This has been triggered by problems encountered in the enforcement of consumer law and competition law, and in the increasing importance of collective redress under the national laws of the Member States and in practice. These initiatives are generally supported by, or even strongly lobbied for, by consumer organisations.[25] Representatives of industry are far more reserved, and point to the risk of abusive litigation. This section will in a nutshell discuss the initiatives.[26]

1. Initiatives at the Sectoral Level

The first policy initiatives in the area of collective redress have focused on the separate areas of consumer law and competition law. The concern here is not judicial cooperation within the meaning of Article 81 TFEU as discussed earlier; the activities in the area are primarily concerned with the enforcement of substantive EU law.[27] The competence for these measures is thus to be found in Article 114 TFEU and in the respective special provisions on consumer law (Article 169 TFEU) and competition law (Articles 101 and 102 TFEU).

---

[24] See on the developments in this area inter alia Xandra E Kramer, 'Cross-border Enforcement in the EU: Mutual Trust versus Fair Trial? Towards Principles of European Civil Procedure' (2011) 2 *International Journal of Procedural Law* 202, 207–15.

[25] See recently *eg* BUEC, EU Action on Collective Redress, Letter sent to President José Manual Barroso, 26 April 2012, calling for concrete legislative action.

[26] See for an overview Duncan Fairgrieve and Geraint Howells (supra note 2).

[27] See also Gerhard Wagner, 'Harmonisation of Civil Procedure' in Xandra E Kramer and CH (Remco) van Rhee (supra note 14) 107.

The current legislative framework already provides for limited collective action in the area of consumer law. As a consequence of Directive 98/27/EC on Consumer Injunctions, national laws of the Member States provide for injunctive relief to stop practices that infringe upon national or EU consumer rules.[28] However, the Directive does not provide for skimming off profits as a result of a violation of consumer rules or *compensatory* relief for consumers. Additional collective actions, including compensatory relief, may be available under the laws of the Member States, and half of the Member States have some form of collective redress available. Several studies have been commissioned by the European Commission to evaluate the existing mechanisms of consumer (collective) redress and the problems that consumers experience in enforcing their rights.[29] These have shown that consumers have relatively little opportunity to make use of the existing mechanisms, and that financing is one of the main concerns.[30] In 2008, a Green Paper on Consumer Collective Redress was published, presenting various options ranging from no additional action to enacting a European collective redress procedure.[31] After a follow-up consultation paper published in 2009, and various hearings and informal meetings, concrete initiatives were suspended.

Also in the area of competition law, policy initiatives are directed at collective redress.[32] Following a 2004 study that concluded that actions for damage as the result of a breach of EU competition rules are 'totally underdeveloped',[33] a Green Paper on Damages Actions for Breach of EU Anti-Trust Rules was published in 2005.[34] This was followed by a White Paper in 2008, containing 'specific proposals to overcome legal and procedural hurdles within the Member States' rules governing antitrust actions for damages'.[35] It mentions a combination of collective redress brought

---

28 Directive 98/27/EC 1 of 19 May 1998 on injunctions for the protection of consumers' interests, OJ 1998, L 166.

29 These studies are available at http://ec.europa.eu/consumers/redress_cons/collective_redress_en.htm#Studies.

30 See also Duncan Fairgrieve and Geraint Howells (supra note 2) 36.

31 European Commission, Green Paper on Consumer Collective Redress, COM(2008) 794 final, 27 November 2008.

32 See for an overview of activities http://ec.europa.eu/competition/antitrust/actionsdamages/index.html.

33 Ashurst, Study on the conditions of claims for damages in case of infringement of EC competition rules, comparative report, 2004.

34 European Commission, Green Paper on Damages Actions for Breach of the EC Antitrust Rules, COM(2005) 672 final, 19 December 2005.

35 European Commission, White Paper on Damages Actions for Breach of the EC Antitrust Rules, COM(2008) 165 final, 2 April 2008.

by representative organisations, such as consumer or trade associations, and collective actions brought by individuals based upon an opt-in model. However, a proposal for a Directive on damages for infringements of competition law of June 2013, makes clear that a sector-specific regulation of collective redress is no longer envisaged.[36]

2. Towards a Coherent (Horizontal) Approach

The above-mentioned policy documents were not received with enthusiasm by all stakeholders and institutions. Industry in particular, but individual Member States and the European Parliament as well, raised concerns on the approach taken by the European Commission. At the same time, several Member States enacted their own rules on collective redress, and notably the Dutch WCAM started to attract cross-border cases and international attention. This led the Commission to look as well at the 'judicial cooperation' side of the coin and to pay attention to the coherence between the sectoral initiatives. An important input to the European debate was the public consultation on a 'Coherent European approach to collective redress' in 2011.[37] This consultation was a joint initiative of DG COMP and DG SANCO, and aims at streamlining the efforts in order to 'facilitate strengthening collective redress (injunctive and/or compensatory) in targeted areas'.[38] At the same time, DG Justice also became involved in the collective redress debate.[39] As Hodges remarked, it is also noteworthy that the terminology changed from 'class action' and 'collective action' to 'collective redress'.[40] Redress is a broader term that does not focus solely or primarily on court action but also on ways to obtain relief. Collective

---

36 Proposal for a Directive on certain rules governing actions for damages under national law for infringements of the competition law provisions of the Member States and of the European Union, COM(2013) 404. This proposal is linked with the Recommendation on collective redress, to be discussed in the next sub-section. The competition proposal expressly leaves it to the Member States whether or not to introduce collective redress actions for the private enforcement of competition law.

37 Commission staff working document. Public Consultation: Towards a Coherent European Approach to Collective Redress, Brussels, SEC(2011)173 final, 4 February 2011.

38 Consultation paper, p 4.

39 The cooperation between these DGs had also been instructed by President Barrosso in 2010, see 'A Coherent European Approach to Collective Redress: Next Steps', Joint information note by Vice-President Viviane Reding, Vice-President Joaquín Almunia and Commissioner John Dalli, SEC(2010) 1192, 5 October 2010.

40 Christopher Hodges, 'The European Approach to Justice and Redress' (2011) *Supreme Court Law Review* 301, 313.

redress is defined as 'any mechanism that may accomplish the cessation or prevention of unlawful business practices which affect a multitude of claimants or the compensation for the harm caused by such practices'.[41]

The Consultation paper explicitly takes into account collective consensual resolution as a means of alternative dispute resolution. It also underlines the need for strong safeguards against abusive litigation, as well as the importance of effective enforcement throughout the EU.[42] Three of the 34 questions posed in the Consultation paper concern the cross-border application of collective redress, and address the possible need for rules on international jurisdiction and on recognition and enforcement. It is specifically these two issues that have raised concern in the cross-border application of the Dutch WCAM procedure, as will be discussed in the next sections. Collective redress is the area in which civil justice competition seems to be most evident, as also *Hess* observed.[43] In the reform of the German KapMuG (*Kapitalanlegermusterverfahrensgesetz*), the German government explicitly referred to the Dutch WCAM to justify an opt-out proceeding in case the parties of the test case proceedings achieve a settlement on behalf of all interested parties.[44] The fact that the Commission's Consultation paper received over 19,000 responses from governments, associations, and other stakeholders, as well as from individuals, underlines the liveliness of the European debate.

In its Resolution of January 2012, the European Parliament showed for the first time a certain willingness regarding the notion of a European collective redress mechanism.[45] The Resolution points out that Europe must refrain from introducing a US-style class action or any system that does not respect European legal traditions.[46] The Parliament remarks that uncoordinated EU initiatives will result in a fragmentation of national procedural and damages laws, and that this will weaken rather than strengthen access to justice. It considers that in the event it is decided that EU action is necessary and desirable, any proposal in this area should take the form

---

[41] Consultation paper, p 3.

[42] Consultation paper, p 6.

[43] Burkhard Hess, 'A Coherent Approach to European Collective Redress' in Duncan Fairgieve and Eva Lein (eds) (supra note 2) 107, 112 and footnote 12 on that page.

[44] See on the amended law that became effective in November 2012: Astrid Stadler, 'Developments in Collective Redress: What's New in the "New German KapMuG"', *European Business Law Review* (forthcoming 2013).

[45] European Parliament Resolution: Towards a Coherent European Approach to Collective Redress Brussels, 2 February 2012. See also the Motion for a European Parliament Resolution (2011/3089(INI)).

[46] Resolution, no 2.

of a horizontal instrument.[47] The Parliament stresses the importance of stringent safeguards, and enlists a range of safeguards that should accompany such a horizontal framework.[48] These concern inter alia standing, the opt-in model as the only acceptable model, the loser-pays principle, and a ban on third-party funding. It further considers that an ADR system should be backed up by the availability of an effective judicial redress system, in order to give incentive to parties to settle.[49]

In June 2013, the Commission released its Recommendation on common principles for injunctive and compensatory collective redress mechanisms in the Member States. It makes clear that a genuine European procedure on collective redress is not feasible in the near future. On the contents, the principles largely coincide with the position in the policy documents mentioned, though third-party funding is not fully forbidden (no. 14–16). It is further provided that any exception to the opt-in principle 'should be duly justified by reasons of sound administration' (no. 21). ADR and settlements are presented as an addition to judicial procedures (nos. 25–28).

In the next section the Dutch system will be described. It is clear that this exclusive settlement system, based on a general opt-out model, does not fit the model the European Parliament and the European Commission envisage.

IV. THE STRANGE CASE OF THE DUTCH WCAM SETTLEMENT

In the EU, the Dutch mass settlement regime is unique, and is often referred to, either as an interesting possible model for Europe or as an exponent of a highly undesirable system. Outside Europe, and especially in the United States, Australia, and Canada, mass settlement also plays an important role, since many class actions end in a settlement.[50] This section will present some of the main features of the Dutch mass settlement regime, to serve as the background for the discussion in the next section with regard to recognition and enforcement of settlements.[51]

---

47 Resolution, nos 15–20.

48 Resolution, nos 20–24.

49 Resolution, no 25.

50 See the contributions in this book by Michael Legg (Chapter 8, Australia), Richard Marcus (Chapter 7, United States) and Jasminka Kalajdzic (Chapter 6, Canada).

51 See for a more detailed elaboration Willem van Boom, 'Collective Settlements of Mass Claims in The Netherlands', in Matthias Casper, Andre Janssen,

1. ADR and Mass Settlements: Key Features of the Dutch WCAM

The development of mass settlement started with the introduction of a collective action in the Civil Code in 1994 (Article 3:305a Dutch Civil Code). This enables incorporated foundations and associations to file claims on behalf of interested persons, in order to protect their rights. However, this provision only allows for declaratory judgments and injunctive relief, and does not permit actions for compensatory claims. In 2005, the Dutch Collective Settlements Act (*Wet Collectieve Afhandeling Massaschade*, abbreviated to WCAM) came into force.[52] It resulted from the shortcomings of the aforementioned provision on collective action, which became evident in the DES affair. This concerned a pharmaceutical product liability case, where many women whose mothers had used this medication during pregnancy suffered damage. The Supreme Court had already established liability, and industry was keen to settle for damages, but a legal mechanism was missing. The WCAM was established to fill this gap.

The WCAM is not a separate act, but consists of provisions spread over the Dutch Civil Code (DCC) and the Dutch Code of Civil Procedure (DCCP). This also characterises the mixed contractual-procedural nature of the mechanism. Four provisions in the DCC (Article 7:907–910) deal with the settlement between parties as such, and six provisions in the DCCP (Article 1013–1018) deal with the court procedure at the Court of Appeal in Amsterdam, which has the exclusive competence to declare the settlement binding. Article 7:907 DCC provides that an agreement concerning the payment of compensation for damages caused by an event or similar events concluded between a foundation or association with full legal competence and one or more other parties who have committed themselves by this agreement to pay compensation for this damage may, at the joint request of the parties, be declared binding by the court on persons to whom the damage was caused, as long as the foundation or association represents the interests of these persons pursuant to its

---

Petra Pohlman and Reiner Schulze (eds), *Auf dem Weg zu einer europäischen Sammelklage*? (Sellier 2009), 171; Tomas Arons and Willem van Boom, 'Beyond Tulips and Cheese: Exporting Mass Securities Claim Settlements from The Netherlands' (2010) *European Business Law Review*, 857; Ianika Tzankova and Hélène van Lith, 'Class Actions and Class Settlements Going Global: The Netherlands', in Duncan Fairgrieve and Eva Lein (eds) (supra note 2) 67. See also Ianika Tzankova and Deborah Hensler in Chapter 4 of this book.

[52] The Dutch government has provided an English summary of the Act and its features, 'The Dutch Class Action (Financial Settlement) Act' ('WCAM'), available at: http://www.rijksoverheid.nl/documenten-en-publicaties/circulaires/2008/06/24/the-dutch-class-action-financial-settlement-act-wcam.html.

articles of association. There is therefore – unlike, for example, in the US class action and settlement system – no 'class member' that represents a group. It is the representative organisation(s) that concludes the settlement agreement with the responsible party, on behalf of the victims (interested parties) that all become bound as a result of the declaration of the court. If they do not wish to be bound, they should make use of the opt-out possibility (Article 908[2] DCC).

Article 7:907 and the following provisions of the DCC list a range of requirements in order to ensure that the interests of each category of victims are adequately safeguarded. Two important elements concern the review of the representativeness of the foundation(s) and association(s) and the review of the reasonableness of the settlement. The law requires that the foundation or association be sufficiently representative,[53] and this should be clear from its statutes.[54] The representative can be either a long-standing foundation or association, or one that is established for the purpose of establishing a settlement agreement. The reasonableness test implies that the court determines whether the level of the settlement amount is reasonable for each category of loss, as well as the ease and speed with which the compensation can be obtained and the possible causes of damage.[55] Interested parties have the right to be heard during the procedure to declare the settlement binding.[56] In practice, the Amsterdam Court of Appeal plays an active role in managing the procedure, and in setting and reviewing the substantive and procedural requirements. In June 2013 a proposal was adopted to introduce several technical improvements, to regulate cases of insolvency of the tortfeasor,[57] and to strengthen several requirements, inter alia those regarding the representativeness, the procedural fairness, and the notification of foreign defendants.[58]

An important element, and one that raises most concerns in the European debate, is the opt-out nature of the decision to declare the settlement agreement binding. If the Amsterdam Court of Appeal declares the settlement binding, it will bind all injured parties falling within the scope of

---

[53] Art 907 (3) (f) DCC.

[54] Art 907 (1) DCC.

[55] Art 907 (3) DCC.

[56] Art 1013 DCCP.

[57] This is in view of the financial crisis, resulting in the insolvency of several banks.

[58] *Wet tot wijziging van de Wet collectieve afwikkeling massaschade*, no 33126 (Law to amend the Collective Settlements Act), adopted on 25 June 2013. The discussion in this section is based on the law as it was, since the new law was only adopted after submission of the text of this chapter.

the settlement agreement. If a person wishes not to be bound, he will have to submit a declaration with the administrator within a time period set by the Amsterdam Court, with a minimum of three months.[59] It is added that the court declaration shall have no consequences for a person entitled to compensation who could not have known of his loss at the time of the announcement if, after becoming aware of his loss, he has notified the administrator of his wish not to be bound.[60] This provision allows for an extension of the opt-out period. In the event that the number of opt-outs is very high, and thus the agreement would be binding for too few persons, the law provides the joint power to cancel the agreement.[61] In practice the number of opt-outs is very low, with the exception of the *Dexia* case (see further below), where a more favourable settlement was available.

Unlike other countries that have the possibility of a mass or class settlement, the Dutch system is based solely on a settlement; a collective action for compensation is not available. It is thus a model of 'settlement without action'. The Dutch legislator has clarified that in the setting up of the WCAM mechanism it was inspired by the US class action and particularly the experience in practice. It deliberately chose to cut out the action part, and provided the following argumentation:

> The WCAM opts for a collective settlement in order to avoid the complications that arise fairly often in American damages class actions. These happen because many of the issues connected with a compensation claim can only be answered individually. They might include, for example, issues of causality, contributory negligence and especially the extent of the damage. Once the legal issues in common have been dealt with, all of the individual victims then have to get involved in the proceedings so as to obtain answers to the issues affecting them individually. The result is that completion of a class action is quite often extremely complex and time-consuming.[62]

The handling of mass settlements has been done satisfactorily until now, as practitioners confirm. Six settlements have meanwhile been established, as displayed in Table 3.1 below.[63]

---

59 Art 908 (2) DCC.

60 Art 908 (3) DCC.

61 Art 908 (4) DCC.

62 See 'The Dutch Class Action (Financial Settlement) Act' ('WCAM') (supra note 52), 4.

63 Court of Appeal Amsterdam 1 June 2006, *LJN*: AX6440 (*DES*); 25 January 2007, *LJN*: AZ7033 (*Dexia*); 29 April 2009, *LJN*: BI2717 (*Vie d'Or*); 29 May 2009, *LJN*: BI5744 (*Shell*); 15 July 2009, *LJN*: BJ2691 (*Vedior*); 17 January 2012, *LJN*: BV1026 (*Converium*). For a concise description of some of these cases, see inter alia Ianika Tzankova and Hélène Van Lith (2012) (supra note 51) 51, 77–81. The number of interested parties is not always clearly reported.

Table 3.1 WCAM settlements

Case/company	Type	Interested parties	Settlement
DES (2006)	Product liability (pharmaceutical)	34,000 (mainly NL residents)	€35 million
Dexia (2007)	Securities lease products	300,000 (4000 residing outside NL, settlement limited to NL residents)	€1 billion
Vie d'Or (2009)	Financial damage bankruptcy (insurance)	11,000 (500 residing outside NL)	€45 million
Shell (2009)	US securities (misleading information)	500,000 (complementary to US settlement, limited to non-US residents residing worldwide)	$352.6 million
Vedior (2009)	Insider trading (merger)	2000 (55 per cent resident outside NL, including the US)	€4.25 million
Converium (2012) (Swiss company)	US securities (misleading information)	12,000 (only 3 per cent NL residents, 8500 Swiss, 1500 UK)	$58.5 million

2. Dutch Settlements and Worldwide 'Ambitions'

Originally, the WCAM was not intended to handle international cases. As was mentioned in the previous sub-section, the DES case triggered its introduction, and this case, as well as the following *Dexia* and *Vie d'Or* cases, concerned primarily Dutch interested parties. However, the mechanism also started to attract transnational (security) cases. This also led the Dutch Ministry of Justice to commission a study on the private international law aspects, which was carried out by the Erasmus University Rotterdam.[64] One of the reasons for class settlements going Dutch is the territorial limitation of class actions having to do with US securities fraud in the well-known *Morrison* of 2010, which concerned an Australian defendant and stocks bought on the Australian exchange market.[65] The

64 WODC report 'The Dutch Collective Settlements Act and Private International Law', 2010, written by Hélène van Lith, supervised by Filip De Ly and Xandra E Kramer. The report is, with minor changes, published at Maklu, 2011.

65 *Morrison v Nat'l Australian Bank*, 130 S Ct 2869 (2010). See inter alia Linda J Silberman, 'Morrison v National Australia Bank: Implications for Global Securities Class Actions' (2010) *Swiss Yearbook of Private International Law* (2010) 123, and in Duncan Fairgrieve and Eva Lein (eds) (supra note 2) 363.

US Supreme Court ruled that non-US plaintiffs buying shares from the Australian defendant on the Australian market ('foreign cubed' claims or 'f-claims') do not have a cause of action under US law. Though there is no official policy in this area, it is clear that the Dutch government, Dutch practitioners, and the Amsterdam Court of Appeal do not regret the global attraction, and do not intend to pose territorial limits. A Dutch financial newspaper picked up the issue of the Netherlands 'hoping' to take over US business'.[66]

Particularly remarkable is the way in which the Amsterdam Court of Appeal established international jurisdiction in the *Converium* case, which has been extensively debated in Dutch doctrine and abroad.[67] In this case, the responsible party was a Swiss-based company and 97 per cent of the parties were non-Dutch residents. Only the representative organizations were Dutch; one of which (Converium Foundations) was established ad hoc to represent the interests of non-US shareholders. The case concerned alleged securities fraud by Converium, a reinsurance company listed on the Swiss stock exchange, but also trading on the New York Stock Exchange. Complementary to a US settlement where non-US parties were excluded, two Dutch settlements were concluded. In an interim decision of 2010, the Amsterdam Court provisionally accepted jurisdiction, and it upheld this in its final decision of 2012, declaring the settlements binding.[68]

The Court gave an extensive reasoning to justify its international jurisdiction. It first explained that the request to declare the settlement binding had two aims: 1) to ensure the enforceability of the obligation to pay compensation; and 2) to establish that the interested parties (beneficiaries) could no longer commence individual proceedings. The Court established its jurisdiction on the basis of the Brussels I Regulation (interested parties domiciled in EU), the Lugano Convention (interested parties domiciled in Switzerland), and domestic jurisdiction rules (interested parties domiciled outside the EU/Lugano States). As in the *Shell* case, the Court considered that the Brussels I Regulation and the Lugano Convention apply, since the issue concerned a 'civil and commercial matter'. It was stated that the interested parties were to be regarded as 'defendants' that in accordance with Article 2 were to be sued in their country of domicile. This provided

---

66 Het Financieele Dagblad, Nederland hoopt stokje VS over the nemen als land van class actions, 17 November 2010.

67 For an overview of jurisdiction and WCAM settlements, see Hélène van Lith, *The Dutch Collective Settlements Act and Private International Law* (Maklu 2011) 27–75.

68 Court of Appeal, 12 November 2010, *LJN*: BO3908 and 17 January 2012, *LJN*: BV1026 (*Converium*).

jurisdiction for the approximately 200 Dutch interested parties. At the same time, this laid the foundation for non-Dutch domiciliaries pursuant of Article 6(1). This provides jurisdiction for defendants in the domicile of one of them, as long as the claims are so closely connected that it is expedient to hear and determine them together to avoid the risk of irreconcilable judgments. The Amsterdam Court considered that it concerned a collection of claims whereby the defendants would – once the settlement was declared binding – no longer be entitled to bring proceedings in any other court. Probably realizing that this basis was a bit weak considering that the other defendants concerned approximately 12,000 persons and the Dutch defendants only 200, the Amsterdam Court found another head of jurisdiction in Article 5(1). It argued that the place of performance of the obligation to pay compensation was in the Netherlands, since the representative organisations were seated in the Netherlands.

This seemingly 'worldwide' jurisdiction with which the Dutch court provided itself faces fierce criticism, both in the Netherlands and abroad.[69] For example, Gidi commented that 'Amsterdam is aggressively vying to establish itself as a hub for worldwide class action settlements'.[70] *Allemeersch*, who also criticizes the reasoning on the jurisdiction, put it more mildly, saying that he prefers 'to believe the Amsterdam judges worked on the basis of sincere belief that their solution was the best possible one in the given circumstances'.[71] It is submitted that the way in which the European jurisdiction rules have been artificially squeezed in order to fit the particularities of the Dutch mass settlement mechanism is not convincing. The Brussels I rules are simply not suited to accommodate a declaratory decision on a settlement between a responsible party who would in traditional litigation be the defendant (but now is to be regarded as the 'plaintiff') and a representative on behalf of victims (interested parties) who would in such a litigation be the plaintiffs, but who are now pushed into the 'defendant's corner'. However, it is hard to believe that the Amsterdam Court sees it as its mission to increase the share of Dutch practitioners in a lucrative business. It emphasized several times that it was acting complementary to

---

69 The literature is abundant. For a critical review in the Netherlands, see inter alia JS Kortmann, *Jurisprudentie Ondernemingsrecht* (JOR) (2011) 460 (no 46); Hélène van Lith, 'Internationale bevoegdheid Nederlandse rechter WCAM-zaak' (2011) *Ondernemingsrecht* 23.

70 Antonio Gidi (supra note 5) 953.

71 Benoit Allemeersch, 'Transnational Class Settlements: Lessons from *Converium*', in Stefan Wrbka, Steven Van Uytsel, Mathias Siems (eds), *Collective Actions: Enhancing Access to Justice and Reconciling Multilayer Interests?* (Cambridge University Press 2012) 364, 384.

the US settlement, where some of the interested parties had been denied access due to the decision to exclude non-US parties. It also explicitly considered the right of access to justice and the right to be heard, as laid down in Article 6 ECHR and Dutch law. Reviewing the aim of the Dutch Settlement Act, the procedural requirements that guarantee that interested parties can be heard, and considering the circumstances, the Court decided that it was just and practical to accept jurisdiction. Nevertheless, it seems advisable to adopt a more reticent approach to the jurisdictional question in future cases.

3. Interim: Old Habits . . .?

It is interesting to note that the pro-activism and pragmatism of Dutch courts and lawyers as well as criticism from European counterparts is not an entirely unique phenomenon. In the 1990s, the Dutch court in The Hague was referred to as trying to establish itself as 'court gate to Europe' in intellectual property cases, by granting 'worldwide' injunctions, particularly in patent cases. Careful consideration at the national level, criticism from abroad, and most of all the *GAT v Luk* and *Roche v Primus* rulings by the European Court of Justice, restrained this practice.[72] At that time, Dutch courts were also liberal in granting provisional measures in cross-border cases, both in intellectual property cases and in cases for interim payments. Again, it was the European Court of Justice that limited the extraterritorial reach of the Dutch court in the *Van Uden v Deco-Line* and the *Mietz* rulings.[73] The Dutch court took these rulings into consideration, and limited its jurisdiction accordingly. In these cases, the Dutch Supreme Court referred questions to the European Court of Justice. It will be interesting to see whether on the next occasion that a settlement has to be declared binding the Dutch court considers it appropriate to refer preliminary questions, and, even more, what the European Court of Justice might decide in such a case.

---

[72] CJEU 13 July 2006, Case C-4/03, ECR I-6509 (*GAT v LuK*); CJEU 13 July 2006, Case C-539/03, ECR I-6535 (*Roche v Primus*). See on this matter Xandra E Kramer, 'Civiele sancties in het internationale geval in Europees perspectief', in Aukje van Hoek *et al* (eds), *Offerhauskring vijftig jaar* (BJU 2012), 73.

[73] CJEU 17 November 1998, Case C-391/95, ECR 1998, I-7091; CJEU 27 April 1999, Case C-99/96, ECR 1999, I-2277. See for these developments inter alia Xandra E Kramer, 'Harmonisation of Provisional and Protective Measures in Europe', in Marcel Storme (ed), *Procedural Laws in Europe. Towards Harmonisation* (Maklu 2003), 305, 312–14.

V. ENFORCING MASS SETTLEMENTS IN THE EU

Until recently, the international debate concerning the recognition and enforcement of class actions and class settlements focused primarily on US judgments. The specificity and opt-out nature of the US class action system led scholars to deny or doubt that these are enforceable in Europe and in Latin America.[74] Not surprisingly, the Dutch court has been willing to recognise a US class settlement.[75] After the *Shell* and *Converium* cases, the attention has shifted to Dutch WCAM settlements, in relation to which similar concerns are raised. This section will focus on the recognition and enforcement of mass settlements in Europe, and in particular those reached under the Dutch WCAM.

1. The Brussels I Regime and Collective Redress

The Brussels I jurisdiction and recognition and enforcement rules are designed with a view to primarily typical two-party litigation. A limited form of aggregate litigation is foreseen in Article 6(1), concerning connected claims where multiple defendants are involved. As discussed earlier, this provision was also used by the Amsterdam Court to establish jurisdiction in the *Converium* case. However, it is doubtful whether in a mass settlement the interested parties (the victims) can be construed as 'defendants' within the meaning of Brussels I. In its 2012 Resolution, the European Parliament points out that a rush to the court (forum shopping) should be prevented, while not jeopardising access to justice. It states that Brussels I should be taken as a starting-point in the event of establishing a horizontal instrument for collective redress.[76]

The Brussels I Regulation does not only fall short in accommodating jurisdiction in collective redress; rules on the recognition and enforcement are also not well suited.[77] In the recast of Brussels I, collective redress and the necessity to include special rules was discussed,[78] but

---

[74] See the literature (supra note 5).

[75] District Court Amsterdam, 23 June 2010, LJN: BM9324 (*SOBI v Deloitte*).

[76] European Parliament Resolution (supra note 45) no 26.

[77] See inter alia Horatia Muir Watt, 'Brussels I and Aggregate Litigation or the Case for Redesigning the Common Judicial Area in Order to Respond to Changing Dynamics, Functions and Structures in Contemporary Adjudication and Litigation' (2010) *IPRax* 111; Burkard Hess, 'Cross-Border Litigation and the Regulation Brussels I' (2010) *IPRax* 116.

[78] See the Green Paper, COM(2009) 175 final, p 11, where it says that 'it should be reflected whether specific jurisdiction rules are necessary for collective actions'.

eventually it was decided not to include a special jurisdiction rule. In the Explanatory Memorandum to the Proposal, collective redress was only mentioned in the course of the abolition of exequatur. The Commission proposed to abolish the grounds of refusal for recognition and enforcement together with the requirement to obtain a declaration of enforceability (exequatur).[79] However, an exception was made for certain collective proceedings. These were – in a seemingly random manner – described as proceedings that concern the compensation of harm caused by unlawful business practices to a multitude of injured parties, and which are brought by either a State, by a non-profit organization whose main purpose and activity is to represent the group, or by a group of more than 12 claimants.[80] The Commission argued this exclusion by stating that the procedures vary widely per Member State in relation to the scope of those procedures, which victims these cover, the (public) authorities involved, and whether they proceed from an opt-in or opt-out model. Mutual trust in this area is apparently lacking. In the new Regulation, as adopted in December 2012, this exclusion is deleted because, although the declaration of enforceability is abolished, the grounds of refusal have been retained as grounds to revoke enforcement.[81]

2. Brussels I and Court 'Judgments'

In relation to the Brussels I Regulation, the question is whether a mass settlement or – more precisely – the decision to declare it binding, as it is construed under the Dutch WCAM procedure, qualifies as a 'judgment' within the meaning of Article 32. In the literature, this question has been answered both in the affirmative and in the negative.[82] A leading ruling

---

79 COM(2010) 748 final.

80 Art 37 (3) of the Commission proposal. See Astrid Stadler, 'Kollektiver Rechtsschutz und Revision der Brüssel I-Verordnung', in Reinhold Geimer and Rolf A Schütze (eds), *Recht ohne Grenzen, Festschrift Kaissis* (Sellier 2012), 951.

81 Arts 39, 45 and 46 Brussels I*bis* (supra note 3).

82 Affirmative inter alia: Maurice V Polak, 'Iedereen en overal? Internationaal privaarecht rond Massaclaims' (2006) *Nederlands Juristenblad* 2346 at 2353; Tomas Arons and Willem van Boom (supra note 51) 880–1; Astrid Stadler, 'Grenzüberschreitender kollektiver Rechtsschutz in Europa' (2009) *Juristenzeitung* 121, 126; Hélène van Lith (supra note 67) 108–11; Axel Halfmeier, 'Recognition of a WCAM Settlement in Germany' (2012) *Nederlands Internationaal Privaatrecht* 176, 178–80. Negative: Horatia Muir Watt (supra note 77) 114 (in relation to class action settlements in general). In doubt: Burkhard Hess, 'A Coherent Approach to European Collective Redress', in Duncan Fairgrieve and Eva Lein (supra note 2) 107, 114; Patrick Wautelet in Ulrich Magnus and Peter Mankowski (eds), *Brussels*

of the Court of Justice is *Solo Kleinmotoren*.[83] In this case (paras 17 and 18), it stated that:

> in order to be a 'judgment' for the purposes of the Convention the decision must emanate from a judicial body of a Contracting State deciding on its own authority on the issues between the parties. (. . .) That condition is not fulfilled in the case of a settlement, even if it was reached in a court of a Contracting State and brings legal proceedings to an end. Settlements in court are essentially contractual in that their terms depend first and foremost on the parties' intention.

As for the Amsterdam Court of Appeal, it can be disputed that it acts on its own authority. It is designated by law to decide on the declaration, but the settlement as such is reached before the declaration is requested. Nevertheless, there is room to regard the settlement approval as a judgment. The granting of the declaration is not just a simple 'yes or no' upon formalities. The Court has to review a whole range of issues, including whether the requirements regarding representativeness have been met, and whether the settlement amount is reasonable for each category of victims. Interested parties are notified and can be heard in the proceedings; these are important requirements in view of the *Denilauler* and *Gambazzi* rulings.[84] Throughout the process of approval, the court plays an active role in managing the case and in setting procedural requirements: for example, regarding notification. It is therefore likely that indeed the decision to declare the settlement binding is to be regarded as a judgment, meaning that it will in principle be recognised and has preclusive effect in other Member States, subject to the applicability of the grounds of refusal. Further, the obligations of the responsible party arising out of the settlement can be enforced. However, the fact remains that the Brussels I provisions do not sufficiently accommodate these atypical proceedings, and the answer will remain uncertain until the European legislator takes measures or the European Court of Justice decides on the matter.

I Regulation (Sellier 2011), comments Article 32, no 39. Stefania Bariatti (supra note 5) focuses only on the question of whether the settlement is to be regarded as a court settlement within the meaning of Art 58 Brussels I (at 331–9), and seems not even to consider it a possibility that the declaration qualifies as a judgment.

83 Case C-414/92 *Solo Kleinmotoren v Boch* [1994] ECR I-2237.

84 Case 125/79 *Denilauler v Couchet* [1979] ECR 1553; Case 394/07 *Gambazzi v DaimlerChrysler* [2009] ECR I-2563.

3 Brussels I and 'Settlements'; The Future Brussels I*bis*

Another question, which is particularly important if the court approval is not to be regarded as judgment, is whether the declaration can be regarded as a 'settlement' within the meaning of Article 58 Brussels I. According to this provision, the settlement is enforceable under the same conditions as authentic instruments. Article 57 regarding authentic instruments refers to the procedure of Article 38 *ff* regarding the enforcement of judgments; however, the only ground of refusal is public policy (Article 57[1] Brussels I).

There appear to be two problems in relation to applying Article 58 to mass settlements, and in particular those reached under the Dutch WCAM. The first one is that this provision requires that the settlement has been approved by a court in the *course of proceedings*. If this requirement is to be understood as having been reached in the course of adversarial proceedings, the Dutch settlement would not be covered.[85] In the earlier referenced *Solo Kleinmotoren* ruling, the European Court of Justice referred to 'an enforceable settlement reached before a court', though this was in the context of distinguishing the settlement in dispute from a judgment. It also emphasized the contractual nature of the settlement in the sense of Article 58, whereas the court approval aims to create preclusive effect for the entire group of interested parties. The mass settlement itself is reached between the representative(s) and the responsible party. In view of this lack of clarity, as was observed in the *Heidelberg* report,[86] the new Brussels I version, Brussels I*bis*, includes a definition in Article 2, sub (b). It defines the court settlement as a settlement 'which has been approved by a court of a Member State or concluded before a court of a Member State in the course of proceedings'. This will definitely cover the court approval of mass settlements, and it is likely that the current Brussels I Regulation will also be interpreted in this light, since the definition is a clarification rather than an amendment.

The second problem with the application of Article 58 Brussels I, and one that the corresponding Article 59 Brussels I*bis* does not resolve, is that it refers exclusively to the *enforcement* of settlements. It provides that settlements enforceable in the Member State of origin shall be enforceable (Brussels I*bis*:

---

85 See also Horatia Muir Watt (supra note 77) 114; Astrid Stadler, 'Die grenzüberschreitende Durchsetzbarkeit von Sammelklagen' in Matthias Casper, Andre Janssen, Petra Pohlman and Reiner Schulze (eds), *Auf dem Weg zu einer europäischen Sammelklage?* (Sellier 2009) 150, 163; Hélène van Lith (supra note 67) 111–15; Axel Halfmeier (supra note 82) 178–80.

86 Burkhard Hess, Thomas Pfeiffer and Peter Schlosser (supra 14) 161.

enforced) in the State addressed (Brussels I*bis*: *in the other Member States*) under the same conditions as authentic instruments. Likewise, Article 57 Brussels I and the corresponding Article 58 in Brussels I*bis* on authentic instruments also only mentions enforcement and not recognition. The reason is that the Brussels provision on settlements is concerned with the enforcement of a settlement agreement as a contract. However, as regards mass settlements, the primary concern is not the enforceability of the settlement between the contracting parties; it is to recognise preclusive effect as a result of the binding nature of the settlement in relation to all the interested parties that did not opt out. For this reason, the provision on settlements is probably of little use to facilitate the mass settlement.

4. Checks and Balances: Grounds of Refusal

If the mass settlement were to be regarded as a judgment under the Brussels I Regulation, its effect can nevertheless be mitigated if the grounds of refusal as laid down in Articles 34 and 35 are invoked. Under the current rules, these grounds can be invoked to appeal the declaration of enforceability (Article 45), or in declaratory proceedings regarding the recognition or where recognition is important as an incidental question (Article 33). Under the Brussels I*bis* Regulation, the exequatur is abolished, but identical grounds of refusal can be applied on application by a party against whom enforcement is sought (Article 46 Brussels I*bis*). On application by an interested party, these grounds of refusal will also apply to the recognition of judgments (Article 45 Brussels I*bis*). In relation to mass limitation, the issue of recognition is most likely to arise when an interested party that did not opt out wishes to initiate individual proceedings in another Member State. Articles 34 and 35 include the public policy exception, improper service, irreconcilability of judgments, and violation of specific exclusive jurisdiction rules. For the purpose of Dutch mass settlements in view of the opt-out character of the procedure, public policy within the meaning of Article 34(1) and proper service as included in Article 34(2) are particularly important. Public policy is also a ground to refuse a settlement within the meaning of Article 58 Brussels I (read in conjunction with Article 57). In view of the criticism on the wide jurisdiction of the Dutch court in the *Converium* case, it is important to note that a violation of the jurisdiction rules in general is not a ground to refuse recognition or enforcement, unless protective (consumer) jurisdiction rules apply.[87]

---

[87] See Art 35 (3) Brussels I. The test of public policy may not be applied to the rules relating to jurisdiction.

In relation to public policy, the starting-point is that the law of the Member State where recognition and enforcement is sought is decisive. However, it must concern a *manifest* breach of public policy. The European Court of Justice has repeatedly ruled that this ground of refusal is to be interpreted strictly.[88] It is not available in the case of a discrepancy between national rules; it should concern a manifest breach of a fundamental principle. A violation of Article 6 ECHR or Article 47 Charter of Fundamental Rights will generally qualify as such. This ground of refusal has been accepted only in incidental cases.[89] Can the opt-out nature of the Dutch mass settlement mechanism be regarded as breaching a fundamental principle? In the Dutch literature, this question has been answered in the negative, and this is backed up by certain non-Dutch scholars.[90] However, most other scholars have expressed serious doubts regarding the compatibility of the opt-out nature with domestic or European public policy.[91] In this context, it is interesting to note that the European Court of Human Rights in relation to Article 6 ECHR dealt with the issue of collective procedures in the case *Lithgow v United Kingdom*.[92] The Court stated that the right to an individual procedure may be limited or restricted if such restriction serves a legitimate goal and is not disproportionate. In a later case, it concluded that Article 6 was not violated, 'since in proceedings involving a decision for a collective number of individuals, it is not

---

[88] See inter alia Case 394/07 *Gambazzi v DaimlerChrysler* [2009] ECR I-2563; Case C-7/98 *Krombach v Bamberski* [2000] ECR I-1935; Case C-38/98 *Renault v Maxicar* [2000] ECRI-2973; Case 145/86 *Hoffmann v Krieg* [1998] ECR 645.

[89] See for an overview of national case law Patrick Wautelet (supra note 82) comments Art 34, nos 33–5.

[90] Arnold RJ Croiset van Uchelen, 'De verbindendverklaring van de WCAM als procesvorm' (2007) *Aansprakelijkheid, Verzekering en Schade* 222, 227; Tomas Arons and Willem van Boom (supra note 51) 881–2; Hélène van Lith (supra note 67) 124–30. See also Axel Halfmeier (supra note 82) 180–3 who concludes that this procedure does not constitute a violation of German public policy.

[91] Specifically in relation to the Dutch WCAM inter alia: Stefania Bariatti (supra note 5) 335–6; Astrid Stadler (supra note 80) 957. In general in relation to opt-out collective redress mechanisms: M Danov, 'The Brussels I Regulation: Cross-Border Collective Redress Proceedings and Judgments' (2010) *Journal of Private International Law* 359, 388–91; Burkhard Hess (supra note 77) 120; Duncan Fairgrieve, 'The Impact of the Brussels I Enforcement and Recognition Rules on Collective Actions', in Duncan Fairgrieve and Eva Lein (eds) (supra note 2) 178–86. See also supra note 5 for literature on the recognition and enforcement of US class actions.

[92] *Lithgow v United Kingdom* (1986) EHRR 329. See also Axel Halfmeier (supra note 82) 182 in this context.

always required that every individual is heard before a court'.[93] The WCAM can be said to fulfil a legitimate goal: namely, to enable compensation of large groups of victims by means of a settlement. The high number of victims and the relatively low value of the claim per victim make individual litigation an unreasonable option. This case law does not explicitly address the opt-out mechanism. It is clear that the European tides are against the opt-out system, as was emphasized as well by the European Parliament in its 2012 Resolution and the Commission Recommendations.[94] This led *Hess* to conclude that 'opt-out mechanisms are not in accordance with current European procedural law'.[95] In spite of the substantive and procedural checks and balances in the Dutch Collective Settlements Act, recognition and enforcement of the decision to declare the settlement binding is therefore not guaranteed in (all) the other Member States.

A specific ground of refusal relates to proper service, enumerated in Article 34(2) Brussels I. It concerns the situation in which the judgment was given in default of appearance, and the document instituting proceedings was not served in a timely manner and in such a way as to enable the defendant to arrange for his defence. The question is whether this provision applies to the Dutch settlements mechanism.[96] Under Dutch law, the decision to declare the settlement binding is not a default judgment, but in view of the autonomous interpretation, this will not be an obstacle.[97] A more important issue is that application of this provision requires that the interested parties can indeed be regarded as defendants within the meaning of Brussels I. If it were to be applicable, within the EU, the Service Regulation would apply. In relation to interested parties that are unknown, or where the domicile is unknown, it is important that all efforts be made to actually reach the defendant.[98] In the *Dexia* case, the Amsterdam Court of Appeal underlined the importance of a proper notice being given to the interested parties by reference to Article 6 ECHR.[99] In this case, the

---

93 *Wendenburg and others v Federal Republic of Germany* (2003) Application no 71630/01.

94 See Section III 2.

95 Burkhard Hess (supra note 77) 120.

96 See also Axel Halfmeier (supra note 82) 183, who concludes that this provision is not applicable.

97 Stéphanie Francq, in Ulrich Magnus and Peter Mankowski (supra note 82) comments Art 34, no 44.

98 See Art 19 Service Regulation and Case C-327/10 *Hypotecní banka asa.s. v Lindner* [2011] ECR X;I-0000; Case C-292/10 *G v Cornelis de Visser* [2012] ECR XI-0000.

99 Amsterdam Court of Appeal 25 January 2007, LJN: AZ7033 (*Dexia*), para 5.2.

Court found it sufficient that the group as a whole had been served properly.[100] However, in later cases the relevant European and international instruments were consistently applied, and extensive efforts were made to serve the parties and to reach unknown parties or parties with unknown domiciles. Particularly in the *Shell* and *Converium* cases, the Court gave strict instructions in relation to the notification.[101] Advertisements were placed in dozens of newspapers, special websites were established, and banners were placed on websites. Though the assessment of an individual case will be a task for the court of the Member State where enforcement is sought, it is submitted that in general the notification requirements are in compliance with the Brussels I and Service Regulation, and should therefore not be an obstacle to the recognition and enforcement of Dutch mass settlements.

VI. CONCLUDING REMARKS

The 'massification' of society, enforcement problems in consumer and competition cases, and the increase of various national forms of collective redress – in particular, mass settlements – have given rise to an intensive European debate. As has been demonstrated in this paper, the recognition and enforcement of mass settlements as such perfectly match the policies within the area of judicial cooperation as expressed in Article 81 TFEU. Mass settlement is a form of alternative dispute resolution, the aim of which is to enhance effective access to justice. The principle of mutual recognition and the strong efforts to promote a free circulation of judgments and extrajudicial decisions fortify their recognition and enforcement. Nevertheless, the European tide and the academic debate do not seem to favour a wide acceptance of mass settlements as they have been reached under the Dutch Collective Settlements Act. However, most of the criticism does not aim at mass settlements as such; it is particularly the opt-out nature of this mechanism as well as the wide international jurisdiction that has been adopted that cause concern. It is submitted that the way in which the Amsterdam Court established its jurisdiction in the *Converium* is not entirely convincing. However, the case also makes clear that the current European legislation, and particularly the Brussels I Regulation,

---

100 Art 1013 (5) DCCP only requires service by ordinary mail. The provisions on service will become stricter once the law to amend this act will enter into force, see (supra note 58).

101 See for a description Hélène van Lith (supra note 67) 86–90.

is ill-suited for this type of procedure. As the analyses in this chapter have shown, the same applies to the rules on recognition and enforcement.

The Commission Communication and accompanying Recommendations have made clear that a vertical instrument is out of the question and that a binding horizontal instrument upon which the Member States can reach agreement is not feasible in the near future. The Recommendations encourage Member States to put an appropriate mechanism in place and provide a framework for such a mechanism. The question still is, whether this framework is the most suitable and whether Member States will change their procedural law in accordance with the Recommendation. Private international law questions, and particularly the issue of recognition and enforcement are not resolved, though in the Communication it is mentioned that the existing rules of Brussels I should be 'fully exploited'.[102] The debates on European collective redress will continue. These discussions touch upon the essence of European civil procedure and enforcement law, the architecture of which has not yet been decided. Meanwhile, national and practical developments will continue. The national legislators will continue to take into account each other's efforts to find legislative solutions for shared practical questions. In addition, national courts applying the procedures in cross-border cases or faced with the question of recognition and enforcement will continue to interpret and maybe sometimes bend the rules to accommodate the purpose.

102 Communication (supra note 4),13.

4. Collective settlements in the Netherlands: some empirical observations

Ianika Tzankova and Deborah Hensler

I. INTRODUCTION

1. General

The Dutch Act on Collective Settlements (WCAM) was introduced in 2005.[1] During the discussions surrounding its introduction, some practitioners expressed the view that the WCAM was going to be a one-day fly.[2] Although it was general in nature, the WCAM was drafted specifically for the resolution of the DES drug case[3] and those practitioners believed that this was such an extraordinary matter that it was unlikely that the same circumstances would be duplicated and the WCAM was going to be used ever again. However, this line of reasoning underestimated the needs of businesses and the creativity of lawyers. The WCAM was still before Parliament when it was announced in the media[4] that Dexia Bank was considering the resolution of the Dexia mass claim matter using the WCAM,[5] which provoked discussions about the scope of the law and the

---

[1] See Dutch Bulletin of Acts and Decrees, 2005, 380. The Act entered into force on 27 July 2005.

[2] Pieter van Regteren Altena, 'De collectieve afwikkeling van de des-zaak in Nederland' in A.I.M. (Toon) van Mierlo and others (eds), *Het wetsvoorstel collectieve afwikkeling massaschade* (Bju 2005) 27–35.

[3] For a detailed discussion of the background of the WCAM and the resolution of the DES case see Ianika Tzankova and Daan Lunsingh Scheurleer, 'The Netherlands. The Globalization of Class Actions' (2009) 622 *Annals of the American Academy of Political and Social Science* 149.

[4] See <http://www.eegalease.nl/index.php?page=/nieuws/main_right.php?nid=68>, accessed 25 February 2013.

[5] Dexia was the first massive consumer mass claim dispute in the Netherlands. For an extensive discussion of the *Dexia* case see Ianika Tzankova, 'Funding of

question whether it was intended to apply on disputes related to financial products and services.

In the years after the enactment of the WCAM it became clear that the act was anything but a one-day fly. Since its enactment in 2005, six collective settlements have been declared binding[6] and each case was a pioneer in its own way. Dexia demonstrated that the WCAM was applicable also in relation to financial products and services. In the Vie d'Or case, which related to the bankruptcy of a life insurer, the Act was applied for the first time under the condition that the contributions of the parties to the settlement fund would not be disclosed to the court. In the Shell case, the WCAM was used for the first time to resolve a securities litigation dispute on a worldwide basis: an application of the law the legislature did not think of when it drafted the WCAM. The Converium case is another securities litigation dispute that was resolved on a worldwide basis, but unlike Shell, in relation to non-Dutch companies. Both rulings, but especially the Converium one, generated a lot of academic and media attention.[7]

The unanticipated broad use of this piece of legislation triggered an evaluation of the WCAM much earlier than is customary.[8] The evaluation related to the private international law aspects of the WCAM,[9] but also to the use and functioning of the WCAM more broadly. It led to draft amendments to improve the act.[10] Some of the proposed amendments are

---

Mass Disputes: Lessons from the Netherlands' (2012) 8.3 *George Mason Journal of Law, Economics & Policy* 577–83.

[6] See *Stichting Converium Securities Compensation v Liechtensteinsche Landesbank* [2012] LJN BV1026 (Converium); *Stichting uitvoering Vedior schikking* [2009] LJN BJ2691 (Vedior); *Shell Petroleum v Dexia Nederland* [2009] LJN BI5744 (Shell); *Stichting Vie d'Or* [2009] LJN BI2717 (Vie d'Or); *Dexia Bank Nederland v Stichting Platform Aandelenlease* [2007] LJN AZ7033 (Dexia); *Stichting DES Centrum v X* [2006] LJN AX6440 (DES).

[7] See for example Axel Halfmeier, 'Recognition of the WCAM Settlement in Germany' (2012) 2 *NIPR* 176–84.

[8] Usually the evaluation of legislation would take place five years after its enactment at the earliest. The evaluations had already started two years after the enactment of the Act.

[9] For a discussion on private international law aspects of the WCAM see generally Hélène van Lith, *The Dutch Collective Settlements Act and Private International Law. Aspecten van Internationaal Privaatrecht in de WCAM* (Ministerie van Justitie 2010), also published on <http://ec.europa.eu/competition/consultations/2011_collective_redress/saw_annex_en.pdf>, accessed 25 February 2013.

[10] See Kamerstukken II 2011–2012, 33 126, nr 2, also published on <https://zoek.officielebekendmakingen.nl/kst-33126-2.html>, accessed 25 February 2013. For a discussion of this legislative proposal see Denise Ozmis and Ianika Tzankova, 'De evaluatie van de WCAM: de kernthema's uitgelicht' (2012) 2 *TvCR* 33–42.

technical in nature and some are a codification of already established practices of the Amsterdam Court of Appeal. However, the draft proposal also contains a few more fundamental changes relating to the role of the judiciary, not only after a settlement is concluded, but also in the stage where parties are negotiating a settlement. The draft proposal caused commotion among the business community. The Dutch *Financial Times* published on its front page 'The Netherlands: paradise for mass claims'.[11]

Apparently, the underlying assumption was that the WCAM leads to more and frivolous litigation, so an *improvement* of the functioning of the WCAM would be even more disadvantageous for businesses. Such reactions originate from a deep misunderstanding of, and a misconception about, the nature, character and the experiences to date with the WCAM. Based on the preliminary results of case studies of the four (out of six) WCAM settlements to date,[12] this chapter will demonstrate that such fear is ungrounded. Furthermore, the chapter will assess whether it is to be expected that the recent legislative proposals to improve the functioning of the WCAM are disadvantageous for businesses and will lead to frivolous litigation. The conclusion is that the proposed legislative amendments are not likely to cause extensive litigation.

2. Mode of Treatment

The structure of this chapter is as follow. After a brief overview of the main features of the WCAM, a brief description of the basic facts of the four cases will follow. The discussion of how the WCAM has been used to date and what can be learned from those experiences will be followed by a discussion of the proposed amendments. The chapter will conclude with a paragraph singling out certain aspects that do deserve the attention of the legislature but have been underappreciated so far.

---

11 'Nederland wordt straks paradijs voor massaclaims; Rijk gaat wetgeving verbeteren' in *Financieele Dagblad* (29 December 2011).

12 This chapter partly builds on the results of case studies conducted in an international collaborative empirical project led by Professors Deborah Hensler (Stanford University/Tilburg University), Christopher Hodges (Oxford Centre for Socio Legal Studies/Erasmus University) and Ianika Tzankova (Tilburg University) examining the functioning of class or group litigation schemes in various countries. Final results of the case studies were presented at the annual Law and Society Conference in Honolulu, Hawaii in June 2012.

II. WCAM

1. Introduction

The Dutch system of collective redress is governed by two sets of rules. The collective action that is general in nature, and not limited to a specific material area of law, has been in force since 1 July 1994. Until now, remedies have been limited to declaratory and injunctive relief. Since its introduction, the collective action has increasingly been used in a variety of cases. Empirical studies or statistics about the use of this provision are lacking but an estimation based on the number of cases reported to date suggests that since 1994 over 100 collective actions have been initiated.

The WCAM was enacted in July 2005. The Dutch legislature was inspired by the US court-approved class settlement regime, but tried to avoid its negative connotation. One of the main reasons why the Dutch business community supported the WCAM probably lies in the fact that, unlike the US class action, the Dutch collective action provisions do not allow actions for damages.[13] Corporations wanted a means of settling damages collectively, but did not want to be forced to settle if they did not want to. Even though not empirically grounded, the fear existed that a mechanism like the US class action for damages might increase the pressure on defendants to settle nuisance value claims.

2. How the WCAM Works[14]

The essence of the WCAM is a settlement reached out of court entered into by a representative organization and one or more parties agreeing to pay compensation to injured persons with the aim of settling all claims at a collective level. The settlement agreement is approved exclusively by the Amsterdam Court of Appeal, with a statutory binding effect on all group members who do not exercise their right to opt out. Once the Court of Appeal approves the settlement and the opt-out period has expired, all claimants who have not exercised their opt-out right are bound by the settlement.

The representative organization entering the settlement on the part of the claiming parties should be an association with full legal competence or a foundation. This could be a longstanding organization or a special

[13] For a detailed discussion of the background of the WCAM and the resolution of the DES case see Tzankova and Lunsingh Scheurleer, *supra* note 3, 149.

[14] See Articles 7:907–7:910 of the Dutch Civil Code.

purpose vehicle. Unlike the collective action that was introduced in 1994, the WCAM contains the requirement that the organization entering into the settlement should be sufficiently representative of the interests of the injured persons who are to benefit from the settlement. Whether the organization meets this requirement depends on the facts and circumstances of the case at hand.

The WCAM proceedings are initiated by means of a joint petition to the Amsterdam Court of Appeal by the organization and the (potential) defendant(s) and/or the parties contributing to or distributing the settlement monies. The beneficiaries of the relevant settlement must then be notified of the content of the agreement, the date and time of the court hearing, and their right to file an objection against the petition and to appear at the hearing. Individual notifications in writing must be sent to known beneficiaries pursuant to applicable regulations and treaties; unknown beneficiaries must be notified by means of the placing of advertisements in newspapers in the relevant jurisdictions. The experiences to date show that the individual notification process that has to be applied pursuant to European regulations and international treaties in the international WCAM cases can be costly.

The right of interested third parties to file objections against the settlement agreement could be seen as a safeguard against a potential abusive use of the WCAM. In four out of the six collective settlements to date, interested parties have filed objections and defenses of various kinds. The Amsterdam Court of Appeal has responded to those objections differently. Some have been promptly rejected at the same time as the binding declaration was issued. Some led to the appointment of an expert to issue an expert opinion on certain issues. To date, all six collective settlements that have been submitted to the Amsterdam Court of Appeal have been declared binding. The Amsterdam Court of Appeal has announced in connection to the *Converium* case that it will act proactively, since principles of due process require protection by the court of the interests of the absent parties. Therefore, it is likely that, even without objectors, the Amsterdam Court of Appeal will take a critical approach towards settlement agreements that have been submitted for approval.

Following the hearing, the court will render its decision, either granting or denying the request to certify the settlement agreement. If the request is granted, the court will also determine the duration of the period during which beneficiaries can exercise their right to opt out. If the court denies the request, appeal (cassation) of the decision is only possible for the petitioners jointly and on limited grounds. The court's decision will be communicated to both known and unknown beneficiaries – the so-called *interested parties* (belanghebbenden). Standing to appeal a denial or an allowance of the request for the approval of the settlement is not granted to interested third parties. According to the Dutch law of civil procedure, interested parties are parties who do not have a general or professional interest in the process, the proceedings or their outcome, but who would be entitled to claim under the settlement agreement, including organizations acting for those interests.

A collective settlement may follow collective litigation in Dutch or foreign courts, or it may simply take place in the shadow of potential litigation, before any lawsuits have been filed or resolved.

The Netherlands is the only European country to date where a collective settlement of mass claims can be declared binding on an entire class on an opt-out basis. Many have interpreted the statute as yet another example of the Dutch consensual culture, but the reality is, as was stated before, that the resolution of a concrete mass claim case has triggered the design of the statute, and at that time it was no longer possible to enact a statute governing only that specific mass claim case, so a general provision had to be introduced.

III. FOUR CASE STUDIES

1. Methodology and Facts

In the time period September 2010–March 2011, over 40 interviews were conducted[15] with parties representing various stakeholders involved in the resolution of the Dexia, Shell, Vedior and Vie d'Or mass disputes. Each interview was scheduled for about an hour but most interviews lasted much longer than that, some even closer to two hours. All interviews followed a common protocol.

The case studies discussed in this chapter were conducted under the umbrella of an international collaborative empirical project examining the functioning of class or group litigation schemes in about a dozen countries, with scholars from North and South America, Asia, Europe and Australia. This chapter discusses some preliminary[16] results of the Dutch case studies.

All four cases related to financial products or services. Dexia resolved claims by Dutch retail investors ('moms and pops') who lost money on an

---

[15] The interviews were conducted by Professors Deborah Hensler and Ianika Tzankova.

[16] The results are preliminary because, according to the case studies protocol we followed, the case narratives that served as the basis for our conclusions are subject to the comments of those who were interviewed.

investment scheme offered by the Dutch subsidiary of Dexia bank. About 300,000 claims were involved and the settlement fund was estimated at EUR 1 billion.[17]

Royal Dutch Shell resolved claims by non-US shareholders worldwide that their shares lost value as a result of Shell's failure to properly disclose information about its oil reserves. The estimated number of claims was 500,000 and the settlement fund was about USD 350 million.

Vedior also resolved claims by US and non-US shareholders worldwide that a failure to timeously disclose information about an acquisition led to loss of share value. The estimated number of claims was 2,000 and the settlement fund EUR 4.25 million.

Finally, Vie d'Or resolved claims of about 11,000 individual policyholders who purchased life insurance policies that included an investment component. The life insurance company went bankrupt and proceedings were initiated against the Dutch State, the Insurers regulator, the accountant and the actuary. After a Supreme Court ruling, a settlement fund of EUR 45 million was established.

2. No Evidence of Extensive Litigation Caused by the WCAM

The use of the WCAM in those four cases appears to be the result of external factors rather than being triggered by its current structure. Shell and Vedior[18] were concerned the spin-off of international securities disputes and aimed at a global resolution of securities claims, although none of those cases had been litigated in the Netherlands. The Shell securities settlement was a spin-off of class actions in the US. The idea to resolve the matter for the non-US investors using the newly implemented WCAM was launched by Shell's in-house counsel at that time, who had extensive experience of dealing with mass torts and resolving those in the US.

Vedior was settled without any form of litigation. The two merging companies simply wanted to deal with potential negative media coverage and move as quickly as possible to the next level after the merger. Based on the interviews, in Vedior the lawyers seem to have latched onto the collective settlement mechanism as a convenient means of quickly resolving claims that stood between the defendant and successful completion of its acquisition.

---

[17] The remedy was that the consumers received a discount on their debt to the company.

[18] Converium, the last WCAM settlement, was not included in the case study but also concerned international securities.

The non-securities claims settlements in Dexia and Vie d'Or have a national background. The WCAM made sure that in those cases, pending extensive collectively and individually commenced litigation came to an end, rather than causing more litigation. Moreover, the extensive litigation in Dexia and Vie d'Or was a result of the strategic choices made by the defending companies, rather than the result of frivolous initiated lawsuits. Dexia had initiated hundreds of individual debt recovery suits against the retail investors as part of a 'total war' scenario of the Belgian-French management, who initially endorsed a more formalistic and strict management approach, whereas in Vie d'Or it was clear from the outset that the State would litigate the case before the Supreme Court, because it wanted a court decision on the standard to be applied with regard to State liability for allegedly failing in regulatory oversight. If the Supreme Court were to have rendered a negative decision, the legislature would have been able to launch new legislation. The Foundation defending the interest of the policyholders anticipated those policy considerations and applied a strategy of getting to the Supreme Court as fast as possible, but without success. All together, the litigation from first instance until Supreme Court took about 13 years.

Moreover, both the Dexia and Vie d'Or settlements were the result of government intervention and political pressure on the companies to resolve the matter. In Vie d'Or, the outcome of the Supreme Court ruling was such that the defendants could have easily decided not to settle at all.

In sum: in all four cases, the idea for and initiative of using the WCAM came from the companies who paid. In one case the representative organization even stated that it preferred to settle without using the WCAM. It considered the use of the mechanisms in that specific case as a waste of time and effort, but the company pushed for the use of the procedure. The conclusion based on these case studies is that the expressed views that the structure or technique of the WCAM leads to extensive litigation are, at the very least, not empirically grounded.

IV. PROPOSED NEW AMENDMENTS: A BALANCED PICTURE

As already stressed in the introduction, the statutory draft proposal to improve the WCAM contains amendments that are technical in nature[19]

---

19 E.g., a stay of pending proceedings until the end of the opt-out period and not until the date of binding declaration.

and amendments that are a codification of already established practices of the Amsterdam Court of Appeal.[20] In addition, it contains a few more fundamental proposals.[21]

The first is the extension of the applicability of the WCAM also to cover bankruptcy proceedings, such as in the DSB Bank bankruptcy matter. This amendment was not included in the first draft proposal, but was added later and has the support of the Association of Dutch Banks. Its rationale was to speed up the resolution of the DSB bankruptcy, in which many Dutch banks were creditors.

The second amendment (preliminary or pretrial hearing) seeks to address criticism made by consumer organizations that the current collective settlement regime does not allow collective actions for damages, leaving the WCAM behind as an entirely voluntary mechanism. The draft proposal contains a provision allowing parties to ask for the assistance of a judge in mass disputes before legal proceedings have been initiated, to explore whether parties could settle, if not the entire dispute then at least part of it. The idea is that an experienced judge or a special master could be helpful in facilitating that process and could bring unwilling defendants to the negotiation table. If the outcome is that a settlement is not a viable option, subsequent proceedings can take place in a more structured and efficient way. This amendment is part of a broader litigation vision and philosophy of the legislature to provide courts and parties with different tools to achieve settlements, preferably out of court, but with assistance of the court. Such settlements should do justice to the legitimate rights and positions of the parties involved. The vision of the legislature is that the shadow of the law can be created in different ways. There are many ways that lead to Rome and a collective action for damages is not the only one.

Another measure that is not part of this proposal, but fits within this philosophy, is a request for a pre-judicial ruling from lower courts to the Supreme Court to rule on questions of law. The lower courts can invoke this provision at their own initiative or at the request of one of the parties. This provision was brought into force on 1 July 2012[22] and would have been able to speed up the resolution of cases like Dexia and Vie d'Or if it had existed at that time.

---

20 E.g., a case management conference prior to the oral hearing to discuss matters of logistics.

21 For an extensive discussion of those, see Ozmis and Tzankova, *supra* note 10, 33–42.

22 See Dutch Bulletin of Acts and Decrees 2012, 65, also published on <https://zoek.officielebekendmakingen.nl/stb-2012-65.html>, accessed 25 February 2013.

Finally, the draft proposal contains an extra requirement on standing to sue in *collective actions*: organizations will now have to show that they are able to sufficiently represent the interests of consumers or of the injured parties.

Given the fact that the first and the third proposals are beneficial for businesses, the interim conclusion should be that even if the second proposal would overall be more beneficial for consumers, that would still make the draft legislative proposal at the very least 'well balanced'. However, some have argued[23] that although the legislature should review the details of the specific provision proposing the 'pretrial hearing', and that it should pay attention to the implementation of the provision in terms of training the courts on how to use it, it serves the interests of both consumers and businesses that are held liable, even though for different reasons.

In sum, the suggested improvements of the WCAM are overall not likely to be disadvantageous for businesses nor will they lead to frivolous suits.

V. ISSUES THAT SHOULD CAUSE CONCERN

Despite the foregoing relatively reassuring outcome of the analysis of the proposed amendments of the WCAM, there are a few issues that do raise worries although they are different from the ones identified by the business community and the media. Those issues are related to the funding of mass disputes and to achieving the right balance between *ad hoc* and longstanding organizations as the driving forces behind the resolution of mass disputes.

1. Funding of Mass Disputes

Although the WCAM was inspired by the US class settlement regime, at least one essential feature of that regime did not make it into the statute: the court's review and approval of class counsel fees, which is one of the safeguards against the potential abuse of collective settlements. Such a requirement was not considered by the Dutch legislator. The latest legislative proposals aiming to improve the WCAM are also silent on this topic. However, it must be noted that when the class counsel fees are being paid out of the settlement fund, as was the case in Converium, the Amsterdam Court will have to review and approve those fees as part of its assessment of the fairness of the settlement agreement. In its consideration of the

---

23 See Ozmis and Tzankova, *supra* note 10, 33–42.

fairness of the conversion settlement with respect to the amount of compensation awarded, which was proportionally considerably lower than the settlement payment for the smaller group of US shareholders, the court heavily relied on the fact that the non-US shareholders had been excluded from the US class, and that it is not plausible that they would therefore have effective remedies in or outside the US absent the settlement agreement. In other words, the difference between the US settlement and the WCAM Converium settlement was not unacceptable, since the legal position of the two groups of shareholders was essentially different and could accordingly be treated differently in terms of settlement outcomes.

The Amsterdam Court also assessed the reasonableness of the US counsel's fees, which represented 20 percent of the settlement payment and was perceived by the objecting parties as excessive and incompatible with Dutch public order. The Amsterdam Court of Appeal dismissed this objection, finding that in the context of determining the fairness of a collective settlement under Dutch law, the court may take into account customary US fee practices, when US law firms are involved and the legal services they provided took place predominantly in the US. Furthermore, the Amsterdam Court of Appeal pointed out that the US lawyer's fees were also thoroughly scrutinized by the US court that approved the US settlement, and that a fee calculated on the basis of the load star method (hourly fees) would lead to a similar remuneration.

Whether an assessment of the counsel fees by the court will take place depends, however, on the design of the settlement agreement, and can therefore be 'manipulated' by the settling parties. If the settling parties agree that the counsel fees are to be paid out of a separate fund, based on a separate agreement, there is no requirement for the court to approve the reasonableness of the counsel fees. Parties can thus manipulate the involvement of the court in such a review through the design of the settlement agreement that is to be declared binding. Statutory provisions that class counsel fees should be presented to and approved by the court in any event increases transparency and is therefore a safeguard against potential abuses.[24]

On a more general level, the questions remain whether an explicit statutory provision with regard to the oversight of funding issues in mass disputes can be omitted, and whether a legal system can afford to be entirely dependent on the competence and discretionary powers of individual

---

[24] Ianika Tzankova and Hélène van Lith, 'Class Actions and Class Settlements Going Global: the Netherlands', in Duncan Fairgrieve and Eva Lein (eds), *Extraterritoriality and Collective Redress* (OUP 2012), 67.

judges deciding on a case-by-case basis whether or not to pay attention to funding dynamics in mass claim disputes. The European Commission has acknowledged that financing in class or group actions is a significant issue,[25] but a vision – let alone concrete proposals – on how access to justice should be preserved while the potential for abuse is avoided, is lacking.

One explanation, in line with European civil law or at least Dutch tradition, for 'rational apathy' with regard to this issue on the part of the legislator and the judiciary, could lie in the concept of contractual freedom, which is viewed as fundamental to many advanced legal systems. Contractual issues should be addressed primarily by the parties involved. The remuneration of the lawyer is a matter of contract between a client and his legal counsel and, as long as there is no conflict between those parties, third parties should not interfere. In collective actions and settlements under Dutch law, the client is a (representative) organization that is deemed capable of dealing with its agent. If and when the client is not satisfied with the financial arrangements and the lawyers' fees, the client can submit a complaint and follow the disciplinary proceedings established by the Dutch Bar Association or (in theory) go to court. Another explanation could be that traditionally in collective actions there is a funding problem on the plaintiff side,[26] so the danger of an overpaid WCAM class counsel is not the first thing that comes to mind. In view of the existing agency costs theories,[27] one may conclude that those explanations are insufficient justifications for disregarding the funding issue under the Dutch system of collective redress.

A final explanation for the absence of a provision on class counsel fees in the WCAM could be that such a provision is not necessary, since the class counsel is being monitored by powerful and sophisticated players, like Consumentenbond (the Dutch Consumers' Organization) and VEB (the Dutch Shareholders' Association), but the increased activism of special purpose vehicles set up by commercially operating entities resembles

---

25 European Commission, *Commission Staff Working Document Public Consultation: Towards a Coherent European Approach to Collective Redress* (SEC 2011 173 final), para 3.5, see also <http://ec.europa.eu/justice/news/consulting_public/0054/sec_2011_173_en.pdf>, accessed 25 February 2013.

26 The Consumentenbond and VEB have to fund collective actions from their members' fees and have limited resources.

27 For a discussion of why the funding of mass disputes is an issue that deserves closer scrutiny and for a demonstration of how various funding mechanisms, traditional and new ones, play out in the Dutch context of mass disputes, see Tzankova, *supra* note 5, 41.

features of the US class action system, for which it has been heavily criticized: the rise of the lawyer without a (tangible) client.

2. Framing the Representative Organization

Recent experiences in the Netherlands with mass disputes show that it is relatively easy to establish an *ad hoc* special purpose vehicle to act in a collective action or settlement. This has strengthened the phenomenon of 'competing organizations', which seems to be an obstacle first for defendants whose litigation strategies require to explore out of court settlement options with groups of claimants, and secondly, for claimants, since it becomes difficult for them to asses which organization to join. What makes it problematic is that special purpose vehicles cannot be absent from the collective redress scene, since longstanding organizations like the VEB and Consumentenbond will not always be inclined or able to facilitate group or collective actions. In addition, special purpose vehicles promote diversity among representative organizations and that should be valued since it prevents a limited number of established longstanding organizations from monopolizing the collective resolution process. Further, an attempt in Shell to contribute to this kind of diversity and extend the WCAM standing requirements to public pension funds (another type of established longstanding interest organization that has been underappreciated in the Netherlands to date) failed. Moreover, in the recent proposed amendments the legislature has explicitly excluded pension funds from being considered as a representative organization under the scope of the WCAM.[28]

There have been some unregulated initiatives aiming to improve the accountability and governance of special purpose vehicles: a Claim Code was drafted by an *ad hoc* Commission[29] and presented in 2011 to the Dutch Ministry of Justice. The Claim Code was the result of a broader consultation that took into account the reactions of various actors professionally involved in collective actions and settlements. In essence, the Claim Code is a set of principles that should apply to special purpose vehicles acting as

---

[28] See Kamerstukken II 2011–2012, 32 612, nr 3, p 14, also published on <https://zoek.officielebekendmakingen.nl/blg-146303.html>, accessed 25 February 2013. See also Ozmis and Tzankova, *supra* note 10, 41.

[29] The Chairman of the Commission was a former president of the Dutch counsel for the judiciary. The Commission included members of the legal profession who have experience with collective actions and settlements, both on the plaintiff and the defendant side, the Consumentenbond (the Dutch Consumers' Association), a law professor who was also one of the Board members of the Foundation that was established in Shell, and a communications adviser.

representative organizations in collective actions or settlements. The Claim Code has five principles relating to the promotion of collective interests without a profit motive: the composition, tasks and working procedure of the Board, the independence and avoidance of conflicts of interests, the remuneration of Board members, and the Supervisory Committee whose task it is to overview the functioning of the Board Members. The Claim Code applies the principle of 'comply or explain'.

This has the potential to add an extra layer of costs and bureaucracy in the functioning of representative organizations and it remains to be seen whether and how it will improve the functioning of the WCAM. In any event the issue of competing special purpose vehicles has not been sufficiently addressed to date by the Claim Code or by the legislator.

With respect to finding the right balance between *ad hoc* and longstanding organizations as the driving forces behind the resolution of mass disputes, Europeans should be careful about relying too heavily on longstanding public interest and consumer organizations to take the lead in the resolution of mass disputes. Currently, the assumption is that limiting standing to act in mass disputes to such organizations offers safeguards against abusive litigation. This appears to be a false assumption and not only for the reasons that are too obvious to point out.[30]

At least one of the case studies revealed that longstanding organizations, once involved in the resolution of a mass dispute, might have to defend a position that advances the interests of only one group of their members. It was reported that the Consumentenbond lost many members after it supported and participated in the WCAM settlement in Dexia, because those members (rightly or wrongly) felt betrayed by the position the Consumentenbond took in that settlement. This has had a negative impact on the willingness of the Consumentenbond to be involved in the future in the collective resolution of mass disputes and has made the Consumentenbond more cautious about doing so – which might not be a good thing.

The bottom line is that eliminating or restricting the role of *ad hoc* organizations where the usual suspects, the established longstanding organizations, are unable or for policy reasons unwilling to act, is a bad idea. On the other hand, longstanding organizations offer a valuable perspective on the mass claim resolution process and contribute to the systems of checks and balances in the same way as *ad hoc* organizations do with respect to

---

[30] E.g., they are underfunded, do not always have the needed expertise, might have other priorities, monopolies are seldom a good idea, there should be checks and balances, etc.

longstanding organizations. A solution to this complex issue in the Dutch financial mass disputes context could be to extend the group of parties allowed to play a more active role in the resolution of mass disputes to public pension funds, who combine the virtues of longstanding and *ad hoc* organizations. And coincidence or not, Eumedion, the Pan-European organization of pension funds, has openly endorsed such a position.[31] This is a story to be continued.

VI. CONCLUSION

When the WCAM was introduced in 2005, it was considered by some to be a one-day fly. The years that followed proved that this assumption was wrong. However, this, in combination with the plans of the Dutch legislature to amend and improve the functioning of the WCAM, has raised different kinds of concerns on the side of the business community. The fear exists that the WCAM promotes frivolous litigation. The case studies of four collective settlements that have been concluded under the WCAM to date reveal that such fear is not well grounded. In the cases settled to date, the use of the WCAM has been invoked at the initiative of the settling companies. Moreover, many of the proposed amendments to improve the functioning of the WCAM are to be considered business friendly. However, there are issues with respect to the resolution of mass disputes that need to be considered, although, as mentioned earlier, they are not the same as the ones identified by the business community or the media so far. Those issues relate to the funding of mass disputes and the framing of the representative organizations. To date, those issues have been underappreciated by the Dutch legislature. It remains to be seen how these will develop in the future.

---

31 See Ozmis and Tzankova, *supra* note 10, 41.

5. Settlement and its pitfalls in England and Wales

Christopher Hodges

The civil procedure system in England and Wales has now had over 12 years' experience with settlement being a formal goal of civil procedure, under the Civil Procedure Rules 1998 (CPR), but settlement has been embedded in the common law system for at least a century. However, the reforms inspired by first Woolf and recently Jackson show that costs rules, funding arrangements, lawyers' culture, and general policy all have significant impact on settlement rates, and when and how settlement occurs.

I. SETTLEMENT AS STANDARD PRACTICE

Although mediation in civil litigation is a relatively recent technique in England and Wales, negotiation and settlement in fact have a far longer history than just 12 years, and have been a common feature of civil litigation for as long as anyone can remember. This phenomenon appears to contrast with the experience of civil law jurisdictions, in which the introduction of mediation is relatively recent, largely initiated by the arrival of the EU Mediation Directive.

Settlement has always been facilitated in common law systems by the intrinsic architecture of their civil litigation procedures, which traditionally rely on parties having control over their cases and, therefore, having knowledge of the facts that are shared between them as the process develops. The need for the parties to have full and non-asymmetrical information is a prerequisite for settlement.

These two factors mean that parties are enabled and empowered to decide whether, and when, to initiate negotiations between them, irrespective of whatever stage the judicial procedure may have reached and generally without disturbing the progress of that procedure. In order to engage in meaningful discussions about the merits of a case, a party has to be in possession of as many facts as possible. That position of knowledge is impeded if the facts are collected by the judge and not fully available to

Table 5.1 County Court statistics (non-family)[1]

Year	Number of claims	Number of defences	Total number of claims allocated to a track
2000	1,965,463	250,442	155,208
2001	1,845,021	255,035	142,781
2002	1,787,061	266,625	142,031
2003	1,765,559	268,042	157,175
2004	1,597,123	261,666	152,913
2005	1,580,511	237,876	159,644
2006	2,157,000	295,372	157,000
2007	2,015,000	341,956	177,000
2008	2,064,000	298,796	164,000
2009	1,879,000	316,000	179,000
2010	1,617.000	291,000	169,000
2011	1,553,983	275,920	170,615

the parties. In these respects, the civil procedures of, for example, Germany and England are opposed paradigms, although in assessing them other considerations also apply, such as the difference that each paradigm produces in costs and duration.

In England and Wales, therefore, it has for many years been the case that individual cases settle. The rule of thumb amongst practitioners has for many years been that over 95 per cent of cases settle. That assumption has more recently been supported by more reliable statistical evidence.[2] Table 5.1 shows, for example, a significant diminution in the number of County Court cases as they proceed through the three stages from issue through defence to allocation to a track. At every stage, the numbers fall because cases are primarily settled (some are withdrawn, but this is anecdotally low). So settlement is not a new phenomenon. What was new, as of 1999

[1] Taken from Annual *Judicial Statistics*, compiled by Naomi Creutzfeldt-Banda.

[2] Her Majesty's Court Service figures suggest that 2.5 per cent of all fast- and multi-track claims are decided at trial, but this figure includes a large number of undefended money claims that proceed straight to judgment without a trial. Of claims that are defended in the fast and multi track, around 25 per cent are decided at trial, but the percentage varies between different types of claim. *Proposals for Reform of Civil Litigation Funding and Costs in England and Wales. Implementation of Lord Justice Jackson's Recommendations*, Ministry of Justice, Consultation Paper CP 13/10, November 2010, para 115, available at http://www.justice.gov.uk/consultations/docs/jackson-consultation-paper.pdf.

when the CPR came into force, was the inclusion in the CPR that settlement is a formal end, and this has realigned civil procedure to a significant extent.

II. PUBLIC POLICY ON SETTLEMENT OF DISPUTES

The reasons for promotion of settlement are not difficult to see. Lord Woolf's basic point was that since the overwhelming proportion of cases settle and are not resolved by a judge, the civil procedure system should not align itself solely to enable the judge to reach a decision, but should primarily enable the parties to reach settlement themselves as soon as possible.[3] Hence, the parties should have access to the relevant information, swapping what each has among themselves right at the start (supported by pre-action protocols on what should be produced for particular types of cases). Such an approach should save public funds in the use of courts. There should also be a cultural public policy benefit: parties should be encouraged to behave in a collaborative manner, and seek to resolve their differences between themselves, rather than adopt aggressive, adversarial behaviour.

Hence, Lord Woolf summarised his policy on the 'new landscape' as having the following features:

> *Litigation will be avoided wherever possible*
> (a) People will be encouraged to start court proceedings to resolve disputes only as a last resort, and after using other more appropriate means when these are available.
> (b) Information on sources of alternative dispute resolution (ADR) will be provided at all civil courts.
> (c) Protocols in relation to medical negligence, housing and personal injury, and additional powers for the court in relation to pre-litigation disclosure, will enable parties to obtain information earlier and promote settlement.
> (d) Before commencing litigation both parties will be able to make offers to settle the whole or part of a dispute supported by a special regime as to costs and higher rates of interest if not accepted.
>
> *Litigation will be less adversarial and more co-operative*
> (a) There will be an expectation of openness and co-operation between parties from the outset, supported by pre-litigation protocols on disclosure and

---

3 Lord Woolf, *Access to Justice: Final Report* (HMSO 1996), available at http://webarchive.nationalarchives.gov.uk/+/http://www.dca.gov.uk/civil/final/contents.htm.

experts. The courts will be able to give effect to their disapproval of a lack of co-operation prior to litigation.

(b) The court will encourage the use of ADR at case management conferences and pre-trial reviews, and will take into account whether the parties have unreasonably refused to try ADR or behaved unreasonably in the course of ADR.. . .[4]

ADR and mediation are not without strong critics.[5] A study of two mediation pilots in the Central London County Court[6] concluded that the motivation and willingness of parties to negotiate and compromise is critical to the success of mediation. The study found persistent rejection of mediation in personal injury cases. Where there is no bottom-up demand, demand can be created by means of education, encouragement, facilitation and pressure accompanied by sanctions or incentives.

In the decade since the Woolf reforms, all UK litigation lawyers have developed expertise in mediation and other ADR techniques. Highly specialised centres of expertise have evolved to train and accredit mediators in different specialisations, and to manage international and domestic ADR, such as CEDR and the City Disputes Panel in London.[7] A Civil Mediation Council provides professional and strategic oversight.[8]

III. PROBLEMS WITH THE CPR REFORMS AND SETTLEMENT

Do pre-action protocols, case management and the other techniques promote settlement? Within a few years of the new CPR regime, anecdotal comments from practitioners, backed by emerging studies,[9] indicated that

---

4 Ibid, Introduction, para 9.

5 Hazel Genn, *Judging Civil Justice* The Hamlyn Lectures 2008 (Cambridge 2010).

6 Hazel Genn, Paul Fenn, Marc Mason, Andrew Lane, Nadia Bechai, Lauren Gray and Dev Vencappa, *Twisting Arms: Court Referred and Court Linked Mediation under Judicial Pressure* (Ministry of Justice 2007), Ministry of Justice Research Series 1/07.

7 http://www.cedr.com and http://www.citydisputespanel.org.

8 http://www.civilmediation.org.

9 Lord Chancellor's Department, *Further Findings: A Continuing Evaluation of the Civil Justice Reforms*, August 2002, at http://webarchive.nationalarchives.gov.uk/+/http://www.dca.gov.uk/civil/reform/ffreform.htm; Tamara Goriely, Richard Moorhead and Pamela Abrams, *More Civil Justice? The Impact of the Woolf Reforms on Preaction Behaviour, Research Study 43* (London: Law Society and The Civil Justice Council, 2002), at https://www.law.cf.ac.uk/research/pubs/reposi-

cases tended to settle at an earlier stage in the procedural process, but the costs of cases were 'front loaded' by having to be incurred before or at the start of the formal processes. The persistence of these views to the end of the decade led to the appointment in 2009 of Lord Justice Jackson to carry out a further review on litigation costs. Jackson's extensive consultations confirmed the 'front loading' charge.[10] He found that around 90–95 per cent of professional negligence claims are settled at the pre-action protocol stage,[11] that there had been a 25 per cent increase in the cost of employers' liability cases between 2000 and 2003 which now settled with more delay,[12] that there were mixed views on the merits of particular protocols, and that a survey of the Technology and Construction Court found that only 6 per cent of claims were settled or discontinued between pre-action protocol correspondence and service of the claim form.[13] Many practitioners' general view after ten years' experience was that informal disclosure under the protocols leads to earlier identification of issues and disposal of weak claims or the improvement of claims, and is easier to comply with than the more formal application for pre-action disclosure under CPR 31.16.[14] However, Jackson was strongly criticised by some on the basis that there was evidence of disproportionate costs in only a small percentage of cases.[15]

Among recommendations on a wide range of issues, including major reform of the means of funding of litigation, Jackson's principal prescription for improving costs matters was the espousal of (enhanced) cost management of cases by judges. The idea was that if costs could be controlled, more cases would be able to be brought, and those that were brought would also be settled earlier, since there would be greater certainty and increased proportionality between costs and sums in dispute. He asserted:

---

tory/557.pdf. Various other studies are summarised in Christos S Konstantinouu, 'Pre-Action Protocols 14 Years on: Have They Been Proven to be Conducive to Settlement?', available at http://papers.ssrn.com/sol3/papers.cfm?abstract_id=2175448.

10 Neil Andrews, 'The Three Paths of Justice: Court Proceedings, Arbitration, and Mediation in England', vol 10 of *IusGentium: Comparative Perspectives on Law and Justice* (Springer Dordrecht Heidelberg Publishers, 2011), at 3.28, p 64.

11 Rupert Jackson, *Review of Civil Litigation Costs: Preliminary Report* (London: TSO, 2009) ('Preliminary Report'), vol II, p 424; Rupert Jackson, *Review of Civil Litigation Costs: Final Report* (London: TSO, 2010) (Final Report), p 352.

12 Preliminary Report, vol I, p 96.

13 Preliminary Report, vol I, p 306, Form 1 Q2.

14 Tim Parkes, 'The Civil Procedure Rules Ten Years On: The Practitioners' Perspective', in Deidre Dwyer (ed) *The Civil Procedure Rules Ten Years On* (Oxford University Press 2009), p 439.

15 Claire McIvor, 'The Impact of the Jackson Reforms on Access to Justice in Personal Injury Litigation' (2011) 30.4 *Civil Justice Quarterly* 411.

> Access to justice is only practicable if the costs of litigation are proportionate. If costs are disproportionate, then even a well-resourced party may hesitate before pursuing a valid claim or maintaining a valid defence. That party may simply drop a good claim or capitulate to a weak claim, as the case may be.[16]

Although a test of proportionality of costs had been introduced under the Woolf reforms,[17] and underlay the whole concept of the fast track for smaller cases, interpretation of the rules led to the re-introduction of the concept of necessity into assessing work done.[18] The rule was that, in applying the (normal) standard basis award of costs, the court would not allow costs that had been unreasonably incurred or were unreasonable in amount,[19] and would only allow costs that were 'proportionate to the matters in issue'.[20] Jackson recommended that the concept of proportionality should prevail on a global basis over the test of reasonableness by enabling disproportionate costs to be disallowed in an assessment of costs on the standard basis. 'Proportionate costs' should be defined by reference to sums in issue, value of non-monetary relief, complexity of litigation, conduct and any wider factors, such as reputation or public importance.[21]

In 2011, the government consulted on a raft of reforms that implemented almost all of Jackson's recommendations and continued the philosophy of resolving more claims through mediation, together with streamlined and lower cost litigation tracks. Some changes were made through the Rules Committee, some by judicial practice, and some in the Legal Aid, Sentencing and Punishment of Offenders Act 2012. The government's primary consideration was to aid economic recovery by saving public expenditure and by promoting 'quicker, cheaper alternative dispute resolution where appropriate'.[22] The major features are:

---

16 Final Report, Ch 4, paras 2.4 and 2.5.

17 The 'overriding objective' requires: 'Dealing with a case justly includes, so far as practicable . . .

(c) dealing with the case in ways which are proportionate –
  (i) to the amount of money involved;
  (ii) to the importance of the case;
  (iii) to the complexity of the issues; and
  (iv) to the financial position of each party.': CPR rule 1.1(2).

18 *Lownds v Home Office* [2002] EWCA Civ 365; [2002] 1 WLR 2450; *Willis v Nicolson* [2007] EWCA Civ 199.

19 CPR rule 44.4(1).

20 CPR rule 44.4(2). See *Henry v News Group Newspapers Ltd* [2013] EWCA Civ 19.

21 Final Report, Ch 3, para 6.1.

22 Consultation paper CP6/2011, *Solving disputes in the county courts: creating a simpler, quicker and more proportionate system. A consultation on reforming*

- expanding significantly non-court appropriate forms of dispute resolution by requiring all cases below the small claims limit to have attempted settlement by mediation, and introducing mediation information/assessment sessions for claims above the small claims limit; requiring all cases below the small claims limit to have attempted settlement by mediation before being considered for a hearing; introducing mediation information/assessment sessions for claims above the small claims limit;[23]
- increasing the upper jurisdiction threshold for small claims (excluding personal injury and housing disrepair) from £5,000 to £10,000, £15,000 or £25,000.[24]
- introducing a simplified claims procedure on a fixed costs basis, similar to that for road traffic accidents under £10,000,[25] for more types of personal injury claim;[26] exploring the possibility of extending the framework of such a scheme to cover low value clinical negligence claims; and examining the option of extending the upper limit of those simplified claims procedures to £25,000 or £50,000;
- introducing a dispute management process and fixed recoverable costs by specific case types up to £100,000.[27]

---

civil justice in England and Wales (Ministry of Justice, 2011) ('Implementation Consultation'), available at http://www.justice.gov.uk/consultations/docs/solving-disputes-county-courts.pdf.

23 In the previous two years more than 10,000 small claims mediation appointments were conducted, for which the settlement rate was 73 per cent, and of over 7,500 users that completed the online survey 98 per cent were satisfied or very satisfied: Implementation Consultation, para 141. Seventy-five per cent of specified debt cases were undefended: ibid, para 90. There were 230,000 property repossession claims in 2009: ibid, para 94.

24 The government favoured an increased cap of £15,000, which would capture 83 per cent of all defended cases currently allocated to a case management track: Implementation Consultation, para 115.

25 Extending the Road Traffic Act (RTA) Personal Injury Scheme from £10,000 to £25,000 would capture around 90 per cent of all RTA PI claims: Implementation Consultation, para 66.

26 This could have a major impact on clinical negligence claims against the National Health Service, which in 2009/2010 appear to total over 10,308 (claims notified to the compensation recovery unit), and total legal costs of claims closed in that year by the NHS Litigation Authority (excluding claims against healthcare professionals not employed by the NHS) of £163.7 million: Implementation Consultation, paras 79 and 80.

27 This extends the pre-existing fixed recoverable cost scheme, which is currently capped generally at £5,000, but £1,000 for personal injury and housing disrepair claims. Although neither the Jackson Report nor the government says this, the fixed costs system in fact copies the tariff system of the German civil litigation system.

The government emphasised the importance of mediation:

> In our view there are many cases which could be better resolved through mediation and do not necessarily require judicial intervention. . . . We propose that this mediation stage should involve the parties in small claims cases being automatically referred to a mediation service. This means that for the first time mediation will be seen as part of the actual court process.[28]

Recognising the element of compulsion in imposing mandatory mediation, the government said:[29]

> We envisage a staged process with fixed costs applying at each stage, with those costs relating to different dispute values and/or different case types. As an example, these stages might be:
>
> 1. **Triage** – what are the initial options available? For example, could the dispute be resolved by referral to an Ombudsman, a Regulator, or a trade association scheme? Or, does the matter require legal advice?
> 2. **Evidence gathering** – if stage 1 has not resolved the dispute, the parties/solicitors would attempt to resolve the matter and to strictly adhere to the timetable and directions set out in the relevant Dispute Management Process.
> 3. **Negotiation/settlement** – essentially a stocktaking stage, where most of the evidence has been gathered and the parties will be required to try to settle the claim via mediation or another dispute resolution process, which could be conciliation, arbitration or the parties arranging a settlement conference.
> 4. **Trial** – where the issue could not be resolved at the settlement stage, the parties would produce joint evidence packs (setting out the efforts made to settle the dispute and the evidence they wish the court to consider), and apply to the court for a final hearing.

Reforms are also to be made in the separate area of labour disputes, by requiring a party (almost always an employee) to notify the Advisory, Conciliation and Arbitration Service (ACAS) and having a mandatory period of conciliation before a claim will be accepted by an employment tribunal.[30]

---

[28] Ibid, paras 149 and 152. The increased use is envisaged of paper-based and telephone determinations, as provided for under the European Small Claims Procedure: ibid, paras 158–62.

[29] Ibid, para 87.

[30] Enterprise and Regulatory Reform Act 2012, section 7. However, there are several other changes inspired not so much by Jackson as by a desire to encourage economic growth by stimulating employers to hire more staff without the risk of being subject to detailed requirements impeding workers being fired.

IV. FINANCIAL INCENTIVES TO SETTLE

The primary mechanism used to promote settlement is through financial incentives and pressures. One cannot make a person negotiate or settle if they do not want to. But a public procedure can include incentives (such as cost-shifting rules) or cost sanctions (such as empowering the court to modify the normal cost-shifting rule where a party has failed to act rationally in entering into negotiations or mediation). Courts have penalised parties in costs for failing to mediate, even at pre-action stage.[31] However, no one can be compelled to mediate,[32] and it can be reasonable to refuse to mediate, for example where the mediation has low prospects of success or trial is imminent.[33]

Cost shifting is the norm in almost all of the many jurisdictions around the world,[34] but its impact on litigants' behaviour is particularly strong in England and Wales for several reasons. First, lawyers costs are comparatively high. Second, they are based on work done on an hourly rate basis, which tends to incentivise rather than limit the amount of work done. Third, the quantum of parties' costs (both client-lawyer costs and *inter-partes* costs) has, until recently, generally only been regulated after the conclusion of a case, and there was little transparency until the end of the case over the size of the exposure to the adverse costs risk. The Woolf and now Jackson reforms have attempted to address these problems through a series of mechanisms, including fixed shiftable costs for smaller cases, production of cost estimates that would cover next stages of large cases and be approved or limited by the judge, and cost capping applications.

The extent of a court's powers to make costs orders is remarkably wide, and the details of costs constitute a complex subject.[35] Many factors may be taken into account under the CPR in departing from the standard 'loser pays' starting-point, and a winning party is normally likely to recover only somewhere between 66 and 75 per cent of his total bill.[36] Gambling over

---

31 *Burchell v Bullard* [2005] EWCA Civ 358.

32 *Halsey v Milton Keynes General NHS Trust* [2004] EWCA Civ 576.

33 *Swain Mason v Mills & Reeve (a firm)* [2012] EWCA Civ 498; *ADS Aerospace Ltd v EMS Global Tracking Ltd* [2012] EWHC 2904 (TCC) (defendant not unreasonable to reject mediation at a late stage in view of repeated earlier attempts to negotiate with claimant, and claimant only offered mediation a short time before trial: claimant ordered to pay defendant's standard costs).

34 Christopher Hodges, Stefan Vogenauer and Magdalena Tulibacka, *The Costs and Funding of Civil Litigation* (Hart/CH Beck, 2010).

35 See John Peysner, 'England' in Hodges, Vogenauer and Tulibacka, *supra* note 34.

36 See CPR 43–48, and the Costs Practice Direction.

costs, and hence promotion of settlement, is encouraged by the rule that a party who fails to receive from the court an amount of damages that exceeds a settlement offer made by the opponent may not be allowed to recover his costs, and might even be ordered to pay the opponent's costs.[37] The rule has given rise to some controversial outcomes:[38] in *Carver v BAA plc*[39] the claimant marginally beat the defendant's offer yet the claimant was ordered to pay the defendant's costs, after the court adopted a wide-ranging view of conduct; in *Jones v Associated Newspapers Ltd*[40] the claimant was awarded £1 more than the offer but was not awarded costs. Jackson said Part 36 is a key element to promote settlement, but recommended that *Carver* be reversed since it put too much pressure on claimants to settle for offers that were not high enough, and the government has been persuaded to overrule *Carver*.

Significant Jackson-inspired[41] reforms have been introduced to the costs rules as of April 2013 that will encourage settlement further. First, there is a new test that costs should be proportionate to the amount in dispute, which takes priority over the tests of reasonableness and necessity.[42] The Court of Appeal has stated that:

> costs budgeting is not intended to derogate from the principle that the court will allow only costs as have been reasonably incurred and are proportionate to what is at stake; it is intended to identify the amount within which the proceedings should be capable of being conducted and within which the parties must strive to remain

and that budgets are 'intended to provide a form of control rather than a licence to conduct litigation in an unnecessarily expensive way. Equally, however, it may turn out for one reason or another that the proper conduct of the proceedings is more expensive than originally expected'.[43]

Secondly, claimants may now initiate Part 36 settlement offers, so

---

37 CPR Part 36, especially r 44.1.

38 See Pablo Cortés, 'A Comparative Review of Offers to Settle – Would an Emerging Settlement Culture Pave the Way for their Adoption in Continental Europe?' (2012) 32.1 *Civil Justice Quarterly* 42.

39 [2008] EWCA Civ 412.

40 [2007] EWHC 1489 (QB).

41 *Reforming Civil Litigation Funding and Costs in England and Wales – Implementation of Lord Justice Jackson's Recommendations. The Government Response* (Ministry of Justice, 2011) ('Jackson Response'), available at http://www.official-documents.gov.uk/document/cm80/8041/8041.pdf.

42 The Civil Procedure Rules, Part 44.4, as amended by the Civil Procedure (Amendment) Rules 2013.

43 *Henry v News Group Newspapers Ltd* [2013] EWCA Civ 19.

opening negotiation at an early stage and pressuring defendants to respond to the merits quickly. Thirdly, enhanced sanctions apply under Part 36 to encourage early settlement, including:

i. An additional amount to be paid by a defendant who does not accept a claimant's offer to settle where the court gives judgment for the claimant that is at least as advantageous as an offer the claimant made to settle the claim. This additional sanction is to be calculated as 10 per cent of damages where damages are in issue, and 10 per cent of costs for non-damages claims;
ii. In mixed (damages and non-damages) claims, the sanction will be calculated as 10 per cent of the damages element of the claim;
iii. However, the sanction under these provisions is to be subject to a tapering system for claims over £500,000 so that the maximum sanction is likely to be £75,000; and
iv. There would only be one sanction applicable for split trials.

Fourthly, certain categories of claimants (all personal injury claims)[44] should be protected by qualified one way cost shifting (QOCS),[45] under which, unless the claimant acts unreasonably,[46] losing claimants would pay their own costs and any success fee, but not pay the winner's costs, and losing defendants would pay the winner's base costs. The aim of QOCS is to reduce the financial risk for the claimant, and hence reduce the need for many claimants to take out after-the-event (ATE) insurance.[47] Claimants would only have to pay defendants if:

(a) the claim is found to be fraudulent on the balance of probabilities;
(b) the claimant has failed to beat a defendant's 'Part 36' offer to settle; or
(c) the case has been struck out where the claim discloses no reasonable cause of action or where it is otherwise an abuse of the court's

---

44 Jackson also suggested that protection could apply in other types of cases (judicial review claims; defamation claims; housing disrepair claims; actions against the police; and professional negligence claims) but the government was 'not persuaded' to extend QOCS: Jackson response, para 27.

45 For the policy on which the Rules are based see *Written Ministerial Statement: Implementation of Part 2 of the Legal Aid, Sentencing and Punishment of Offenders Act 2012: Civil Litigation Funding and Costs* (Ministry of Justice, amended 17 July 2012), available at http://www.parliament.uk/documents/commons-vote-office/July_2012/10-07-12/11-MOJ-Civil-Litigation-Funding.pdf.

46 Jackson Consultation, para 136.

47 Jackson Consultation, paras 85 and 132.

process (or is otherwise likely to obstruct the just disposal of the proceedings).

QOCS protection would apply in relation to claims that are discontinued during proceedings, subject to (a) above. A defendant of modest means faced with a wealthy claimant could apply at the beginning of a case for the cap on the claimant's costs recovery to be lifted altogether or increased.[48] QOCS only applies to individuals and not commercial organisations.[49] It is unclear whether it would apply to civil society bodies like consumer associations, who may be active in collective proceedings: the government notes that some NGOs have substantial assets and should not be afforded costs protection. Trade unions and consumer associations are able to recover costs from opponents on a notionally self-insured basis: this would no longer be permitted.[50]

Fifthly, a strengthened regime of cost management of litigation is imposed, implementing the principle of proportionality. For smaller cases, regimes of fixed shiftable costs are imposed or extended.[51] For all multi-track (i.e., larger and more complex) cases,[52] from 1 April 2013 parties must file and exchange costs budgets, and the court may both cap and manage the costs, backed by severe sanctions for transgressions by parties and lawyers, unless there is good reason.[53] Practitioners expect that enhanced

---

[48] Jackson Consultation, para 164.

[49] Jackson Consultation, para 152.

[50] Jackson Consultation, para 94.

[51] The Civil Procedure Rules, Part 44.5, as amended by the Civil Procedure (Amendment) Rules 2013.

[52] Automatic costs management does not apply in the Admiralty and Commercial Courts, or to all cases in the multi track in the Chancery Division, Technology and Construction Court and the Mercantile Courts where, at the date of the first costs management conference, the sums in dispute exceed £2 million, excluding interest and costs, except where the court so orders: *Costs Management in the Chancery Division and the Specialist Lists in the Queen's Bench Division: Amendment to CPR Rule 3.12 (1)* (Judiciary of England and Wales, 18 February 2013), available at http://www.judiciary.gov.uk/JCO%2fDocuments%2fPractice+Directions%2fcosts-budgeting-announcement-draft-direction-cpr-rule-3-12.pdf.

[53] The Civil Procedure (Amendment) Rules 2013. A cost cap limits the amount of future costs (including disbursements) which a party may recover under a subsequent order for costs. A pilot costs management scheme was introduced in October 2009 in relation to defamation proceedings, now embodied in Practice Direction 51D (the Defamation Proceedings Costs Management Scheme), under which the court approves a budget submitted by parties and will not depart from it unless satisfied that there is good reason to do so, 'The function of the budget is to ensure that the costs incurred are not only reasonable but proportionate to what is at stake.' *Henry v News Group Newspapers* [2013] EWCA Civ 19.

budgeting will have a cooling effect on clients' approaches to litigation, and hence encourage swifter settlements.

V. SETTLEMENT IN MULTI-PARTY ACTIONS

There should be no reason in theory why settlement should not occur in large or multi-party cases as it does in individual cases. The incentives that arise under the cost-shifting risk are the same for any type of case, but perhaps even more so for collective cases, since the sums involved are generally very large. However, large multi-party actions (MPAs) give rise to particular problems on settlement.

What has happened in practice? In reviewing the position on MPAs, one should start by recognising that the incidence of cases, and types of cases, has changed over the past three decades or so. This appears to be due to (a) the incidence of underlying problems, (b) the availability of funding for lawyers to investigate and pursue multiple and often complex cases, (c) the ability of the judge to exercise effective management over what is a large and complex litigation, and advance its resolution, whether by cases falling out, settlement or decision, and (d) the availability of pathways for dispute resolution that are alternative to courts, which may be cheaper, quicker or otherwise more attractive. Let us examine these points in turn.

1. Incidence of Cases and Types

Data from the Legal Services Commission identified 955 applications for a Group Litigation Order (GLO) in the 15 years to 2004, 52 GLOs between 2000 and 2005 (this might only capture cases in which a request for funding has been made to the LSC), and a dramatic fall in the number of multi-party actions after 2002, down to only four in 2006–2007.[54] To September 2007, the LSC records showed that the most numerous cases related to child abuse (156), health, medical and pharmaceuticals (34), and prisoners (27). The MPA position went remarkably quiet in the later 2000s, but has unsurprisingly picked up with a series of financial claims and cases over press invasion of privacy.

Almost all of the initial multi-party product liability cases were defended, with little attempt at settlement, and their claimants failed before full

---

[54] Reproduced at Christopher Hodges, 'Global Class Actions Project. Country Report: England and Wales', Appendices, at http://globalclassactions.stanford.edu/sites/default/files/documents/England_Country%20Report.pdf.

trial.[55] Negotiated settlements were reached in only a small number of cases.[56] Defendants defended the cases as a matter of principle in the belief that the merits of the vast majority of individual claims brought were at best low. Most individual claimants withdrew or were struck out before trial. However, since then, other types of claims have been successfully settled,[57] notably the care homes child abuse cases, holiday or transport cases,[58] some (not all) medical device implant cases, and other one-off cases such as mass murder by healthcare professionals.

A representative procedure applies to damages claims in the Competition Appeal Tribunal, under which the consumers' association 'Which?' may act as representative claimant.[59] Only one case has been brought under this procedure, involving replica football T-shirts.[60] The case settled, but there is widespread misinformation over what transpired. The popular account was that the opt-in procedure impeded sufficient claimants joining the class, whereas the more important factor was that reputation damage in the market had previously forced the defendant to offer voluntary compensation to many customers, and the scheme that was agreed with the claimant therefore only attracted a small number of takers.[61]

It seems that different types of case have had different settlement profiles. A significant proportion of the MPAs in the period from 1995 to 2005 involved child abuse in care homes (after successful prosecutions) and transport crashes. In these cases, liability is usually not the major issue, and cases usually settle. In contrast, there was a series of claims from the 1980s till mid 2000s involving allegedly defective products, predominantly medicines but sometimes medical devices, tobacco or sofas containing toxic materials. In some of these cases (sofas and some medical devices), liability was not in issue, but in many of the medicines cases, and the tobacco cases, defendants denied liability or causation, and made clear that they would usually fight all the way, even when faced with the 'legal aid blackmail' situation.

---

55 See the case studies in Christopher Hodges, *Multi-Party Actions* (Oxford University Press, 2001).

56 Notably Myodil contrast medium, Opren, haemophiliacs with HIV, Gamagard, human growth hormone.

57 Information provided by participants at the conference on Group Actions held at the Centre for Socio-Legal Studies, Oxford on 14 December 2006.

58 L Christian, 'Rail Crash Litigation – Southall and Ladbrooke Grove' [2001] *JPIL* 4/01, 339–55.

59 Competition Act 1998, s 47A and B.

60 See http://www.which.co.uk/reports_and_campaigns/consumer_rights/campaigns/Football%20shirts/index.jsp.

61 See Hodges, *supra* note 55.

A recurring feature of the medical product cases has been that the claimant group (often assembled as a result of a 'media bandwagon') tends to comprise individuals whose individual cases had widely differing merits, whether on issues of liability, causation, or under the 'development risks' defence. All such issues are often difficult to establish in medical product liability claims. The lesson is that there is a need to investigate and scrutinise the merits of individual cases at the start. However, the claimants' lawyers may not have the funding to do this, or a full understanding until later in the case of the medical criteria that should be applied, and it may not help their negotiating position to weed out cases from what otherwise appears to be a large group. The overall position from the medicines and more recent financial investment cases is that large defendants do not implode when faced with a mass of claims but can decide to fight on both generic and individual issues. This means that general settlements are less likely to occur.

Lawyers play the central part in the negotiations. The Myodil case was run outstandingly well by its claimant lawyer, who carried out an internal audit on claims, as a result of which the class slimmed from 3,000 to 342, and the defendants then settled. In many other cases, defendants fought on and often won overall, possibly with a small number of meritorious cases being pulled down by the existence of a mass of poor cases and difficult generic issues.

It is important to note that large cases often end in some *ad hoc* compensation scheme arrangement under which the rights, entitlement, causation and quantum of damage of each individual is established on an individual basis. These schemes have arisen both under voluntary settlements (such as the medicine Eraldin) and after the court has determined the liability of a defendant but before quantum has been determined for every claimant (such as various diseases of miners).[62] Special insurance or compensation arrangements also exist for particular categories of victims, such as for creditors of failed financial institutions,[63] or policyholders in the failed company Equitable Life,[64] or vaccine damage.[65] These schemes sometimes only provide for partial compensation, rather than full indemnity.

---

[62] Schemes include noise induced hearing loss (NIHL), some asbestos related conditions, pneumoconiosis, chronic obstructive pulmonary disease (COPD) and vibration white finger (VWF): see http://www.decc.gov.uk/en/content/cms/funding/coal_health/coal_health,aspx.

[63] The Financial Services Compensation Scheme, at http://www.fscs.org.uk.

[64] A special fund, arranged by HM Treasury after pressure from the Parliamentary and Health Service Ombudsman.

[65] A one-off tax-free payment of £120,000 under the Vaccine Damage Scheme.

2. Availability of Funding

Funding is essential for large cases and claimant lawyers have long argued that the absence of funding is the main problem in bringing mass litigation. The forensic reason is that, given the size of the required investment in costs and the size of the adverse costs risk, the total amount of funding required for a mass case of any size is significant and not easily available, and there is therefore considerable risk to funds invested, even without taking into account the 'adverse costs gamble'.

Three periods can be identified.[66] First, there was a 'golden age' for MPAs under the legal aid arrangements until the government closed the tap in the mid 1990s. One of the major reasons why there was extensive multi-party litigation in this first period[67] was that where claimants were funded by the state through legal aid, the one-way cost shift applied, under which the state would effectively be reimbursed its costs if the party it funded won, but if the defendant won he was effectively unable to recover any costs either from the claimant or the state. This situation was known as 'legal aid blackmail'.[68]

During this first period, the attentions of both claimant and defence lawyers were primarily focused on persuading the Legal Aid Board to fund – or not to fund – a large case. The court's role was almost secondary. The Legal Aid authorities' concern not to waste public funds on unjustified cases, or on unnecessary work in the (highly expensive) cases that they did fund, produced some difficult situations. For example, the level of bureaucratic reporting by the funded lawyers to the Legal Aid Board imposed a considerable burden. Further, the level of control over what steps should be taken next in a case, and at what cost, became intense and sometimes debilitating. Claimant lawyers complained of micro-management by the authorities, and being impeded from having the flexible discretion to make relevant tactical decisions. Some tensions occurred when judges objected to their managerial authority appearing to be usurped in having to bow to decisions on whether the next steps in a case should be dictated by what

---

66 The changing funding arrangements and the 'costs war' between claimants and insurers are described in Christopher Hodges, John Peysner and Angus Nurse, *Litigation Funding: Status and Issues* (Centre for Socio-Legal Studies, Oxford and Lincoln Law School, 2012), 15–37, available at http://www.csls.ox.ac.uk/documents/ReportonLitigationFunding.pdf.

67 See the case studies in Hodges, *supra* note 55.

68 For an explanation of how the Legal Aid Act 1988, s 18(4) worked, see Hodges, *supra* note 55, p 308.

the court considered necessary or what the Board would fund (the court usually won this uneasy stand-off).

Secondly, after legal aid was largely deconstructed,[69] from 1995 until 2010 there was a period of privatised funding based on Conditional Fee Agreements (CFAs).[70] However, claimants were exposed to the normal cost-shifting rule. That change was perhaps the most important factor that reduced the flow of multi-party actions over the succeeding decade. In order to cover claimants' exposure to potential liability for opponents' costs, legal expenses insurance (LEI) was required, either pre-existing policies or a new form of ATE policy. From 1999,[71] the government made CFA success fees and ATE premiums recoverable from losing or settling defendants, and this had a significant fuelling effect on individual claims but far less so on MPA cases. Lawyers were not attracted to CFA cases with large risks, and ATE premiums were extremely high. Administering cases with multiple individual LEI policies was practically impossible. In this period, MPAs and GLOs almost wilted away.

During this period, however, two series of scandals occurred involving uncontrolled 'claims farmers', who used high-pressure marketing to attract claimants in supposedly mass claims, or simply submitted fraudulent claims. Many of the individual claims that were put forward were not verified, and defendants/insurers faced a difficult choice on whether to fight or just settle because it was cheaper. The first example occurred in early 2000s when claims management companies that had formed to exploit the recoverability of CFA success fees and ATE premiums (TAG and Claims Direct) collapsed after failing to verify the validity of individual claims.[72] The government was forced to introduce a regulatory regime for claims management businesses.[73]

---

69 Successive restrictions have been imposed over many years on eligibility criteria, and imposition of rationing and budgetary constraints. The latest merits test is in The Civil Legal Aid (Merits Criteria) Regulations 2013/104.

70 Under a CFA, there is a basic fee based on work done charged at an hourly rate, and a success fee based on a percentage of the basic fee. A proportion of the basic fee, subject to court control, is recoverable from a losing opponent. There are certain regulatory requirements governing CFAs, and success fees are capped at 100 per cent of the basic fee.

71 Access to Justice Act 1999.

72 See Hodges, Peysner and Nurse, *supra* note 66, 21ff.

73 Compensation Act 2006, Part 2. See *Claims Management Services Regulation: Baseline Study*, Department for Constitutional Affairs, April 2007; Mark Boleat, *Claims Management Regulation. Impact of Regulation. Third Year Assessment* (Ministry of Justice, 2010), available at http://www.justice.gov.uk/publications/docs/cmr-impact-assessment0710.pdf.

The second scandal occurred at the end of the decade, when intermediaries marketed services to bring claims based on financial scandals that had become widely publicised, notably the failure of mutual Equitable Life, mis-selling of payment protection insurance (PPI), or road traffic or other personal injury accidents. The market was vibrant,[74] abuse had reached epidemic proportions,[75] and the Information Commissioner brought criminal proceedings. Pursuant to a Jackson recommendation, the widespread practice of lawyers paying referral fees to insurers and claims managers has been banned.[76]

In 2010, Jackson found that the CFA recoverability regime was one of the major drivers of excessive costs,[77] and persuaded the government to undertake radical changes to funding options and costs rules. CFA success fees and ATE premiums were made irrecoverable, so that source of funding should also wilt. Claimants would in future have to deduct such costs from their damages recovered. This has been the position in Scotland, where it has not caused difficulty.[78] In order to balance the diminution in value of claimants' damages that would be caused by having to pay for their lawyers' success fees and ATE premiums, Jackson proposed that general damages should rise by 10 per cent.[79]

Instead, in further privatisation of funding, we are at the commencement of a third period of litigation funding, in which regulated contingency fees

---

74 Between 1 October 2011 and 30 September 2012, a total of 477 claims management companies surrendered their authorisation. During the same period 283 claims management companies had their authorisation cancelled. However, these market exits were countered with 568 new market entrants: *Consultation. Regulation fees paid by claims management companies* (Ministry of Justice, 2012) https://consult.justice.gov.uk/digital-communications/claims-management-companies-fees/consult_view.

75 *CAB evidence briefing: The claims pests – CAB evidence on PPI and claims-management companies* (Citizens Advice Bureau, November 2012), available at http://www.citizensadvice.org.uk/index/policy/policy_publications/er_legal/the_claims_pests.htm.

76 Claims Management Regulator's Conduct of Authorized Persons Rules 2007. *Claims Management Regulation: Approach and Enforcement of the Referral Fee Ban* (Ministry of Justice, November 2012), available at http://www.justice.gov.uk/downloads/claims-regulation/cmr-referral-fee-ban.pdf.

77 *Final Report*, para 3.26.

78 Lord Gill's *Report of the Scottish Civil Courts Review* (2009) para 96.

79 Jackson Consultation, para 100. In *Simmons v Castle* [2012] EWCA Civ 1039 the Court of Appeal announced a rise in the level of general damages for personal injury, nuisance, defamation and all other tort claims that cause suffering and inconvenience by 10 per cent.The Association of British Insurers challenged this but lost.

and third-party litigation funding are to be permitted. Contingency fees are called Damages Based Agreements (DBAs), and extended from prior use in Employment Tribunal cases (where they had given rise to concern about abuse by lawyers[80]) to general use from April 2013.[81] Third Party Litigation Funders are now well established in the UK, but choose to invest primarily in major commercial cases.[82] Funders have made clear that they are currently not particularly attracted to funding multiple individual cases, save in particular circumstances where the investment risk is low, such as cartel damage cases that follow a regulatory agency's finding of infringement (and hence liability will essentially be difficult to defend, and settlement is highly likely). The response to calls for regulation of third party funding has so far been a self-regulatory code.[83]

What will happen now? Will the new regime of DBAs, Litigation Funding, QOCS and the other complex costs rules generate an increase in litigation, and MPAs? Many people expect so, and the QOCS protection for personal injury cases will clearly support product liability and transport disaster cases. The strong costs rules discussed above that force early settlement should pressure swift investigation and settlement of cases. However, the QOCS rules may not incentivise proper investigation of the merits of individual claimants' cases. Some highly contentious litigation can be anticipated.

---

80 Regulating Damages Based Agreements, Consultation Paper 10/09 (Ministry of Justice, 2009) available at http://www.justice.gov.uk/consultations/docs/regulating-damages-based-agreements.pdf; leading to revised regulation under the Coroners and Justice Act 2009 and the Damages-Based Agreements Regulations 2010. See Practice Note at http://www.lawsociety.org.uk/productsandservices/practicenotes/damagesbasedagreements.

81 The Legal Aid, Sentencing and Punishment of Offenders Act 2012 section 45 inserts into section 58AA of the Courts and Legal Services Act (1990) a new section 6(A), under which rules of court may make provision with respect to the assessment of costs in proceedings were a party in whose favour a costs order is made has entered into a damages-based agreement in connection with the proceedings. Costs would be recovered from the opponent on a conventional basis, on the Ontario model. Any excess over the sum recoverable on a normal hourly rate basis would be paid by the client: Jackson Consultation, para 234.

82 See Hodges, Peysner and Nurse, *supra* note 66, 21ff. Cento Veljanovski, 'Third Party Litigation Funding in Europe' (2012) 8 *Journal of Law, Economics & Public Policy* 405.

83 *The Association of Litigation Funders of England and Wales: Code of Conduct for Litigation Funders* (Civil Justice Council, November 2011), available at http://www.judiciary.gov.uk/NR/rdonlyres/75D4F49E-BDC6-40BC-B379-B5A1DA82BED9/0/CodeofConductforLitigationFundersNovember2011.pdf.

3. Case Management

Effective case management by expert judges can clearly promote settlement, and do so at the right time. In the common law system generally, the insistence on addressing the information asymmetry issue between the parties as soon as possible promotes settlement. In large cases, judges can assist by ensuring that the facts and law that are needed for a rational view of the merits to be taken can be identified and addressed on a 'critical path analysis'. In some cases, therefore, judges may clear the path by deciding an issue of law that enables resolution,[84] or may reach decisions on test cases that can be applied to other cases.

In individual actions, different courts have experimented with case management techniques over the past decade and in some cases longer, with a view to moving cases along and encouraging settlement. The Commercial Court, for example, has long and extensive experience of handling big cases, and has a reputation for demonstrating a degree of flexibility that is greater than in some other courts. However, concern over costs and delays by the mid 2000s led to a series of recommendations over the adoption of further innovations in procedure.[85]

The series of claims arising out of the Buncefield oil depot explosion were the first cases to test the new techniques: judges in the Commercial Court and the Technology and Construction Court were involved in succession and adopted an interventionist style of management, and issued lengthy directions, imposing strong pressure on parties to settle quickly, without outstanding results.[86] It is noteworthy that the judges refused to adopt the GLO procedure, since they were able to rely solely on the courts' flexible case management powers. This case involved a large number of commercial property, economic loss, household property and personal injury claims that arose from the explosion, which were processed in groups.

---

[84] A notable example occurred in the unauthorised bank overdraft charges disputes, where the Supreme Court's decision on a provision in the Unfair Terms in Consumer Contracts Regulations 1999 brought extensive litigation and claims in the Financial Ombudsman Service to an unexpectedly swift end: *Office of Fair Trading v Abbey National plc and Others* [2009] UKSC 6.

[85] *Report and Recommendations of the Commercial Court Long Trials Working Party* (Judiciary of England and Wales, 2007), at http://www.judiciary.gov.uk/Resources/JCO/Documents/Reports/rep_comm_wrkg_party_long_trials.pdf.

[86] Naomi Creutzfeldt-Banda and Christopher Hodges, 'Buncefield' in Deborah Hensler, Christopher Hodges and Ianika Tzankova (eds), *Class Actions in Context: How Economics, Politics and Culture Shape Collective Litigation* (Edward Elgar, forthcoming).

Case management in MPAs in fact preceded Woolf by some time. Woolf merely crystalised existing practice into a rule in very general terms. Judges have shown themselves robust in managing GLOs. The purpose of a GLO is to provide case management of claims that give rise to common or related issues.[87] The principal tension is that claimants wish to have generic issues decided first, whereas defendants often wish to focus on individual claims, since those positions represent the relative strengths and weaknesses of each side. Judges usually resist a theoretically generic approach, and want to decide 'real cases', so tend to favour defendants' positions. In a recent example,[88] the judge rejected the shutting out of individual circumstances since that would pre-judge some issues and produce a hypothetical decision. He denounced as 'moral blackmail' the suggestion that certain parties would only pursue the case if it were to be processed on a certain basis.

4. Alternative Dispute Resolution Pathways

Roughly contemporaneously with the revision of the CPR in the late 1990s, another separate major development was occurring that went largely unnoticed by lawyers and academics until recently.[89] This was the growth of extra-court dispute resolution mechanisms, ranging from ombudsmen, complaint and arbitration mechanisms under business codes of business practice for certain sectors, to in-house customer complaint mechanisms for many retailers and manufacturers, and to powers for regulators to facilitate restorative solutions.

The development of these 'ADR' pathways has coincided with the crisis in public funding since 2008. The crisis has forced the government to make deep cuts in courts' and legal aid budgets,[90] towards development of various types of private funding for litigation, but also caused a significant shift in emphasis away from courts and lawyers towards ADR. The Minister of Justice set out the new policy:

---

87 CPR 19.10.

88 *Tew and others v BoS (Shared Appreciation Mortgages) No 1 plc and others* [2010] EWHC 203 (Ch).

89 Christopher Hodges, Iris Benöhr and Naomi Creutzfeldt-Banda, *Consumer ADR in Europe* (Hart 2012).

90 The Ministry of Justice's target in 2010 was a real reduction of 23 per cent in its budget, worth nearly £2bn in 2012–15. *Consultation Paper, Proposals for Reform of Legal Aid in England and Wales*, November 2010 ('Legal Aid Consultation'), para 1.3, available at http://www.justice.gov.uk/consultations/legal-aid-reform-151110.htm.

> I believe that this has encouraged people to bring their problems before the courts too readily, even sometimes when the courts are not well placed to provide the best solutions. This has led to the availability of taxpayer funding for unnecessary litigation. There is a compelling case for going back to first principles in reforming legal aid. . . .
>
> To continue like this is unsustainable, and I want to use these lessons as an opportunity for fundamental reform of the scheme. I want to discourage people from resorting to lawyers whenever they face a problem, and instead encourage them, wherever it is sensible to do so, to consider alternative methods of dispute resolution which may be more effective and suitable. I want to reserve taxpayer funding of legal advice and representation for serious issues which have sufficient priority to justify the use of public funds, subject to people's means and the merits of the case.

The objective is:

> These proposals complement the wider programme of reform to move towards a simpler justice system: one which is more responsive to public needs, which allows people to resolve their issues out of court without recourse to public funds, using simpler, more informal, remedies where they are appropriate, and which encourages more efficient resolution of contested cases where necessary. But these legal aid proposals are not dependent on the implementation of those wider reforms.[91]

The government states that 'to help establish the right balance' it has been guided by various considerations, beginning with, 'the desire to stop the encroachment of unnecessary litigation into society by encouraging people to take greater personal responsibility for their problems, and to take advantage of alternative sources of help, advice or routes to resolution'.[92]

The implications of the 'consumer ADR' (CDR) aspects of this transformation are discussed in Part B of this book. The result of the establishment and growth of these CDR mechanisms has been to capture many consumer-to-business disputes, which have therefore shifted away from lawyers and courts. This development is now virtually irreversible, and CDR systems already process some mass disputes, for example in financial services, telecoms and utilities cases, and their capacity to do so will increase. However, this dispute pathway revolution has yet to seep into the consciousness of many lawyers and the general public.

In a highly significant development in late 2012, the government *rejected* the option of a collective action or litigation mechanism for resolution of consumer claims, and instead favoured regulatory and ADR/CDR

---

91 Legal Aid Consultation, para 1.5.
92 Legal Aid Consultation, para 2.11.

techniques.[93] The reasons cited were that private enforcement, whether individual or collective redress mechanisms, are slow, expensive and frequently ineffective in delivering compensation to consumer victims. The government expressed concern:

> about the scope for such mechanisms to create incentives for intermediaries, the economic cost of such intermediation and the very heavy burden which a proliferation of such cases may impose on businesses. In particular, in the consumer law area, much of the law is based on general principles rather than detailed provisions, and private collective redress could lead to abundant litigation on fine points of law, creating high costs for business, which would then raise prices for consumers as a whole. By contrast, public enforcers would only take action under the Enterprise Act 2002 in the public interest and would only generally prioritise action if the breach were both significant and clear. Businesses would be given the opportunity to resolve any complaint informally, before court action would be considered.[94]

Earlier in 2012, however, the government had proposed a combination of ADR, regulatory powers and a class action mechanism for dealing with (and encouraging more) competition damages claims.[95] The regime that may eventually emerge may differ from these proposals. This proposal was

---

[93] *Civil enforcement remedies: consultation on extending the range of remedies available to public enforcers of consumer law* (Department for Business Innovation and Skills, 2012), at http://www.bis.gov.uk/assets/biscore/consumer-issues/docs/c/12-1193-civil-enforcement-remedies-consultation-on-extending.

[94] Consultation, para 3.10. In relation to the reference to 'incentives for intermediaries', there has been considerable disquiet about the activities of claims intermediaries in relation to the largest current compensation challenge, namely mis-selling of payment protection insurance (PPI) products by financial institutions. Many PPI claims are being brought through the courts and especially the Financial Ombudsman Service. Claims intermediaries have marketed their services heavily. However, a significant number of claims have been brought by intermediaries that are unsubstantiated, and some fraudulent, necessitating regulatory action. See recently *Claims Management Regulation. Proposals for amendment to the Conduct of Authorized Persons Rules* (Ministry of Justice, August 2012); *CAB evidence briefing: The claims pests – CAB evidence on PPI and claims-management companies* (Citizens Advice Bureau, November 2012); *Claims Management Regulation: Approach and Enforcement of the Referral Fee Ban* (Ministry of Justice, 2012); *Payday Lending Compliance Review. Interim Report* (OFT, 2012), OFT1466.

[95] *Private Actions in Competition Law: A Consultation on Options for Reform* (Department for Business Innovation & Skills, 2012), ('the Consultation') at http://bis.gov.uk/assets/biscore/consumer-issues/docs/p/12-742-private-actions-in-competition-law-consultation.pdf. Implementation proposals in Consumer Rights Bill 2013, s 82 and Schedule 7.

significantly influenced by a desire to compete with the litigation settlement regime in The Netherlands.[96]

The current situation is that of competition between different intermediaries, who each want to make money but each of which adopts the pathway that will maximise their income. Thus, lawyers use courts rather than Ombudsmen; claims handlers have flooded the Financial Ombudsman Service (FOS). There is a high level of consumer abuse and detriment. Every week many citizens receive several texts, calls and emails enticing one to register to claim 'your compensation entitlement' for 'your accident' or PPI or whatever.

These intermediaries feed claims both to courts and the CDR system. For example, claims about losses alleged with financial products can be directed to the FOS, and quantified at just under £500, which until 2012 was the sum that the defendant bank had to pay to the FOS in costs on processing any case beyond an initial stage, irrespective of its outcome. The claims intermediaries' calculation would be that the bank would settle the case immediately for the claimed sum, and the intermediary could take its percentage fee out of the winnings.

VI. SETTLEMENT: A GAP IN JUDICIAL OVERSIGHT?

In stark contrast to the rules of class actions in the most active jurisdictions, the English and Welsh GLO rule and practice is that there is no requirement for the court to approve a settlement, or to scrutinise its fairness. This is a striking omission, difficult to justify, and should be remedied.

The absence of practical client control over an MPA is striking. In contrast to active class action regimes in other jurisdictions, in which a representative plaintiff only nominally gives instructions to the legal team, control under the English MPA model nominally rests with every one of the individual claimants, since the MPA consists of an aggregation of individual claims. In effect, therefore, in a claimant group of any size, the individuals have no effective individual voice, and their interests are not represented by any one of them. All tactical decisions are taken by the legal team. Of course, professional requirements require lawyers to keep

96 *Plan for Growth: Promoting the UK's Legal Services Sector* (Ministry of Justice and UK Trade and Investment, 2012); *Dispute Resolution in London and the UK 2012* (The City UK, 2012).

their clients informed of relevant developments and to seek instructions, certainly in relation to settlement issues. However, it is curious that there appears to have been little dissent by individual or sub-groups of claimants that their individual positions have been adversely affected. The potential for conflicts of interest between clients and lawyers or funders over financial issues, and between sub-groups of clients, is a clear risk. Such risks will only worsen with the advent of DBAs and independent litigation funding. The absence of arrangements for transparency, accountability and independent governance by a trustee[97] or the court is a major failure of democratic accountability.

VII. CONCLUSIONS

This analysis has shown that settlement has long been an integral part of civil dispute resolution in England and Wales, and since 1999 has been enshrined in the rules and culture of litigation and of litigation lawyers. New reforms in 2013 will increase systemic and judicial pressure for settlement.

However, the incidence of mass litigation is clearly linked with the availability of funding and the prevailing costs rules. The history of successive changes in those rules demonstrates a perennial problem of the need for balance, and how difficult it is to achieve. When it is difficult for claimants (and their lawyers) to finance running litigation and to finance the adverse costs risk, cases are not brought. Conversely, when claimants' 'access to justice' is increased, lawyers generate collective litigation, which has been associated with a significant number of meritless claims, at least in some types of claims, which are not weeded out since that costs money and claimants' strategic priorities are to maximise the class so as to maximise pressure for settlement. Counter-intuitively, some large defendants (possibly because manufacturers rather than insurers were making the strategic decisions) chose in English cases to defend and not settle, and did so with considerable success.

The 'bandwagon' effect of mass publicity can exacerbate the ability and merits of settlement by attracting a range of cases with varying merits. There, therefore, remains the concern that either people are compensated when they should not be if a mass settlement is reached, maybe delivering less than full compensation to those who deserve it but are 'dragged down' by what might be called minimal harmonisation, or the number of

[97] See Hodges, *supra* note 55.

bad cases has the result that a settlement is not reached so the good cases go uncompensated. This is not good for justice or confidence in a justice system. It points to the need for scrutiny of individual merits, either when cases join the group, or when individuals are paid as part of a settlement. It is interesting to note that ombudsmen/CDR procedures and *ad hoc* settlement schemes can process individual claims, especially those forming part of generic or mass problems, efficiently. Some thought should be given to how courts and alternative structures might be combined to overcome the merits-verification and processing problems.

6. Class actions and settlement culture in Canada

Jasminka Kalajdzic

I. INTRODUCTION

Corporate and governmental wrongdoing can affect large numbers of people. Such wrongdoing has an institutional victim as well; mass harm exerts enormous pressure on civil justice systems to provide efficient but fair procedures for redress. In this context, settlement of mass disputes is easily understood as a common good. Yet settlements involving hundreds or thousands of claims, often across jurisdictions, raise concerns about the substantive fairness of the compromise reached by lawyers, and the ability of the court system to ensure meaningful oversight. Unburdening the judicial system of mass claims comes at a price; how much rough justice are we prepared to accept?

As the contributions to this book illustrate, the difficulty of balancing these competing interests is ubiquitous.[1] Canadian class action settlement practice is no exception. In this chapter, I first explore the realities of this form of litigation, and to some extent debunk the myth that class actions inevitably result in large monetary settlements. I then turn to a brief discussion of the incentives and disincentives to settle large claims, for both plaintiffs' lawyers and defendants. In Part III, I describe and critique the judicial framework for the approval of proposed settlements. I finish by pointing out the lack of alternatives to class proceedings and conclude that, although not perfect, the Canadian class action settlement system stands as a model for consideration by other jurisdictions wrestling with the problem of mass disputes.

---

[1] Christopher Hodges and Astrid Stadler, Introduction, in this volume, Chapter 1.

II. FACTS AND STATISTICS: THE (ASSUMED) PREVALENCE OF CLASS ACTION SETTLEMENTS

It is often said that 'most' class actions settle,[2] raising the spectre that unmeritorious claims are commenced for the purpose of blackmailing defendants into submission. Most recently, such sentiments were expressed[3] in relation to the largest auto manufacturer class action settlement in history: Toyota agreed to pay $1.4 billion to resolve class actions by car owners who claimed the value of their vehicles declined as a result of a massive recall due to acceleration problems in several models.[4] Notably, however, NASA, the National Highway Safety Administration and private technical tests conducted by experts on the vehicles' electronic throttle systems all showed that the systems were not defective.[5] Despite the lack of evidence of liability, the company announced that it was settling the litigation in the best interests of its shareholders, employees and customers.[6]

That 'most' class actions settle is probably empirically true in Canada, in that more cases are certified as class proceedings than are rejected, and more certified actions settle than go to trial. Statistical data is still very difficult to find in a jurisdiction where court documents are not electronically available. According to the authors of a leading text on class actions,

---

2 See eg Daryl-Lynn Carlson, 'The search for plaintiffs' (*Financial Post*, 30 June 2010) <www.financialpost.com/search+plaintiffs/3218545/story.html> accessed July 2, 2010: 'The majority of class actions that are certified by courts are settled prior to reaching trial.'

3 See eg Robert Bostelaar, 'It seems class-action craziness will only accelerate' (*The Ottawa Citizen*, 27 December 2012) <http://www.ottawacitizen.com/business/seems+class+action+craziness+will+only+ accelerate/7749814/story.html>.

4 Associated Press, '$1-billion-plus settlement with Toyota gets preliminary approval in U.S.' (*The Globe and Mail*, 31 December 2012) <http://www.theglobeandmail.com/globe-drive/new-cars/auto-news/1-billion-plus-settlement-with-toyota-gets-preliminary-approval-in-us/article6805420/>. The settlement value was subsequently raised to $1.63 billion and received final approval on July 19, 2013: Bill Callahan and Edvard Pettersson, 'Toyota Settlement of Acceleration Cases Wins Approval' (Bloomberg, 20 July 2013) <http://www.bloomberg.com/news/2013-07-19/toyota-settlement-of-acceleration-cases-wins-approval.html>.

5 Stephen Harner, 'The Toyota class action settlement and economic justice in America's "mixed" economy' (*Forbes*, 2 January 2013) <http://www.forbes.com/sites/stephenharner/2013/01/02/the-toyota-class-action-settlement-and-economic-justice-in-americas-mixed-economy/>.

6 W.J. Hennigan, 'Toyota settlement in sudden-acceleration case will top $1 billion' (*Los Angeles Times*, 26 December 2012) <http://www.latimes.com/business/autos/la-fi-toyota-to-pay-at-least-12-billion-to-settle-suddenacceleration-lawsuit-20121226,0,7432292.story>.

however, of the 470 certification decisions issued by Quebec courts up to 2008, 268 cases were granted certification.[7] As of September 2011 in Ontario, the class was successful in 114 out of 181 contested certification hearings, while another 141 cases were certified on consent, usually as part of a settlement.[8] Similar statistics exist in British Columbia.[9]

As with certification statistics, determining rates of settlement is also an imprecise art. Ontario's Chief Justice Warren Winkler has observed that the settlement rate in class actions is consistent with that of ordinary civil litigation, which currently stands at approximately 96 per cent.[10] The rate of class action settlement is actually lower, however, since not all proposed class actions are certified, and only certified actions are capable of being settled. Furthermore, while it may have been true five years ago that the majority of all certified actions settled, most Canadian lawyers and judges agree that, increasingly, the current trend is to take certified cases to trial or summary judgment on the merits.[11]

In any event, whatever the precise statistics, one cannot equate high settlement rates with blackmail or improvident bargains.[12] As is discussed in Part III, there is a concerted judicial effort across the Canadian civil justice system to settle litigation before trial, for reasons of scarce judicial resources, high litigation costs, and improved access to justice.[13] The settlement of class actions, therefore, is of a piece with a broader litigation culture, in which case management and mediation encourage pre-trial resolution of complex disputes. Moreover, there is little evidence of mis-

---

7 Ward Branch, *Class Actions in Canada* (loose leaf, Canada Law Book, 2008), 22–1.

8 Ibid.

9 Ibid. As of September 2011, there have been 43 certifications on consent, 56 successful contested certification motions, and 24 defeated certification motions.

10 Warren K. Winkler, 'Civil Justice Reform – The Toronto Experience' (speech given at the University of Ottawa, Faculty of Law, 12 September 2007) <http://www.ontariocourts.on.ca/coa/en/ps/speeches/ civiljusticereform.htm>.

11 Drew Hasselback, 'Class action battles to shift to trial court from motions hearings' (*Financial Post*, 28 November 2012) <http://business.financialpost.com/2012/11/28/class-action-battles-to-shift-to-trial-court-from-motions-hearings/>.

12 Ward K. Branch and Don Montrichard, 'Exposing the "Litigation Blackmail" Myth' (2005) <http://www. branchmacmaster.com/storage/articles/exposing_the_litigation_blackmail_myth.pdf>. The authors point out that the settlement rates in both ordinary and class action litigation are roughly the same, and argue that class actions settle for many of the same reasons that other litigation does, namely, to avoid the risk, uncertainty and expense associated with prolonged trials (at 11).

13 The arguments are familiar. See Marc Galanter and Mia Cahill, '"Most Cases Settle": Judicial Promotion and Regulation of Settlements' (1994) 46 *Stan L Rev* 1339.

conduct within the class action bar, and support for class actions as an institution remains high on both sides of the bar.[14]

III. INCENTIVES TO SETTLE

Apart from overt encouragement from judges to settle class actions, there are many implicit incentives built in to the class action system to achieve pre-trial resolution of class actions. For plaintiffs' counsel, the existence of the two-way cost rule – a significant feature that differentiates the Canadian system from its American counterpart – creates a powerful disincentive to launch unmeritorious claims or to risk going to trial.[15] Importantly, the law reform paper that proposed a statutory class action scheme in Ontario recommended that special cost rules be adopted for class actions, on the basis that exposure to costs would stagnate the regime.[16] Although the imposition of costs on unsuccessful plaintiffs has not spelled the predicted demise of class actions, there is little doubt that costs have significantly influenced the class action dynamic in Canada. Responding to the argument that adverse costs would deter plaintiffs from bringing meritorious class actions, Justice Perell wrote:

> For good or for evil, any litigation chill is already built into the system selected by the Legislature. The Legislature advertently imposed the normal rules about costs notwithstanding the view of the Ontario Law Reform Commission that the question of costs was 'the single most important issue' that the Commission considered in designing a class action procedure. In the Commission's view, the matter of costs affected not simply the efficacy of class actions, but the more fundamental question of whether class actions should be utilized at all. In rejecting the recommendation of the Commission, the Legislature decided that there is to be some restraints on the access to justice available through a class action procedure. The Legislature did not recommend any so-called access to justice discount.

---

[14] Jasminka Kalajdzic, W.A. Bogart and Ian Matthews, 'Class Actions in Canada: Country Report Prepared for the Globalization of Class Actions Conference' (2009) 622 *Annals of the American Academy of Political and Social Sciences* 41, 47–8.

[15] The two-way costs rule, also known as the English Rule, creates the presumption that the losing party in the litigation bears the costs of both parties. Note that Ontario, New Brunswick, Nova Scotia and Alberta have two-way costs regimes in class actions. Quebec's rules limit such costs to a modest tariff. In the rest of Canada the parties bear their own costs.

[16] Ontario Law Reform Commission, *Report on Class Actions* (Toronto: Ministry of Attorney General, 1982) 647 [citations omitted]. The majority of the commissioners recommended a modified no-costs rule for class actions pursuant to which costs would only be ordered against an unsuccessful party in extraordinary circumstances.

> I suspect that neither the Law Reform Commission nor the Legislature foresaw the sometimes breath-taking claims for costs in class actions for what is supposed to be just an interlocutory procedural motion. This lack of foresight may explain why courts have infused the jurisprudence about costs in class proceedings with the idea that in the exercise of the court's discretion, a judge should have regard to the purposes of the class actions legislation. This discretion is helpful, but it must be exercised within the directive of the Legislature that the normal rules and policies about costs are to apply to class proceedings.[17]

The 'loser pays' costs regime, coupled with the considerable resources committed by defendants to defend against certification motions, have resulted in very large costs awards for what is, at bottom, merely a procedural motion.[18] Certification costs as high as $740,000 have been awarded against unsuccessful defendants,[19] and $525,000 against unsuccessful plaintiffs.[20] Even more daunting, plaintiffs who are unsuccessful at trial face costs orders in the millions of dollars.[21] In reality, these costs are rarely paid by the representative plaintiffs themselves, but by their lawyers, a third-party litigation funder, or the Class Proceedings Fund (in Ontario) or le Fonds[22] (in Quebec).[23] When lawyers themselves, or their financiers, are responsible

---

17 *Cavanaugh v Grenville Christian College* [2012] CanLII 47233 (ON SC), paras 37, 38.

18 Ibid, para 33; *Dell Computer Corp. v Union des consommateurs* [2007] SCC 34 (CanLII) para 103.

19 *McCracken v Canadian National Railway Company* [2010] ONSC 6026; overturned on other grounds *McCracken v Canadian National Railway Company* [2012] ONCA 445 (CanLII).

20 *Fresco v Canadian Imperial Bank of Commerce*, 2010 ONSC 4724, overturned on other grounds 2012 ONCA 444, leave to appeal dismissed 2013 CanLII 14331 (SCC). The plaintiff initially lost the certification motion, but won on appeal. The Class Proceedings Fund, a non-profit entity established by the Law Foundation of Ontario to assist class action plaintiffs with disbursements, had indemnified the representative plaintiff and would therefore have been liable to pay the costs award if the plaintiff had lost the appeal. For information about the Fund, see the Law Foundation website: <http://www.lawfoundation.on.ca/cpcabout.php>.

21 See eg *Smith v Inco* [2012] ONSC 5094, in which the trial judge awarded the successful defendant costs in the sum of $1.7 million, approximately half of what the defendant requested. The defendant has sought leave to appeal the costs order.

22 Le Fonds d'aide aux recours collectifs is Quebec's non-profit entity for distributing financial assistance to class action plaintiffs, in return for a percentage of any monies recovered by the class; see the organization's website <http://www.farc.justice.gouv.qc.ca/>.

23 In *McCracken v Canadian National Railway Company* [2010] ONSC 6026

for adverse costs, a negotiated settlement may be far more attractive than the uncertain outcome of a trial.

Quite apart from the risk of adverse costs, plaintiffs' lawyers are also always exposed to the risk of non-payment of their own fees; unlike European jurisdictions, Canadian class action lawyers universally work on a contingency fee arrangement, pursuant to which they are paid only in the event of success, out of the settlement or judgment proceeds. Given that class action litigation routinely takes several years to reach certification, pre-trial discovery and then trial, the possibility that thousands of hours of work may be unpaid is another significant incentive to reach a reasonable compromise. Unlike the United States, Canadian courts cannot award treble damages, and are very cautious about punitive damages; the potential upside of a trial, therefore, is not the lottery described by class action critics.[24] Moreover, despite the existence of a fee agreement which fixes a contingency fee, class counsel fees must be approved by a judge.[25] Canadian courts have shown little hesitation in reducing the fee contemplated in the agreement between class counsel and the representative plaintiff.[26] There is little certainty in fees, therefore, even in the event of success.

For their part, defendants are also incentivized to settle mass disputes, albeit for different reasons than those which operate vis-à-vis plaintiffs. The usual advantages of settlement of any litigation obtain; corporations may prefer to put an end to litigation uncertainty, remove the liability from their books, preserve their brand, and focus executive resources on the business of the firm rather than on defending a lawsuit.[27] Commercial considerations are as important, if not more, than legal ones. This exercise

---

(CanLII) [para 7] Justice Perell referred to the ordering of costs against a representative plaintiff as a 'fiction', in that plaintiffs themselves are 'always' indemnified against such costs:

> And it is well known that if the plaintiff is unsuccessful in obtaining certification or if the class is ultimately unsuccessful, the plaintiff will be insulated from costs liability by having obtained funding from the Class Proceedings Fund of the Law Foundation of Ontario or by having obtained an indemnity agreement from class counsel. (The existence of these indemnity agreements is also well known, but their disclosure is often resisted).

24 Terry Carter, 'A Lesson Learned' *ABA Journal* (May 1998) 70–73.

25 See eg Ontario's Class Proceedings Act, 1992, S.O. 1992, c 6, s 32.

26 See eg *Sutts, Strosberg LLP v Atlas Cold Storage Holdings Inc*, 2009 ONCA 690.

27 Laura Kupcis, 'Defence Strategy: Settle or Fight?' (*Claims Canada Magazine*, December 2007) <http:// www.claimscanada.ca/issues/article.aspx?aid=1000219433>.

in risk management is of the same kind, important, albeit of a different magnitude, than other, non-representative litigation. Precisely because the stakes are so high, corporate defendants will often resist certification vehemently, and engage in all manner of procedural, interlocutory court proceedings. But in the end, only negotiated settlements can guarantee corporate defendants that a dispute will be resolved within the limits of their insurance coverage, and avoid the inherent uncertainty of an adjudication process.

IV. JUDICIAL APPROACHES TO SETTLEMENT APPROVAL[28]

All Canadian class proceedings statutes require that settlements be vetted by a judge; once approved, the settlement is binding on all class members, unless they opt out.[29] Some statutes are silent as to whether notice of the proposed settlement must be given to the class members, while others explicitly encourage judges to consider ordering such notice.[30] Nevertheless, a practice has developed to require counsel to publish notice of the settlement fairness hearing in order for possible objectors to make written submissions or to appear at the hearing. The number of objectors who appear in Canadian fairness hearings is relatively small, and those who do argue against a proposed settlement are rarely successful.[31]

The statutes are silent as to what factors the court is to consider in assessing the proposed settlements, but fairly detailed criteria have emerged from the courts' jurisprudence. There is little, if any, divergence of approach with respect to the role of the court, and the standards to be applied, in assessing the fairness, reasonableness and adequacy of a proposed settlement. Courts have consistently applied the following framework of analysis:

---

[28] This section is adapted from parts of an article previously published by the author entitled 'Access to a Just Result: Revisiting Settlement Standards and Cy Près Distributions' [2010] 6:1 *Can Class Action Review* 217 [hereafter 'Access to a Just Result'].

[29] See eg Ontario's Class Proceedings Act, 1992, SO 1992, c 6, s 29.

[30] See eg Class Proceedings Act, RSBC 1996, c 50, s 35 (5); Class Proceedings Act, SNS 2007, c 28, s 38(5).

[31] Jasminka Kalajdzic, 'Access to a Just Result', supra note 28, 217, 232–7.

(a) to approve a settlement, the court must find that it is fair, reasonable, and in the best interests of the class;
(b) the resolution of complex litigation through the compromise of claims is encouraged by the courts and favoured by public policy;
(c) there is a strong initial presumption of fairness when a proposed class settlement, which was negotiated at arm's-length by counsel for the class, is presented for court approval;
(d) to reject the terms of the settlement and require the litigation to continue, a court must conclude that the settlement does not fall within a zone of reasonableness;
(e) a court must be assured that the settlement secures appropriate consideration for the class in return for the surrender of litigation rights against the defendants. However, the court must balance the need to scrutinise the settlement against the recognition that there may be a number of possible outcomes within a zone or range of reasonableness. All settlements are the product of compromise and a process of give and take and rarely give all parties exactly what they want. Fairness is not a standard of perfection. Reasonableness allows for a range of possible resolutions. A less than perfect settlement may be in the best interests of those affected by it when compared to the alternative of the risks and costs obligation;
(f) it is not the court's function to substitute its judgment for that of the parties or to attempt to renegotiate a proposed settlement. Nor is it the court's function to litigate the merits of the action or, on the other hand, to simply rubber-stamp a proposal;
(g) the burden of satisfying the court that a settlement should be approved is on the party seeking approval; and
(h) in determining whether to approve a settlement, the court takes into account a number of factors . . . [including the likelihood of recovery and the proposed terms of settlement].[32]

The list of factors contemplated by (h) has also remained constant since first enumerated by Sharpe J. (as he then was) in *Dabbs*.[33] Ontario's current Chief Justice described the factors this way in *Gilbert v Canadian Imperial Banks of Commerce*:

---

[32] *Nunes v Air Transat AT Inc* [2005] CanLII 21681 (ON SC), para 7 (per Cullity J).

[33] *Dabbs v Sun Life Assurance of Canada* (1998) 40 OR (3d) 429 (Ont Ct (Gen Div)).

> There are a number of factors, not all to be given equal weight, which are to be considered in determining whether to approve a settlement. *These include likelihood of success, degree of discovery, the terms of the settlement, recommendation of counsel, expense and duration of litigation, number of objectors, presence of arms length bargaining, extent of communications with the class and the dynamics of the bargaining.*[34]

Winkler J's list of factors to be considered in assessing the fairness, reasonableness and adequacy of settlement remains the standard for judges in fairness hearings. Other judges continue to use the same list, but have offered two additional criteria: the recommendation of neutral parties, and the absence of collusion.[35]

Not surprisingly, the operative principle in the approval exercise is that the settlement must be fair in an overall sense; it need not be the optimal result, nor must it be reasonable vis-à-vis particular class members. Still, three of the elements of the framework for settlement approval are troubling. First, public policy is said to favour the compromise of claims. Second, there is a 'strong' presumption that the proposed settlement is fair and reasonable.[36] Third, the nature and number of objectors are to be considered, and therefore class members have the right to be heard. In each of these three areas there is room for possible reform.

a. Public Policy Favours Compromise

Public policy in Canada clearly favours settlement of all civil litigation, including class actions, on the basis that negotiated settlements avoid the expense and length of trials and allow for creative resolutions of disputes beyond the winner-takes-all outcome of adjudication. There is also institutional self-interest involved: settlements reduce the strain on overbur-

---

34 *Gilbert v Canadian Imperial Banks of Commerce* [2004] CanLII 34176 (ON SC) paras 11 [emphasis added]; to the same effect, see *Vitapharm Canada Ltd v F. Hoffmann-LaRoche Ltd* (2006) 74 OR (3d) 758 (ON SC), paras 111, 113. In British Columbia a slightly different formulation of essentially the same factors is summarized in the 'Jeffery four questions', referring to *Jeffery v Nortel Networks Corp* (2007), 68 BCLR (4th) 317 (BC SC) para 28.

35 *Bilodeau v Maple Leaf Foods Inc* [2009] OJ No 1006 (On SC), para 47 (per Perell J) and *Lawrence v Atlas Cold Storage Holdings Inc* [2009] CanLII 55128 (ON SC)(per Lax J).

36 *Nunes v Air Transat AT Inc*, supra note 32 para 7; *Vitapharm Canada Ltd v F. Hoffmann-LaRoche Ltd*, supra note 34, para 110. In the interest of full disclosure, I point out that I was counsel for the plaintiffs in *Vitapharm* on the carriage motion, but had no involvement with the case thereafter, and not at the time Cumming J. granted the certification and settlement approval motion.

dened court systems.[37] Courts overwhelmingly favour settlement of class actions.[38] They do so for practical considerations regarding scarce judicial resources, as well as a normative belief that settlement enhances access to justice. As one judge stated at the outset of his discussion regarding the approval of a settlement,

> there is an additional, and powerful, reason to support the implementation of the [Settlement] Agreements in this case: the overriding public interest in encouraging the pre-trial settlement of civil cases. This laudatory objective has long been recognized by Canadian courts as fundamental to the proper administration of civil justice. . . . Furthermore, the promotion of settlement is especially salutary in complex, costly, multi-party litigation.[39]

The settlement of a significant proportion of class actions is therefore not only judicially encouraged, but an expected feature of our justice system.

A policy favouring settlement of collective actions, however, must be tempered with an acknowledgment of the peculiar features of representative litigation.[40] Plaintiffs' lawyers are the driving force behind class actions, and are largely unencumbered by the usual constraints of client instruction and oversight. Indeed, class counsel need not have the support of

---

37 *Sparling v Southam Inc* (1988) 66 OR (2d) 225, [1988] OJNo 1745 (HCJ), para 17; *Loewen, Ondaatje, McCutcheon & C v Sparling* [1992] 3 SCR 235, 259.

38 I know of only three Ontario cases where the proposed settlement was rejected: *Epstein v First Marathon Inc* [2000] CanLII 22797 (ON SC), *McCarthy v Canadian Red Cross Society* [2001] OJ No 567 (SCJ) and *Gould v BMO Nesbitt Burns Inc* [2007] OJ No 847 (SCJ). *McCarthy* was ultimately settled once the parties revised the agreement to address the concerns expressed by Winkler J in the earlier decision: *McCarthy v Canadian Red Cross Society* [2001] OJ No 2474 (SCJ). The settlement in *Gould* was also ultimately approved after additional material was filed by the parties at the request of Cullity J: *Gould v BMO Nesbitt Burns Inc* [2007] OJ No 1095 (SCJ). Similarly, initially rejected settlements in Quebec were ultimately approved: *MG v Association Selwyn House* [2009] QCCS 989 (CanLII); *ACEF-Centre v Bristol-Myers Squibb Co* [1995] JQ No 1970 (SC). Most recently, in *Kidd v The Canada Life Assurance Company*, 2013 ONSC 1868, an attempt by the parties to amend a previously approved settlement was rejected by the court, partly on the basis of some class members' objections.

39 *Vitapharm Canada Ltd v F. Hoffmann-LaRoche Ltd*, supra note 34, para 112.

40 For a discussion of the ethical challenges to which class action litigation gives rise, see Jasminka Kalajdzic, 'Self-Interest, Public Interest and the Interests of the Absent Client: Legal Ethics and Class Action Praxis' (2011) 49 *Osgoode Hall L J* 1 [hereafter 'Class Action Praxis'].

the representative plaintiff in order to submit a proposed settlement for judicial approval;[41] class counsel's professional obligation is to advance the best interests of the class, not those of any one class member.[42] That said, the class has been described as the 'absent client', in that it is usually impossible for counsel to consult with each class member, let alone seek instructions from each of them.[43]

Voluminous materials are filed with the court as part of the settlement approval process. Both plaintiffs' and defence counsel have a duty to make 'full and frank disclosure of all material information' to the court relevant to the fairness determination, including all agreements and understandings between lawyers and class members, and any facet of the settlement that may adversely affect members of the class.[44] Whether full disclosure is actually made is likely impossible to gauge. Varying degrees of judicial scrutiny are brought to bear in the exercise of review, with some judges indicating that they must scrutinize proposed settlements 'closely',[45] and others stating that it 'is not necessary to delve deeply into the course of the negotiations between the parties and their counsel. [. . .] I should give considerable deference to the recommendation of class counsel.'[46]

---

[41] In *Berry v Pulley* [2011] ONSC 1378 (CanLII) [93] Justice Perell held that settlement offers must be delivered to representative plaintiffs, who have the authority to accept or refuse the offer; in the event that class counsel believes those instructions not to be in the best interests of the class, they may seek directions from the court (at para 93). But see *Richard v British Columbia* [2007] BCSC 1107 (CanLII), [2007] BCCA 570, where class counsel was removed as solicitors of record for having failed to follow one of two representative plaintiffs' instructions regarding settlement. For a critique of this decision see Jasminka Kalajdzic, 'Class Action Praxis', supra note 40 1, 19–22.

[42] In *Ward-Price v Mariners Haven Inc* [2004] CanLII 13951 (ON SC) 7. At para 7, Justice Nordheimer stated:

> At the same time, it seems to me that it is indisputable that a solicitor and client relationship must exist between counsel for the representative plaintiff and the members of the class once the membership of the class has been fixed. At that point, counsel for the representative plaintiff is clearly counsel to the class as certified with all of the duties and obligations that arise under a solicitor and client relationship with respect to the class members including the obligation to represent the class members 'resolutely and honourably' [citations omitted].

[43] Jasminka Kalajdzic, 'Class Action Praxis', supra note 40, 10–12.

[44] *McCarthy v Canadian Red Cross Society* [2001] OJNo 2474 (SCJ), paras 19–21.

[45] *Dabbs v Sun Life Assurance of Canada*, supra note 33.

[46] *Garland v Enbridge Gas Distribution Inc* [2006] CanLII 36243 (ON SC), para 28.

b. Presumption of Fairness

In this context, I[47] and others[48] have criticized the presumption of fairness that operates in a settlement approval hearing on the basis that the judge faces the onerous and rather unique task of approving a settlement, and thereby extinguishing individual litigation rights, on behalf of hundreds or thousands of class members who are both figuratively and literally absent. In doing so, judges exercise what one author has likened to a fiduciary duty.[49] Furthermore, the judge exercises her approval function in a proceeding that is marked by an adversarial void: plaintiff and defence counsel, having negotiated a hard-fought settlement, have common cause to secure approval of the settlement and are therefore unlikely to point out the settlement's deficiencies.[50] Moreover, as courts have repeatedly recognized, both sets of counsel have a personal financial interest in having the settlement approved, and are therefore in a conflict of interest.[51] Given these dynamics, and the court's weighty task in ensuring that the settlement is fair and in the best interests of the class, a presumption of fairness is not appropriate.

c. Objectors

Finally, the case law makes clear that objectors have a right to be heard and to participate, in one form or another, in the settlement approval hearing. Although the fairness of a proposed settlement is to be judged by reference to the best interests of the class as a whole, and not vis-à-vis the interests of any one class member, the views of class members are 'certainly relevant and entitled to great weight'.[52] Nevertheless, an examination of the case law reveals that few objectors are ultimately successful in convincing the judge to amend or reject a proposed settlement.[53] Even where objectors are found to raise legitimate concerns about the settlement, courts either respond

---

47 Jasminka Kalajdzic, 'Access to a Just Result', supra note 28.

48 Catherine Piche, *Fairness in Class Action Settlements* (Carswell, 2011).

49 Ibid.

50 *Smith v National Money Mart* [2010] ONSC 1334 (CanLII), paras 26–33.

51 *Dabbs v Sun Life Assurance of Canada*, supra note 33 at para 33 ('The recommendation of class counsel is clearly not dispositive as it is obvious that class counsel have a significant financial interest in having the settlement approved'). See also *Fantl v Transamerica Life Canada* [2008] CanLII 17304 (ON SC) at para 49.

52 *Vitapharm Canada Ltd v F. Hoffmann-LaRoche Ltd*, supra note 34, para 179.

53 Jasminka Kalajdzic, 'Access to a Just Result', supra note 28 217, 232–6.

that dissatisfied class members may opt out of the settlement, or repeat that it is the very nature of compromise that less than perfect solutions are reached.[54]

Objectors typically are asked to file written objections. They have the right to adduce evidence, but only as it relates to the issues raised in the objection. They have no right to oral or documentary discovery, but in principle, may cross-examine deponents at the fairness hearings themselves.[55] In some cases class counsel have voluntarily provided relevant documents to objectors. The lack of access to documentary evidence renders it very difficult for any objector to mount a serious, substantive argument in opposition to the terms of the settlement.

In addition, there are no significant financial incentives to intervene in a fairness hearing. Objectors who choose to retain their own counsel are obligated to pay them, with the possibility of only partial indemnity costs payable by class counsel in the event the objectors are successful.[56] Objectors are not entitled to a 'bonus' and are therefore treated no differently than any other class member.

Finally, beyond the procedural and financial disincentives to mounting meaningful opposition to a proposed class settlement, there is the issue of class member apathy. The smaller the individual stake in the class proceeding, the less interested a class member is likely to be in monitoring the fairness of the proposed settlement, a phenomenon which contributes to the adversarial void:

> Our system of justice is based on the basic tenet that the court will be able to reach the most informed, considered, impartial and wise decision after presiding over the confrontation between opposing parties, in which each side can identify issues, lead evidence, cite law, discuss policy considerations, and seek to undermine the position of the other. Motions for the approval of settlements and class counsel fees in class proceeding depart from this basic tenet as a matter of routine. They usually proceed unopposed in large part because individual class members often have too small a stake to be compelled to participate.[57]

How best to improve class member participation in fairness hearings has not been discussed in Canadian legal and judicial circles, but it is evident that the current procedure does not create many incentives for robust

---

54 *Griffin v Dell Canada Inc* [2011] ONSC 3292 (CanLII), paras 28, 39.

55 *Dabbs v Sun Life Assurance of Canada*, supra note 33, paras 18–27.

56 *Sutts, Strosberg LLP v Atlas Cold Storage Holdings Inc*, supra note 26.

57 *Smith Estate v National Money Mart Company* [2011] ONCA 233 (CanLII) para 15.

participation. It is unlikely that court-appointed counsel will be offered to represent objectors, given the current fiscal realities of civil justice systems across Canada. Ultimately, great faith must be placed in the veracity of counsel and the probing eye of the settlement approval judge.

d. Prognosis

Judges are cognizant of the difficult task they undertake when assessing the fairness of a proposed class settlement. They perform a delicate balancing exercise between two fundamental but competing policy interests:

> This task is not an easy one, for the directly involved parties will have chosen to reach agreement rather than pursue all of the merits of their respective positions. This leaves the court from which approval has been sought in the position of attempting to ensure that absent class members' interests are protected properly without having all of the information that a fully adversarial process would yield. At the same time, the court will not wish to be too zealous in scrutinizing a settlement for fear of discouraging adverse parties from attempting to fashion their own agreement in light of their own perceptions of their respective interests.[58]

While some have suggested improving the rigour of the settlement approval process by, for example, appointing an amicus curiae,[59] questions regarding who will pay for such third parties and concerns about prolonging the court process unnecessarily appear to have stalled any concerted reform effort.

In the absence of a court monitor or amicus charged with bringing a third-party, neutral assessment of a proposed settlement, judges are left with an onerous task. Yet the jurisprudence has matured sufficiently so that it is clear judges are sensitive to the ethical minefield of class action praxis. A specialized class action bar, with its own reputational interests to protect, is less likely to engage in malfeasance. At the same time, a specialized class action bench[60] is increasingly sophisticated in its understanding of the dynamics at play. Judges recognize the peculiar conflicts of interest that pervade class action settlements:

---

58 McCarthy Tétrault, *Defending Class Actions in Canada* (CCH *Canadian Limited*, 2002), 147–8.

59 *Smith Estate v National Money Mart Company*, supra note 57, paras 15–31.

60 In some Canadian provinces, judges are appointed to serve on the class proceedings list for a number of years, and thereby develop an expertise in this area of the law.

> As is well known, the settlement of class actions raises very difficult ethical problems for class counsel because of the inherent conflicts of interest that arise because class counsel has an enormous financial interest in the class members' causes of action. There is also the potential conflict of interest of class counsel of having legal and ethical responsibilities to class members whose interests are not homogeneous.[61]

Because judges acknowledge these risks, there is good reason to have faith in their ability to mediate them.

Despite the inherent conflicts, there is a general consensus within the bar and the judiciary that Canadian class action settlements are reasonable and avoid the perceived excesses of the US system. There is little evidence of 'sweetheart' or blackmail settlements in either the scholarly literature or the popular press, and it appears that Canadian courts are alive to the potential dangers of class action abuse. Indeed, only one case is routinely referred to as a 'strike suit',[62] a lawsuit filed only for its settlement value, without any or adequate evidence of actual wrongdoing on the part of the defendant, but which the defendant will settle because of the sheer cost of defending even an unmeritorious claim. Judicial scrutiny is the bulwark against unfettered self-interest. According to the Ontario Court that dismissed the strike suit, '[t]he requirement of judicial approval is . . . [the] means of dealing with the potential for abuse of process in specific class proceedings.'[63]

V. CONCLUSION: IF NOT CLASS ACTIONS, WHAT?

Whatever the imperfections of the class action system in Canada, it remains the only viable recourse for many consumer disputes.[64] Unlike the European Union which has been traditionally reliant upon publicly enforced regulatory models,[65] English-speaking Canada has less robust statutory consumer

---

61 *Berry v Pulley*, supra note 41, para 80 (Perell J).

62 *Epstein v First Marathon Inc* [2000] CanLII 22797 (ON SC).

63 Ibid, para 35.

64 Craig Jones, 'Litigate or Regulate? The Elusiveness of an Effective Consumer Protection Regime' (2013) 53 *Can Bus L J* 360; Jasminka Kalajdzic, 'Public Goals by Private Means & Public Actors Protecting Private Interests: A Response to Professor Jones' (2013) 53 *Can Bus L J* 371.

65 Christopher Hodges, Iris Benöhr and Naomi Creutzfeldt-Banda, *Consumer ADR in Europe* (Hart 2012).

protection, and a very weak enforcement culture.[66] Whether intended – as is the case with British Columbia's *Business Practices and Consumer Protection Act*[67] – or a *de facto* result of limited government funding of public agencies, the enforcement of consumer protection standards has largely been outsourced to private citizens. Class arbitration, while possible in theory, has no foothold in Canada, primarily because of industry resistance to this form of dispute resolution.[68] Mandatory arbitration clauses in consumer contracts have been hotly litigated for the past decade, and have since been banned in some provinces on the basis that to deny recourse to court adjudication (specifically class proceedings) would be to foreclose the only realistic avenue of justice for wronged consumers.[69]

Class actions, therefore, are an important element of Canada's legal architecture. Economic incentives and public policy support the settlement of mass actions, while the statutory requirement of court oversight mitigates against the possibility of class action abuse and blackmail settlements. Unlike the settlement of most individual litigation and almost all private arbitration, class action settlements must be judicially approved. The usual benefits of public scrutiny and the requirement of written reasons, therefore, provide important checks on lawyers' self-interest in what is clearly entrepreneurial litigation.

---

66 Jacob Ziegel, 'Class Actions to Remedy Mass Consumer Wrongs: Repugnant Solution or Controllable Genie? The Canadian Experience' (2008–2009) 27 *Penn St Int'l L Rev* 879. Quebec's civil law system is somewhat more conducive to a rules-based system of consumer protection.

67 SBC 2004, c 2. Section 172 of the Act dispenses with privity of contract and creates a public interest cause of action for anyone to bring a suit enforcing the standards of the Act and obtaining equitable relief. For a discussion of the Act and consumer arbitration jurisprudence in Canada, see Shelley McGill, 'Consumer Arbitration After *Seidel v Telus*' (2011) 51 *Can Bus* LJ 187, 203.

68 See eg *Griffin v Dell Canada Inc.* [2010] ONCA 29 (CanLII) at para 60 where the Court of Appeal describes the defendant company's contractual stipulation that all consumer disputes be submitted to individual arbitration as 'simply seeking to exploit the inefficiency of arbitrating individual claims'. The Court found a class action by Dell's customers to be more efficient and ultimately denied a stay of the class proceeding. Leave to appeal to the Supreme Court of Canada was dismissed in *Dell Canada Inc v Thaddeus Griffin* [2010] CanLII 27725 (SCC).

69 McGill, supra note 67.

7. America's dynamic and extensive experience with collective litigation

Richard Marcus

I. INTRODUCTION

At a conference in Moscow in September 2012, Professor Walker introduced a plenary session on Cultural Dimensions of Group Litigation by asking 'Who's Afraid of US-style Class Actions?'[1] Her panel included academics from Australia, Brazil, Belgium, Canada, the UK, Italy, the Netherlands, Russia and Sweden. She elaborated on the theme as follows:

> US-style class actions have become a flashpoint for debate over group litigation and the collective redress regimes emerging around the world. Everyone wants to develop better ways for consumers and others who suffer loss from mass harms to receive compensation for claims that are too small to litigate individually. Everyone wants to improve the means for encouraging responsible conduct on the part of those who might cause such harms. But everyone, at least outside the United States, seems also to agree that they do not want to adopt US-style class actions in their systems.[2]

Professor Walker's provocative introduction takes up where Professor Hodges left off in his recent book on European class and representative actions,[3] for that book is largely occupied with working through the ways in which European countries can try to accomplish the goals Professor Walker identifies without falling into the errant ways of the US class action.

In short, the US experience is both a target for criticism and a source of ideas that might be usefully adopted or adapted. As is known to all, that experience is very extensive, but it has hardly been constant over the last

---

1 Janet Walker, 'General Report' in Dmitry Maleshin (eds), *Civil Procedure in Cross-Cultural Dialogue: Eurasia Context* (Statut Pub House 2012) 413.

2 Ibid. 413–14.

3 Christopher Hodges, *The Reform of Class and Representative Actions in European Legal Systems* (Hart 2008).

15 years or so. To the contrary, it has been dynamic and is still changing. The American class action rule was the focus of important amendments in 2003, and study is ongoing about possible further changes to that rule.[4] At the same time, other methods of resolving mass or collective claims have emerged in the US that may eclipse the class action in importance.

Those outside the US who are considering ways of handling similar problems could benefit from fuller knowledge about what has been going on. Providing an exhaustive chronicle is beyond the scope this chapter. American class actions are the subject of multi-volume treatises in the US, and full books consider the complications of some of the other techniques addressed below. But the broad strands of development can be sketched much more briefly. That is my goal here; for those outside the US, a general appreciation of what has happened there may be more instructive than a voluminous detailed report, whether the learning from that instruction is used to identify things to emulate or things to avoid.

II. THE BACKGROUND

The American class action grew out of the practices of the Equity courts in England,[5] but was relatively unimportant until Rule 23 of the Federal Rules of Civil Procedure[6] was extensively amended in 1966, creating what has been recognized to be the 'modern' US class action. Until that time, few class actions had been litigated, and some involved in rewriting the rule in 1966 say that the future impact of the revised rule was little appreciated. But in one respect the debate about those changes was prescient. One member vehemently opposed expanding the American class action because he thought it would be 'contrary to fundamental principles of fairness,' and would create 'insidious incentives' for 'class counsel willing to settle an action on less than most favorable times.'[7] Despite these forebodings, the 1966 revisions were largely a leap into the unknown because

---

[4] As Associate Reporter of the US Judicial Conference's Advisory Committee on Civil Rules, I was a primary drafter of the 2003 amendments, and I serve as Reporter of the committee now considering further possible changes to that rule. In this chapter, however, I speak only for myself and not for the Advisory Committee or anyone else.

[5] For a careful review of this history, see Stephen Yeazell, *From Medieval Group Litigation to the Modern Class Action* (Yale Univ Press 1987).

[6] Fed R Civ P 23.

[7] John K Rabiej, 'The Making of Class Action Rule 23 – What Were We Thinking?' 24 *Miss Col L Rev* 323, 335 (2005) (describing the 1960s debates in the Advisory Committee about changing Rule 23).

there had been very few class actions and there was no particular basis to think that there would be a surge in use of the class-action device.

Over the ensuing quarter century, the US class action waxed and waned; initially there seemed much enthusiasm for using it to its fullest potential, and in reaction a series of restrictive rulings curtailed its use,[8] so that by the late 1980s some predicted that it would fade from the scene. To take a prominent illustration, in 1988 an article in the *New York Times* entitled 'The Rise and Fall of the Class Action Lawsuit,' quoted the then-Reporter of the Advisory Committee on Civil Rules as saying that American class actions had 'had their day in the sun and kind of petered out.'[9] The article suggested that the class action was passing from the American litigation scene.

For the most part, class actions during this period addressed claims for employment discrimination, antitrust violations, and securities fraud. Opposition to their use generally originated in the business community, and strong support came from the civil rights community and, as time went by, more forcefully from the growing and prospering 'private attorney general' sector of the private American bar. One might say that, as the success of anti-discrimination efforts gathered momentum, the broad anti-discrimination suit became less significant.[10] Meanwhile, with the election of Ronald Reagan as President in 1980, the US government downplayed antitrust enforcement, leading to a striking decline in the frequency of antitrust class actions, which often rode the 'coattails' of a governmental prosecution. Securities fraud class actions remained highly significant, leading Congress to pass the Private Securities Litigation Act[11] in 1995. Although these kinds of class actions were certainly significant, it is unlikely that they would have generated the sort of momentum for reform that has emerged in the US due to later developments.

---

[8] For a chronicle of these developments, see Arthur Miller, 'Of Frankenstein Monsters and Shining Knights: Myth, Reality, and the "Class Action Problem"' 92 *Harv L Rev* 664 (1979).

[9] Douglas Martin, 'The Rise and Fall of the Class Action Lawsuit' *New York Times* (New York, 8 Jan 1988).

[10] See John Donohue and Peter Siegelman, 'The Changing Nature of Employment Discrimination Litigation' 43 *Stan L Rev* 983, 1019–21 (1991) (reporting that by the 1980s class actions had declined significantly in importance as methods of enforcing anti-discrimination provisions in court).

[11] Private Securities Litigation Reform Act of 1995, 109 Stat 737 (1995). Some provisions of this legislation are addressed in note 68 *infra*.

III. THE CONTEMPORARY US CLASS-ACTION SCENE

Beginning in the 1980s, the class action started to evolve. One sort of class action that had increasing importance could be called the 'consumer class action.' In a sense, this sort of class action could have been close to the ideal some cited leading up to the 1966 amendments as a prime objective for strengthening the class action. As Chief Justice Burger articulated in a Supreme Court decision in 1980:

> The aggregation of individual claims in the context of a classwide suit is an evolutionary response to the existence of injuries unremedied by the regulatory action of government. Where it is not economically reasonable to obtain relief within the traditional framework of a multiplicity of small individual suits for damages, aggrieved persons may be without any effective redress unless they may employ the class-action device.[12]

But even such cases could invite possibly abusive practices. These claims frequently built on legislative regulations of various businesses that authorized injured consumers to sue, often breaking with the American Rule that each party must pay its own lawyer and permitting successful plaintiffs to recover their attorney fees from the defendant, and often guaranteeing a minimum recovery sufficient to induce consumers to file such suits. That minimum was often large enough that a class action on behalf of all consumers affected by the practice could involve a huge potential recovery, quite possibly something the legislature did not intend, since sometimes the violations involved seemed somewhat technical. The courts were wary about imposing those sorts of crippling liabilities on defendants guilty of technical violations.[13]

A second type of class actions could be broadly labeled 'mass tort class actions.' This kind of action had actually been foreseen to some extent when the rule was revised in 1966. It seems that the sort of 'mass tort' the framers had in the mind in the 1960s was quite a bit more limited than the

---

12 *Deposit Guaranty National Bank v Roper*, 445 US 326 (1980).

13 See, eg, *Katz* v *Carte Blanche Corp*, 496 F2d 747 (3d Cir 1974), a suit brought as a class action asserting claims under the federal Truth in Lending Act on behalf of 700,000 credit card holders. Because there was a $100 minimum recovery, the suit was for 'substantially in excess of Carte Blanche's net worth' even though the likelihood of recovery was very low. Ibid. 751. The appellate court held that the class action should not be certified because having a class action was not a 'superior' method of adjudication.

most prominent versions that appeared a quarter century later.[14] Even that prospect was sufficient to prompt a warning in the Advisory Committee Note about employing the class action in mass tort situations:

> A 'mass accident' resulting in injuries to numerous persons is ordinarily not appropriate for a class action because of the likelihood that significant questions, not only of damages but also of liability and defenses to liability, would be present, affecting the individuals in different ways. In these circumstances an action conducted nominally as a class action would degenerate in practice into multiple lawsuits separately tried.[15]

A very different sort of mass tort litigation gripped the US courts by the 1980s – personal injury suits brought by workers exposed to asbestos on the job. This sort of mass tort presented a much greater challenge to the courts than the sort the reformers in the 1960s worried might be forced into the class-action format. The injuries resulting from exposure to asbestos could take many forms, and some of them were significantly affected by other activities, such as smoking. In addition, it was possible (particularly using X-ray examinations) to detect 'pleural thickening' in the lungs of many exposed to asbestos who had manifested no actual health problem as a result. Altogether, these circumstances presented significant challenges to American tort law, and different US states reacted in different ways. One focus was the statute of limitations period with 'latent diseases' like those due to exposure to asbestos. Another was the question whether 'fear of cancer' could itself be a viable present tort claim for somebody who had not suffered any actual health problem.

Putting aside those challenges to tort law, it was abundantly clear by the late 1980s that the growing mountain of asbestos cases presented a very serious challenge to the US court systems. The tocsin was sounded by the 1982 decision of Johns Manville, one of America's leading companies, that it had to file a petition in bankruptcy court to forestall the prospective financial consequences for the company of tort litigation. In ensuing years, more and more companies in this field seemed destined for bankruptcy. As a federal appellate court explained in 1986 while upholding certification of a class action on behalf of workers claiming injury due to exposure to asbestos:

---

14 For example, the most vigorous opponent to providing for even potential class action treatment for mass torts during the 1960s debates reported 30 years later that the idea of a big case was 'the Grand Canyon airplane crash.' See John K Rabiej (supra note 7), 323 n 4 (quoting John Frank, a member of the Advisory Committee during the 1960s).

15 Advisory Committee Note to 1966 Amendments to Fed R Civ P 23 (b) (3).

> The courts are now being forced to rethink the alternatives and priorities by the current volume of litigation and more frequent mass disasters. If Congress leaves us to our own devices, we may be forced to abandon repetitive hearings and arguments for each claimant's attorney to the extent enjoyed by the profession in the past.[16]

At the same time, partly due to the American jury system and partly to divergences in state law, the outcomes for different plaintiffs began to seem 'more like roulette than jurisprudence.'[17] A possible solution was found in the class-action rule. In the early 1990s, creative American lawyers crafted nationwide settlements of asbestos personal injury cases that treated all class members similarly no matter what state they came from. As I said at the time, this initiative seemed to promise 'mass tort reform via Rule 23.'[18]

These developments together explain why the late 1980s forecast that the class action would vanish from the American scene was so wrong. As the Chair of the Advisory Committee on Civil Rules told Congress in 1997, what had actually happened was far different: 'The use of class actions is transforming the litigation landscape. [. . .] Class actions are being certified at unprecedented rates, and they are involving a substantial number if not a majority, of all American citizens.'[19]

Since then, the trend lines seem consistent with this description. Although the full impact of recent decisions enforcing arbitration clauses[20] cannot be predicted with certainty, it can be said that class actions have become more frequent in the US during the last 15 years than they were in 1997. As two American lawyers put it in 2002:

> the class action device has changed from the more or less rare case fought out by titans of the bar in top financial centers of the nation to the veritable bread and butter of firms of all shapes and sizes across the country.[21]

---

16 *Jenkins* v *Raymark Indus Inc*, 782 F2d 468, 473 (5th Cir 1986).

17 *In re School Asbestos Litigation*, 789 F2d 996, 1001 n3 (3d Cir 1986) (quoting state-court judge).

18 Richard Marcus, 'They Can't Do That, Can They? Tort Reform Via Rule 23' 80 *Cornell L Rev* 858 (1995). Eventually, the Supreme Court invalidated those settlements. See *Ortiz v Fibreboard Corp*, 527 US 815 (1999); *Amchem Products Inc v Windsor*, 521 US 591 (1997).

19 See 'Senate Subcommittee Holds Hearing on Class Action Litigation Reform' 66 USLW 2294 (18 Nov 1997) (quoting Judge Paul Niemeyer).

20 See *infra* Part IV 5.

21 Benjamin Reid and Chris Coutroulis, 'Checkmate in Class Actions: Defensive Strategy in the Initial Moves' 28 *Litigation* 21, 21 (Winter 2002).

IV. A QUARTER CENTURY OF REFORM EFFORTS FOR THE US CLASS ACTION

After completing its revision process in 1966, the Advisory Committee resolved to leave the class-action rule alone, and did not consider any changes to it for 25 years.[22] In 1991, the US Judicial Conference – prompted in large measure by the challenges of mass tort class actions – asked the Advisory Committee to consider further changes to the rule. That prompt led to a dozen years of work on revisions to the rule, culminating in amendments that went into effect in 2003. More recently, the Advisory Committee has resumed analysis of possible further changes to the rule. Meanwhile, Congress itself has become involved by adopting legislation moving more class actions to federal court and addressing some perceived failings of current class-action practice.

1. The Settlement Evaluation Problem

The idea of a lawsuit is to get a decision from a court about whether the defendant is liable to the plaintiff. The reality of a lawsuit in the US is that such a judicial resolution usually does not occur. Instead, most lawsuits are 'settled.' That settlement can occur early in the pretrial proceedings, or could be reached only while the case is on appeal, after the trial court has reached a final judgment. The customary notion is that the parties are best able to make decisions about whether to proceed with litigation or reach a compromise; traditionally that was not the judge's concern.[23]

As recognized immediately, however, the settlement problem under the 1966 version of Rule 23 presented challenges for this attitude.[24] Although there may sometimes be uncertainty about whether settlement decisions in some cases are mainly made by the party or the lawyer,[25] at least that was not the court's problem. A lawyer who 'settled' a suit without authority from the client could be the subject of bar discipline or even a malpractice

---

22 See John K Rabiej (supra note 7), 328.

23 The alternative dispute resolution movement, which also gained force in the US in the 1980s, prompted a general shift toward settlement by judges. For a 1980s introduction to these issues, see Jethro Lieberman and James Henry, 'Lessons from the Alternative Dispute Resolution Movement' 53 *U Chi L Rev* 424 (1986).

24 See text accompanying note 7 supra (reporting on concerns about 'insidious incentives' for class counsel in the settlement situation).

25 See Deborah Hensler, 'Resolving Mass Toxic Torts: Myths and Realities' (1989) *U Ill L Rev* 89, 92 (describing how lawyers tend to exercise actual control in such situations).

suit by the client, because the client is supposed to be the 'principal' and the lawyer is merely an 'agent' who (under US ethics rules) cannot be given final authority to accept a settlement. But the judge presiding over the 'settled' case did not have to worry because the lawyer was authorized to act for the client in taking actions in the lawsuit.

The assumed relationship between the client as principal and the lawyer as agent does not work in class actions. The lawyer is authorized to take actions on behalf of the class members because the court so directs by certifying a class, not because the client has so authorized. That might not be so unnerving if the 'clients' became formal class members only by electing to join, often called the opt-in method. But the 1966 revision of the rule instead adopted an opt-out approach, meaning that all class members are bound unless they affirmatively exclude themselves.[26] For many in Europe, this arrangement raises serious autonomy issues, but from an American perspective (imbued with an appreciation of the role of class actions in enforcing regulatory provisions that otherwise might lack teeth), the autonomy interest of a consumer in a $50 claim seems nonexistent. To the contrary, the only value of litigation may be in the class setting.[27]

The solution was to empower and require the judge to take on new and difficult tasks in reviewing the content of proposed settlements in class actions. As adopted in 1966, Rule 23 (e) therefore said that a class action could be dismissed only with the judge's permission. The problem was that it said nothing more about how the judge was to make this decision.[28] The courts responded in the common law method by developing case law that required judges to determine whether the settlement was fair, reasonable, and adequate.

Saying judges were to do such scrutiny did not make the job easy. Under the American adversary system, the judges might have only limited knowledge about the case; they were supposed to get that knowledge, as they needed it, from the competing presentations of the adverse parties. But by

---

26 See Fed R Civ P 23 (c) (providing that all class members are bound by the judgment unless they have excluded themselves from the class when permitted to do so by the judge, and requiring that opportunity to exclude only in some types of class actions).

27 See supra text accompanying note 12 (quoting Supreme Court recognition that small claims may have no value unless they are part of a class action).

28 The Advisory Committee Note offered only the following explanation about this requirement: 'Subdivision (e) requires approval of the court for the dismissal or compromise of any class action.' No further guidance was provided by the framers of the revised rule.

the time the settlement proposal was before them, both sides were urging the same thing, hardly compatible with the adversary ideal. Some notice about the proposed settlement to the class members was usually required (sometimes individualized mailed notice), and they could object. That might provide something like an adversary presentation, but the objectors were in a way fighting an uphill battle because the lawyers the judge already knew were allied against them and in support of the settlement. So one impulse would be to empower objectors, perhaps by guaranteeing them a chance to take discovery (usually an absorbing activity in American courts) in support of their objections.

But the objectors were often not the the most savory of sorts. Under a 2002 decision by the Supreme Court, objectors could appeal approval of the settlement over their objections.[29] Because the appeals process could last several years, this prospect could give the objecting lawyer considerable leverage to extract concessions, either for the objecting class member or (possibly) for himself (in the form of a fee for 'improving' the settlement with some cosmetic changes). One judge used an opinion to denounce 'professional objectors who seek out class actions to simply extract a fee by lodging generic, unhelpful protests.'[30]

At the same time, one could not assume that objectors were up to no good and that the settlement was the best deal for the class members. The worry about a 'reverse auction', in which defendants defeat class actions brought by vigorous plaintiff lawyers by 'settling' other class actions (on behalf of the 'same' class) with unsavory lawyers willing to accept a settlement for a pittance provided they got a handsome attorney fee, seemed to have been realized in some instances.[31] These worries became particularly pointed when the settlement provided the class members with 'coupons' for a discount on more of defendant's products but provided class counsel with hard cash in an amount calculated on the assumption that the coupons were really worth their face value. Those arrangements could be regarded as marketing programs by defendants, and often seemed to lead

---

29 *Devlin v* Scardelletti, 536 US 1 (2002).

30 *Shaw v Toshiba America Information Systems, Inc*, 91 F Supp 2d 942, 973 (ED Tex 2000).

31 See *Reynolds v Beneficial National Bank*, 288 F3d 277 (7th Cir 2002) (federal-court settlement for nationwide class approved in setting suggesting that the goal of defendants was to defeat a Texas state-court suit that promised a much larger recovery). See also *Matsushita Electrical Industry Co v Epstein*, 516 US 367 (1996) (plaintiff lawyers in state-court case settled securities class action there for pennies per share even though a federal-court class action offered the prospect of much higher recoveries).

to minimal actual use of the resulting coupons; it could appear that only the lawyers got anything of value from the suit.

In sum, it could not be said in the abstract that either class counsel or the objectors should be clothed with a presumption of good intentions.

2. Reforms to Address Settlement

After much consideration, the 2003 amendments to Rule 23 (e) expanded its directives about the settlement-approval process by prescribing that the court should use the 'fair, reasonable, and adequate' standard previously articulated by the case law,[32] requiring the court to give notice 'in a reasonable manner' to class members of the proposed settlement,[33] and explicitly authorizing class members to object to the proposed settlement.[34] Because of the concern that the defendant and class counsel might have made 'under the table' arrangements about other things, it also directed the proponents of the settlement to 'file a statement identifying any agreement made in connection with' the proposed settlement.[35] Due to worries that objectors might seek to exploit their objections for personal gain, the amended rule also states that they may withdraw their objections only with the court's approval.[36] In addition, a very controversial provision specifies that the court may insist that class members be granted a right to opt out once the settlement terms are known as a condition for approving the settlement.[37]

Besides improvements in the rule provisions on the settlement-approval process, there have been additional changes that address the concerns that have emerged about class settlements. Until 2003, there was no provision about class counsel in Rule 23; instead, courts addressed the question of

---

32 Fed R Civ P 23 (e) (2).
33 Fed R Civ P 23 (e) (1).
34 Fed R Civ P 23 (e) (5).
35 Fed R Civ P 23 (e) (3).
36 Fed R Civ P 23 (e) (5).
37 Fed R Civ P 23 (e) (4). One proposed rule change, not adopted, would have made such a 'second opt-out' right mandatory in all class actions in which the original time to opt out had already passed. The controversy was due, in part, to the experience that lawyers who opposed class action settlements had sought to promote opting out in the past, either instead of presenting objections in court or in addition to presenting such objections. Sometimes these lawyers were called 'opt-out farmers' because they sought to harvest a crop of opt-outs. The defense response to such strategies, and to concerns about ensuring that the binding effects of class settlements are extensive enough, has been to provide by agreeent that defendants may withdraw from the settlement if more than a certain number of class members opt out.

who should be the lawyer under a rule provision focused on whether the class representative would adequately represent the class.[38] New Rule 23 (g), added in 2003, provides that the court must appoint class counsel and provides criteria for making that appointment.[39] Rule 23 (g) (4) then makes it clear that '[c]lass counsel must fairly and adequately represent the interests of the class.'[40]

Because attorney fees are often a crucial factor in the management of class actions, new Rule 23 (h) addresses those awards to class counsel, and requires that the class be given notice of the motion for a fee award, and that any class member may object to that award.[41] The court also may direct applicants for the position of class counsel to propose terms for a potential fee award before they are appointed.[42]

These rule changes were supplemented by provisions of the Class Action Fairness Act, adopted by Congress in 2005.[43] One thing this Act did was to make it easier for class actions to be in federal court. In some instances, it seemed that plaintiff lawyers were filing class actions in 'magnet' state courts in which they had found receptive judges; particularly given the adoption of the new rule provisions noted above, Congress concluded that it would be preferable to facilitate having class actions handled under those new provisions.[44]

But the legislation went beyond expanding federal-court jurisdiction and added further provisions regulating settlement of class actions. Reacting to the concern that 'coupon' settlements may serve the interests only of the lawyers, Congress directed that judges be especially vigilant in scrutinizing such settlements, and that attorney fee awards be limited in such cases.[45] Another provision sought to provide the judge with input

---

38 Fed R Civ P 23 (a) (4) (providing that one prerequisite to certifying a class is that 'the representative parties will fairly and adequately protect the interests of the class').

39 Thus, Rule 23 (g) (1) (A) says that the court must consider four topics – the work counsel did in identifying or investigating potential claims in the action, counsel's experience in handling class actions and this type of claim, counsel's knowledge of the applicable law, and the resources counsel will commit to representing the class. Rule 23 (g) (1) (B) then says the court may additionally consider 'any other matter pertinent' to whether class counsel would do a good job.

40 Fed R Civ P 23 (g) (4).

41 Rule 23 (h) (1), (2).

42 Fed R Civ P 23 (g) (1) (C).

43 Class Action Fairness Act 2005, Pub L No 109-2, 119 Stat 4 (codified in scattered sections of 28 USC).

44 For discussion, see Richard Marcus, 'Assessing CAFA's Stated Jurisdictional Policies' 156 *U Pa L Rev* 1765 (2008).

45 28 USC 1712.

from the 'appropriate state official' by directing that notice be given to such officials, who may act to protect the interests of class members in their states.[46] The idea is that this public participation could provide a backstop to objections by class members. Although one law professor predicted 'a high degree of public participation in class action settlements, especially by the Attorneys General of the states,'[47] it has not led to a high rate of public participation.[48]

3. The Certification Problem

American class-action practice relies on the judge not only to scrutinize proposed settlements but also to determine whether the case should be a class action at all. In many other countries contemplating some form of group litigation, judges likely would not have to shoulder such tasks because 'standing' to initiate such litigation is bestowed only on recognized organizations. Moreover, such organizations might be expected to have internal arrangements that would serve to promote group interests and to provide group members with a voice in making group decisions in a way that might not be true of the American class-action model. Yet it seems unavoidable that there could be concerns about the goals or orientation of recognized organizations, and also the potential of contending organizations each seeking to 'appropriate' particular claims as their own for purposes of litigation. Whether one is contemplating such an arrangement, therefore, or contemplating something more along the lines of the American model, considering the US experience with this authorization process seems worthwhile.

The early experience after 1966 stressed simplicity in class certification. As written then, the rule required certification 'as soon as practicable' and directed that class certification be decided before there was any decision on the merits of the case. The goal of these provisions was to avoid 'one-way intervention,' which might happen if the class members did not have to decide whether to opt out until after the judge had ruled on who would win the law suit; class members could then be expected to opt out if the outcome were unfavorable and stay in if it were favorable, a result felt to be unfair to defendants.[49]

Partly due to time pressures, the American courts soon developed the

---

46 28 USC 1715.

47 Laurens Walker, 'The Consumer Class Action Bill of Rights: A Policy and Political Mistae' 58 *Hast LJ* 849, 850–1 (2007).

48 See Peter Geier, 'State AGs Eschew CAFA Review' *National Law Journal* (23 Oct 2006).

49 See Rabiej (supra note 7), 332–3.

view that they would have to pass on class certification without addressing the merits of the case. Yet it seemed that determining whether there were 'common questions' applicable to all the class members,[50] and deciding whether the proposed class representative was 'typical' of class members[51] called for considering just those things. Evaluating the merits to decide certification unnerved judges, however, and could undermine an effort to constrain discovery before certification was decided.

The result was that, for a time, American judges ruled that defendants could not challenge the legal sufficiency of even the named plaintiff's claim until the court had decided whether to certify the class. And sometimes courts adopted rules of thumb that seemed to invite overbroad certification. A leading example was a lower court's rule that in employment discrimination cases a plaintiff alleging one kind of discrimination could expand the case to encompass an 'across the board' challenge to all the employer's allegedly discriminatory practices.[52]

Were class certification a relatively unimportant ruling, this state of affairs might have been quite satisfactory. But the recurrent reality is that certification is a critical decision. If certification were denied, it was said, that would be the 'death knell' of the suit, something readily understood in a consumer case where the individual claims are small.[53] Indeed, in the view of some judges, certification of a class might mean that a case became a 'bet the company' litigation, enabling plaintiffs to coerce a substantial settlement without regard to the strength of their claims on the merits.[54] Whether this scenario is frequently true can certainly be debated,[55] but there is no doubt that the concern has become very salient among American judges.

---

50 See Fed R Civ P 23 (a) (2).

51 See Fed R Civ P 23 (a) (3).

52 *Johnson v Georgia Highway Express, Inc*, 417 F2d 1122, 1124 (5th Cir 1969).

53 See supra text accompanying note 12 (quoting the Supreme Court's recognition of the importance of class action status in such a case). But in *Coopers & Lybrand v Livesay,* 437 US 463 (1978), the Supreme Court ruled that a decision denying class certification would not be immediately appealable even if it might signal the death knell of the case. The later adoption of Fed R Civ P 23 (f), described below, made such review possible after that amended rule became effective in 1998, and permitted the development of a much richer body of appellate law on certification.

54 A leading example of this reasoning is Judge Posner's decision in *In re Rhone-Poulenc Rorer, Inc*, 51 F3d 1293 (7th Cir 1995) (worrying about irresistible settlement pressure due to class certification, due to the potential exposure, even though all indications were that the defendant would likely win at trial).

55 See Charles Silver, '"We're Scared to Death": Class Certification and Blackmail' 78 *NYU L Rev* 1357 (2003) (challenging the notion that class certification actually is such a potent development as many others claimed).

The result has been that American judges became more exacting in their decisions whether cases were proper class actions, often stressing scrutiny of the common features of the claims of various class members and weighing whether they were common enough to justify combined litigation. For one thing, the notion that 'merits' discovery should be deferred until after certification was decided fell out of favor.[56] Gradually, the courts became more exacting; in a leading 2008 decision the US Court of Appeals for the Third Circuit held that a court must weigh opposing evidence and make 'findings' on all class-certification issues, such as the existence of common questions, before certifying a class.[57] During its 2012–13 Term, the US Supreme Court decided two cases raising related issues, but much remains unresolved.[58]

One way to approach this set of problems would be to revise the class-certification criteria. In 1996, proposed revisions to those criteria were published for public comment.[59] But the proposals prompted very strong opposition, and they were shelved. Nevertheless, in 1998 Rule 23 was amended to add Rule 23 (f),[60] authorizing immediate appellate review of class-certification decisions. Before that, it was usually difficult or impossible to obtain such review of these critical decisions. Among other things, that meant that there was very limited appellate authority on how the certification criteria should be applied. Rule 23 (f) provided an avenue for appellate supervision, and it has repeatedly been used to permit the courts of appeals to weigh in about those decisions before final judgment is entered, as in the cases described in the preceding paragraph. Although some have argued that this innovation worked to the advantage of defendants challenging certification,[61] it seems difficult to favor entirely untrammeled discretion to make these critical decisions. So the

---

[56] See *Szabo* v *Bridgeport Machines, Inc*, 249 F3d 672 (7th Cir 2001) (noting that '[b]efore deciding whether to allow a case to proceed as a class action [. . .] a judge should make whatever factual and legal inquiries are necessary under Rule 23').

[57] *In re Hydrogen Peroxide Antitrust Litigation*, 552 F3d 305 (3d Cir 2008). For analysis, see Richard Marcus, 'Reviving Judicial Gatekeeping of Aggregation: Scrutinizing the Merits on Class Certification' 79 *Geo Wash L Rev* 324 (2011).

[58] See Amgen, Inc. v. Connecticut Retirement Plans and Trust Funds, 133 S. Ct. 1184 (2013) (affirming certification of securities fraud class action); Comcast Corp v. Behrend, 133 S. Ct 1426 (2013) (reversing certification of antitrust class action).

[59] See Proposed Rules, 167 FRD 523, 539 (1996).

[60] Fed R Civ P 23 (f) (permitting review at discretion of court of appeals).

[61] See Robert Klonoff, 'The Decline of Class Actions' 90 *Wash U L Rev* (forthcoming 2013) (reporting that, 'in terms of sheer numbers, Rule 23 (f) has served primarily as a device to protect defendants' because they have obtained review more frequently, and prevailed more frequently when review was granted).

common law method has gradually refined the Rule 23 criteria for class certification.[62]

The impulse to regulate trial court certification decisions was somewhat reinforced by features of the 2003 amendments to Rule 23. One changed the timing directive about when the certification decision must be made from 'as soon as practicable' to '[a]t an early practicable time.'[63] Another removed a provision in the 1966 version that permitted 'conditional' certification, seemingly authorizing the judge to defer addressing the hard issues until later. The amended rule also requires the court, on certification, to 'define the class and the class claims, issues, or defenses.'[64] The Committee Note accompanying these changes observed that the court may want to insist that the lawyers provide a 'trial plan' showing how the class action could actually be tried.[65] Though that notion may seem odd, given that class actions are so rarely tried, it does tend to focus attention on whether there really are sufficient common features to permit combined adjudication.

It seems unavoidable that more intense scrutiny of the propriety of class certification is resulting in increased expense for the parties and more work for the judges, and resulting in denial of class certification more often than had been true under the former less-demanding regime.[66] For those not firmly in the camp of either the plaintiffs or the defendants, these outcomes cannot easily be characterized as good or bad. Given the unquestioned importance of certification, it seems that courts should be careful about granting it. But given the reality that lawyers who bring these cases are taking a risk of incurring high costs without any recompense, there is at least a nagging concern about whether it has become too difficult or too

---

[62] This upsurge in appellate refinement of certification criteria has not necessarily produced national uniformity, however. American lawyers generally agree that some US circuit courts of appeals are much more receptive to class certification than others. This belief seems to have prompted forum-shopping by American lawyers in the wake of the Class Action Fairness Act. Now, rather than filing their cases in 'magnet' state courts, they may be favoring 'magnet' US circuits. See Emery Lee and Thomas Willging, 'The Impact of the Class Action Fairness Act on the Federal Courts: An Empirical Analysis of Filings and Removals' 156 *U Pa L Rev* 1723, 1759 Fig 6 (2008) (showing that after the Act broadened federal-court jurisdiction the number of class actions in the Fourth Circuit increased by about 30 percent, while in the Ninth Circuit the number of federal-court class actions increased by nearly 500 percent).

[63] Fed R Civ P 23 (c) (1) (A).

[64] Fed R Civ P 23 (c) (1) (B).

[65] See Committee Note to 2003 amendments to Fed R Civ P 23 (c).

[66] See Marcus (supra note 57), 355–64.

costly, thereby crippling the utility of the device to provide class compensation and enforce the law.[67]

Many might regard this experience as showing that the American approach is flawed, and that a method that confers authority to initiate group litigation instead on 'recognized' organizations is preferable.[68] But there seem at least some grounds for uneasiness with that route as well. One is that organizations that can profit from successfully bringing such cases may have a temptation to initiate 'bet the company' litigation to extract rich settlements, just as plaintiff lawyers do in the US. Some may subscribe to the view that non-government organizations (NGOs) are uniformly wholesome, but we must recall that at least some (for example al-Queda) are not.

Putting aside organizational malevolence, it can surely happen that organizations could compete with one another in raising money through group litigation if there is a payoff for the group for doing so. If there is no potential payoff for the group that initiates such litigation, it is difficult to see what incentive an organization would have to do so, particularly in a 'loser pays' system in which it might be at risk for defendant's costs of suit if the case were unsuccessful. If one wants to have a vibrant group litigation sector (as America surely does), one needs to think about incentives. And one needs also to recognize that incentives alone are not likely to

---

[67] An important related issue is that the American courts regard 'settlement class certification' as permissible on a reduced showing of compliance with at least some of the requirements for certification of a class for full litigation. See *Amchem Products, Inc v Windsor* 521 US 591, 619 (1997) (recognizing that 'settlement is relevant to a class certification'). The proper calibration of this certification decision is a matter of intense debate.

[68] Although the US has many voluntary associations that pursue shared causes, and they sometimes have recognized standing to sue for their members, that option has not widely supplanted the class action model. Instead, a similar impulse found expression in the US in the adoption of the Private Securities Litigation Act in 1995. That legislation builds on the idea that a 'lawyer-centric' model for securities fraud class actions should be replaced with a 'client-centric' model. The Act therefore requires the court to designate a 'lead plaintiff' as 'most capable of adequately representing the interests of class members,' and directs that this person should presumptively be the class member or group of members with 'the largest financial interest in the relief sought by the class' 15 USC 78u-4(a)(3)(B). This lead plaintiff would then select class counsel, something of an inversion of the customary class action reality in which the lawyer found the 'client' instead of the other way around. Although this 'empowered client' method may work for securities fraud class actions, it dos not seem to hold promise for very many other sorts of class actions. See Jill Fisch, 'Lawyers on the Auction Block: Evaluating the Selection of Class Counsel by Auction' 102 *Colum L Rev* 649, 726–7 (2002) (explaining that a similar method would not work for mass tort litigation).

provide enough regulation of the use of group litigation without some official determination (as by having the judge make a class-certification decision) about whether the device has been properly employed in a given case. As a consequence, it may be easier to frown at the difficulties American courts encounter in making class-certification decisions than to escape them while adopting some dynamic form of group litigation.

4. The Reform 'Agenda' for the Future

For a quarter century after the 1966 revision of the class-action rule, there was no change to the rule. During the 20 years since then, there have been several rule amendments and some important legislative developments also. It takes time for changes to sink in, and it may be too soon to embark on a set of further changes. But that possibility does at least exist. In 2011, the Advisory Committee created a Rule 23 Subcommittee to analyze current issues and try to identify areas for possible rule changes. After initial study, that Subcommittee identified some topics that seemed to deserve study, including the handling of merits issues during class certification and the proper application of those criteria in the settlement context.[69] It is far too early presently to forecast whether any further rule changes will result from this study, but important to note that there is ongoing study.[70]

5. The Privatization Possibility

None of the discussion above addresses what some see as the most significant American development regarding class actions, which is the growing importance of arbitration as a method for side-stepping class-action litigation altogether. Under a series of decisions of the US Supreme Court,[71] it has come to seem possible that companies may be able to include provisions in contracts with their customers that require arbitration and forbid arbitrators to permit class-wide arbitration. For some time critics of this trend have warned that it heralds the demise of class actions in American

---

69 See Agenda Book, Advisory Committee on Civil Rules (22–23 March 2012) 449–75, available at <www.uscourts.gov/RulesAndPolicies/rules/archives/agenda-books/committee-rules-civil-procedure.aspx>.

70 It bears note that Congress continues to pay attention to class-action developments. On 1 June 2012, a committee of the House of Representatives held a hearing on class-action practice. Details can be found at <http://judiciary.house.gov/hearings/Hearings%202012/hear_06012012.html>.

71 See, eg, *AT&T Mobility v Concepcion*, 131 S Ct 1741 (2011).

courts.[72] Thus far, those predictions have not proved true; class actions continue to be filed.

V. THE MDL ROUTE

Those who fixate on the American class action miss a large part of the story. Beginning around the same time that Rule 23 was revised in the 1960s, the US federal courts embarked on another experiment that has grown prominent in handling mass tort and other collective litigation. It began when a number of high executives of electrical equipment companies were sentenced to prison in the early 1960s for price fixing, and thousands of suits were filed across the country to recover for overcharges due to this price fixing. Anticipating this avalanche of litigation, the US Judicial Conference authorized creation of a special committee of judges to supervise discovery, and in 1962 Chief Justice Earl Warren appointed a Coordinating Committee for Multiple Litigation of the United States District Courts.[73] This ad hoc body succeeded in avoiding chaos that might otherwise have resulted from divergent and conflicting discovery demands in different cases, and it was roundly applauded.

Congress responded by institutionalizing the experiment in 1968, creating the Judicial Panel on Multidistrict Litigation.[74] This body, made up of seven federal judges from around the country, has authority to transfer cases involving overlapping factual elements to a single judge, who is authorized to supervise all pretrial activity in the cases.[75] This 'transferee' judge has broad powers, including entering orders that would govern the conduct of the trial if the case were returned to its original jurisdiction for trial.[76] It has given rise to an acronym (MDL for multidistrict litigation)

---

[72] For warnings about this outcome, see Myriam Gilles and Gary Friedman 'After Class: Aggregate Litigation in the Wake of *AT&T Mobility v Concepcion*' 79 *U Chi L Rev* 623 (2012); Myriam Gilles, 'Opting Out of Liability: The Forthcoming Near-Total Demise of the Modern Class Action' 104 *Mich L Rev* 373 (2005).

[73] For a review of this history, see Richard Marcus, 'Cure-All for an Era of Dispersed Litigation? Toward a Maximalist Use of the Multidistrict Litigation Panel's Transfer Power' 82 *Tul L Rev* 2245 (2008).

[74] See 28 USC 1407 (creating and regulating the Judicial Panel on Multidistrict Litigation).

[75] For a review of the activities of the Panel, see John Heyburn, 'A View From the Panel: Part of the Solution' 82 *Tul L Rev* 2225 (2008) (review of the Panel's work by its Chair, Judge John Heyburn).

[76] See, eg, *In re Blood Factor VIII or IX Concentrate Blood Products Litigation*,

that has even assumed the status of a quasi verb, for lawyers speak of whether it would be a good idea 'to MDL' a given set of cases.[77]

As with modern Rule 23, it is difficult now to determine whether the framers of this new judicial body foresaw in the 1960s the importance it would assume in later decades. MDL litigation surely lacks the reach of class actions. It is limited to pending cases, and cannot capture the claims of those who have not yet sued. For that reason, it enmeshes more lawyers than class actions, which could go forward on the initiative of a single lawyer. Yet for more than 20 years American lawyers have compared the values of the class actions and MDL consolidations.[78] More recently, lawyers have begun to look longingly at MDL treatment as a more promising method of securing combined litigation than class actions.[79]

Judges have also begun to see MDL proceedings as alternative vehicles for disposing of dispersed litigation. Judge Weinstein, long an innovative leader in handling complex litigation, suggested in 2006 that Congress pursue this possibility:

> It may be useful for Congress to consider expanding the Class Action Fairness Act from class actions to at least some national MDL, non-Rule 23, aggregate actions. As use of the class action device to aggregate claims has become more difficult, MDL consolidation has increased in importance as a means of achieving final, global resolution of mass national disputes.[80]

Not to be left out of the act, many states have created similar institutions to consolidate related cases pending in their state courts.[81] The popular press has begun to notice the growing importance of MDL proceedings. In 2010, for example, an article in the *Wall Street Journal* noted: 'In recent years, thousands of suits filed across the U.S. in some of the biggest

169 FRD 632 (N D Ill 1996) (transferee judge enters order limiting number of expert witnesses parties could call at trial).

77 For a discussion of this sort of rumination from the perspective of defendants, see Mark Hermann, 'To MDL or Not to MDL? A Defense Perspective' 24 *Litigation* 43 (Summer 1998).

78 See Charles Silver, 'Comparing Class Actions and Consolidations' 10 *Rev Lit* 495 (1991).

79 See Edward Sherman, 'The MDL Model for Resolving Complex Litigation If a Class Action is Not Possible' 82 *Tul L Rev* 2205 (2008) (observing that the 'increasingly stringent requirements' for class certification have prompted increased attention to MDL proceedings as an alternative route to resolution).

80 *In re Zyprexa Products Liability Litigation*, 238 FRD 539, 542 (E D N Y 2006).

81 See Amanda Bronstad, 'The States Are Getting In on the MDL Action' *Nat LJ* (19 Sep 2011), 12.

product liability and personal injury cases – from harmful diet drugs to smelly Chinese drywall – each have been consolidated into "multidistrict litigation" cases.'[82]

An article in the *National Law Journal* noted further that '[t]he number of cases winding their way through the multidistrict litigation (MDL) process across the country has more than doubled during the past decade, inundating the MDL panel.'[83] Indeed, some plaintiff lawyers have lamented that the Panel seems less inclined to transfer and centralize litigation than in the past, leaving the individual plaintiff lawyer 'out on her own.'[84]

There certainly are examples of the power of MDL proceedings to achieve combined resolution of huge outbursts of litigation. Surely the most prominent example grew out of litigation involving the painkiller Vioxx, which was taken off the market when it was linked to an increased risk of heart attacks and strokes. The MDL Panel transferred all the federal-court cases to a single federal judge in New Orleans. That judge then invited state-court judges from California and New Jersey who were presiding over cases consolidated by the transfer mechanisms of those states to collaborate in efforts to resolve all the cases throughout the country under a voluntary non-class settlement program. This effort eventually yielded a $4.85 billion settlement agreement to which some 99 percent of claimants subscribed, an extreme version of 'opting in.'[85]

Whether this model will be followed more frequently in the future remains to be seen. The circumstances in Vioxx may have singularly invited such treatment, since the drug had been removed from the market and there was a short latency period. Combined with the application of statutes of limitations, that permitted the parties to be fairly certain there was not a significant number of additional potential claims they did not know about. The settlement also involved some innovative aspects that might not invite imitation. For one thing, the agreement required the plaintiff lawyers to strongly recommend that all their clients take the deal, and almost required them to 'fire' the clients if they did not. In addition, in the exercise of his 'equitable' power, the federal judge regarded himself in this 'quasi

---

82 Dionne Searcey, 'Many Wary as Consolidated BP Suit Advances' *Wall St J* (13 Sept 2010).

83 Amanda Bronstad, 'Swelling Docket Challenges System' *Nat LJ* (20 Sep 2010).

84 See Leslie O'Leary, 'Out on Your Own' Trial (Nov 2010) at 36, bemoaning the failure of the Panel to order transfer in *In re Shoulder Pain Pump-Chondrolysis Products Liability Litigation* 571 F Supp 2d 1367 (JPML 2008).

85 For a description of this activity, see Sherman (supra note 79), 2213–16.

class action' to have the power to regulate the fees the plaintiffs had to pay their lawyers, and to reallocate some of those fees to the lead counsel he had appointed to handle the plaintiff side of the combined litigation. From the perspective of the other plaintiff lawyers, who had contracts with their clients entitling them to receive a certain percentage of any recovery, the judge's actions reducing what they received and then directing some of it to other lawyers, raised serious questions about judicial power.

For the present, however, the main point is to appreciate that the US class action is not the only model for mass resolution of litigation. Probably it has emerged in the US due to the distinctive American bar, with its wide reliance on the contingency fee for personal injury cases and freedom from the risks associated with a 'loser pays' rule on attorney fees. But those interested in a full consideration of the American model must consider the 'quasi class action' along with the real one.

VI. THE 'MASS ACTION' POSSIBILITY

Nor does the MDL option exhaust the American bag of litigation tricks. An even simpler option can sometimes exist and usher in something that looks a lot like class actions and 'quasi class action' MDL proceedings. The prospect that permissive party joinder could do so was sufficient to prompt Congress to equate such suits with class actions in the Class Action Fairness Act. That Act says that a 'mass action' is 'a civil action [. . .] in which monetary relief claims of 100 or more persons are proposed to be tried jointly on the ground that the plaintiffs' claims involve common questions of law or fact.'[86]

It seems that other countries permit joinder of parties on terms similar to those in the US.[87] But it also seems that most Europeans would regard the possibility of such mass joinder to permit lawyers to create a case similar to an American class action as absurd. Suggesting that it could happen suggests also that something like American class actions could occur in other legal systems without any special new procedural arrangements.

Such things certainly have happened in US courts, however. Consider two consolidated suits brought in state courts in Texas in the 1990s and

---

86 See 28 USC 1332(d)(11)(B)(i).

87 See, eg, Peter Murray and Rolf Stürner, *German Civil Justice* (Carolina Academic Press 2004) 201–2; Nicolo Trocker, *Civil Justice in Italy* (Nagoya Univ Press, 2010) 173–5; Miklos Kengyel and Viktoria Harsagi, *Civil Justice in Hungary* (Nagoya Univ Press 2009) 79.

removed to federal courts by defendants. The two suits alleged that defendant uranium companies were legally responsible for personal injuries and property damages suffered in towns near their operations. One was brought on behalf of more than 1,000 individual plaintiffs, and the other for approximately 600 additional individual plaintiffs.[88]

These cases were not handled in the normal manner by the assigned judge; instead, the judge employed a more aggressive management plan that might sound similar to what some European judges would employ in civil cases. The judge employed what has come to be known as a *Lone Pine* order, named after the New Jersey state court case that first used this method of handling such a multitude of claims.[89] The order required each plaintiff to provide supporting information on his or claim at the outset in order to proceed. When plaintiffs submitted over 1,000 identical form affidavits, the judge dismissed their cases, and the appellate court affirmed. Other courts have ruled similarly.[90]

Probably the hypothetical possibility that such group litigation could be created using existing permissive joinder would not make it likely to occur in most countries in Europe, even though the joinder rules look like the American rules, both because the bar is organized in such a different manner, and because of the loser-pays rule on costs. Nonetheless, if Europe wants to move more toward group litigation and to learn from the American experience, it may be useful to consider the role of such measures as *Lone Pine* orders. On that score, the judge in the Vioxx litigation[91] offered thoughtful comments on how to approach these problems:

> In crafting a *Lone Pine* order, a court should strive to strike a balance between efficiency and equity. *Lone Pine* orders may not be appropriate in every case and, even when appropriate, they may not be suitable at every stage of the litigation. For example, in the present case, a *Lone Pine* order may not have been appropriate at an earlier stage before any discovery had taken place since little was known about the structure, nature and effect of Vioxx by anyone other than perhaps the manufacturer of the drug. But this case is no longer in its embryonic stage. It has existed in state courts for over seven years and in this Court for over three years, and much discovery has taken place. In this MDL, the Plaintiffs' Steering Committee has established and organized a document

---

88 *Acuna* v *Brown & Root, Inc*, 200 F3d 335 (5th Cir 2000).

89 *Lore v Lone Pine Corp*, 1986 WL 637507 (NJ Super Ct 1986).

90 See, eg, *Avila v Willits Environmental Remediation Trust*, 633 F3d 828 (9th Cir 2011), affirming the district judge's use of a variety of claims screening devices in a suit brought on behalf of more than 1,000 plaintiffs for alleged environmental contamination in an industrial facility in the town of Willits, California.

91 See supra text accompanying note 85 for a description of the resolution of this litigation.

> depository to house materials produced by [defendant] Merck and has made those materials available to Plaintiffs' counsel in individual cases. In total, Merck has produced over 22 million pages of documents. Hundreds of depositions have taken place. [. . .] Six bellwether trials have been held in this MDL as well as fourteen other trials in various state courts throughout the country. [. . .] For nearly a decade, Plaintiffs' counsel throughout the country have been studying, exploring, and discovering all of the effects of Vioxx on the human body [. . .].
>
> The Court finds that at this advanced stage of the litigation, it is not too much to ask a Plaintiff to provide some kind of evidence to support [his or her] claim that Vioxx caused [him or her] personal injury, whether that injury be deep vein thrombosis, a heart attack, an ulcer or some other malady. Surely if Plaintiffs' counsel believe that such claims have merit, they must have some basis for that belief; after all this time it is reasonable to require Plaintiffs to come forward and show the basis for their beliefs and show some kind of basic evidence of specific causation.[92]

VII. CONCLUDING OBSERVATIONS

Just as it has not ended in Europe, so the debate about group or class litigation is not over in the US. Consider, for example, the rueful recent observations of a *New York Times* columnist:

> Class-action lawsuits have been denounced by businesses for decades, and some of their arguments are compelling. We've all heard of settlements in which lawyers take home millions in fees and consumers wind up with piddling sums, often in the form of coupons. Recently, Ferrero U.S.A. settled lawsuits brought by two moms who said they were deceived by health claims made on jars of the chocolate hazelnut spread Nutella. Yes, if you bought Nutella thinking it was spinach in a jar – actually even if you bought it because you find it delicious – you are a winner.
>
> Is that really the most efficient way to deal with a reportedly misleading health claim? Maybe the Federal Trade Commission could have handled that one.[93]

Maybe the EU regulatory arrangements can handle such claims adequately also. But as Professor Keleman has recently noted, the EU may be coming to rely more on private enforcement,[94] and the interest in some form of

---

92 *In re Vioxx Products Liability Litigation*, 557 F Supp 2d 741, 744 (E D La 2008).

93 David Segal, 'A Rising Tide Against Class-Action Suits' *New York Times* (6 May 2012).

94 R Daniel Keleman, *Eurolegalism: The Transformation of Law and Regulation in the European Union* (Harv Univ Press Cambridge 2011) 9.

group litigation in Europe suggests strongly that traditional regulation is not sufficient. So it may be that the litigation future for Europe will look more like the US than the litigation past. Meanwhile, there are some indications that class actions may be flowing from the US to Professor Walker's home – Canada.[95] As these developments unfold, this chapter on the American experience can hopefully serve to inform consideration of ways to handle similar problems of group litigation in other countries, even though it barely scratches the surface of an immense body of American law and experience.

---

[95] See Tanya Monestier, 'Is Canada the New Shangri-La of Global Class Actions?' 32 *Nw J Int'l Law & Bus* 365 (2012). See also Merritt Fox, 'Securities Class Actions Against Foreign Issuers' 64 *Stan L Rev* 1173 (2012).

8. Mass settlements in Australia

Michael Legg

I. INTRODUCTION

Mass settlements are most common and most regulated in Australia in relation to 'class actions' or 'representative proceedings' under Part IVA of the Federal Court of Australia Act 1976 (Cth) (the FCA Act). In the Multiplex shareholder class action, Finkelstein J observed:[1]

> It goes without saying that the court should encourage the settlement of class actions and other complex cases. Perhaps more than most cases, class actions lend themselves to compromise because of the uncertainty of their result, difficulties of proof, complexities in the assessment of damages, as well as the expense of a long trial.

It is no surprise that settlement of class actions is the most common way in which they are resolved.[2] Further, class action settlements have been for substantial sums of money, including $200 million for a shareholder class action and $120 million for a cartel class action.[3] A share of these recoveries will be taken by lawyers and/or litigation funders. As a result this chapter will focus on the settlement of class actions in the Federal Court of Australia by examining the requirements for settlement that flow from the representative nature of the class action and highlighting some of the continuing controversies around how settlement operates in this context. The chapter will also briefly examine non-class action mass settlements.

---

1 *P Dawson Nominees Pty Ltd v Brookfield Multiplex Limited (No 4)* [2010] FCA 1029, 2. See also *Regent Holdings Pty Ltd v State of Victoria* [2012] VSCA 221, 20.

2 See Vince Morabito, *An Empirical Study of Australia's Class Action Regimes – First Report* (December 2009) 30–36.

3 Examples of Australian class action settlements are set out in Table 8.1 to this chapter.

II. BACKGROUND

1. Australian Class Action Regimes

Class actions have existed in Australia since the addition in 1992 of Part IVA to the FCA Act which provided for 'representative proceedings' at the Federal level.[4] On 28 June 2010 the Federal Court issued Practice Note CM 17, 'Representative Proceedings Commenced under Part IVA of the Federal Court of Australia Act 1976' which after extensive consultation with the legal profession commenced on 5 July 2010 (Practice Note CM 17). Practice Note CM 17 provides extensive guidance on the conduct of class actions in the Federal Court, including in relation to settlement.

In Australia's six states, only two have class action regimes. In Victoria, a procedure for 'group proceedings' was inserted in Part 4A of the Supreme Court Act 1986 (Vic) with effect from 1 January 2000.[5] The Victorian provisions are almost identical to the FCAA, including adopting the same numbering of sections. In New South Wales (NSW) Part 10 was inserted into the Civil Procedure Act 2005 (NSW) so as to make 'representative proceedings' available in NSW courts.[6] Part 10 commenced on 4 March 2011. The NSW procedures are similar to the FCA Act but some changes were introduced in response to case law developments in the Federal Court.[7] In jurisdictions other than the Federal Court, Victoria and NSW there is no comprehensive modern class action procedure. However, representative actions based on the former practices of the United Kingdom's Court of Chancery are available in these jurisdictions to run pseudo-class actions.[8] The representative action also remains in the Federal

---

[4] Federal Court of Australia Amendment Act 1991 (Cth) (FCAA) which commenced on 4 March 1992.

[5] Courts and Tribunals Legislation (Miscellanous Amendments) Act 2000 (Vic).

[6] Courts and Crimes Legislation Further Amendment Act 2010 (NSW).

[7] See Dorne Boniface, Miiko Kumar and Michael Legg, *Principles of Civil Procedure in New South Wales* (2d ed, Thomson Reuters 2012) paras 7.180, 7.250, 7.470, 7.660.

[8] See Uniform Civil Procedure Rules 1999 (Qld), Chapter 3 Division 4 rules 75–7, Supreme Court Rules 1987 (SA), r 34 (applies to actions commenced before 4 September 2006) and Supreme Court Civil Rules 2006 (SA), Chapter 5 Part 1 Division 3, rules 80–84 (applies to actions commenced on or after 4 September 2006), Supreme Court Rules 2000 (Tas), Part 10 Division 5, rules 335–6 and Rules of the Supreme Court 1971 (WA), Order 18, rule 12. South Australia's model varies considerably from the Court of Chancery model but is neither a detailed class action regime.

Court and Victoria, but not NSW.[9] This chapter will focus on the FCA Act.

2. Federal Court Class Actions

In the Federal Court of Australia proceedings are commenced by the applicant, who also performs the role of representative party, against one or more respondents. Proceedings commenced pursuant to the FCA Act usually have three hurdles to overcome: complying with the requirements for commencing the proceedings (seven or more persons with claims arising out of the same, similar or related circumstances that give rise to a substantial common issue of law or fact),[10] complying with the additional pleading requirements (identifying the group and specifying the common questions)[11] and avoiding being discontinued (the costs are excessive as compared to separate proceedings; the relief sought can be obtained without resort to a representative proceeding; the representative proceeding is not an efficient and effective means of dealing with the claims; or it is otherwise inappropriate that the claims be pursued by means of a representative proceeding – all subject to the interests of justice).[12]

The FCA Act also adopts an opt-out approach so that group members do not have to consent or agree to participate, but rather, if an entity falls within the group definition they are a group member, subject to being given an opportunity to exclude themselves from the proceedings prior to trial.[13] The opt-out approach means that some, perhaps many, group members are not specifically identified, which presents a particular challenge for settlement. The development of litigation funding in Australia has seen group definitions employed that gave rise to a closed class.[14] A

---

9 Federal Court Rules 2011 (Cth) r 9.21, Supreme Court (General Civil Procedure) Rules 2005 (Vic) Order 8 r 2 and Michael Legg, 'Shareholder Class Actions in Australia – The Perfect Storm?' (2008) 31 *UNSWLJ* 669, 695–6. The NSW representative action was contained in Uniform Civil Procedure Rules 2005 (NSW) r 7.4 and 7.5 that were repealed by the Courts and Crimes Legislation Further Amendment Act 2010 (NSW) Schedule 6.4.

10 Federal Court of Australia Act 1976 (Cth) s 33C.

11 Ibid, s 33H.

12 Ibid, s 33N

13 Ibid, s 33J.

14 Michael Legg, 'Reconciling Litigation Funding and the Opt Out Group Definition in Federal Court of Australia Class Actions – The Need for a Legislative Common Fund Approach' (2011) 30 *CJQ* 52, 53. The closed class approach is favoured by litigation funders because it allows them to require each group member to accept the terms of their funding agreement.

closed class involves a class action being commenced on behalf of a group specifically created for, and prior to, the commencement of the class action. The class is closed or limited by reference to the group members having entered into a litigation funding agreement with a named funding company. The right to opt out must still be ensured, but the group members are known.[15]

3. Legal Costs and Litigation Funding

The usual costs rule in Australian litigation is that a losing party is liable for the other side's costs, albeit only a portion of the costs actually incurred.[16] This is referred to as 'the loser pays' or 'costs follow the event' and is usually given effect procedurally through an adverse costs order. The rule is modified in relation to class actions as the costs rule applies to the applicant/representative party only and not to the group members.[17]

The funding of class actions traditionally relied on the lawyer for the applicant providing legal services on a 'no win – no fee' basis so that legal fees only became payable if a successful outcome was achieved. In some circumstances the lawyers would also charge an 'uplift fee' which was usually expressed as an additional percentage, usually the statutory maximum of 25 per cent, of the legal fees incurred.[18] This approach removed the disincentive to an applicant commencing proceedings because they would incur the legal costs of the proceedings. However, it did not remove the disincentive created by the risk of being personally liable for an adverse costs order.

Litigation funding developed in relation to class actions because it addressed both disincentives: incurring legal costs and the risk of an adverse costs order. In a typical litigation funding arrangement, the funder (usually a commercial entity) will enter into an agreement with the applicant and some or all of the group members. The funder pays the costs of the

---

15 *Multiplex Funds Management Ltd v P Dawson Nominees Pty Ltd* (2007) 164 FCR 275; [2007] FCAFC 200, 142, 150; and Michael Legg, *Case Management and Complex Civil Litigation* (Federation Press 2011) 220–2.

16 *Ruddock v Vadarlis* (2001) 115 FCR 229 11; and *Hughes v Western Australia Cricket Association (Inc)* (1986) ATPR 40-748, 48,136. See also Victorian Law Reform Commission, Civil Justice Review – Report 14 (2008) 648 estimating that only 60–70 per cent of costs are recovered.

17 Federal Court of Australia Act 1976 (Cth) s 43(1A).

18 See eg *Johnson Tiles Pty Ltd v Esso Australia Ltd* [1999] FCA 1363; *Cook v Pasminco Ltd (No 2)* [2000] FCA 1819, 39, 54; and *Courtney v Medtel Pty Limited (No 5)* [2004] FCA 1406, 56. It is illegal for a lawyer to charge a fee by reference to the recovery achieved in the proceedings.

litigation (such as the lawyer's fees, disbursements, project management and claim investigation costs) and usually accepts the risk of paying the other party's costs in the event that the claim fails through providing the plaintiff with an indemnity. In return, if the claim is successful, the funder will receive a certain percentage of any funds recovered by the litigants either by way of settlement or judgment, and the litigants will assign the funder the benefit of any costs order they receive. The share of the proceeds is agreed with the litigants, and is typically between one-third and two-thirds of the proceeds (usually after reimbursement of costs).[19] Litigation funding was endorsed by the High Court of Australia in *Campbells Cash and Carry Pty Ltd v Fostif Pty Ltd* (2006) 229 CLR 386 and has subsequently been subject to court oversight and limited government regulation.[20]

III. SETTLEMENT MUST BE APPROVED BY THE COURT

Settlements are usually viewed as a form of contract in which the parties can confidentially settle their dispute in whatever way they agree upon. The fairness of the settlement amount is not examined provided the parties are competent and not under any disability. In class actions the settlement is argued to require judicial oversight because the lawyer for the group is potentially an unreliable agent of the group and the group is unable to effectively monitor the lawyer. In terms of principal (group) and agent (lawyer), the principal has too little at stake to expend resources monitoring the agent and the agent has superior information. Traditional adversarial positions dissipate in the settlement approval context and the judge must be alive to the possibility of conflict and collusion – the applicants' lawyers may collude with respondents and there may be conflict between the representative party and other group members or between sub-groups.[21] In the Australian context the advent of litigation funding adds to, or alters, the above concerns because the funder may be able to monitor the lawyers but it may also

---

19 Legg, supra note 14.

20 Michael Legg, Edmond Park, Nicholas Turner and Louisa Travers, 'The Rise and Regulation of Litigation Funding in Australia' (2011) 38 *N Ky L Rev* 625, Wayne Attrill, 'The Future of Litigation Funding in Australia' in Michael Legg, *The Future of Dispute Resolution* (Lexis Nexis 2012), Chapter 16 and Australian Securities and Investments Commission, *Regulatory Guide 248: Litigation schemes and proof of debt schemes: Managing conflicts of interest* (April 2013).

21 Michael Legg, 'Judge's Role in Settlement of Representative Proceedings: Lessons from United States Class Actions' (2004) 78 *ALJ* 58, 68 cited in *Courtney*

collude with those lawyers and be an unreliable agent for group members. Consequently, it is essential that the court exercise a critical supervisory role to ensure that a settlement is in the interest of all the group members.[22]

The FCA Act therefore provides the court with the power, indeed the responsibility, to examine the terms upon which a representative proceeding is being settled or discontinued.[23] Section 33V provides:

> (1) A representative proceeding may not be settled or discontinued without the approval of the Court.
> (2) If the Court gives such an approval, it may make such orders as are just with respect to the distribution of any money paid under a settlement or paid into the Court.

Consequently, the representative proceeding may not be settled or discontinued without the approval of the court. In addition, the notice provision, section 33X provides:

> Unless the Court is satisfied that it is just to do so, an application for approval of a settlement under section 33V must not be determined unless notice has been given to group members.

Reference should also be made to section 33ZF which gives the court the power to 'make any order the Court thinks appropriate or necessary to ensure that justice is done in the proceeding', as this provision is relied upon by the Court to allow it to address novel issues that arise as part of a settlement.[24]

---

v Medtel Pty Ltd (No. 5) (2005) 212 ALR 311, 38. See also *Mercedes Holdings Pty Ltd v Waters (No 1)* (2010) 77 ACSR 265; [2010] FCA 124, 9 ('since the representative parties and their lawyers are at the coalface of the suit where time, stress and money are being consumed in the furnace of litigation, it is natural that their inclination towards settlement may be affected by a just appreciation of their own positions. Those positions, and the allied interests accompanying them, may not wholly coincide with those of the members of the class. It is to superintend that inherent tension that s 33V erects a requirement for court approval of settlements and discontinuances').

[22] *Australian Competition and Consumer Commission v Chats House Investments Pty Ltd* (1996) 71 FCR 250, 258; *Williams v FAI Home Security Pty Ltd (No 4)* (2000) 180 ALR 459; [2000] FCA 1925, 22, 31–5, *Tasfast Air Freight v Mobil Oil* [2002] VSC 457, 4; *P Dawson Nominees Pty Ltd v Brookfield Multiplex Limited (No 4)*, supra note 1, 4; *Pharm-a-Care Laboratories Pty Ltd v Commonwealth of Australia (No 6)* [2011] FCA 277, 20.

[23] *Taylor v Telstra Corporation Ltd* [2007] FCA 2008, 56; *Mercedes Holdings Pty Ltd v Waters (No 1)*, supra note 21 (dealing with discontinuance); Practice Note CM17, 10.

[24] Legg, supra note 15, 234–5.

IV. WHAT IS A SETTLEMENT?

A settlement has been defined in *Tongue v Council of the City of Tamworth* as follows:[25]

> In ordinary parlance, for a claim to be settled, it must have been compromised. However, law dictionaries suggest that the element of compromise is not a necessary ingredient. As is said in Butterworth's Australian Legal Dictionary at 1073, when a matter has been settled, the parties have reached some kind of agreement and no longer require the Court to deliberate between them. Another dictionary states that a 'settlement' means 'an agreement ending a dispute or law suit'.

This broad reading of settlement is appropriate in the class action context for the reasons requiring court approval discussed above, namely to protect absent group members and prevent conflict and collusion. A more limited view of settlement would take a sub-set of actions outside of the court's purview.

Section 33V has been interpreted as applying to a settlement in full, against any respondent, or in relation to any single substantive claim.[26] Section 33V has also been interpreted as requiring approval to settle only some of several claims, or against some of several respondents.[27] The concern with this approach is that it can have the result of increasing costs as there need to be notices and fairness hearings in relation to each settlement. However, a settlement by an individual group member with a respondent has been found not to require approval under section 33V.[28]

A further, specific regime exists for when the representative party settles his or her own claim but not the claims of the group. The representative party retains standing to continue the action in his or her representative capacity should they wish to.[29] If the applicant wishes to withdraw as representative party they require leave of the court and notice of the application to withdraw must first be given to group members.[30] This is because the aim is to find a replacement representative party. However, the possibility that there will be no applicant is not a barrier under section 33W to the exercise of the power to grant leave to the representative party

---

25 *Tongue v Council of the City of Tamworth* [2004] FCA 1702, 32 citing *Transport Accident Commission v Coyle* (2001) 3 VR 589, 27.

26 *Australian Competition and Consumer Commission v Chats House Investments Pty Ltd*, supra note 22, 258. See also *King v AG Australia Holdings Ltd* (2002) 121 FCR 480, 40–2.

27 *Bray v F Hoffman-La Roche Ltd* [2003] FCA 1505, 23.

28 *Courtney v Medtel Pty Ltd* (2002) 122 FCR 168, 44–6.

29 Federal Court of Australia Act 1976 (Cth), s 33D(2).

30 Ibid, ss 33W and 33X(1)(c).

to withdraw. An unwilling party cannot be forced to litigate against his or her will. Consequently, the proceedings may cease to be able to be pursued as a class action.[31]

V. SETTLEMENT APPROVAL STEPS

Settlement usually involves a three-step process. First, a settlement agreement is negotiated and executed. This will contain essential caveats such as approval by the court pursuant to section 33V.[32] It may annexe the orders to be sought from the court as part of the settlement process. The second step is usually approaching the court for the approval of a notice to group members advising of the terms of the settlement and the date for the subsequent settlement approval hearing. Alternatively, and much less common, the court may be approached for an order that notice be dispensed with. The third step is the settlement approval or fairness hearing at which group members can provide objections and the settlement is formally approved or disapproved. In some settlements, the court may retain jurisdiction while the settlement is allocated and distributed so as to be able to monitor this process.

1. Notice

The practice of the Federal Court is to require the applicant to give prior notice to group members advising of the application.[33] Although notice may be dispensed with if just to do so.[34] Practice Note CM 17 provides guidance as to the content of the notice by specifying that it should usually include:[35]

---

[31] *Tongue v Council of the City of Tamworth*, supra note 25, 36–8.

[32] *Jarra Creek Central Packing Shed Pty Ltd v Amcor Ltd* [2011] FCA 671, 17 and *Paxtours International Travel Pty Ltd v Singapore Airlines Ltd* [2012] FCA 426, 16. There may also be other caveats such as the settlement amount not exceeding a specified amount: *Dorajay Pty Ltd v Aristocrat Leisure Ltd* (2008) 67 ACSR 569; [2008] FCA 1311, 3, 7.

[33] Federal Court of Australia Act 1976 (Cth) ss 33X(4) and 33Y; *Pharm-a-Care Laboratories Pty Ltd v Commonwealth (No 6)* [2011] FCA 277, 18; *P Dawson Nominees Pty Ltd v Brookfield Multiplex Ltd (No 4)*, supra note 22, 5; Practice Note CM17 ,10.2.

[34] Federal Court of Australia Act 1976 (Cth) ss 33X(4); *Vernon v Village Life Ltd* [2009] FCA 516, 42, 76.

[35] Practice Note CM17, 11.5. See also Peter Cashman, *Class Action Law and Practice* (Federation Press, 2007) 351 and Legg, supra note 21.

(a) a statement that the group members have legal rights that may be affected by the proposed settlement;
(b) a statement that an individual group member may be affected by a decision whether or not to remain as a group member (where the opt-out date has not already passed or where there is a further opportunity to opt out);
(c) a brief description of the factual circumstances giving rise to the litigation;
(d) a description of the legal basis of the claims made in the proceedings and the nature of relief sought;
(e) a description of the group on whose behalf the proceedings were commenced;
(f) information on how a copy of the statement of claim and other legal documents may be obtained;
(g) a summary of the terms of the proposed settlement;
(h) information on how to obtain a copy of the settlement agreement;
(i) an explanation of who will benefit from the settlement;
(j) where all group members are not eligible for settlement benefits – an explanation of who will not be eligible and the reasons for such ineligibility;
(k) an explanation of the Court settlement approval process;
(l) details of when and where the Court hearing will be and a statement that the group member may attend the Court hearing;
(m) an outline of how objections or expressions of support may be communicated, either in writing or by appearing in person or through a legal representative at the hearing;
(n) an outline of any steps required to be taken by persons who wish to participate in the settlement (in the event that affirmative steps are required);
(o) an outline of the steps required to be taken by persons wishing to opt out of the settlement if that is possible under the terms of the settlement; and
(p) information on how to obtain legal advice and assistance.

The courts have observed that it is of importance that any notice be both accurate[36] and expressed in as plain and simple language as is consistent with the information sought to be communicated,[37] because a misleading or

---

36 *Williams v FAI Home Security Pty Ltd (No 3)* [2000] FCA 1438, 24.
37 *McMullin v ICI Australia Operations Pty Ltd* (1998) 156 ALR 257, 260; *Courtney v Medtel Pty Ltd* [2001] FCA 1037, 10–11.

inaccurate notice may impact the decision of a group member.[38] The form of the notice is also important as it will impact whether group members have the content of the notice brought to their attention. An example of the forms of notice employed is provided by the Corrugated Cardboard cartel class action where the settlement notice was published in national newspapers, emailed, sent by post, placed on the applicant's lawyer's and court's websites, as well as being the subject of company announcements to the stock exchange and media reports.[39] Consequently, the form and content of the notice will be frequently subject to close attention by the parties and the court.[40]

2. Application for Approval

An application for approval of a proposed settlement is made by motion on notice supported by affidavit.[41] This can be made at the same time that notice is sought or after the court has approved the giving of notice. If the former, the application will need to be stood over to the date of the settlement approval hearing.

The orders which are commonly sought include: (a) approval of the proposed settlement, (b) approval of legal fees and disbursements, (c) approval of the reimbursement of costs incurred by the applicant or nominated group members, (d) approval of any scheme for distribution of the settlement payment (e) confidentiality of evidence provided in support of the settlement; and (f) disposing of the proceeding (eg by dismissing the application).[42] The affidavit in support will usually address:[43]

(a) how the settlement complies with the criteria for approving a settlement;
(b) why the proceedings have been settled on particular terms;
(c) the effect of those terms on group members (ie the quantum of damages they are to receive in exchange for ceasing to pursue their claims and whether group members are treated the same or differently and why);

---

38 *King v GIO Australia Holdings Ltd* [2001] FCA 270 , 14–15.

39 *Jarra Creek Central Packing Shed Pty Ltd v Amcor Ltd*, supra note 32, 57–8, 127.

40 *Pharm-a-Care Laboratories Pty Ltd v Commonwealth (No 6)*, supra note 22, 11.

41 Ibid, 7.

42 Practice Note CM17 ,11.3.

43 Ibid, 11.4.

(d) the means of distributing settlement funds;
(e) the terms of fee and retainer agreements including the reasonableness of legal costs;
(f) a response to any arguments against approval of settlement raised by group members;
(g) any issues that the court directs be addressed;
(h) a hearing of the application for settlement approval, including consideration of any group members' objections to the settlement and an order dealing with costs.

Additional affidavits may be needed to respond to such matters as group member objections or issues raised by the court.

3. Settlement Approval Hearing

There will be a settlement hearing for the judge to consider the evidence in relation to section 33V and to determine if the orders sought should be made. If the settlement is approved there will follow various steps to administer the settlement, including identifying the group members, if this has not previously occurred, calculating each group member's claim and distributing payments.

VI. IDENTIFYING GROUP MEMBERS

A prerequisite for some settlements will be the 'closing of the class' to identify group members. For others group members may be already known due to the group definition (ie a closed class) or the nature of the claims. For yet others the settlement may proceed on the basis that a specified sum will be allocated to group members who come forward as part of the settlement distribution process (discussed below). Where a class action employs a traditional opt-out group definition it will be necessary to 'close' the class because '[u]ntil the class of participating group members is closed and the members of the closed class identified there can be no final settlement and no distribution of settlement monies to members of the class'.[44]

---

[44] *Dorajay Pty Ltd v Aristocrat Leisure Ltd*, supra note 32, 13. See also Rachael Mulheron, 'The Case for an Opt-out Class Action for European Member States: A Legal and Empirical Analysis' (2009) 15 *Columbia Journal of European Law* 409, 431 n 127 ('There are, essentially, only three scenarios where an opt-out action will never "convert" to an opt-in action: where the class (a) loses on common issues relevant to liability; (b) wins on common issues or liability, and thereafter damages

However, closing the class is controversial because it requires group members to take an affirmative step, which they may not do because of misunderstanding,[45] not receiving the notice, laziness or because they do not wish to claim because of a defect in their cause of action[46] or because their losses do not make it worthwhile expending the time completing the forms. The effect of a group member not identifying themselves and providing the necessary information is that they are ineligible to participate in the settlement. It will also mean that their claims are extinguished, unless the court excludes those persons from the group or provides a further opportunity to opt out.[47] Extinguishing all group members' claims achieves finality in relation to the subject matter of the class action proceedings. However, orders allowing some persons to opt out or be excluded from the group may create a risk for respondents that a sub-set of group members can commence separate proceedings, thus undermining the certainty that the settlement would otherwise provide.[48] Further, the goal of access to justice for those facing social or economic barriers may only be facilitated up until there is the prospect of receiving compensation if they do not take the required affirmative steps.[49]

The practical ramification of the above conundrum is to ensure that the notices to group members are well publicised and as clear and straightforward as possible.[50] It is also highly desirable that the class is only closed once there is a settlement on foot because knowing the outcome of

---

are awarded upon an aggregate basis and the entire amount is distributed cy-près; or (c) wins the common issues or liability, and thereafter the damages can be awarded without any proactive steps being taken by the class members, because the defendant has the information to make direct credits or refunds').

45 Empirical research of opt-out notices suggests misunderstanding is a significant problem: Vince Morabito, *An Empirical Study of Australia's Class Action Regimes – Second Report* (September 2010) 33.

46 *King v AG Australia Holdings Ltd (formerly GIO Australia Holdings Ltd)* [2003] FCA 980, 4.

47 *Williams v FAI Home Security Pty Ltd (No 5)* [2001] FCA 399, 10 (redefining the group so as to exclude persons who did not particpate in the settlement); *Courtney v Medtel Pty Limited (No 4)* [2004] FCA 1233, 15 (providing an opportunity to opt out of a settlement).

48 Damian Grave, Ken Adams and Jason Betts, *Class Actions in Australia* (2d ed, Thomson Reuters, 2012) 14.540.

49 The use of a closed class does not address this problem but rather exacerbates it by excluding those facing social or economic barriers at the commencement of proceedings when less is known about the prospects of success and the quantum of any settlement: Legg, supra note 14, 60.

50 See Legg, supra note 21, 67 discussing the US Federal Judicial Center's project on class action forms.

the proceedings will be an important factor for a group member in determining whether to take the time to complete and return forms.[51] If meaningful notice has been given then a court can close the class and extinguish outstanding claims with greater comfort that no injustice has taken place.

VII. ASSESSING REASONABLENESS OF PROPOSED SETTLEMENT

Despite the importance of settlement approval, section 33V makes no express reference to the criteria for approving settlement. Consequently the courts developed their own criteria for approving settlement, namely (1) to assess whether the proposed settlement or compromise is fair and reasonable and adequate having regard to the claims made on behalf of the group members who will be bound by the settlement;[52] and (2) 'to be satisfied that any settlement or discontinuance of representative proceedings has been undertaken in the interests of the group members as a whole, and not just in the interests of the applicant and the respondent'.[53]

The fair and reasonable and adequate requirement was further explained by reference to the 'nine factor test' applied in the United States Court of Appeals for the Third Circuit, namely (1) the complexity and duration of the litigation; (2) the reaction of the class to the settlement; (3) the stage of the proceedings; (4) the risks of establishing liability; (5) the risks of establishing damages; (6) the risks of maintaining a class action; (7) the ability of the defendants to withstand a greater judgment; (8) the range of reasonableness of the settlement in light of the best recovery; and (9) the range of reasonableness of the settlement in light of all the attendant risks of litigation.[54]

---

[51] *Pharm-a-Care Laboratories Pty Ltd v Commonwealth (No 6)*, supra note 22, 14.

[52] See *Williams v FAI Home Security Pty Ltd (No 4)*, supra note 22, 19–20, *Jarrama Pty Ltd v Caltex Australia Petroleum Pty Ltd* [2004] FCA 1114, 11; *Haslam v Money for Living (Aust) Pty Ltd (admin apptd)* [2007] FCA 897, 17.

[53] *Australian Competition and Consumer Commission v Chats House Investments Pty Ltd*, supra note 22, 258; *Lopez v Star World Enterprises Pty Ltd* [1999] FCA 104, 15; *Darwalla Milling Co Pty Ltd v F Hoffman-La Roche Ltd (No 2)* (2006) 236 ALR 322, 30 and 31.

[54] *Williams v FAI Home Security Pty Ltd (No 4)*, supra note 22, 19 citing *Re General Motors Corporation Pick-Up Truck Fuel Tank Products Liability Litigation* (3d Cir 1995) 55 F3d 768, 785. See also *Jarrama Pty Ltd v Caltex Australia Petroleum Pty Ltd*, supra note 52, 10 and *Courtney v Medtel Pty Ltd (No 5)*, supra note 21, 39–40.

The reference to adequacy and the nine-factor test attracted some criticism.[55] Some Federal Court judges then started to refer to whether a settlement was fair and reasonable.[56] Practice Note CM 17 now sets out the test as follows:[57]

> When applying for Court approval of a settlement, the parties will usually need to persuade the Court that:
> (a) the proposed settlement is fair and reasonable having regard to the claims made on behalf of the group members who will be bound by the settlement; and
> (b) the proposed settlement has been undertaken in the interests of group members, as well as those of the applicant, and not just in the interests of the applicant and the respondent/s.
>
> When applying for Court approval of a settlement the parties will usually be required to address at least the following factors:
> (a) the complexity and likely duration of the litigation;
> (b) the reaction of the group to the settlement;
> (c) the stage of the proceedings;
> (d) the risks of establishing liability;
> (e) the risks of establishing loss or damage;
> (f) the risks of maintaining a representative proceeding;
> (g) the ability of the respondent to withstand a greater judgment;
> (h) the range of reasonableness of the settlement in light of the best recovery;
> (i) the range of reasonableness of the settlement in light of all the attendant risks of litigation; and
> (j) the terms of any advice received from counsel and/or from any independent expert in relation to the issues which arise in the proceeding.

The above factors have been applied on numerous occasions.[58]

---

[55] See *Darwalla Milling Co Pty Ltd v F Hoffman-La Roche Ltd (No 2)*, supra note 53, 32–9.

[56] *Vernon v Village Life Ltd*, supra note 34, 45 and *Fowler v Air Services Australia* [2009] FCA 1189, 21. Other judgments have put the test in the negative: *Hobbs Anderson Investments Pty Ltd v Oz Minerals Ltd* [2011] FCA 801, 4 ('identify any features of the proposed settlement or compromise that are obviously unreasonable or unfair').

[57] Practice Note CM17, 11.1–11.2.

[58] See eg *Jarra Creek Central Packing Shed Pty Ltd v Amcor Ltd*, supra note 32, 68–77; *Pharm-a-Care Laboratories Pty Ltd v Commonwealth (No 6)*, supra note 22, 20–7, 37.

1. Reliance on Lawyers

The Federal Court has observed that 'the task of the court in considering an application under section 33V is indeed an onerous one' and is a task 'in which the court inevitably must rely heavily on the solicitor retained by, and counsel who appears for, the applicant to put before it all matters relevant to the court's consideration of the matter'.[59]

Reliance on the lawyers is premised on the duties that they owe to group members. In relation to the applicant and those group members who have retained the lawyers, that is they are clients of the lawyer, the solicitor-client relationship will give rise to fiduciary duties.[60] The duty to the absent group members is said to be to conduct the proceedings in a way that is consistent with the interests of those group members. The duty also arises as a result of a fiduciary relationship.[61] Consequently, the lawyer is required to act in good faith and avoid conflicts of interest in relation to both clients and absent group members.

A practice has developed where the solicitor for the applicant will provide an affidavit in which they address each of the above factors listed in Practice Note CM 17 relevant to the instant litigation. They will also provide a written opinion as to the fairness and reasonableness of the proposed settlement that focuses on the prospects of success of the litigation. The opinion is exhibited to an affidavit made by the solicitor but includes an application for an order that the exhibited opinion be confidential and not required to be served on the respondents so as to maintain the client's legal privilege which attaches to the advice. The opinion is then made

---

[59] *Lopez v Star World Enterprises Pty Ltd*, supra note 53, 16. In the Victorian context see *Pathway Investments Pty Ltd v National Australia Bank Limited (No. 3)* [2012] VSC 625, 3.

[60] *Maguire v Makaronis* (1997) 188 CLR 449, 463.

[61] *King v AG Australia Holdings Ltd*, supra note 26, 489; *Bray v F Hoffman-La Roche Ltd*, supra note 27, 15; *Dorajay Pty Ltd v Aristocrat Leisure Ltd* [2009] FCA 19, 8. See also Grave, Adams and Betts, supra note 48, para 6.255. The decisions tend to assume, rather than decide, that a fiduciary relationship exists, but applying the criteria for establishing a fiduciary relationship according to the High Court of Australia, it is clear that there is vulnerability of the group member to the lawyer's power or vulnerability necessitating reliance (*Hospital Products Ltd v United States Surgical Corp* (1984) 156 CLR 41 at 142 per Dawson J; *Mabo v Queensland (No 2)* (1992) 175 CLR 1, 200–1 per Toohey J and *Breen v Williams* (1996) 186 CLR 71, 134) and a power held by the lawyer to affect the interests of the group members in a real or practical sense (*Hospital Products Ltd v United States Surgical Corp*, 68 per Gibbs CJ, 96–7 per Mason J).

available to the judge at the return of the motion.[62] As a result the court then has 'evidence' upon which it can make its findings.

Attempts have been made to suggest that:

> the respondent's lawyers should also bear some responsibility for ensuring that the court has all the information that objectively describes the merits of the case and brings to the court's attention the obstacles to recovery and the benefits to be derived from the proposed settlement.[63]

Despite these observations, anecdotal evidence suggests that respondents rarely actively gather evidence or make submissions in relation to a settlement, but rather, simply express their support.[64] The approval process takes place without an opposing voice seeking to identify aspects of the settlement that are unfair or unreasonable. The adversarial process that relies on each party bringing forward the evidence that supports their case does not apply, thus making the onerous nature of the judicial task apparent.

2. Objections by Group Members

The lack of objections by group members has been seen as a sign that a settlement is not opposed and is a factor in favour of the settlement being fair and reasonable.[65] However:

> Where some group members object to a settlement or compromise and state their reasons for doing so, it is appropriate for the court to have regard to those

---

62 See eg *Wright Rubber Pty Ltd v Bayer AG (No 3)* [2011] FCA 1172, 9; *Hobbs Anderson Investments Pty Ltd v Oz Minerals Ltd*, supra note 56, 17–19, 25–7; *Jarra Creek Central Packing Shed Pty Ltd v Amcor Ltd*, supra note 32, 154–62 (which also included an opinion from an expert witness); *P Dawson Nominees Pty Ltd v Brookfield Multiplex Ltd (No 4)*, supra note 1, 14. The absence of an opinion from counsel has been raised as a 'matter of concern': *Peterson v Merck Shaerpe & Dohme (Aust) Pty Ltd (No 6)* [2013] FCA 447, 23.

63 *P Dawson Nominees Pty Ltd v Brookfield Multiplex Ltd (No 4)*, supra note 1, 4.

64 *Pharm-a-Care Laboratories Pty Ltd v Commonwealth (No 6)*, supra note 22, 49. An exception appears to be the Storm Financial class action settlement where the Court received opinions from counsel for both the applicant and the settling respondent: *Richards v Macquarie Bank Limited (No. 4)* [2013] FCA 438, 13.

65 *Clime Capital Ltd v Credit Corp Group Ltd (No 3)* [2012] FCA 218, 23 ('Another matter of significance is the absence of any objection to the proposed settlement agreement from any group members. The authorities make it clear that this is a factor which should be given considerable weight').

> reasons as a point of reference by which to determine matters of fairness and reasonableness.[66]

Reliance on a lack of objections has been identified as problematic because silence may not equate to acquiescence bur rather reflect the high cost of objecting compared to the benefit to be obtained, or result from group members being unaware of the settlement, having insufficient information or miscomprehending the settlement notice.[67]

Some federal court judges have refined the understanding of a lack of objections. In the Multiplex shareholder class action, Finkelstein J observed that 'it is dangerous to assume that silence equals assent as class members with only a very small stake in the action have little incentive to object' but in the instant case a lack of objections could be given more weight as most group members were institutional investors who had in-house legal departments, were experienced investors and were better placed to assess the benefits of the settlement.[68] In the Corrugated Cardboard cartel class action, although it was acknowledged that some Group Members may have only a small stake in the action, comfort was obtained from all group members being 'business owners who should be able to assess the benefits (or disadvantages) of the settlement'.[69]

While better resourced and more informed group members are better placed to object if they wish, the collective action problem persists in that the objector incurs costs alone in aid of a benefit that accrues to all group members. The costs for institutional investors may be greater than for individuals as they must give up the relative anonymity provided to group members and take centre stage in a settlement hearing. Institutional investors such as banks and insurance companies may not wish to be seen as litigating against other corporations with whom they have a current or future relationship, there may be concerns at being identified as having made an unsuccessful investment, or more general reputational concerns such as being associated with class action litigation.[70]

When objections are made they usually occur without legal assistance

---

66 *Hobbs Anderson Investments Pty Ltd v Oz Minerals Ltd*, supra note 56, 4.

67 See Christopher Leslie, 'Significance of Silence: Collective Action Problems and Class Action Settlements' (2007) 59 *Fla L Rev* 71 and Catherin Piche, 'A Critical Reappraisal of Class Action Settlement Procedure in Search of a New Standard of Fairness' (2009–2010) 41 *Ottawa L Rev* 25, 36–7.

68 *P Dawson Nominees Pty Ltd v Brookfield Multiplex Ltd (No 4)*, supra note 1, 23.

69 *Jarra Creek Central Packing Shed Pty Ltd v Amcor Ltd*, supra note 32, 124.

70 Michael Legg, 'Institutional Investors and Shareholder Class Actions: The Law and Economics of Particpation' (2007) 81 *ALJ* 478, 481–2.

and are expressed to be against the amount of the settlement, the amount of legal fees or due to some idiosyncratic feature of the group member's claim.[71] These objections almost never result in a settlement being rejected. Often this is because the objection involves a misunderstanding or is put forward without any evidence, compared to the affidavits from the lawyers for the applicant on prospects of success, fairness of settlement and reasonableness of fees.[72] A reliance on a lack of objections and the poor quality of the objections that are made supports the use of appointing a guardian for group members, which is discussed below.

3. Litigation Risk

The existence of 'litigation risk' is a factor that carries significant weight, with the court being a factor that the parties and the court are expressly directed to consider by Practice Note CM17. Litigation risk refers to 'the vagaries of litigation and the risks of failure as well as the expense to be incurred in protracted litigation'.[73] Litigation risk exists in all proceedings because documentary evidence may be incomplete or a witness may forget or not be believed.[74] In class actions that risk is often higher because of the novelty of the law and the need at some point to quantify losses. In Australian shareholder and cartel class actions the law in relation to causation and damages is unsettled.[75] There is also the prospect of cost and

---

[71] *Pharm-a-Care Laboratories Pty Ltd v Commonwealth (No 6)*, supra note 22, 34–5; *Hobbs Anderson Investments Pty Ltd v Oz Minerals Ltd*, supra note 56, 31–8. The only case that the author is aware of where objections by group members were successful in having a settlement rejected was *Tongue v Council of The City of Tamworth*, supra note 25 where over half of the group members opposed the settlement.

[72] See eg *Hobbs Anderson Investments Pty Ltd v Oz Minerals Ltd*, supra note 56, 33 (complaint about legal costs rejected when compared to affiadvit of an independent costs lawyer), 37 (complaint about loss of claim against auditors but proposed claim was from company for an indemnity and would not increase the quantum of the claim).

[73] *Jarra Creek Central Packing Shed Pty Ltd v Amcor Ltd*, supra note 32, 95. See also *Wright Rubber Pty Ltd v Bayer AG (No 3)*, supra note 62, 12; *P Dawson Nominees Pty Ltd v Brookfield Multiplex Ltd (No 4)*, supra note 1, 24.

[74] See eg *Jarra Creek Central Packing Shed Pty Ltd v Amcor Ltd*, supra note 32, 90 ('The Respondents' written openings point to what are said to be discrepancies in the evidence of the witnesses and possible gaps in the proofs . . .').

[75] See *P Dawson Nominees Pty Ltd v Brookfield Multiplex Ltd (No 4)*, supra note 1, 15–17; *Hobbs Anderson Investments Pty Ltd v Oz Minerals Ltd*, supra note 56, 9–10; *Kirby v Centro Properties Ltd (No 6)* [2012] FCA 650, 4 (causation and damages in shareholder class actions is uncertain); *Darwalla Milling Co Pty Ltd v*

delay due to the need for extensive discovery,[76] or because novel points of law are likely to be appealed.[77] In the Multiplex shareholder class action Finkelstein J referred to this as the 'bird in the hand' approach[78] and observed that the parties in that class action were 'well served' by reliance on that approach.[79]

The problem with too great a focus on litigation risk is that when a court compares the uncertainties that inform litigation risk with the certainty of settlement, the settlement almost always is an attractive option. This can undermine the judge's ability to critically assess a settlement and lead to too ready an acceptance of the settlement put up by the parties. This is not to say that judges should be in the habit of trying to extract 'better' settlements or consider that they know more about the litigation risk in a particular case than the parties' legal representatives.[80] However, in large and complex litigation, such as class actions, litigation risk is inherent but it should not be allowed to provide a smokescreen for a settlement that overly discounts potential recoveries in aid of settlement approval.

VIII. LEGAL FEES, LITIGATION FUNDERS AND OTHER PAYMENTS

1. Legal Fees

When a settlement is reached it is usual for it to include the payment of the legal costs incurred by the applicant. Australian courts have power to

---

F Hoffman-La Roche Ltd (No 2), supra note 53, 48, *Jarra Creek Central Packing Shed Pty Ltd v Amcor Ltd*, supra note 32, 98–113 (quantum of damages in a cartel class action involves uncertainty). See also Ross Drinnan and Jenny Campbell, 'Causation in Securities Class Actions' (2009) 32 *UNSWLJ* 928; Andrew Watson and Jacob Varghese, 'The Case for Market-Based Causation' (2009) 32 *UNSWLJ* 948; Brooke Dellavedova and Rebecca Gilsenan, 'Challenges in Cartel Class Actions' (2009) 32 *UNSWLJ* 1001; Graeme Edgerton, 'Cartel Damages and the Passing On Defence: A comparative analysis' (2009) 17 *CCLJ* 56.

[76] *Darwalla Milling Co Pty Ltd v F Hoffman-La Roche Ltd (No 2)*, supra note 53, 52.

[77] *Kirby v Centro Properties Ltd (No 6)*, supra note 75, 4.

[78] This is a reference to the proverb 'A bird in the hand is worth two in the bush'.

[79] *P Dawson Nominees Pty Ltd v Brookfield Multiplex Ltd (No 4)*, supra note 1, 24. See also *Pharm-a-Care Laboratories Pty Ltd v Commonwealth (No 6)*, supra note 22, 37.

[80] *Darwalla Milling Co Pty Ltd v F Hoffman-La Roche Ltd (No 2)*, supra note 53, 50.

regulate costs agreements between a solicitor and a client.[81] In the class action context, the power in section 33ZF has been interpreted as allowing for the supervision of costs agreements with lawyers.[82] Accordingly, it has been accepted that the amount to be paid to the lawyers, including disbursements, must be approved by the court.[83]

To satisfy the court that the costs amount payable to the lawyers should be approved it has become common practice to supply an affidavit from an independent costs expert who is able to opine as to the reasonableness of the costs and disbursements incurred by the lawyers for the applicant.[84] Frequently the costs amounts awarded are large, especially in comparison to the settlement amount. The courts place significant reliance on the evidence of the independent costs expert.[85] However, they also consider the general circumstances of the litigation. In the Aristocrat shareholder class action, Stone J referred to:

> the duration of the proceeding, . . . the complexity of the matter and novelty of the issues raised, and what senior counsel for the applicant described at the trial as the 'years of interlocutory skirmishing' leading up to the hearing.[86]

The Australian approach to legal fees has the advantage that they require court approval and thus justification must be provided. The downside is not that the review of legal fees is outsourced to a costs expert, but that the costs expert is retained by the lawyers seeking the fee award. The expert may become dependent on the lawyers for repeat work, which is unlikely to continue if legal fees are substantially reduced. The process could be improved without any increase in cost if the court appointed the costs expert and the expert owed their allegiances solely to the court.

2. Payments to Litigation Funders and Equalisation Orders

The payments to litigation funders can consume a large proportion of any class action settlement. However, the ability to supervise or alter contractual relations involving a litigation funder is less clear compared to the

---

81 *Woolf v Snipe* (1933) 48 CLR 677.

82 *Johnson Tiles Pty Ltd v Esso Australia Ltd* (1999) 94 FCR 167, 35–7.

83 Ibid, 39; *Reiffel v ACN 075 839 226 Pty Limited (No 2)* [2004] FCA 1128, 11.

84 *Courtney v Medtel Pty Ltd (No 5)*, supra note 21, 59.

85 *Dorajay Pty Ltd v Aristocrat Leisure Ltd*, supra note 61, 30

86 Ibid, 31. See also *Taylor v Telstra Corporation Ltd*, supra note 23, 73 ('settlement was reached only about two weeks before the hearing that a substantial amount of work has gone into the preparation of the case').

position of lawyers as the funder is not an officer of the court and the fee arrangements are not amenable to the court's taxation of costs process.[87] Consequently, the fees charged by litigation funders have rarely been examined when a settlement is approved. The exception is the Pharm-a-care class action where Flick J observed that:

> Some reservation, however, was expressed during the course of the hearing (and still remains) as to the extent to which this court should scrutinise both the quantum of monies proposed to be paid to a litigation funder and the percentage that that amount bore to the overall settlement.

But his honour did not conduct an examination preferring instead to observe that the percentage to be paid to the litigation funder was below what had been charged in other class actions.[88] Significantly though, Flick J did find that the court had power pursuant to section 33ZF to approve a settlement subject to the litigation funder's fee being limited to a particular amount.[89]

While the courts have been slow to conduct an examination of the fee paid to the litigation funder, the courts have endorsed the use of a 'funding equalisation factor'. In class actions involving funded and unfunded group members so that the funded group members are contractually obliged to pay a percentage of their recovery to a litigation funder but the unfunded group members are not, the applicant will often seek a 'funding equalisation factor' by which non-funded class members will have deducted from their entitlement an amount equal to the commission payable to the litigation funder by the funded group members which is then redistributed across all group members.[90] The 'funding equalisation factor' is argued to prevent unfunded group members free-riding, ie obtaining the benefit

---

87 See eg *Kirby v Centro Properties Ltd*, supra note 75, 42.

88 *Pharm-a-Care Laboratories Pty Ltd v Commonwealth (No 6)*, supra note 22, 38–9.

89 Ibid, 42. See also *Kirby v Centro Properties Ltd (No 6)*, supra note 75, 10 (in a terse judgment Middleton J stated 'To the extent that other monies are to be paid, including commissions under the terms of litigation funding agreements, . . . I also regard these as appropriate and reasonable to be paid in the manner proposed').

90 *Dorajay Pty Ltd v Aristocrat Leisure Ltd*, supra note 61, 17; *P Dawson Nominees Pty Ltd v Brookfield Multiplex Ltd (No 4)*, supra note 1, 26–8; *Modtech Engineering Pty Ltd v GPT Management Holdings Ltd* [2013] FCA 626, 55–61 where approval of a litigation funder taking a commission from unfunded group members' recoveries equivalent to the amount agreed to be paid by funded group members was rejected by the court. Instead the commission was to be deducted from unfunded group members' recoveries and added back to the Settlement Sum and distributed pro rata to all group members.

of the proceedings without contributing to their cost. However, the court's power to make such awards has not been identified. Presumably sections 33V(2) and 33ZF may be pressed into service but the requirements to do what is just would require more than a simple redistribution of funds based on a free-riding argument.

The 'funding equalisation factor' has some similarities with the common fund approach used in the United States, where the lawyers are awarded a percentage or component of the settlement fund created as a result of the class action.[91] However, the common fund approach involves an assessment by the court of what is a reasonable payment. In Australia the unfunded group members are saddled with whatever percentage the funded group members agreed to and without court oversight. Now that litigation funding has become a pervasive component of class actions the court needs to subject the terms of that funding to greater scrutiny as part of the settlement approval process.

3. Additional Payments and Deductions

Applicants and nominated group members have sought reimbursement and/or out-of-pocket expenses for the time expended providing instructions, monitoring the litigation and in the preparation of the evidence in the case in the interests of group members as a whole. Courts have been prepared to order that such payments be paid from a settlement prior to calculating the amounts to be distributed to group members.[92]

This type of application was considered for the first time in the Vitamins cartel class action. The reservations expressed there by Jessup J included: not having any method by which the claims could be verified such as is the case with legal costs and that claims did not 'sufficiently discriminate between time and expenditure which related to the organisation and preparation of the claimants' own cases, on the one hand, and time and expenditure which had a truly representative purpose, on the other hand'.[93] Equally, Jessup J accepted that it would be reasonable for a person who had incurred expense for the benefit of all group members to receive some degree of compensation. There was also a suggestion that

---

91 Legg, supra note 14, 63–9.

92 *Jarra Creek Central Packing Shed Pty Ltd v Amcor Ltd*, supra 32, 143–52; *Darwalla Milling Co Pty Ltd v F Hoffman-La Roche Ltd (No 2)*, supra note 53, 74–93.

93 *Darwalla Milling Co Pty Ltd v F Hoffman-La Roche Ltd (No 2)*, supra note 53, 75, 80–1. See also *Modtech Engineering Pty Ltd v GPT Management Holdings Ltd*, supra note 90, 67, 70–71.

such compensation was necessary to encourage people to take on the role of the representative party, but this was rejected.[94] In a subsequent cartel class action it was observed that in litigation not involving a class action a successful party was not entitled to be paid for time spent in the conduct of litigation.[95]

The validity of the reimbursement of applicants and nominated group members turns on the representative nature of class actions creating an exception to the usual rule that parties are not be paid for their time conducting litigation. The issue is vexed because the FCA Act chose not to address the issue despite dealing with liability of legal costs between the applicant and group members,[96] yet at the same time gave the court the power in section 33ZF to make any order needed to ensure justice is done. Consequently any reimbursement for time spent or expenses incurred must have been done solely for the benefit of the group and not in aid of the applicant's own claim. Most, if not all, of the work undertaken by an applicant will serve dual purposes because the applicant's claim is meant to be the vehicle by which the common questions relevant to the group's claims are resolved.[97]

IX. DISTRIBUTION OF SETTLEMENT FUNDS

In the Corrugated Cardboard cartel class action the five main features of a distribution scheme were set out:

> The first is the appointment of [the applicant's lawyers] as court appointed administrator. The second is the establishment of a procedure for the identification and verification of Group Members who are entitled to participate in the Settlement. The third is the assessment of claims by Participating Group Members and the identification of the formula by which claims are to be assessed and determined. The fourth is the establishment of a dispute resolution mechanism. The fifth is the provision for supervision of the Scheme by the court.[98]

The court will maintain jurisdiction over settled proceedings to be able to monitor and approve steps involving the calculation and distribution of

---

94 Ibid, 76, 86.

95 *Jarra Creek Central Packing Shed Pty Ltd v Amcor Ltd*, supra note 32, 149.

96 Federal Court of Australia Act 1976 (Cth) ss 33ZJ and 43(1A).

97 See Practice Note CM 17, 2.2.

98 *Jarra Creek Central Packing Shed Pty Ltd v Amcor Ltd*, supra note 32, 23. See also *Dorajay Pty Ltd v Aristocrat Leisure Ltd*, supra note 61, 20.

group member's claims and payment to the solicitors (and possibly third parties such as accountants) undertaking the settlement administration.[99] While the distribution of the settlement is a mechanical task it is also very significant in terms of the fairness of a settlement as it determines whether participation in the settlement is allowed and the actual payment to be received.

An example of a distribution scheme involving a shareholder class action is provided by the GIO case where the scheme is an annexure to the judgment approving settlement.[100] The scheme involved the applicant's lawyers identifying a final list of group members based on those who had retained the lawyers directly and those who had completed a 'Form C' that had been employed to close the class.[101] The lawyers ensured that those people met the criteria for group membership and advised them of the number of shares that they were recorded as holding. An opportunity was provided to contest this data. Where correspondence was returned as undeliverable steps were taken to locate another address for the person. The scheme also provided persons who were not regarded as being group members to challenge that designation. Approximately 838 people who were not included as group members contacted the lawyers claiming they should participate in the settlement.[102] Almost all of these people had not completed and returned Form C. The inclusion or exclusion of persons from the settlement was resolved by the court. The reasons for this included a change of address resulting in the form not being received, being away from home at the time the form was sent, incorrectly recorded as having opted out or as being clients of the applicant's lawyer so that no form was provided, forms returned before the deadline but received after the deadline and medical reasons. Where these circumstances were made out the person was included in the settlement. Persons who alleged that they lost Form C, did not comprehend it, forgot to return it or were too busy to return it were not included. Similarly, those that sought to be included but provided no

---

99 *Pharm-a-Care Laboratories Pty Ltd v Commonwealth (No 9)* [2011] FCA 1111. The fees earned in administering the fund can be very lucrative. In the Aristocrat shareholder class action the applicant's lawyers were paid about $960,000. See Michael Legg, 'The Aristocrat Leisure Ltd Shareholder Class Action Settlement' (2009) 37 *ABLR* 399, 405.

100 *King v AG Australia Holdings Ltd (formerly GIO Australia Holdings Ltd)*, supra note 46, Annexure A. See also Justice Michael Moore, 'Ten Years Since King v GIO' (2009) 32 (3) *UNSWLJ* 883 where the judge who case managed the GIO case describes and reflects on the proceedings.

101 *King v AG Australia Holdings Ltd (formerly GIO Australia Holdings Ltd)*, supra note 46, 7 explains the Form C process.

102 Ibid, 13.

information as to their claim or the reason for not having returned Form C were excluded.[103] At the end of this process a final list of group members was created. The lawyers then calculated the loss incurred on the shares held by each group member compared to the takeover offer that they had not accepted because of misleading conduct. This total loss was then compared to the settlement fund to devise the relative proportion of losses that each group member should recover. The lawyers' costs in administering the fund were to be approved by the court and deducted from the settlement fund to the extent those costs exceeded the interest accruing on the settlement sum prior to its distribution.

In a settlement distribution scheme often the most difficult aspect is the calculation of the group members' loss.[104] In shareholder class actions based on breaches of disclosure to the market it is necessary to calculate the 'true' value of the securities compared to what they were trading at.[105] In cartel class actions it is necessary to calculate the effect of the cartel on prices so as to identify the overcharge paid by group members.[106] As a result some form of multiple regression analysis is employed to devise a statistical model for identifying loss. However, settlement distribution schemes and the models they employ often 'operate according to broad rules of thumb' and those rules 'may not reflect the actual experience of particular group members' so that a particular group member may obtain a better, or a worse, outcome than if the litigation was pursued to judgment and damages were awarded to each group member according to its actual loss and damage.[107] Equally, further precision short of an actual litigated outcome can often only be achieved with further cost and delay. There is a trade-off between precision and cost that must be managed so as to ensure settlement funds are distributed fairly.

---

103 Ibid, 19–70 and Annexure B. The late return of forms to participate in a settlement was also dealt with at length in the Aristocrat shareholder class action: *Dorajay Pty Ltd v Aristocrat Leisure Ltd*, supra note 32.

104 *Darwalla Milling Co Pty Ltd v F Hoffman-La Roche Ltd (No 2)*, supra note 53, 46.

105 *Clime Capital Ltd v Credit Corp Group Ltd (No 3)*, supra note 65, 11. See also Bernard Murphy and Andrew Watson, 'Negotiations and Settlement – 2010 Multiplex Debrief' *Lexis Nexis Shareholder Class Action Masterclass*, Sydney, 18 October 2010 pp 6–9.

106 *Jarra Creek Central Packing Shed Pty Ltd v Amcor Ltd*, supra note 32, 40–52.

107 *Darwalla Milling Co Pty Ltd v F Hoffman-La Roche Ltd (No 2)*, supra note 53, 60.

X. GUARDIAN FOR GROUP MEMBERS INTERESTS

The responsibility for the approval of a settlement, including protecting group members' interests, is an onerous and important role for the presiding judge. A potential reform to aid the judge is the use of a guardian for group members.[108] This concept has been advocated because it allows for the court to 'create an adversary contest'[109] which would otherwise be lacking, for representation of the interests of absent group members, monitoring of the parties, and assistance to the court in understanding the mechanics and ramifications of the settlement.[110]

In Australia in both the GIO and Aristocrat shareholder class actions a 'contradictor' was appointed to represent the putative group members who sought to be included in the settlement but had failed to return a necessary form by the specified date.[111] The contradictor was thought necessary because the lawyers for the applicant and group members were arguing against inclusion. The contradictor was a senior barrister who was paid by the lawyers for the applicants. In an early food poisoning class action settlement that provided for the applicant's solicitor to administer the settlement fund but without any mechanism for reviewing the allocation of payments to group members, Finkelstein J queried whether such an attempt to oust the court's jurisdiction was permissible but did not decide the question as he had not heard from a contradictor.[112]

It has been accepted that in the analogous area of court approval of a pecuniary penalty agreed between a regulator and a respondent that a contradictor may be beneficial. In *Minister for Industry, Tourism and Resources v Mobil Oil Australia Pty Ltd* the Federal Court was asked to approve an agreed penalty following breaches of the Petroleum Retail Marketing Sites Act 1980 (Cth). On appeal, the Full Federal Court observed that if

---

[108] Sylvia Lazos, 'Abuse in Plaintiff Class Action Settlements: The Need for a Guardian During Pretrial Settlement Negotiations' (1985) 84 *Mich L Rev* 308; Edward Cooper, 'The (Cloudy) Future of Class Actions' (1998) 40 *Ariz L Rev* 923, 950 and Edward Brunet, 'Class Action Objectors: Extortionist Free Riders or Fairness Guarantors' (2003) *U Chi Legal F* 403, 464–71.

[109] Judith Resnik, 'Money Matters: Judicial Market Interventions Creating Subsidies and Awarding Fees and Costs in Individual and Aggregate Litigation' (2000) 148 *U Pa L Rev* 2119, 2161.

[110] Brunet, supra note 108, 466–7.

[111] *King v AG Australia Holdings Limited (formerly GIO Australia Holdings Ltd)* [2003] FCA 1420, 15 and *Dorajay Pty Ltd v Aristocrat Leisure Limited*, supra note 32, 11.

[112] *Lopez v Star World Enterprises Pty Ltd*, supra 53, 20.

the absence of a contradictor inhibits the court in the performance of its duties, it may seek the assistance of an amicus curiae or of an individual or body prepared to act as an intervener.[113] A guardian or contradictor could be usefully employed in Australian class actions on a more extensive basis. This follows due to the limitations on the adversarial process through lack of participation by respondents in critiquing the fairness and reasonableness of settlements, including the quantum of legal fees and litigation funding fees, while reliance on objectors (if there are any) is problematic. A guardian given access to the necessary information and required to act in the interests of the group members can provide a valuable critique or outright objection to a settlement that may otherwise be unavailable.

XI. FACILITATING SETTLEMENT – CIVIL DISPUTE RESOLUTION ACT

The Civil Dispute Resolution Act 2011 (Cth) (the CDR Act) requires an applicant who commences proceedings in the Federal Court to file a 'genuine steps statement' at the time of filing the application unless the proceedings are excluded under Part 4 of the Act.[114] Class actions are not ordinarily excluded. The statement must specify, inter alia, the steps that have been taken to try to resolve the issues in dispute between the applicant and the respondent.[115] The steps to be taken are not prescribed; rather, the steps are at the discretion of the parties. Examples of such steps include:[116]

- notifying the other person of the issues that are, or may be in dispute and offering to discuss them with a view to resolving the dispute;
- providing relevant information and documents to the other party to enable the other person to understand the issues involved and how the dispute might be resolved; and
- considering whether the dispute could be resolved by a process facilitated by another person including alternative dispute resolution (ADR).

A respondent who is given a copy of a genuine steps statement filed by an applicant in the proceedings must file a genuine steps statement before

---

113 *Minister for Industry, Tourism and Resources v Mobil Oil Australia Pty Ltd* [2004] FCAFC 72, 58, 72.

114 Civil Dispute Resolution Act 2011 (Cth) s 6.

115 Ibid, s 6(2)(a).

116 Ibid, s 1(c).

the hearing date specified in the application. The respondent is required to agree or disagree with the steps set out in the applicant's genuine steps statement.[117]

An eligible court may, in performing functions or exercising powers in relation to civil proceedings before it, including making orders as to costs, take account of whether a genuine steps statement was filed, and whether genuine steps were actually taken.[118] The CDR Act has the potential to facilitate settlement of class actions through the exchange of information, especially on the quantification of loss which is often unable to be reliably estimated by a respondent, and through prompting the early resort to ADR. Although largely voluntary, the CDR Act when applied to class actions operates in a context where Practice Note CM17 already requires an initial case management conference that aims to promote the exchange of information so as to identify the issues in the litigation and whether the matter should be referred to ADR.[119] Opportunities for considering settlement and employing processes to facilitate settlement are available prior to, and shortly after, the commencement of class action proceedings.

XII. MASS SETTLEMENTS WITHOUT A CLASS ACTION

A prominent example of a mass settlement outside of the class action framework was the Storm Resolution Scheme. This was an ADR scheme set up by Australian banks after the collapse of Storm Financial Limited during the global financial crisis. Storm Financial was one of the biggest financial planning networks in Australia, with 115 staff, $4.5 billion of funds under management and 14,000 clients. It convinced most of it clients to acquire significant debt, from various banks, to fund investments in the stock market. When the market crashed not only were those investments lost, but for many who had used their homes as collateral, the family home was at risk.[120]

The Commonwealth Bank of Australia (CBA), National Australia Bank and ANZ bank negotiated resolution schemes with the law firm Slater & Gordon that were available to bank customers who alleged losses resulting from the collapse of Storm Financial. The details of the scheme are not

---

117 Ibid, s 7.

118 Ibid, ss 11, 12.

119 Practice Note CM 17, 3.4.

120 Paul Barry, 'In the Eye of the Storm: The Collapse of Storm Financial', *The Monthly* (February 2011).

publicly available but in relation to CBA they included the following elements:[121]

- Payment by CBA of its client's legal fees to a maximum of $5000
- CBA clients represented by 40 law firms independent of CBA
- Use of test cases to establish the principles for deriving settlement offers
- Disclosure of documents and facts about each claimant by CBA
- The assessment of the test cases by an independent panel composed of a retired High Court judge, a retired Federal court judge and a barrister
- Financial and non-financial components were included in the resolution including adjusting home loan terms, writing off interest payments and providing permanent tenancies to allow claimants to stay in their homes
- Claimants being able to accept offers, make counter-offers, seek evaluation of an offer from the independent panel and reject an offer.

Twelve months after the start of the resolution scheme more than 900 of the 1120 claims lodged with Slater & Gordon had been finalised, about 100 accepted that they had no claim and others were still going through the process.[122] When completed the total monetary compensation paid was estimated to be about $132 million, but there were other benefits such as interest waivers, reduced interest rates and flexible payment arrangements.[123] The advantage of the resolution scheme was explained by one journalist as being that it drew 'much of the political heat, the consumer anger and reputational damage from the issue and contained the final costs to a few hundred million'.[124]

However, the resolution scheme did not prevent the Australian Securities & Investments Commission (ASIC) or other CBA clients commencing legal proceedings against CBA, the latter by way of a Federal Court class action on behalf of 238 clients.[125] ASIC's proceedings were based on a statu-

---

121 Legg, supra note 15.

122 Slater and Gordon Media Release, 'Slater & Gordon settles 900 Storm CBA claims' (7 September 2010).

123 Australian Securities & Investments Commission, ASIC and CBA Storm Financial Settlement (4 October 2012) 1–2.

124 Duncan Hughes, 'Two Ways of Tackling Storm Damage', *The Australian Financial Review* (26 June 2009) 58.

125 *Sherwood v Commonwealth Bank of Australia (No 2)* [2012] FCA 1030, 5.

tory cause of action, the existence of an unregistered management investment scheme, and sought to increase compensation for Storm Financial investors. ASIC also commenced proceedings against banks, not including CBA, based on breach of contract, unconscionable conduct and liability as a linked credit provider of Storm Financial.[126] The class action was able to be commenced on behalf of those CBA clients that had not entered into settlement agreements through the resolution scheme which contained clauses that barred further proceedings.

ASIC subsequently settled its proceedings against CBA on the basis that CBA would make available a further $136 million in addition to what had been paid under the ADR scheme. ASIC has calculated that when this additional amount is added to the original payment, CBA's customers that participate in the settlement will receive 55 per cent of their total loss.[127] The class action continues. It seems that the resolution scheme did not give CBA the finality it would have liked nor capped costs and compensation amounts within a relatively short time frame. However, the proactive nature of the resolution scheme does appear to have assisted in limiting reputational damage and fostering positive client relationships.

XIII. CONCLUSION

Australia has had a class action procedure since 1992 which has resulted in the process for settlement being well tested and, to a significant degree, standardised in relation to some causes of action. This is reflected in the Federal Court being able to provide significant guidance as to how settlement approval will be undertaken in Practice Note CM 17. Nonetheless, the reasons for requiring court approval, such as the risk of conflicts of interest, collusion and outcomes that are not for the benefit of absent group members, remain. The settlement approval process, including the process for the distribution of settlement funds, requires close and careful scrutiny. Reforms that can aid the court in fulfilling the onerous responsibilities of approving class action settlements should be explored.

---

126 See ASIC's Storm Financial website: https://storm.asic.gov.au/.

127 Australian Securities & Investments Commission, supra note 123, 1–2.

Table 8.1 Sample Federal Court of Australia settlements

Case Name	Case Type	Settlement Amount (inclusive of lawyers' and litigation funders' fees)	Lawyer Fees	Litigation Funder Fees	Comments
Lopez v Star World Enterprises Pty Ltd [1999] FCA 104	Product liability – food poisoning	\$1.45m	\$700,000	No funder	Respondent insolvent
Williams v FAI Home Security Pty Ltd (No 5) [2001] FCA 399	Product liability – home alarm systems	\$910,000	\$415,000	No funder	Legal fees agreement included a 25 per cent uplift but this was not charged
King v AG Australia Holdings Ltd (formerly GIO Australia Holdings Ltd) [2003] FCA 980	Shareholder class action re misleading statements in a takeover	\$112m	\$15m	No funder	Legal fees included a 25 per cent uplift
Courtney v Medtel Pty Limited (No 5) [2004] FCA 1406	Product liability – pacemakers	\$4.7m (estimated)	\$2.3m	No funder	Legal fees included a 25 per cent uplift
Guglielmin v Trescowthick (No 5) [2006] FCA 1385	Shareholder class action re disclosure to market and in a prospectus	\$3m	\$1.55m	No funder	Respondent's insurance was limited and would be exhausted by defence costs
Darwalla Milling Co Pty Ltd v F Hoffman-La Roche Ltd (No 2) [2006] FCA 1388	Vitamins cartel	\$41m	\$10.5m	No funder	
Taylor v Telstra Corporation [2007] FCA 2008	Shareholder class action re disclosure to market	\$5m	\$1.25m	No funder	

Dorajay Pty Ltd v Aristocrat Leisure Ltd [2009] FCA 19	Shareholder class action re disclosure to market	$144.5m	$8.5m	$35m	Settlement occurred after trial
P Dawson Nominees Pty Ltd v Brookfield Multiplex Ltd (No 4) [2010] FCA 1029	Shareholder class action re disclosure to market	$110m	$11m	Not disclosed as litigation funder was based offshore	
Pharm-a-Care Laboratories Pty Ltd v Commonwealth (No 6) [2011] FCA 277	Misfeasance in public office and negligence relating to regulatory action taken by the Therapeutic Goods Administration	$67.5m	$5m	$24m	
Jarra Creek Central Packing Shed Pty Ltd v Amcor Ltd [2011] FCA 671	Corrugated Cardboard cartel	$120m	$25m	No funder	Largest cartel class action settlement in Australia
Wright Rubber Pty Ltd v Bayer AG (No.3) [2011] FCA 1172	Rubber Chemicals cartel	$1.5m	$1.1m	No funder	Second respondent was bankrupt. Part of settlement was in common stock that had to be sold
Hobbs Anderson Investments Pty Ltd v Oz Minerals Ltd [2011] FCA 801	Two shareholder class actions re disclosure to market	$60m ($39m and $21m)	$3.1m and $1.8m	$15m and another amount not disclosed by the funder	
Kirby v Centro Properties Ltd (No 6) [2012] FCA 650	Three shareholder class actions re disclosure to market with additional claims against directors and the auditor	$200m ($150m for two class actions and $50m for the other)	$21.1m for two class actions and $10.06m for the other	$60m for two class actions and another not disclosed by the funder	Largest shareholder class action settlement in Australia

9. The legislation and judicial practice of China's group action

Zhang Wusheng and Liao Haiqing

I. THE LEGISLATION ON CHINA'S GROUP ACTION PROCEEDINGS

The Civil Procedure Law of the People's Republic of China (CPL) promulgated in 1991 and revised in 2007 and 2012, established for the first time a system of representative proceedings (perceived as a group action system), which has remained in use. Article 53 of CPL provides that:

> If the persons comprising a party to a joint action are large in number, the party may elect representatives from among themselves to act for them in the litigation. The acts of such representatives in the litigation shall be valid for the party they represent. However, modification or waiver of claims or admission of the claims of the other party or pursuing a compromise with the other party by the representatives shall be subject to the consent of the party they represent.

Article 54 of CPL provides that:

> Where the subject matter of action is of the same category and the persons comprising one of the parties is large but uncertain in number at the commencement of the action, the people's court may issue a public notice, stating the particulars and claims of the case and informing those entitled to participate in the action to register their rights with the people's court within a fixed period of time. Those who have registered their rights with the people's court may elect representatives from among themselves to proceed with the litigation; if the election fails its purpose, such representatives may be determined by the people's court through consultation with those who have registered their rights with the court. The acts of such representatives in the litigation shall be valid for the party they represent; however, modification or waiver of claims or admission of the claims of the other party or pursuing a compromise with the other party by the representatives shall be subject to the consent of the party they represent. The judgments or written orders rendered by the people's court shall be valid for all those who have registered their rights with the court. Such judgments or written orders shall apply to those who have not registered their rights but have instituted legal proceedings during the period of limitation of the action.

Chinese scholars tend to divide class actions into two categories depending on whether the number of the plaintiffs is certain or not at the commencement of the action: representative proceedings with a certain number of persons and representative proceedings with an uncertain number of persons. In addition, the newly revised Civil Procedure Law of the People's Republic of China, which came into effect on 1 January 2013, adds a provision on "Public interest litigation". Article 55 of the CPL provides that:

> Relevant bodies and organizations prescribed by the law may bring a suit to the people's court against such acts as environmental pollution, harm of the consumer's legitimate interests and rights and other acts that undermine the social and public interest.

II. COURT HANDLING OF GROUP ACTIONS IN CHINA

From the perspective of judicial practice in group disputes, the representative proceedings that have a certain number of persons, as stipulated in Article 53 of CPL, are used in many courts to varying degrees. However, a significant downward trend has developed in recent years, especially in some developed areas and central cities, where these kinds of representative proceedings have largely disappeared. In contrast to proceedings under Article 53, representative proceedings with an uncertain number of persons, as stipulated in Article 54 of CPL, are seldom found in China's judicial practice. In general, most courts prefer more flexible ways to resolve group disputes, depending on the actual circumstances and their own understanding of the case, other than positively adopting the representative proceedings model. As far as the author is aware, the main approaches to group action cases currently adopted by civil courts in China include the following:

(1) Independent case registration and combined hearings (including the situation that all the cases are heard in a one-off combination or heard in stages and in groups). Many courts in China regard these kinds of cases as "series cases".[1] The courts usually try the group

---

[1] In judicial statistics, this approach is referred to as X group actions involving X cases, or X series involving X cases, etc. For example, Shanghai First Intermediate People's Court accepted and heard 21 group actions, involving 771 cases, which include 15 group actions about collective property disputes, involving

action cases with relatively few claimants involved in combination, by holding one hearing for all the cases, so that all the individual litigants can enter an appearance (most of the litigants who are appearing in court will sit in the public gallery).[2] In hearing group action cases that have a larger number of claimants involved, and which give rise to sharper contradictions,[3] hearings will usually be held in several stages and the parties appearing in court will also be restricted, depending on the capacity of the court, whether the entrusted agents of the parties are the same,[4] and the need for maintaining the court order.

(2) Independent case registration and individual case hearing. At present, most of China's group action cases are registered independently. The mode of the hearing can be an individual case hearing, a combined hearing, or a partially combined hearing, depending on the specific circumstances of the disputes. Generally speaking, each divisional hearing lasts a relatively short time (including where one judge hears different cases in succession and several judges hear the same series of cases). The issues that arise in the disputes become ascertained and the opinions of the judge become clarified (they usually find a way to reach a consensus when cases are heard individually by different judges), hearings of subsequent cases become simpler. Several cases are usually heard within half a day, given the short duration of court time that is available for each case.

(3) Model suits. Despite the absence of legal provisions, regulations or theories on model suits in China, courts have also explored a series

---

556 cases; two group actions about the compensation arrangements for household relocation, involving 111 cases; four group actions about labor disputes, involving 41 cases; one group action about disputes over adjacent buildings blocking sunlight, involving 58 cases; and one group action about compensation for loss caused by the expiration of a lease contract, involving five cases, etc. See Shen Li, 'The Difficulties and Solutions Adopted by People's Courts in Hearing Group Action Cases', *Shanghai Judging Practices*, No 4, 2005, 49.

2 Owing to limited space in courtrooms, only those elected as representatives and the attorneys sit at the plaintiff/defendant stand, and other litigants sit in the public gallery. The advantage of this arrangement is that the representatives, attorneys and even the judges can ask for opinions and can investigate particulars at any time from all of the litigants, and those sitting in the public gallery can express their opinions with the permission of the court.

3 The term 'sharper contradictions' refers to situations where antagonism between two parties is very strong. If the case is not appropriately handled, overreactions like blockading the door of the courts or other official buildings may be triggered.

4 Cases represented by the same attorney usually will be heard together.

of practices to deal with group disputes that are similar to the model suits in foreign nations. This approach has been applied extensively in labor disputes, disputes between property owners and real estate developers, property owners and property management companies, as well as minority shareholders and companies or dominant stockholders. The most usual approach is that potential litigants with claims based on similar circumstances, or litigants who have already filed similar lawsuits, will come to court and sit in the gallery. On the basis that they have reasonably adequate expectations regarding the outcome of the court decision, the majority, including litigants for the specific case on trial, will choose to reach a settlement or mediation agreement[5] with the other party through the coordination of judges (including explanations of the points of law that arise). Sometimes the numerous parties will even jointly sponsor one or several of the claimants in filing an initial lawsuit. This indicates that the first cases that arise and their judgments have wider impact in solving multiple disputes in later cases.

(4) Representative proceedings are the litigation approach established by the CPL to process group disputes. Representative proceedings with an uncertain number of claimants, as stipulated in Article 54 of CPL, rarely appear in judicial practice in China, whereas representative proceedings with a certain number of claimants, as stipulated in Article 53 of CPL, are still being applied to some extent by most of the courts in China.

These are the main forms of action that courts in China are now practicing in dealing with group action cases. In practice, these forms are intersecting, integrating and applied together in judicial practice. For instance, in the cases against Daqing Lianyi Petro-chemical Co., Ltd where there were more than 800 plaintiffs, the approaches were really diversified, including being registered as independent actions, joint actions (less than ten people), and a group action (more than ten people). In the process of registering and hearing the cases, the court can divide a case involving numerous plaintiffs into several cases with fewer plaintiffs, or hear several cases in combination at the same time.

---

[5] The court will not try the cases that have already been filed. The litigants will withdraw their suits through settlement or the court will issue a Mediation Statement. For those who have not filed lawsuits, the parties can drop the case through settlement or the court will issue a Mediation Statement through the rapid case registration mechanism.

III. COURT MEDIATION AS THE PREDOMINANT WAY OF DEALING WITH GROUP ACTION CASES

Judgment and court-based mediation are the two main ways of handling civil cases.[6] The relationship between contentious court decisions and mediation is also a controversial issue among scholars in China. Because of the working principle of "mediation first and combination of mediation and trial" proposed by the Supreme Court in 2008,[7] many courts devote great efforts to promoting court-based mediation. This causes a series of controversies. Generally, three different academic viewpoints exist. One argument in favor of "mediation first" is prevailing in practice,[8] and is also supported by some scholars. For example, Professor Fan Yu thinks:

> the estimation that court-based mediation is superior to judgment is not only the courts' judicial response to social demands, but also in line with the global trend towards mediation. This idea is a significant breakthrough in traditional legal thinking and judicial traditions, and it also reflects an advance and reflection in relation to the development of human society and the rule of law.[9]

A contrary viewpoint is also found. Some scholars hold that the judicial policy of "strengthening mediation" leads, on the one hand, to the

---

[6] Court-based mediation presided over by a judge in China has a lot in common with the judge's active promotion of settlement between both litigants in Western countries. First, both of them can happen at any stage (or main stages) during the proceedings; secondly, they can have effects which are similar to a judgment in some way; and thirdly, judges in both proceedings will conduct the negotiation and try to persuade the parties. Based on these similarities, Taiwan scholar Yang Jianhua considers that despite their different names, the court-based mediation in CPL of mainland China is essentially the same as the settlement of action in Taiwan. The difference is, however, that Chinese judges are more active and forceful than Western judges in promoting the settlement between both parties. Thus, a large percentage of mediation agreements in China are entered against litigants' intentions.

[7] SPC (Research Office of Supreme People's Court) Official Interview on Certain Opinions of the Supreme People's Court on Further Implementation of the Principle of "Mediation first and combination of mediation and trial", see the website of Supreme People's court at www.court.gov.cn2010-06-28 08:13:00.

[8] See Gao Gao, Huang Jianzhong, 'Firmly Implementing the Working Principle of "Mediation First and Combination of Mediation and Judgment', *People's Court Daily*, 28 June 2010, 2; Li Jinggang, Zu Xianhai, 'Vigorously Strengthening the Court-based Mediation', *People's Court Daily*, 12 April 2008, 1.

[9] See Fan Yu, 'Legitimacy and Development Trend of Mediation', *People's Court Daily*, 15 October 2009, 5.

situation that people's rights cannot be safeguarded by the law and people become increasingly dissatisfied with the legal system, and, on the other hand, distorts the social structure and encourages people to politicize disputes as far as possible, puts pressure on the nation in a way that harms social stability and solicits extra-legal advantages from the nation.[10] Others consider mediation as characteristic of a rule-by-men society. The viewpoint there is that court judgments are beneficial to the development and realization of law and the establishment of a rule-by-law society. Thus, emphasis on mediation is increasingly and seriously prejudicing the rule-by-law undertaking, which is in its infancy in China.[11]

Mediation has been getting more attention in recent years with a vigorous push by courts at all levels.[12] This has been especially so in group action cases, where mediation is far more appreciated than a court judgment. The reasons for the wide use of mediation are not only that mediation is beneficial and appropriate to avoid complicated issues in potential lawsuits, to economize on litigation costs, to increase proceedings' efficiency and to save judicial resources (these reasons being aligned with those of many other countries), but they also fit into the specific circumstances in current

---

10 See Xu Yun, 'The Reflection on "Mediation First" – Taking Theory of Civil Trial Structure as Analytical Framework', *Academic Research*, No 4, 2010, 26–38.

11 See Zhou Yongkun, 'On the Impact of Forcible Mediation upon the Rule By Law and Justice Enforcement', *Science of Law (Journal of Northwest University of Political Science and Law)*, No 3, 2007, 47–58; Zhang Wusheng, Xiao Guoyu, 'The Relationship Between Court Judgment and Mediation, *Tribune of Political Science and Law*, No 6, 2012, 168–74.

12 Why is mandatory mediation severe in the process of court-based mediation? The author thinks the reason is related to the traditional civil procedure system. In traditional civil litigation mode in China, the judge plays a leading role in the confirmation and adjudication of claims, collection and taking of evidence, termination of the proceedings, and the formation of judgments. Under this system, the judge is inclined to impose his/her will on both litigants as a result of an imbalance of the power. When the judge as adjudicator also conducts mediation, compulsion will exist overtly or covertly. For example, the judge can communicate with both parties and their agents, making both of them believe that there is a high possibility of losing the lawsuit if they refuse mediation. So the parties have little choice but to accept mediation. Are there any reasons for a judge's preference of mediation? Apart from the advocacy of judicial policies, it is not necessary for the judge to give any reasons for the decision in the Statement of Mediation, there is no appeal when it comes into effect, and a retrial is unlikely to happen. These characteristics influence judges in favor of mediation and minimize potential risks for them. To tackle these problems, the legislative and judicial departments are promoting a mediation system without involving judges in cases in which complaints have already been filed to the courts. Thus, there is a convergence to widespread judicial ADR (alternative dispute resolution) in the rest of the world.

China. "Petitions by letters and calls", which impose great influence over judgments, have peaked recently.

Petitions by letters and calls, also known as "appealing to the higher authorities", is a Chinese-specialized way of resolving disputes. It mainly refers to the activities of citizens, legal persons and other organizations reporting situations or submitting opinions, proposals or requests to state organs at all levels, through letters, e-mails, phone calls, faxes or personal visits. The petitions are dealt with by the relevant organs according to the law. The Party and government organizations at various levels, legislatures, judicial departments, enterprises and institutions have been staffed with professional personnel, or have set up offices, to handle petitions by letters and calls. Given the fact that China has not achieved full judicial independence, the state organs' opinions, especially those of higher level state organs, can have a significant and even decisive influence on ongoing lawsuits or judgments.

If the judgment fails to meet with general acceptance by the group litigants, it may cause many petitioners based in different localities to appeal to the higher authorities for help. Some of them will assemble in front of the State's organs or even blockade the door of the official buildings, which affects the normal operation of the these institutions and social harmony, and, of course, also endangers the stability of the effective judgments.[13] Mediation becomes the preferred method in group action cases to address contradictions and settle matters after the conclusion of cases. Securities group actions have the greatest impact among the group action cases in China. The cases of Dongfang Electronics Co., Ltd and Guangxia (Yinchuang) Industrial Co., Ltd, in both of which the companies were sued by their shareholders for damages based on false statements relating to securities, are two typical cases with significant impacts on all the individual disputes, which were settled through mediation. A brief explanation of these two cases will now be given, to illustrate how group disputes in China are resolved.

Case I

The case involved 6,989 stock investors who filed lawsuits against Dongfang Electronics Co., Ltd (Dongfang Eletronics) for false statements

---

[13] Unlike the usual court-based mediation, the group is in a powerful position in this kind of court-based mediation. But this is not true for all of the group action cases. For example, in the two securities cases we introduce below, most of the litigants are geographically dispersed and live far away from the court that has jurisdiction. This means that the group is unlikely to appeal to a higher authority. Thus, the court will feel less pressure to try the cases.

in the securities market.[14] It is so far the civil compensation case with the largest number of plaintiffs in China. Since the plaintiffs in this case lived in many different provinces and cities, it was the local attorneys instructed by the plaintiffs that filed the lawsuits with the Qingdao Intermediate People's Court. Considering the diverse locations of the plaintiffs and the difficulties in adjusting differences of opinion, on 24 September 2006, attorneys from 17 law firms representing different plaintiffs decided to establish the "legal delegation for plaintiffs in negotiating the settlement of Dongfang Electronics case". This committee operated on the basis of achieving consensus through consultation, and the attorneys elected three representatives to conduct negotiations. This was the first example of an attempt to operate through the election and concrete operation of attorney representatives. In the meantime, the court also adopted an unprecedented innovation by designing a special software program to accurately calculate the compensation for each investor.

On 28 July 2007, the Qingdao Intermediate People's Court held a collective mediation meeting for the Eastern Electronics case, which was mainly attended by attorneys. The mediation plan was announced at the meeting and the plaintiffs[15] and defendant signed the "Framework of Mediation Agreement". The final "Detailed Mediation Agreement" specified the exact amount of compensation for each investor and the court then issued the "Civil Mediation Statement". According to the "Civil Mediation Statement", the defendant listed company (Dongfang Electronics) would then come to the Shenzhen Branch of "China Securities Depository and Clearing Corporation Limited" to go through the formalities for non-trading transfer of the agreed shares to the stock accounts of the relevant investors and select an appropriate date for public circulation. Compensation was limited to the actual losses, which included the loss of investment differences calculated on the basis of the implementation date, exposure date and a benchmark date of false representation confirmed by Qingdao Intermediate People's Court, plus stamp duty, commissions and interest, after deducting systemic risks. That is to say, the amount of the compensation for plaintiffs was 100 percent compensation after deduction of systemic investment risks. On 6 September 2007, Qingdao Intermediate

---

14 Dongfang Electronics Co., Ltd is an enterprise listed on Shenzhen Stock Exchange (Stock Code: 000682, abbreviation: Eastern Electronics) and a key enterprise in Shandong Province.

15 The plaintiffs in this case lived in different cities and provinces across the country. Most of them instructed local attorneys to handle their litigation, so a mediation agreement was mainly signed by the attorneys and only a few litigants signed it in person.

People's Court declared that, apart from disqualified plaintiffs, about 6,800 plaintiffs had accepted the mediation agreement. The stocks compensated by the defendants were transferred to the accounts of the plaintiffs over subsequent months.

The main reason for this successful mediation was the new wave of a great bull market, which created an opportunity to settle the case through the transfer of stocks. From the viewpoint of Dongfang Electronics, concluding the case was very helpful for the improvement of its image. Dongfang Electronics therefore began to take an active attitude towards mediation. This case had been dragging on for years, and both the plaintiffs and their attorneys were completely exhausted both physically and mentally. So it was the unanimous desire of all litigants to settle the case as soon as possible. Since the mediation offered full compensation, and compensation awarded by a court judgment would have been the same as was proposed in the mediation agreement, there was no question but that the plaintiffs would accept the mediation. Thus, thanks to the considerable amount of work done by the judges and the concerted efforts contributed by various litigants, the Dongfang Electronics cases were all settled through mediation.

During the process of mediation, the opinions of most of the litigants, who lived in many different locations, were expressed through their attorneys. However, the court took a leading part in this process, and the role played by the attorneys was in fact quite limited. For individual claimants who were not satisfied with the mediation agreement, theoretically the law did not prohibit them from opting out and pursuing their individual claims, but they would have been confronted with a lot of difficulties and so it happened rarely.

Case II

This civil compensation case involved 847 stock investors filing lawsuits against Guangxia (Yinchuang) Industrial Co., Ltd (Guangxia (Yinchuan) for false statements in the securities market.[16] By the end of July 2002, Yinchuan Intermediate People's Court started to put the cases on record after Guangxia (Yinchuan) was disclosed in the media as a defendant to these mass claims and then penalized by China Securities Regulatory Commission for serious false statements. By the time the limitation period

---

[16] Guangxia (Yinchuang) Industrial Co., Ltd (Stock Code: 5557, Abbreviation: Guangxia Yinchuan Company) is the first listed company in the Ningxia Hui Autonomous Region.

for action ran out, the court had accepted 103 cases, involving 847 investors with total claims of approximately 181 million Yuan.

Only a few litigants actually filed lawsuits against Guangxia (Yinchuan) within the prescribed litigation period, which was undoubtedly good news for the defendant, as the amount of compensation would be very small because many other free-riding complainants could not join the litigation.[17]

However, even though the amount of compensation in individual cases was small, it was very hard to recover the money.[18] The plaintiffs had no choice but to wait patiently.

Some breakthroughs were made in the spring of 2006, and by May 2007, after five years, the damages cases against Guangxia (Yinchuan) were completely concluded. Surprisingly, it was the defendant, Guangxia (Yinchuan) who proactively designed and promoted the compensation plan. The main reason that Guangxia (Yinchuan) adopted this strategy was the fact that its decision makers were deeply aware that for a listed company the influence of paying off bank debt worth 200–300 million Yuan could not be compared to the impact of clearing debts worth 100 million Yuan owed to small- and medium-sized investors.[19] Moreover, it is easier for listed companies in China to negotiate with bank creditors, because many banks have divested debts to asset management companies. For the listed companies, the biggest problems are caused by debt disputes with small- and medium-sized investors, because their behavior tends to be more influential on fundamental matters and even on the share price. The possibility of solving the problem quickly through the judicial procedure

---

[17] The characteristics of a limited amount of compensation and numerous victims in securities litigation leads to the "free-rider" problem, ie potential plaintiffs tend to file lawsuits after witnessing the winning of litigation filed by others, so as to control their exposure to litigation costs.

[18] There are two main reasons why the defendant is not able to offer such limited compensation: First, the defendant lacks debt-paying ability, so the final compensation is provided in the form of stocks rather than money; second, the defendant occupies an obvious advantage in the proceedings, since the securities cases are under the jurisdiction of a people's court in the place where the defendant is located. Generally, defendants have great influence in their local areas, the courts are subject to the local Party and government organizations in many aspects, and local protectionism exists in local courts to varying degrees. So even if the defendant is insolvent, a bankruptcy procedure is unlikely to occur.

[19] If a decision has to be made between paying off bank debt and compensating the loss of the small- and medium-sized investors, a listed company in China will choose the latter as being in its best interests.

was deemed to be advantageous to the restructuring of ST Guangxia (Yinchuan).[20]

The core of the solution proposed by Guangxia (Yinchuan) was that the consideration paid by non-tradable share owners to the plaintiffs was 10 Yuan for 2.2 shares, which was equivalent to 37 percent of the actual loss of the plaintiffs. The plaintiffs' acceptance of this would be deemed to be acceptance of the settlement agreement. For the defendant, the 37 percent compensation amount was calculated as being precisely the bottom line that would guarantee initial costs, but it was considered as a ridiculously low loss ratio by the plaintiffs. Because of the multiple crises suffered by the defendant, the plaintiffs would be at risk of getting nothing if they missed this chance. Therefore, half of the plaintiffs had no choice but to accept this compensation agreement. The other half of the plaintiffs, who refused to accept this agreement, continued the lawsuit and were finally paid the same amount as proposed in the settlement agreement, after a first trial and a trial on appeal.[21] The actual compensation for the plaintiffs in this case was not as bad as predicted. In fact, it was better than expected. Although the plaintiffs only got 37 percent of the actual loss under the plan proposed by Guangxia (Yinchuan), the fundamental value of ST Guangxia was greatly improved and its share price continued to rise with the bull market of 2007. Therefore, most of the investors' losses were completely compensated.

IV. THE EFFECT AND TREND OF GROUP ACTIONS IN CHINA

1. Efficient Handling of a Group Action Case involving Thousands of Farmers who Filed a Lawsuit against the Fengzhan Flour Processing Factory in Huojia County

In China, legislation on a group action is relatively advanced compared with civil law countries. In judicial practice, some group action cases have achieved the goal of low litigation costs and high litigation efficiency, and prompted increased interest in this procedure. For instance, as reported in the People's Court Daily of 13 September 2004, the court of Huojia County

[20] See Li Rui, 'The Case For False Statement against Guangxia (Yinchuan): Hearing After a Five-Year Wait', *Morning News*, 24 November 2006.

[21] See Zhang Wusheng, 'Different Judgments on Similar Cases – Comment on the Civil Compensation Case against Guangxia (Yinchuang) for False Statements', (2010) *Journal of East China University of Political Science and Law*, No 2, 38–47.

in Henan Province, had created a sound legal environment for increasing the income of farmers since the beginning of that year. The court promised to take prompt action in registration, hearing, evidence preservation, judgment and enforcement of the cases that the interests of farmers had been harmed. A group action case involving more than 1,000 claimants was triggered when the property owner of Fengzhan Flour Processing Factory in Fengzhuang Town closed the factory after illegally having sold all the preserved wheat under the counter and having paid nothing to the local residents. When five representatives came to the court to file a lawsuit, with a civil complaint full of inked thumbprints and the signatures of 1,055 people, the court registered the case immediately and delayed charging litigation fees. The court also immediately sealed up the plants and equipment of Fengzhan Flour Processing Factory, worth 300 thousand Yuan, at the request of the plaintiffs. A judgment was rendered within 30 days, holding that the defendant must compensate the economic loss of the plaintiffs.

2. Efficient Handling of a Group Action Case involving over 3,000 Peach Famers who Filed Lawsuits against an Intermediary Dealer in Wuxi

a) The facts of Wuxi peach farmers' case

Despite the limited number of cases of representative proceedings with an uncertain number of claimants, there are some excellent examples which illustrate how the procedure works. One of these was the debt case filed by over 3,000 peach orchard workers from Yangshan Town, Huishan District, Wuxi, against the intermediary dealer Mr Yang for default on payment for honey peaches.[22] From June to September in 2004, the peach orchard workers in the peach production areas in Yangshan Town, Wuxi, delivered harvested peaches to the intermediary dealer Mr Yang as usual. Mr Yang was responsible for selling the peaches to Metro Market and RT-Mart, etc. in Shanghai. They made an oral agreement that payment would be made on a monthly basis. But from June to October thousands of workers got nothing from Mr Yang. After fruitless efforts requesting payment, the workers collectively appealed to the government of Yangshan Town. Under the guidance of the government of Yangshan Town, the workers resorted to law and filed lawsuits against Mr Yang on 4 November 2004. After the acceptance of this case, Huishan Court decided to adopt the procedure of "representative

---

22 The case was detected by the author during a field investigation on mass claims, see Zhang Wusheng, et al, *Theory and Case Analysis of China's Group Action* (Law Press China 2009) 283.

proceedings with an uncertain number of claimants" as stipulated in Article 54 of CPL. On 30 November 2004, the court posted up over 50 notices across the neighborhood where the peach orchard workers lived, inviting them by 30 December 2004 to register in the peach market in Yangshan Town and submit relevant formal written documents, such as receipts for peaches sold and copies of their ID cards.

By that date, 3,964 peach farmers had registered their claims with the court. The total amount of the payments claimed exceeded 1.13 million Yuan, and individual claims varied from 9 Yuan to 10,000 Yuan. A long-standing association of peach farmers organized the election of three individuals (Mr Wang, Mr Zhou and Mr Yu) as representatives for the plaintiffs. They were expected to proceed with the litigation on the basis of consensus through consultation. They instructed Mr Zhou Jianpeng as their legal representative (voluntary representation), who was a legal worker (without a lawyer's certificate) in Yangshan Legal Service Office in Huishan District, Wuxi. The court proceeding of this group action was officially opened on 10 January 2005. The defendant had no objection to the facts presented in the case. However, he argued that he had not deliberately defaulted on the payments to the farmers. He said that the problem was caused by the supermarkets' failure to pay him, and he would pay the workers immediately as soon as the supermarkets paid their debts. The court closed the hearing and entered a judgment in favor of the plaintiffs on the same day, since the case was clear. The judge sent a notice to assist in the enforcement against the supermarkets after the judgment came into force. When two supermarkets paid Mr Yang, sums due to the peach workers were deducted and transferred to them. Over the following days, the court contacted the peach farmers to get their peach payments by putting up announcements, issuing notices and making telephone calls, and so on. It took only four months from the start of the lawsuits by the peach farmers on 4 November 2004 to the judgment of first trial on 1 January 2005, and then to enforcement.

This case is the most influential representative proceedings case with an uncertain number of claimants, which has been tried so far in China. The reasons why Article 54 is rarely used by courts are as follows. First, the Supreme Court clearly stipulated that people's courts should not accept civil compensation cases arising from false statements in the form of a group action.[23] Second, informing the potential plaintiffs by way of issuing

23 Article 4 of the 'Notice of the Supreme People's Court on Issues Concerning Acceptance of Civil Compensation Cases Arising from False Statement in Securities Market' provides that "with regard to civil compensation cases arising from false

a public notice will increase the influence and scale of group disputes, and attract a lot of attention from the media and the public. This would lead to the courts' reluctance to adopt this form of action.

b) Reasons for applying Article 54 CPL

The Wuxi case is also a landmark case among group action cases in China. Why, then, was Huishan Court willing to adopt this form of procedure? The author thinks it is directly connected to the characteristics of this case. First, the facts were not complicated, the debt was clear and the defendant was solvent. It was unlikely that the court would be in an awkward situation here, where numerous plaintiffs were very angry about getting nothing from a defendant after the class had been confirmed. Second, the defendant had no special background in attracting public attention. The defendants in large-scale group action are usually large enterprises, companies, and sometimes even the Party and government organs. Because of a lack of judicial authority, the courts will take many extra-legal factors into consideration when dealing with group disputes. While the defendant in this case was an ordinary intermediate dealer, the court did not have to be aware of attracting too much attention. The failure to pay the workers was because of the supermarkets' failure to pay the defendant. Accordingly, enforcement to some extent meant helping the defendant get the money from the supermarkets. Thus, the court was able to make an impartial judgment without pressure from the defendant. Third, the adoption of representative proceedings with uncertain claimants in this case was helpful in resolving the dispute rapidly and in maintaining stability of the local society. These workers had already made a collective appeal to the Higher Government before filing the lawsuit, and the Government wished to see the disputes being settled as soon as possible through litigation. If the court had registered the cases independently and conducted an individual hearing in each case, as frequently happens in many other places, a lot of potential plaintiffs with small claims would have had difficulties in filing a lawsuit,[24] and this might also have brought other troubles or even civil instability.

---

statements, people's courts shall accept the cases in the form of separate actions or joint action, and shall not accept such cases in the form of group action". The "group action" herein refers to the representative proceedings with an uncertain number of persons as stipulated in Art 54 of CPL.

24 The losses suffered by many individual plaintiffs in this case were very small, in the tens of Yuan, or at most a few hundreds Yuan. Litigation cost is an obstacle to filing individual lawsuits.

3. Existing Problems and Trends with Group Actions in China

The common characteristics of the previous two cases are that the facts were simple, the debts defaulted on by the defendants were clear, and the defendants had no special privileges. These are also the main reasons why these two cases were dealt with in such a short time. However, these kinds of cases only account for a small proportion of mass claims in China. Worsened by the considerable lag of the legal infrastructure and credit system in China, group disputes that are triggered by the same or similar illegal behavior and involve the interests of numerous people have greatly exceeded those in developed countries in numbers, in frequency and with respect to the malicious intent of the infringers. China has become one of the nations with the largest number of group action cases in the world, but a considerable proportion of them have not been handled properly. The author considers that the main reasons for the existing problems in group action cases in China are as follows.

First, most of the group action cases are registered independently or being handled separately, which is adversely affecting the values and functions of the group action mechanism and is increasing litigation costs for the litigants in safeguarding their legal rights. The objectives of group actions are realized to the greatest extent by utilizing the class to change litigation patterns and in affecting the balance of power between the parties so that they can confront each other equally on a level playing field. Sanctions for wrongdoing by infringers will inevitably be affected adversely, and more larger scale infringements will be triggered, if the representative proceedings are held under restraint.

Second, Chinese courts hold a negative attitude towards representative proceedings and restrain the application of this mechanism. This is closely related to the lack of judicial authority. Courts become overcautious and indecisive, thus affecting the independent exercise of their judicial power, since defendants in group cases usually enjoy extensive political influence in local areas and courts are usually dependent on the local governments in terms of the management of human, financial and material resources.

Last, but not least, inadequate punishment of infringers and the low cost of infringements gamble away deterrent effects on organizations and individuals as potential infringers. They are not yet aware of the importance of abiding by the laws, and this is closely related to the large-scale and frequent outbreak of group disputes. In recent years, public clamor for change in the situations mentioned previously in this chapter has been growing stronger and stronger. The establishment of public interest litigation is a response to such clamor from governmental legislation departments. Legislators intend to restrict the growing problems raised in large-scale group disputes by integrating group action and public interest litigation. But then again, concerted efforts from all walks of life will be needed to address the problems. The establishment of judicial authority plays a decisive role, which in turn is intimately associated with reform of the political system in China.

PART B

Consumer alternative dispute resolution

10. The origins and evolution of consumer dispute resolution systems in Europe

Naomi Creutzfeldt

I. INTRODUCTION: IDENTIFYING CDR

Alternative dispute resolution (ADR) is the umbrella term given to a set of methods for resolving disputes without the need for a determination by a court. This rather broad definition[1] includes various types of dispute resolution pathways and techniques that characterize the ADR landscape in the EU today.[2] The term ADR is used as a generic name, but causes confusion, since it can describe both a series of techniques and at least two different architectures within which those techniques are applied. Some greater clarity is required.

A variety of different but related ADR techniques has developed. These

---

1 The definition offered in EU documents is equally broad '. . . dispute resolution procedures which are designed as an alternative to resolving a dispute in a court. [. . .] It covers out-of-court mechanisms that lead to the settling of a dispute through the intervention of a third party', Consultation paper On the use of Alternative Dispute Resolution as a means to resolve disputes related to commercial transactions and practices in the European Union (2011); ('ADR entities') 'These entities aim at resolving, out-of-court, disputes arising between parties, through the intervention of an entity (eg arbitrator, conciliator, mediator, ombudsman, complaints board)', Regulation (EC) No 2006/2004 and Directive 2009/22/EC (Directive on consumer ADR) 2.

2 The focus of this chapter is on consumer to business (C2B) dispute resolution. See Christopher Hodges, Iris Benöhr and Naomi Creutzfeldt-Banda, *ADR in Europe* (Hart 2012); *Study on the Use of Alternative Dispute Resolution in the European Union* (Brussels, Civic Consulting 2009); Jules Stuyck, Evelyne Terryn, Veerle Colaert, Tom Van Dyck, Neil Peretz, Nele Hoekx and Piotr Tereszkiewicz, *Study on Alternative Means of Consumer Redress other than Redress Through Ordinary Judicial Proceedings* (Catholic University of Leuven, 17 January 2007) published April 2007, para 384, hereafter 'Leuven Study'.

techniques may include[3]: Arbitration, adjudication, mini-trial, binding advice, ombudsman procedure, conciliation, early neutral evaluation, facilitation, conciliation, fact-finding, negotiation, dialogue forums. Some or all of these techniques can be deployed within, or alongside, traditional court-based or arbitration-based dispute resolution systems.[4] But the focus of this chapter is on a separate architectural structure of dispute resolution that has emerged in Europe for the resolution of consumer-to-business (C2B) disputes.[5] That architecture typically involves in-house customer care functions, and external ombudsmen or dispute resolution schemes that form part of business sectors' codes of business practice. The new architecture has been referred to as 'Consumer ADR', but since use of the acronym ADR in that context can give rise to confusion over whether what is being described is ADR in the court-like context, it is preferable to use a different name: accordingly, in this chapter the acronym CDR is adopted for the new architecture. Almost all of the 'ADR techniques' can be found in the CDR schemes. Indeed, in many CDR models, there is a tiered structure of procedures, in which techniques are escalated, such as from direct negotiation, to mediation, with a final option of arbitration.[6] The process is influenced by the nature of a decision, if it is binding or non-binding on the parties.[7]

There is both considerable diversity of different approaches, architectures and techniques of CDR models across the EU, and also considerable similarities.[8] The current position is a kaleidoscope, but one that, Member States are agreed, offers considerable potential for effective

[3] See Klaus J Hopt and Felix Steffek (eds), *Mediation: Principles and Regulation in Comparative Perspective* (OUP 2012) 16; Christopher Hodges et al (supra note 2) 403–9.

[4] A list of different meanings of ADR was also published by the UK Office of Fair Trading in 2010, which includes: in-house complaints procedures, mediation, conciliation, arbitration, adjudication, ombudsman schemes and legal mechanisms. *Mapping UK Consumer Redress: A Summary Guide to Dispute Resolution Systems* (Office of Fair Trading 2010), <http://www.oft.gov.uk/shared_oft/general_policy/OFT1267.pdf> accessed 18 December 2012.

[5] See Christopher Hodges et al (supra note 2).

[6] See Iain Ramsay, 'Small Claims Courts in Canada: A Socio-legal Appraisal', in CJ Whelan, *Small Claims Courts. A Comparative Study* (Oxford Clarendon Press 1990).

[7] For different models see Christopher Hodges et al (supra note 2) 406, 407.

[8] 'The multiplicity and contradictory nature of the applied concepts in the legal systems indicate that a productive classification of the procedures requires moving beyond aspects of terminology to focus on functional distinctions', Klaus J Hopt and Felix Steffek (supra note 3) 16.

dispute resolution and hence for supporting the vibrancy of the EU market. A major watershed has been reached with the EU legislation on consumer ADR[9] and online dispute resolution (ODR).[10]

CDR has existed in parts of Europe for some decades, but has only recently become important at the level of European dispute resolution policy, and done so with considerable force. This chapter seeks to identify the origins of CDR in Europe, so as to give a better understanding of the forces at work and the strength of likely future developments. The key issue for the future is: will CDR fade away, or will it largely replace lawyers and courts, or will they continue to co-exist? The analysis here identifies a series of different origins, forces and developments that have collectively contributed to the growth of CDR. It looks at the failure of court-based civil procedure systems to deliver accessibility to justice for C2B disputes, the development of ADR techniques within civil procedure systems, cultural aspects that favour resolution of problems through collaborative rather than adversarial means, the impact of increasing regulation of the EU market and the importance of consumers in that market, the advent of new technology for both selling and dispute resolution (and the integration of these two modes), the impact of choice for consumers and businesses in relation to pathways for dispute resolution, and the ability of CDR systems to resolve mass problems better than court-based systems.

Each of these factors, and no doubt others, have contributed to the position today that CDR is on the verge of forming a central pathway, and probably the major if not exclusive pathway, for resolution of B2C disputes in Europe. Each factor has had an effect, and many have run in parallel (which makes analysis of the individual strands somewhat of a challenge). Although the factors are considered individually below, it is the congruence of all these factors that has given CDR its power, innovative force and enormous potential.

---

9 Directive 2013/11/EU of the European Parliament and of the Council of 21 May 2013 on alternative dispute resolution for consumer disputes and amending Regulation (EC) No 2006/2004 and Directive 2009/22/EC (Directive on consumer ADR) OJ 2013 L165/63.

10 Regulation (EU) No 524/2013 of the European Parliament and of the Council of 21 May 2013 on online dispute resolution for consumer disputes and amending Regulation (EC) No 2006/2004 and Directive 2009/22/EC (Regulation on consumer ODR) OJ 2013 L165/1.

II. TIMELINES IN THE DEVELOPMENT OF ADR

In order to explain the development of the ADR/CDR phenomenon, it is necessary to identify the major historical events and innovations. Various scholars have recognized that the techniques of what we currently call 'ADR' were regarded as merely 'normal DR' many centuries ago, and still exist today in many parts of the world, not only in aboriginal or tribal societies.[11]

The concept of an ombudsman as an out-of-court dispute resolution pathway originated in Sweden; a parliamentary ombudsman was established by the Swedish Constitution in 1809. The Parliament appointed a representative to deal with problems in the absence of the king. This was the birth of the public sector ombudsman, looking after the interests of both the king and of citizens by means of investigating complaints about maladministration. Following the Swedish example, the concept of a 'middle-man' between citizens and government institutions has become increasingly popular over recent decades to the point where it is now a highly significant and permanent feature of the legal systems in many parts of the world as a flexible and adjustable means to solve disputes. [12] This is significant, because it means every European state is familiar with a non-court investigative and dispute-resolution system as a general proposition, even though these are in the realm of public/administrative law, for disputes between citizens challenging the state. The EU established the institution of a European ombudsman in 1995 as a means for citizens to raise complaints about EU administration. In the late 20th century, the private ombudsman model was established on a similar notion to counteract the imbalance of powers between consumers and business. A form of private sector ombudsmen exists in every EU Member State today.[13]

A major breakaway from courts in providing an alternative pathway for civil disputes was arbitration. The world of arbitration was established for commercial disputes for reasons mainly to do with confidentiality, but also in some cases reducing cost. This method was so successful and widely adopted that it is the primary means of resolving commercial disputes of

---

11 Michael Palmer and Simon Roberts, *Dispute Processes – ADR and the Primary Forms of Decision Making* (Butterworths 1998).

12 See Trevor Buck, Richard Kirkham and Brian Thompson, *Ombudsman Enterprise and Administrative Justice* (Ashgate 2010); Mary Seneviratne, *Ombudsmen Public Services and Administrative Justice* (Butterworths LexisNexis 2002).

13 <http://ec.europa.eu/consumers/redress_cons/schemes_en.htm> accessed 15 January 2013.

any size. Well-established arbitration systems operate in parallel with court systems.

In Europe, development of non-court ADR pathways (CDR) started to occur in the 1960s. It cannot have been coincidental that the rise of consumerism, expressed within the expansion of consumer protection law and rights, occurred at that time. The evolution of CDR does not seem to have been linked particularly with dissatisfaction with the courts. In all the Nordic states, CDR procedures emerged *instead of* courts for consumer disputes, alongside consumer advice mechanisms. In the Netherlands, the *Geschillencommissie* complaint boards developed from the 1960s as an inherent part of the unique national architecture by which standard terms and conditions for business practice within a sector were agreed under the aegis of the State Council, and negotiated between the consumers' association(s) and the trade association for each relevant business sector. Over 40 years, more and more sectors joined this model until by 2012 roughly 50 sectors were covered, each with its own dispute resolution board (and in the financial services sector also an ombudsman as an extra initial tier).[14] These Nordic and Dutch CDR systems for C2B disputes all initially adopted an arbitration panel model, but added on conciliation techniques as a first stage. In the Nordic states, the determination of the arbitration panel has not been binding on either party, whereas in the Netherlands it only occurs pursuant to a formal arbitration agreement, which is therefore binding on both parties. Arbitration models also developed in Spain and Portugal.

Ombudsmen models began to emerge from 1986 in the United Kingdom's financial services sectors (merged in 2000 into the statutory Financial Ombudsmen Service),[15] and in Germany with the Insurance Ombudsman in 2001. In both those countries, the model was seen to work and was copied for other sectors in the later 2000s. The ombudsman model incorporated an initial conciliation stage followed by a decision stage, even if in many cases the decision was not binding.

An ombudsman model is based on a permanent structure headed by an individual. An alternative model involves a dispute resolution function that is 'attached' to a business code of practice, typically operated by a particular trade association for its members. This model grew strongly in the UK from the 1970s, spurred by increasingly competitive markets and rising

---

14 See Franziska Weber and Christopher Hodges 'The Netherlands' in Hodges et al (supra note 2) Ch 6.

15 See Naomi Creutzfeldt-Banda, Christopher Hodges and Iris Benöhr 'The United Kingdom' in Hodges et al (supra note 2) Ch 11.

standards of consumer expectations. The Dutch 'standard terms and conditions' model is identical in function to the British 'code of practice' model. The British CDR-with-code model again typically adopted arbitration by independent panels or individuals (usually barristers), and increasingly also adopted conciliation as a first stage.[16] A leading example was created for the travel sector by ABTA as far back as the 1950s. By the 1990s, British trade codes were seen to be self-serving for their traders and not to offer sufficient protection for consumers. The result was concerted formal pressure to raise standards by establishing an official benchmark standard for the contents of codes and their associated dispute resolution functions.[17]

It will be seen that there remains no standard approach to the architecture of CDR within the various schemes in the Member States. Similarly, there is no standard approach on adoption of techniques (arbitration, conciliation, etc). National CDR Systems are still developing and flexible, as are their techniques, procedures and sector coverage. But there is a strong trend towards a tiered model based on the stages of traders' in-house customer care schemes, triage and conciliation by a third party body, and finally a determination on the merits by an independent person or panel.[18]

III. ALTERNATIVE DISPUTE RESOLUTION WITHIN THE ACCESS TO JUSTICE THEORY

In the late 20th century, emerging markets and the wave of liberalization and privatization of public services that occurred in the western world led to the introduction of alternatives to the state judicial system.[19] The access to justice literature provides a theoretical framework for the debate about alternative dispute resolution. In the 1970s, Cappelletti saw ADR as 'the third wave' of development of 'access to justice in modern societies', as part of the international access to justice movement:[20]

---

16 Ibid.

17 Consumer Codes Approval Scheme: Core Criteria and Guidance 2008 <www.oft.gov.uk/shared_oft/Approvedcodesofpractice/oft390.pdf> accessed 20 November 2012.

18 See Christopher Hodges et al (supra note 2) 359.

19 Loukas A Mistelis, 'ADR in England and Wales: A Successful Case of Public Private Partnership' in Nadja M Alexander (ed), *Global Trends in Mediation* (Kluwer Law International 2nd ed 2006) 139–80.

20 Mauro Cappelletti and Bryant Garth (eds), *Access to Justice in the Welfare State* (European University Institute 1981); Mauro Cappelletti, 'Alternative Dispute Resolution Processes within the Framework of the World-Wide Access-to-Justice Movement' (1993) 56 *Modern Law Review* 3, 282–96.

> The access-to-justice movement, as a theoretical approach, while certainly rooted in the realistic criticism of formalism and legal dogmatic, tends toward a vision more faithful to the complexity of human society. While the normative component of the law is not denied, it is seen as one element, and quite often not even the principal one of the law. The primary element is the people, with all their cultural, economic and psychological features. Moreover, the institutions and processes are prominent in this realistic vision. The result of the access-to-justice approach is a 'contextual' conception of the law.[21]

This horizontal approach of law in context focuses on the right to effective access to justice[22] as a basic requirement, 'the most basic human right, of a system which claims to guarantee legal rights' for citizens. For the first time in EU law, the concept of access to justice was constitutionalized in the Lisbon Treaty.[23] Further, a recognition of ADR as an important part of civil procedure was established.[24]

IV. ADR WITHIN CIVIL PROCEDURE

Undoubtedly, national CDR Systems and their procedures have been influenced by the developing concepts of what an ADR/CDR pathway would look like in the specific national context. Courts, as the main setting in which justice is sought, are subject to well-established norms.[25] Within the relatively young standards that apply to the CDR approach, rules and quality criteria are still to be clearly defined and established, and interlinked with the standards that apply to courts or any other form of dispute resolution.

The expansion of ADR within traditional dispute resolution mechanisms, namely civil procedure and court systems, in the second half of the

---

21 Mauro Cappalletti (supra note 20) 283.

22 See Lisbon Treaty, chapter 3 *Judicial Cooperation in Civil Matters*, Article 65 6; Article 6 of the European Convention of Human Rights guarantees the right to access to justice and a fair trial.

23 Detailed discussion: Maria Elvira Mendez Pinedo, 'Access to Justice as Hope in the Dark in Search for a New Concept in European Law' (2011) 1 *International Journal of Humanities and Social Sciences* no 19; Eva Storskrubb, *Civil Procedure and EU Law: A Policy Area Uncovered, Studies in European Law* (OUP 2008).

24 Mauro Cappelletti (supra note 20) 287 et seq; Mauro Cappelletti and Bryant Garth, 'Access to Justice: The Newest Wave in the Worldwide Movement to Make Rights Effective' (1978) 27 *Buffalo Law Review* 181.

25 Denis Galligan, *Due Process and Fair Procedures: A Study of Administrative Procedures* (Clarendon Press 1996).

20th century gathered momentum in the United States of America before it did in Europe.[26] The motivation in the US was a common criticism of the role of the state and its institutions which, in turn, led to general questioning of conceptions of judgment and settlement in the 1960s.[27] In the next decade, the debate shifted towards the disadvantages of court trials and adjudication and the benefits of settlement.[28] The notion of informal justice and the critique of informalism entered the debate in the 1980s.[29] The debate focused on the context of resolving disputes avoiding lawyers and without reference to the law,[30] and the term 'ADR' spread.[31] A further impact of this wider debate was that academic lawyers began to refer to dispute 'processes' rather than litigation or adjudication, and that the word 'dispute' acquired a wider meaning.[32]

In Europe, some jurisdictions became increasingly dissatisfied with the efficiency of their national civil procedure systems. The cost problem of court litigation became acute in a number of jurisdictions.[33] This was not a particular issue in Germany or Austria, which have enjoyed efficient and low-cost civil procedure systems since the 19th century. But it was a problem for England and Wales, and even for various other civil law jurisdictions. Debate about ADR in the UK was fully developed in the 1990s with a focus on litigation mania[34] and a crisis in civil justice, which constituted a serious threat to maintaining access to justice.[35] Reforms of

---

26 Mauro Cappelletti and Bryant Garth (supra note 20) 142–8.

27 Michael Palmer and Simon Roberts (supra note 11) 25–6.

28 Warren E Burger, 'Agenda for 2000 ADR – Need for Systematic Anticipation', (1976) 70 *Federal Rules Decisions* 92–4.

29 Mirjan R Damaska, *The Faces of Justice and State Authority* (Yale University Press 1986); Richard L Abel (ed), *The Politics of Informal Justice, vol 1: The American Experience; vol 2: Comparative Studies* (Academic Press 1982).

30 James S Auerbach, *Justice without Law? Resolving Disputes Without Lawyers* (OUP 1983); Derek Bok, 'A Flawed System of Law and Practice Training' (1983) 33 *Journal of Legal Education* 570–85; Leonard L Riskin and James Westbrook, *Dispute Resolution and Lawyers* (West 1987); J S Murray, A S Rau and E Sherman, *Processes of Dispute Resolution: The Role of Lawyers* (Foundation Press 2nd ed 1996).

31 Michael Palmer and Simon Roberts (supra note 11) 25–6; Deborah Hensler, 'Our Courts, Ourselves: How the Alternative Dispute Resolution Movement is Reshaping our Legal System', (2003) 108 *Penn State Law Review* 165–97.

32 Peter Stein, *Legal Institutions: The Development of Dispute Settlement* (Butterworths 1984).

33 Christopher Hodges, Stefan Vogenauer and Magdalena Tulibacka, *The Costs and Funding of Civil Litigation: A Comparative Perspective* (Hart 2010).

34 Brian Markesinis, 'Litigation-Mania in England, Germany and the USA: Are We So Very Different?' (1990) 49 (2) *Cambridge Law Journal* 233–76.

35 Adrian S. Zuckerman, *Civil Justice in Crisis. Comparative Perspectives of Civil*

civil procedure stimulated not only the development of ADR schemes but also the formal incorporation of mediation and similar techniques (under the title of ADR) into the civil procedure system.[36] For example, the major reforms of the civil procedure system introduced through the Civil Procedural Rules in 1999 were made under the title of reforming 'access to justice'.[37]

From the late 1990s, the attention of the European Commission began to be directed to civil justice issues, and the fact that disparities in national civil procedure systems constituted barriers to trade, and hindered cross-border trade because they impeded cross-border dispute resolution. A slow programme of harmonization had begun.[38] As part of this process, mediation was mandated to be incorporated into all national civil procedure systems from 2012 under an EU Mediation Directive.[39]

However, the trend under which national court systems became increasingly unable to handle small consumer claims, because the procedures were too expensive or slow or not user-friendly, only continued unsolved. Attempts at both national levels and at EU level to introduce further procedural reforms continued. One example was the small claims procedure.[40] However, this has not been a notable success, at least for cross-border claims: the recent ECC Report[41] shows that the EU Small Claims mechanism has not been taken up by users in significant numbers. It is too bureaucratic, not user-friendly and uncertain.

Procedure (OUP 1999); Hazel Genn, *Paths to Justice: What People Do and Think About Going to Law* (Hart 1999); Hazel Genn and Alan Paterson, *Paths to Justice Scotland: What People in Scotland Think and Do about Going to Law* (Hart 2001).

36 Erhard Blankenburg, 'The Infrastructure for Avoiding Civil Litigation: Comparing Cultures of Legal Behavior in The Netherlands and West Germany' (1994) 28 *Law & Society Review* (4) 789–808.

37 Lord Woolf, *Access to Justice – Interim Report to the Lord Chancellor on the Civil Justice System in England and Wales* (The Stationery Office June 1995) ch 1; *Final Report – Access to Justice* (July 1996). Key problems Lord Woolf identified in the interim report in 1995 were cost, delay and uncertainty. In 1996 the report suggested a restructuring of the rules of civil procedure, implemented as the CPR in 1999.

38 Eva Storskrubb (supra note 23); Christopher Hodges, 'Europeanisation of Civil Justice: Trends and Issues' (2006) 1 *Civil Justice Quarterly* 96–123.

39 Directive 2008/52/EC on certain aspects of mediation in civil and commercial matters [2008] OJ L 136/3; Klaus J Hopt and Felix Steffek (supra note 3).

40 Council Regulation (EC) 861/2007 establishing a European small claims procedure [2007] OJ L199/1.

41 ECC-NET European Small Claims Procedure (Report September 2012). <http://ec.europa.eu/consumers/ecc/docs/small_claims_210992012_en.pdf> accessed 20 November 2012.

The absence of a clearly efficient option for resolution of small and consumer claims was a strong spur to the development of CDR. We therefore need to examine the place of CDR within the development of consumer protection: the 2011 CDR initiative was after all instituted by DG SANCO rather than DG JUSTICE.

V. BUSINESS DRIVERS TO SPREAD CDR

The overall level of consumer detriment, as reported by consumers, was estimated in 2012 to be £3.08 billion in the UK alone.[42] Studies found that there is a clear barrier for consumers to seek redress, due to duration, cost and complex procedures of courts which, as a result, does not allow effective access to justice.[43]

Consumer confidence is an essential ingredient to good business. There are some striking examples of how business sectors have realized that provision of effective dispute resolution systems has been necessary to maintain consumer trust and relationships. First, the German insurance sector concluded that insurance issues were too complicated for consumers to understand how to navigate through them, and there was a need to maintain relationships with customers rather than see them break down whenever any issue arose. This led the sector to establish a very successful ombudsman scheme.[44] Many countries now have CDR systems for insurance and financial services, the former underpinned by EIOPA Guidelines on Best Practices in Complaints Handling by Insurance Undertakings.[45]

A second example occurred in the UK motor sector, the Office of Fair Trading (OFT) claimed that millions of pounds were lost by consumers because there was a high volume of complaints about the motor sector registered by Consumer Direct and Trading Standards officials. The OFT challenged the Society of Motor Manufacturers and Traders (SMMT)[46]

---

[42] Consumer Focus Report, *Consumer Detriment 2012* <http://www.consumerfocus.org.uk/files/2012/10/TNS-for-Consumer-Focus-Consumer-Detriments-20121.pdf> accessed 28 November 2012.

[43] DG SANCO Study on the use of Alternative Dispute Resolution in the EU (Berlin Civic Consulting 2009); Leuven Study (2007).

[44] See Iris Benöhr, Christopher Hodges and Naomi Creutzfeldt-Banda, 'Germany' in Hodges et al (supra note 2) Ch 4.

[45] Guidelines on Complaints Handling by Insurance Undertakings (EIOPABoS 12/069); Report on Best Practices by Insurance Undertakings in Handling Complaints (EIOPABoS 12/070) (2012).

[46] SMMT is an independent trade association that has promoted the interests of the UK automotive manufacturers since 1902. The motor vehicle trade associa-

to reduce the high level of complaints. In 2005 the National Consumer Council[47] threatened to institute a competition law super-complaint[48] against the car sector over service and repair problems. This resulted in the creation of a series of modernized codes for the industry. Talks between OFT, SMMT and the government led to the creation of a conciliation scheme within the new car code (the service and repair code and the vehicle warranty products code followed) that covered the whole industry. They then went through the CCAS approval stages.[49]

In a third example, the UK trade association for the consumer package travel sector, ABTA, established a Code of Conduct from the 1950s to distinguish its members from their competitors and to help ensure high standards of customer service. It also had the added bonus for members of ensuring that they had not inadvertently broken the law as it incorporates all relevant legal requirements. The code enables ABTA to enforce self-regulatory pressure on its members; if the members are in breach of the code then a code investigation can be opened. The code now operates according to Directive 90/314/EEC on Package Travel and Holiday Tours in the Domestic Legislation of EC Member States.[50]

Individual businesses with major brands to protect have also developed in-house dispute resolution facilities as part of their 'customer care' facilities, to maintain their reputations and market shares.[51] These trends have occurred in parallel with the geographical expansion of markets, and the rise of standards of quality and safety for products and services. A parallel example is the development not just of the 'front end' of enhanced selling techniques but also the 'back end' of the development of product recall systems from the 1990s.[52] Now, *all* big retailers with major brand reputations to maintain seek extensive and constant feedback from their customer base about their products and services (good or bad) so they can react accordingly. In-house 'customer care' and complaint departments

---

tions developed codes of practice in the 1970s. Since the creation of the CCAS the codes have been updated or created to gain OFT recognition.

47 Now part of Consumer Focus.

48 Under the Enterprise Act 2002 s 11.

49 The Consumer Codes Approval Scheme (CCAS) is run by OFT. <http://www.oft.gov.uk/OFTwork/consumer-protection/campaign11-12/consumercode> accessed 5 December 2012.

50 The Package Travel Directive (PTD) came into effect in 1990 and its provisions were introduced into UK law through the Package Travel Regulations (PTR) in 1992.

51 Christopher Hodges, 'Best Practice in Customer Care in the UK' in Christopher Hodges et al (supra note 2) Ch 12.

52 See Directive 2001/95/EC on general product safety [2002] OJ L11/4.

within many large traders have become substantial in size and sophistication, and highly effective in attracting and resolving customer issues (e.g. Boots the Chemist in the UK[53]).

Business lawyers report that an important motivation for the development of these examples of 'in-house ADR' and CDR was specifically to prevent disputes escalating, increasing the costs of resolution through involving lawyers and courts, in trying to prevent problems appearing in the media, and especially to retain customers. In recent years, whilst some sectors believe they can handle almost all customer issues in-house and very rarely receive a court proceeding, some others increasingly realize that having an external long-stop of a more formal national CDR scheme can be beneficial to avoid lawyers and courts, and retain customer adherence. These considerations have led the CDR phenomenon to spread horizontally across Member States. There are some core sectors where CDR is surprisingly consistent across states, such as insurance, financial services, telecommunications, energy, travel, motor vehicles and motor hire.

VI. CONSUMER PROTECTION IN THE EU SINGLE MARKET

The development of EU consumer protection legislation since the 1960s is well known.[54] For many years, attention was directed exclusively at substantive rules of consumer protection law. Recently, however, concern has arisen about redress, and how the rules are to be enforced. These issues were heightened by focusing on the economic power that consumer purchasing can bring to generating growth and employment in the internal market. Accordingly, enhancing consumer redress became a concern of the European Commission. Initial EU consumer legislation on redress focused on enforcement measures, such as the Injunctions Directive[55] and the administrative enforcement system (the CPC Regulation).[56]

A special Eurobarometer on consumer empowerment in 2011 found that only 2 per cent of European consumers who encounter a problem end up

---

[53] Christopher Hodges (supra note 51).

[54] Stephan Weatherill and Geraint Howells, *Consumer Protection Law (Markets and the Law)* (Ashgate 2nd ed 2005).

[55] Directive 98/27/EC on injunctions for the protection of consumers' interests [1998] OJ L 166/51.

[56] Regulation (EC) No 2006/2004 on cooperation between national authorities responsible for the enforcement of consumer protection laws (the Regulation on consumer protection cooperation) [2004] OJ L364/1.

taking this to a court.[57] Reasons for this vary; for example, the consumers might have already found a solution for their problem through contacting the seller, and some state that the sum in question is too small to justify the effort to invest time and money. One explanation is that consumers do not like courts.[58] There is a lack of trust; a feeling of inferiority to business; anxiety about the complex and formal court process, and the costs involved. All these factors pose a psychological barrier leading consumers to avoid courts. In contrast, an ADR/CDR procedure is less formal and 'people appear to value the opportunity to present their case in a less constrained manner than is often possible in courts'.[59]

The considerable size of the EU single consumer market makes it essential to find appropriate mechanisms to solve disputes. The EU Consumer Commissioner said in 2012, 'Consumers who want to take advantage of the opportunities offered by the Single Market need to be able to rely on a variety of effective and efficient means of redress'.[60]

As discussed above, civil procedure systems in EU Member States have not managed to establish effective avenues to justice that can provide remedies for small claims,[61] despite recent changes of introducing a mediation directive[62] and a cross-border European small claims procedure.[63] The main challenges for cross-border transactions are differences in legislation between Member States, language barriers and varying costs. This, in turn,

---

57 Special Eurobarometer 342 Consumer Empowerment (2011) 184 <http://ec.europa.eu/consumers/consumer_empowerment/docs/report_eurobarometer_342_en.pdf> accessed 20 November 2012.

58 Hazel Genn, *Paths to Justice: What People Do and Think About Going to Law* (Hart 1999); 'How Europeans Trust Courts and Police' (People in Nordic countries have a high level of trust in the police and courts, while people in Eastern European countries tend to be the least trusting of justice institutions, according to recent findings from the ESRC-supported European Social Survey, 14 February 2012) findings from the ESRC-supported European Social Survey (ESS) <http://www.esrc.ac.uk/impacts-and-findings/features-casestudies/features/19793/how-europeans-trust-courts-and-police.aspx> accessed 7 December 2012.

59 Richard A Enslen, 'ADR: Another Acronym or a Variable Alternative to the High Cost of Litigation and Crowded Court Dockets? The Debate Commences' (1988) 18 *New Mexico Law Review* 1.

60 See (supra note 41) John Dalli (European Commissioner for Health and Consumer Policy) 6.

61 See Christopher Hodges, 'New Modes of Redress for Consumers: ADR and Regulation' *Oxford Legal Studies Research Paper No. 57/2012* University of Oxford – Centre for Socio-Legal Studies 2012 <http://papers.ssrn.com/sol3/papers.cfm?abstract_id=2126485> accessed 20 December 2012.

62 Directive 2008/52/EC.

63 Regulation (EC) 861/2007.

has a wider impact on access to justice for EU citizens,[64] a fundamental right that faces many challenges, one basic one being that citizens do not know about alternative pathways and therefore do not use them, or the pathways do not yet exist.[65]

From around 2000, the EU started to establish cross-border networks specialized in facilitating dispute resolution, whether through the courts or any ADR option. The European Consumer Centre Network[66] (ECC-NET) consists of 29 centres throughout Europe, including Iceland and Norway. The aim of the Network is to provide information on consumer rights in Europe and assist in cross-border disputes.[67] Although ECC offices were intended, initially, to refer consumers to court systems, they quickly found that CDR systems were far more effective, and they themselves began to develop a strong facilitative mediation-conciliation role, avoiding courts.

FIN-NET is a financial ADR network covering the EU, Iceland, Liechtenstein and Norway. They handle disputes between consumers and financial services providers. FIN-NET was launched by the European Commission in 2001. By the end of 2011, FIN-NET had 56 members, national ADR schemes, covering 21 Member States' financial sectors.[68]

Debate about mass disputes, involving multiple consumers who have the same issue with one or a small number of traders, has been strong since the mid 2000s.[69] The initial focus was firmly on collective action procedures in courts, but the more people looked at the class action paradigm of the US, the more concern rose over issues of the potential for abuse arising out of

---

[64] The special Eurobarometer 195 *European Union Citizens and Access to Justice* (2004) found that citizens experienced limits to access to justice through the cost of the legal procedure in comparison to the value of the product or service.

[65] Study on the use of Alternative Dispute Resolution in the European Union of 16 October 2009 <http://ec.europa.eu/consumers/redress_cons/adr_study.pdf> accessed 15 December 2012 56–63; 112–15; 120–1.

[66] The ECC network is a result of the merger in 2005 of the two existing consumer protection networks: the Network for the extra-judicial settlement of consumer disputes (EEJ-Net) and the Network of Euroguichets <http://ec.europa.eu/consumers/redress_cons/> accessed 25 November 2012.

[67] The number of cases handled by the ECC-Net is consistently high. In total, the ECC-Net has helped consumers in about 416,000 cases since its creation in 2005.

[68] See European Commission FIN-NET activity report 2011 (Brussels June 2012) <http://ec.europa.eu/internal_market/fin-net/docs/activity/2011_en.pdf> accessed 17 December 2012.

[69] Christopher Hodges, *The Reform of Class and Representative Actions in European Legal Systems: A New Framework for Collective Redress in Europe* (Hart 2008).

conflicts of interest and high costs of intermediaries, and delay.[70] The fact that various existing CDR systems were, meanwhile, delivering effective, swift and cheap collective redress to consumers was noted. For example, the UK Financial Ombudsman Service handled 1,012,371 initial enquiries and complaints from consumers between April 2010 and March 2011, of which 104,597 were about payment protection insurance.[71] Their systems can identify trends and cases that are similar in nature and group them into mass cases. This led to the realization that the real practical and effective solution to the issue of consumer redress lies not with court procedures and collective actions but with CDR, and was a major influence in the European Commission's CDR/ODR proposals of 2011.

VII. ADR AS PART OF THE REGULATION OF EUROPEAN MARKET SECTORS

The creation of the EU single market inherently relies on the creation of harmonized regulatory structures.[72] As the EU has adopted regulation, it was anticipated that the imposition of a raft of new regulatory requirements and rising standards would give rise to a potential for a large number of consumer disputes with traders. In addition, when an ADR mechanism is linked with regulatory and other market control mechanisms, significant data on market behaviour is captured and fed back to regulators and the market. This feedback mechanism can provide a powerful means of behaviour control of traders, triggering regulatory enforcement, and raising standards.[73]

The legislation creating the regulatory structures has increasingly included a requirement for traders to have a dispute resolution function, and it has adopted the 'ADR model' for the resolution of these C2B

---

70 For more detail about why collective actions have not been brought in European jurisdictions: Rebecca Money-Kyrle and Christopher Hodges, 'European Collective Action: Towards Coherence?' (2012) *Maastricht Journal of European and Comparative Law* 477–504.

71 Financial Ombudsman Services Annual Review 2010/11 <http://www.financial-ombudsman.org.uk/publications/ar11/index.html> accessed 10 January 2013.

72 Giandomenico Majone, *Regulating Europe* (Routledge 1996); Fabrizzio Cafaggi and Horatia Muir Watt (eds), *The Regulatory Function of European Private Law* (Edward Elgar 2009).

73 Christopher Hodges, Iris Benöhr and Naomi Creutzfeldt-Banda, 'Consumer-to-business Dispute Resolution: The Power of CADR' (2012) 13 *ERA Forum*, 199–225.

disputes, first *encouraging* and later *requiring* traders to have ADR facilities.[74] During the last decade, detailed regulatory requirements have spread across all the major business sectors of the single market, and with them 'ADR' (which can now be seen to be CDR). The sectors involved encompass financial services, telecoms, postal services and energy.

An example of the difficulty of finding a definition for ADR/CDR is mirrored in the use of language that the directives apply. They take a very broad approach to what ADR is, leaving a lot of scope for interpretation. For example, the sectors in which ADR mechanisms are *required* (telecom[75]; energy[76]; consumer credit[77]; and payment services[78]) are shown in Box 10.1.

BOX 10.1 REQUIREMENTS FOR OUT-OF-COURT DISPUTE SETTLEMENT IN EU SECTORAL REGULATION

Telecom (2009/136/EC)

Article 34(1) 'Member States shall ensure that transparent, non-discriminatory, simple and inexpensive out-of-court procedures are available for dealing with unresolved disputes between consumers and undertakings providing electronic communications networks and/or services arising under this Directive and relating to the contractual conditions and/or performance of contracts concerning the supply of those networks and/or services. Member States shall adopt measures to ensure that such procedures enable disputes to be settled fairly and promptly and may, where

[74] See Iris Benöhr, 'Consumer ADR at EU level' in Christopher Hodges et al (supra note 2) 10.

[75] Directive 2009/136/EC amending Directive 2002/22/EC on universal service and users' rights relating to electronic communications networks and services, Directive 2002/58/EC concerning the processing of personal data and the protection of privacy in the electronic communications sector and Regulation (EC) No 2006/2004 on cooperation between national authorities responsible for the enforcement of consumer protection laws [2009] OJ L 337/11.

[76] Directive 2009/72/EC concerning common rules for the internal market in electricity and repealing Directive 2003/54/EC [2009] OJ L 211/55.

[77] Directive 2008/48/EC on credit agreements for consumers and repealing Council Directive 87/102/EEC [2008] OJ L133/66.

[78] Directive 2007/64/EC on payment services in the internal market amending Directives 97/7/EC, 2002/65/EC, 2005/60/EC and 2006/48/EC and repealing Directive 97/5/EC [2007] OJ L 319/1.

warranted, adopt a system of reimbursement and/or compensation. Such procedures shall enable disputes to be settled impartially and shall not deprive the consumer of the legal protection afforded by national law. Member States may extend these obligations to cover disputes involving other end-users.'

Energy (2009/72/EC)
Article 13 'Member States shall ensure that an independent mechanism such as an energy ombudsman or a consumer body is in place in order to ensure efficient treatment of complaints and out-of-court dispute settlements.'

Consumer Credit (2008/48/EC)
Article 24 Out-of-court dispute resolution: 'Member States shall ensure that adequate and effective out-of-court dispute resolution procedures for the settlement of consumer disputes concerning credit agreements are put in place, using existing bodies where appropriate. Member States shall encourage those bodies to cooperate in order to also resolve cross-border disputes concerning credit agreements.'

Payment Services (2007/64/EC)
Article 83 Out-of-court redress: 'Member States shall ensure that adequate and effective out-of-court complaint and redress procedures for the settlement of disputes between payment service users and their payment service providers are put in place for disputes concerning rights and obligations arising under this Directive, using existing bodies where appropriate. In the case of cross-border disputes, Member States shall make sure that those bodies cooperate actively in resolving them.'

Regardless of the broad account of what an ADR/CDR scheme is, a central aspect of the sectoral regulation is that the regulators (transport, financial services, telecom and energy) play an important role in watching the market. This is backed by EU legislation that gives regulators more powers to 'issue binding decisions, carry out investigations and impose effective, proportionate and dissuasive penalties'.[79] In the energy sector, for example, the regulators have powers and duties to monitor the

[79] See Directives No 2009/72/EC and No 2009/73/EC [2009] OJ L 211 55, 94.

development of competition and to ensure improved consumer protection and information.

This phenomenon has been largely invisible to anyone who is not familiar with the structure and workings of each respective sector (people who specialize in financial services know about financial CDR, and so on, but not necessarily about energy), so the quiet spread of CDR across many sectors has until recently been almost invisible. This 'vertical CDR spread' can now be seen, especially when joined up with the 2011 horizontal consumer ADR proposals, as constituting a coherent pan-EU CDR matrix. The aim of the ADR directive[80] and ODR regulation[81] is to create a full horizontal ADR coverage throughout the Union which will enable consumers to enjoy the benefit of the European single market and feel protected when buying goods and services.

VIII. ONLINE TRADING AND ODR

The Internet has created a world of online trade and e-commerce. This constantly growing market,[82] like any other market, relies on consumer satisfaction and trust to work effectively. However, there are perceived difficulties in resolving complaints relating to online transactions (domestic and cross-border) that are obstructing the growth of the market.[83] Similar to the reasons discussed above why ADR/CDR poses an attractive alternative pathway for resolving low value disputes, online dispute resolution (ODR) is better suited to e-commerce complaints than the regular court system. One of the key issues addressed in the Digital Agenda for Europe,[84] launched by the Commission in 2010, is consumer protection. Within this, one objective is to improve ADR systems and propose an

---

[80] Directive 2013/11/EU of the European Parliament and of the Council of 21 May 2013 on alternative dispute resolution for consumer disputes and amending Regulation (EC) No 2006/2004 and Directive 2009/22/EC (Directive on consumer ADR) OJ 2013 L165/63.

[81] Regulation (EU) No 524/2013 of the European Parliament and of the Council of 21 May 2013 on online dispute resolution for consumer disputes and amending Regulation (EC) No 2006/2004 and Directive 2009/22/EC (Regulation on consumer ODR) OJ 2013 L165/1.

[82] Commission Staff Working Document Report on cross-border e-commerce in the EU SEC(2009)283 final.

[83] See Pablo Cortes, 'Developing Online Dispute Resolution for Consumers in the EU: A Proposal for the Regulation of Accredited Providers' (2010) 19 *International Journal of Law and Information Technology* 1.

[84] COM (2010) 245 A digital agenda for Europe.

EU-wide online redress tool for e-commerce and improve access to justice online:[85]

> Fragmented digital markets
> Europe is still a patchwork of national online markets, and Europeans are prevented by solvable problems from enjoying the benefits of a digital single market. Commercial and cultural content and services need to flow across borders; this should be achieved by eliminating regulatory barriers and facilitating electronic payments and invoicing, dispute resolution and customer trust. More can and must be done under the current regulatory framework to weave a single market in the telecoms sector.[86]

ODR[87] developed out of, and is based on, ADR, in particular arbitration; ODR represents the merging of IT and ADR. Common ODR methods for B2C disputes involve automated negotiation, assisted negotiation, mediation, arbitration and small claims court procedures.[88] For both ADR and ODR alike there is no single method that would be applicable to all types of consumer complaints. This produces a variety of approaches and different methods throughout the Member States. ODR is widely used by private online companies such as eBay, PayPal and Amazon.[89] Arguably, they would not have been so successful without the confidence-building support of an online DR system to support the online trading system. Therefore the European Commission has adopted ODR as an idea because it wants strongly to support the development of digital trading within the EU. Additionally, UNCITRAL is deliberating on an ODR system for global e-commerce[90].

In light of the requirements for a pan-EU ODR platform, it makes sense to use and build upon models that are already in place. The ODR regulation applies to cross-border (trader is in Members State A and consumer resides in Member State B when purchasing the product[91]) e-commerce disputes. Consequently, the proposal suggests that ECC-NET carries out

---

85 Ibid 13.

86 Ibid 5.

87 See: Julia Hörnle, *Cross-Border Internet Dispute Resolution* (Cambridge University Press 2009); Pablo Cortes *Online Dispute Resolution for Consumers in the European Union* (Routledge 2011).

88 Pablo Cortes (supra note 87) Ch 20.

89 See: Colin Rule, *Online Dispute Resolution For Business: B2B, E-Commerce, Consumer, Employment, Insurance, and other Commercial Conflicts* (John Wiley & Sons 2002); Ethan Katsh and Janet Rifkin, *Online Dispute Resolution* (Jossey-Bass 2001).

90 <http://www.uncitral.org/pdf/english/workinggroups/wg_3/26th_WG_III/wp_117_e.pdf>.

91 See definition COM(2011) 794, Draft article 4 (e).

the function of being the 'keeper of the ODR gateway' and collecting all the complaints and then delegating to national ADR schemes and/or accredited ODR providers. Cross-border trade is being slowed down by the lack of effective means to resolve disputes.[92] This, in effect, translates into no appropriate access to justice for European consumers. ADR/ODR can fill this gap.

IX. NATIONAL CULTURES OF SETTLEMENT

In considering both the historical development and the ongoing endeavour of creating EU-CDR, it is important to draw attention to the specific and significant differences in national cultural approaches to settlement of disputes. These differences have clearly shaped the architecture and influenced the development of the various national models. Equally, in the process of harmonization of legal requirements in the EU, the contextual approach cannot ignore national and cultural complexities that are in a continuous process of change and development. In other words, an important part of understanding the challenges to a harmonized pan-EU approach is to consider nationally distinctive sets of legal cultures.[93] Legal culture (and political culture) is made up of a mixture of institutions and behaviour patterns:

> Political and legal culture inform specific institutional arrangements and at times give them meaning. Culture, including political and legal culture, is never static. It may inform the specific institutional arrangements, but, in turn, it is itself informed, shaped, and modified by the arrangements in a continuous cycle of interaction.[94]

National (legal) culture plays a big part in the process of building a system that is compatible and useable throughout the EU respecting its diversity. Legal culture is often viewed as the foundation for unique characteristics of a legal system, on which CDR is based and developed. Taking the national context into consideration helps understand why the ADR/CDR models have developed the diverse ways they have. The cultural approach to dispute settlement plays a role in consumers' basic expectation and

---

92 Ibid 7.

93 David Nelken, 'Defining and Using the Concept of Legal Culture' in E Örücü and David Nelken (eds), *Comparative Law: A Handbook* (Hart 2007).

94 Joseph Weiler, 'The Political and Legal Culture of European Integration: An Exploratory Essay' (2011) 9 *Int J Constitutional Law* 678–94.

acceptance of a DR model. The following examples demonstrate this. The Nordic countries and the Netherlands have a clear approach towards settlement rather than adversarial solutions to disputes. This is mirrored in the similarity of the ADR/CDR systems in the Nordic countries. Sweden's consumer protection forms a large part of a general (cultural) approach of avoiding courts and being in favour of settlement.[95] As a result Sweden has a wide range of alternative methods to resolve consumer disputes, almost none of which go through courts, and an associated range of no-fault compensation schemes. Similarly, the Netherlands has a strong national culture of settlement. There is comprehensive ADR/CDR sector coverage, through the *Geschillencommissie* (consumer complaints boards), a centrally organized structure. It provides quality and standard control as well as flexibility to accommodate sectorial variations.[96] Further, there is a 'solidarity-like' approach of negotiation between consumers and trade associations. The origins of this approach could derive from a cultural trait of conflict-avoiding approaches to disputes,[97] as well as a clearly identifiable tendency to solve disputes outside of courts.[98]

Considering the approach of different patterns of legal culture, Blankenburg[99] found, comparing Dutch and German litigation behaviour, that:

> after having excluded explanations on the basis of substantive law as well as legal consciousness, the observed differences in litigation behaviour can only be accounted for by the different infrastructure of institutions which facilitate judicial remedies side by side with alternatives to avoid formal procedures.

This resonates with the point made above, that the Dutch legal culture provides more alternatives of out-of-court settlement and thereby a sophisticated 'avoidance infrastructure', which leaves the citizens with more

---

[95] See D Rustov, *The Politics of Compromise* (Princeton University Press 1955); W Dowsett, 'Pragmatism in Politics (With Reference to Swedish Democratic Practice)' (1967) 39 *The Australian Quarterly* No 3, 49–64; Thomas Anton, 'Policy-Making and Political Culture in Sweden' (1969) 4 (Issue A4) *Scandinavian Political Studies* 88–102.

[96] It provides a faster, cheaper and effective alternative to the courts. See Franziska Weber and Christopher Hodges '*The Netherlands*' in Christopher Hodges et al (supra note 2) Ch 6.

[97] Geert Hofstede, *Culture's Consequences: Comparing Values, Behaviours, Institutions, and Organizations across Nations* (Sage Publications 2nd ed 2001); Erhard Blankenburg and Freek Bruinsma, *Dutch Legal Cultures* (Kluwer 1994).

[98] Marc Tuil, 'The Netherlands' in Christopher Hodges, Stefan Vogenauer and Magdalena Tulibacka (supra note 33) 401.

[99] Erhard Blankenburg, 'Patterns of Legal Culture' (1998) 46 *The American J of Comp L* 1.

options of DR mechanisms, whereas in Germany the court system is the common pathway to solve a dispute. Although this is only one perspective, it offers an explanation of the cultural influence on complaint behaviour. There are, of course, a variety of additional factors that influence the development of ADR/CDR in Member States (e.g. legal fees, legal aid, court systems, trust in the legal system).

The UK has a very developed CDR system that has spread sectorally without a standardized approach. The various CDR models are visible and generally known to the consumers. However, some gaps in coverage exist. There is a strong culture of self-regulation in the UK which, in turn, established public regulatory authorities that provide a solid base for ADR/CDR models to develop. There are ombudsmen working alongside sectorial regulators, some have statutory mandate; the Financial Ombudsman Services were set up in 2001 as a result of the Financial Services and Market Act 2000[100]; the Pensions Ombudsman was created by an Act of Parliament in 1991; The Legal Services Ombudsman for England and Wales created by the Office for Legal Complaints under the Legal Services Act 2007 and opened in 2010.

In contrast to the Nordics, the Netherlands and the UK, the CDR landscape in Germany is very patchy and in the early stages of its development. There are significant gaps in sector coverage and also those sectors that have ADR schemes are not fully covered, e.g. banks. Germany has a distinct and well-established structure of lawyers that give legal advice and a civil procedure system that is widely known and used. This suggests that the comparative efficiency of the court system in Germany slowed the development of CDR. Unlike the German example, the court system in the UK is expensive[101], complicated to use, typically involves lawyers, takes a long time to process complaints and is made more inaccessible through legal aid cuts.[102] One could argue that as a way of experimenting with dispute resolution pathways to avoid the court costs and accompanying burdens for consumers,[103] a side effect was that ADR is now well

---

[100] Various ombudsmen existed before the FOS was created and were merged into the FOS through the Financial Service and Markets Act 2000, introducing major regulatory reorganization.

[101] John Peysner, 'England and Wales' in Christopher Hodges, Stefan Vogenauer and Magdalena Tulibacka (eds) (supra note 33) 313.

[102] Rupert Jackson, *Review of Civil Litigation Costs: Final Report* (The Stationery Office London 2010).

[103] See: K Economides, 'Reading the Waves of Access to Justice', paper presented at seminar on 'Justice and Citizenship' (Rio de Janeiro, Brazil, September 1997).

established in the UK. In other words, unlike the German court system, the evolution of the British court system has been very conducive to the development of ADR/CDR pathways.

In summary, a few Member States have a long tradition of CDR (the Netherlands and Nordic countries), but models and procedures vary significantly between Member States. They range from industry mediation schemes (France: in-house *médiateurs*); private trade association and consumer association codes (UK: SMMT/ABTA); public arbitration schemes (Spain: consumer arbitration model[104]); to ombudsman schemes (UK and spreading in Germany). These schemes are typically limited to national boundaries and might not be appropriate for cross-border disputes.

X. CONCLUSIONS

This chapter has discussed various trends in the development of alternative models of consumer dispute resolution in the EU. The current state of ADR/CDR models in the EU is a paradox: one of great differences but at the same time considerable similarities. At national level, different stages of development and a diverse range of models were developed as a reaction to sectorial and national trends/legislation. The national development of CDR models has been overtaken by the requirements in sectorial regulations. The patterns of ADR/CDR developments that arise from sectorial coverage can be compared to the development within other areas of consumer law in the EU. There is an existing vertical sectorial regulation (e.g. product safety regulation) followed by a horizontal level of regulation (e.g. the general product safety directive).[105] This is the path that CDR is hoped to develop in the future, slowly joining up the picture to reach full horizontal coverage throughout the EU.

An important detail in getting closer to a classification within the complex world of ADR is that the introduction of mediation into the court system is commonly called the 'ADR phenomenon'. This is not, as such, the CDR phenomenon, and the two are often confused. In other words, this ADR in-court system is, in fact, a different world to that of CDR. The difference is that the CDR system aims to deal with claims that would typically not be brought in the court system in many Member States. The Member States are required to implement the ADR/ODR rules

104 Christopher Hodges et al (supra note 2) 209–28.

105 Christopher Hodges, *European Regulation of Consumer Product Safety* (OUP 2005).

by 2015. The ADR rules will ensure that disputes over contractual issues between consumers and traders will be settled outside the courts by means of ADR/CDR systems. All Member States are required to cover all sectors, with the exception of higher education and health. The ODR regulation will bring to life an EU-wide single entry point for disputes arising from online B2C transactions. This platform is envisaged not only to operate in all official EU languages but also to link all the national ADR bodies.

As the EU is formed of a rich mixture of countries and cultures it will prove a large challenge and take time to integrate CDR models into the national framework. In other words, although CDR is an attractive pathway for consumers, especially for small value claims, to obtain access to justice, the question arises if the existing variations (both cultural and procedural) between the Member States require more consideration and a more flexible approach to the expected ADR/CDR framework.

11. Out-of-court settlement of consumer disputes in financial services[1]

Iris Benöhr

I. INTRODUCTION

Alternative dispute resolution (ADR) has become a topical issue as part of the process of improving access to justice and has developed extensively in the financial services sector. [2] Extrajudicial settlements are often viewed as cheap and expeditious alternatives to court dispute resolution procedures in consumer matters. As a result, the EU has become increasingly active in promoting ADR, adopting a wide range of measures which include Recommendations, Directives and, more recently, sector specific guidelines. Despite the gradual Europeanization of this area, a comparison of consumer ADR schemes in the financial services sector shows a wide range of national approaches, including arbitration, ombudsmen, mediation and conciliation schemes. Furthermore, persistent challenges in terms of availability and quality of financial services schemes remain. This chapter will provide a comparative perspective on key consumer ADR measures that apply to financial services dispute resolution in the EU and in three Member States. It will focus in particular on the insurance sector, where the numbers of complaints have grown in some countries and where a complex system of specialized schemes has been developed.

1 This chapter draws on previous work by the author, published in Christopher Hodges, Iris Benöhr and Naomi Creutzfeld-Banda, *Consumer ADR in Europe* (Hart Publishing, Oxford, 2012) and in European Policy Analysis, Sieps (April, 2013).

2 According to the European Commission's Consultation Paper, ADR mechanisms cover out-of-court schemes that lead to the settling of a dispute through the intervention of a third party, such as an arbitrator, a mediator or an ombudsman. See the Consultation 'On the Use of Alternative Dispute Resolution as a Means to Resolve Disputes Related to Commercial Transactions and Practices in the European Union' 2011, para 6.

Finally, this chapter will outline the recent proposals by the European Commission on Consumer ADR and on Online Dispute Resolution (ODR), assessing possible implications for dispute resolution in financial services.

II. OUT-OF-COURT DISPUTE RESOLUTION IN FINANCIAL SERVICES

The enlargement and progressive integration of the European market offers consumers a wider choice of financial services providers.[3] Facilitated by the Internet, consumers now undertake an increasing number of financial transactions in the Union, and this inevitably results in a growing number of cross-border complaints. However, if a complaint cannot be resolved directly with a financial services provider, the consumer is often reluctant to pursue a case in court, due to litigation costs and complex and lengthy procedures, for disputes which often involve small monetary claims.[4] In this context, out-of-court mechanisms are regarded as important alternatives to court procedures, because they generally help to settle conflicts in a fast and amicable way. This is particularly relevant in financial disputes, where the parties are often locked into a long-term contractual relationship.

Given these convenient properties of out-of-court mechanisms, in the last decade a number of ADR measures have been adopted in the EU to facilitate consumer access to justice. Moreover, the recent financial crisis placed a renewed focus on consumer protection and on effective enforcement in the financial sector, resulting in the adoption of new guidelines for complaint handling in the insurance field and stronger supervision of the financial market.[5]

Despite these innovations, important gaps in coverage in the financial services area remain and differences in quality standards are persistent

---

[3] See eg the European Commission's Consultation Document, Alternative Dispute Resolution in the Area of Financial Services, 2008, 3.

[4] See OECD, *Recommendation on Consumer Dispute Resolution and Redress* (Paris, OECD, 2007).

[5] At the international level the World Bank issued a document on 'Good Practices for Financial Consumer Protection', June 2012. In the EU see the Guidelines on Complaints-Handling by Insurance Undertakings, issued by the European Insurance and Occupational Pensions Authority (EIOPA) in 2012.

across the EU.[6] The following section explores key EU measures which have a bearing on consumer ADR in financial services.[7]

1. Key EU Measures

The EU established rules for financial services operators, in order to enhance effective consumer protection in the key areas of financial services including banking,[8] insurance[9] and securities dealing.[10] In relation to ADR, the EU has adopted a number of general and sector-specific measures of voluntary and binding natures, which are relevant for out-of-court settlements of financial disputes.

Historically, the first types of general measures were non-binding Recommendations, adopted in 1998 and 2001. They established a number of minimum guarantees, such as transparency and effectiveness, which ADR schemes should offer to their users.[11] Both Recommendations have positively influenced a large number of national consumer ADR schemes, promoting quality standards, including in financial services.[12]

An important change of attitude came in 2008, when the EU adopted a *binding* measure in the form of a Directive on Mediation in Civil and Commercial Matters. This Directive aims to foster the amicable settlement of disputes by encouraging the use of mediation, and by ensuring a sound

---

6 Hans-W. Micklitz, Norbert Reich and Peter Rott, *Understanding EU Consumer Law* (Intersentia, 2009) 341.

7 See more in Iris Benöhr, 'Alternative Dispute Resolution in the EU', in Christopher Hodges, Iris Benöhr and Naomi Creutzfeld-Banda, *Consumer ADR in Europe* (Hart, 2012), pp. 5–11.

8 Eg Directive 2008/48/EC of 23 April 2008 on credit agreements for consumers, OJ L 133/66-92, 22.5.2008.

9 For example, Directive 2002/92/EC on insurance mediation of 9 December 2002 OJ L 009, 15/01/2003.

10 For example, Directive 2004/39/EC on markets in financial instruments of 21 April 2004, OJ L 145, 30.4.2004.

11 Commission Recommendation of 30 March 1998 on the principles applicable to the bodies responsible for out-of-court settlement of consumer disputes, OJ 115, 17/04/1998, 31–34; Commission Recommendation (EC) 2001/310 on the principles for out-of-court bodies involved in the consensual resolution of consumer ADR, OJ L 109, 56.

12 The Commission has developed a database with more than 500 ADR schemes, which, according to Member States, meet the Commission's quality criteria, complying with the Recommendations: see http://ec.europa.eu/consumers/redress_cons/schemes_en.htm.

relationship between mediation and judicial proceedings.[13] It establishes common EU rules on key aspects of civil procedure and makes cross-border dispute resolution in civil and commercial matters more effective, ensuring a balanced relationship between mediation and judicial proceedings.

At the same time, in contrast with older Directives that rarely mentioned out-of-court dispute resolution, the EU adopted a large number of measures, specifically directed at financial services, which *encourage* or even *require* Member States to establish out-of-court dispute resolution procedures. Measures that *encourage* Member States to establish ADR schemes are, for example, the Distance Marketing of Financial Services Directive,[14] the Insurance Mediation Directive[15] and the Markets in Financial Instruments Directive (MiFID).[16] In turn, EU measures *requiring* that adequate and effective ADR schemes are put in place are the Consumer Credit Directive[17] and the Payment Services Directive.[18]

Finally, a number of networks were created to facilitate the resolution of cross-border consumer complaints; for example FIN-NET, a network specializing in financial services complaints, discussed in the next section.

2. Financial Services Complaints Network

The Commission has set up a specific dispute resolution network of national ADR bodies for financial services, called FIN-NET (Financial Services Complaints Network). This network was established in 2001 and deals with ADR cross-border disputes between consumers and financial services providers, covering the European Union, Norway, Iceland and Liechtenstein.[19] The objective of FIN-NET is to provide consumers

---

13 Directive (EC) 2008/52 on certain aspects of mediation in civil and commercial matters, [2008], OJ L 136/3.

14 Directive 2002/65/EC concerning the distance marketing of consumer financial services, [2002], Art 14.

15 Directive 2002/92/EC on insurance mediation (Article 11[1]), OJ L 9, 15.1.2003, Article 11.

16 Directive (EC) 2004/39 on markets in financial instruments, [2004] OJ L 145/1, 33.

17 Directive (EC) 2008/48 on credit agreements for consumers, [2008] OJ L 133/66, 66.

18 Directive (EC) 2007/64 on payment services in the internal market, [2007] OJ L319/1, 32.

19 See ec.europa.eu/internal_market/finservices-retail/finnet/index_en.htm.

with easier access to ADR schemes in cross-border cases through the cooperation and assistance of national ADR bodies.[20] It also aims to improve the quality of ADR schemes and ensure that they operate under a common set of principles.[21]

If a consumer has a complaint against a service provider from another country, the FIN-NET member in the consumer's country will help to identify the relevant complaint scheme in the provider's country. Furthermore, it will provide information about the scheme and its complaint procedure.[22] If the consumer then decides to file a complaint, the FIN-NET member will transfer it to the relevant scheme in the provider's country, or suggest that the consumer files a complaint directly with the cross-border scheme. In order to be admitted as a member of FIN-NET, a scheme must provide out-of-court settlement of disputes between consumers and service providers.[23] In addition, it has to comply with the quality requirements set out in Commission Recommendation 98/257/EC of 30 March 1998.[24] This means that it must observe the seven principles of the Recommendation (independence, transparency, adversarial procedure, effectiveness, legality, liberty and representation).[25]

A 2009 evaluation report commissioned by DG Internal Market and Services showed that FIN-NET can work well in specific cases.[26] However, the report also revealed significant gaps in the coverage of the network. For instance, some EU Member States had no ADR schemes for particular financial services sectors, and a number of schemes were not members of FIN-NET. Importantly, they were sometimes not members because they did not comply with the ADR quality standards set out in the Commission Recommendation 98/257/EC.[27] This indicated that consumers still often face barriers to settling financial services disputes out of court, due to a lack of availability or quality in ADR schemes.

---

[20] *Report on the Evaluation of FIN-NET* (2009, Centre for Strategy & Evaluation Services, commissioned by DG Internal Market and Services).

[21] Ibid.

[22] See ibid.

[23] A Memorandum of Understanding links FIN-NET members, including a declaration of intent on cross-border co-operation between the parties. See ec.europa.eu/internal_market/fin-net/members_en.htm.

[24] Commission Recommendation (EC) 98/257 on the principles applicable to the bodies responsible for out-of-court settlement of consumer disputes, [1998] OJ L 115/31.

[25] www.fin-net.eu.

[26] *Report on the Evaluation of FIN-NET* (2009, Centre for Strategy & Evaluation Services, commissioned by DG Internal Market and Services).

[27] Ibid, 19–20.

3. The New Regulatory Framework in Financial Services and Consumer Protection

In the wake of the financial crisis, the European Commission presented several reforms in the financial sector in 2010 focusing on four core principles. One of them concentrated on 'strengthened responsibility and consumer protection' to restore confidence in the financial market. The other principles were: transparency in the financial market, effective supervision through new independent authorities and enforcement, and enhanced resilience and financial stability.[28] In order to strengthen consumer protection, the EU has also started to reassess a number of EU measures affecting consumers in the financial services sector.[29] The aim is to revise the regulatory framework, in order to restore consumers' confidence in financial markets and prevent unfair or risky market behaviour.

Furthermore, as a result of the EU reforms, three new supervisory authorities were established and became operational at the beginning of 2011: the European Banking Authority (EBA); the European Insurance and Occupational Pensions Authority (EIOPA); and the European Securities and Markets Authority (ESMA). These three authorities are responsible for supervising different financial areas at the micro-financial level, covering banking, insurance and occupational pensions and securities. In addition, the European Systemic Risk Board (ESRB) was established to provide macro-prudential oversight of the financial system, by monitoring and assessing possible risks to financial stability. All four bodies form part of a European system of financial supervisors, which also includes the Member States' supervisory authorities and which aims to strengthen the EU supervisory framework of the financial sector.

In this overall system, the three bodies responsible for consumer protection are EBA, EIOPA and ESMA, which were given specific powers and tasks for this purpose. Their regulations expressly state that they 'shall take a leading role in promoting transparency, simplicity and fairness in the market for consumer financial products or services across the internal market' (Article 9).[30] They can do this by different means, including

---

[28] Communication from the Commission of 2 June 2010 – Regulating financial services for sustainable growth [COM(2010) 301 – Not published in the Official Journal].

[29] See more at the European Commission's website, DG Internal Market: http://ec.europa.eu/internal_market/finances/committees/index_en.htm.

[30] Regulation 1093/2010 establishing a European Banking Authority;

collecting, analysing and reporting on consumer trends, reviewing and coordinating financial literacy and education initiatives and by developing training standards for the industry. Furthermore, they have to monitor financial activities and 'may adopt guidelines and recommendations with a view to promoting the safety and soundness of markets and convergence of regulatory practice'. If financial activities threaten the orderly functioning and integrity of financial markets they may also temporarily prohibit or restrict certain financial activities in the Union in specific circumstances. While these provisions do not expressly mention out-of-court settlement of consumer disputes, EIOPA has already adopted a relevant initiative in order to improve complaint handling in the financial insurance sector, as discussed in the next section.

4. Guidelines on Complaints-Handling by Insurance Companies

In 2012 EIOPA has issued Guidelines on Complaints-Handling by Insurance Undertakings,[31] under which undertakings are expected to facilitate out-of-court settlement in the insurance sector. The guidelines are addressed to the national authorities responsible for the supervision of complaints-handling procedures by insurance companies. The national authorities should integrate the guidelines into their regulatory and supervisory framework, unless they can provide a reasoned answer for not doing so.

The guidelines cover seven main points. First, they promote the establishment of complaints management policies, which should be formalised in written form and follow fair and transparent procedures, preventing for example conflicts of interest. Furthermore, they require the insurance undertakings to register complaints internally and to provide clear information on complaints to the national authority or ombudsman. The guidelines also require that insurance companies address recurring problems that are uncovered by the complaints. Finally, they provide guidance on transparent procedures and timely complaints handling, requiring for example that a reasoned reply is given to the complainants.

These guidelines are accompanied by a complementary report on voluntary best practices aiming to promote effective customer protection

---

Regulation 1094/2010 establishing a European Insurance and Occupational Pensions Authority; Regulation 1095/2010 establishing a European Securities and Markets Authority (adopted on 24 November 2010).

[31] See EIOPA's Guidelines on Complaints-Handling by Insurance Undertakings, EIOPA-Bos-12/069, 14 June 2012.

and to facilitate convergence among supervisory approaches.[32] Besides directly strengthening consumer protection by upholding basic standards, such as impartiality, transparency and responsiveness, EIOPA's 2012 Report and Guidelines for the insurance sector may set a precedent and inspire similar approaches in related areas. Moreover, they can induce convergence at the European level on certain quality standards. At present, however, the European landscape is still relatively variegated, as we will see in the next section, which compares ADR schemes in the insurance sector.

III. A COMPARISON OF ADR SCHEMES IN THE FINANCIAL INSURANCE SECTOR

At the Member State level, important national reforms of civil procedure have encouraged the development of ADR schemes.[33] As a result, at least 750 national ADR schemes currently exist, according to a recent study commissioned by the EU.[34] Many of them focus on sectors which present a high number of disputes, such as the financial services and telecommunication sectors.[35] Some of the ADR mechanisms show common characteristics while others vary considerably in their procedures and functions, as the next section on ADR in the insurance sector will show. They represent an important step to facilitate access to justice and yet a number of shortcomings still prevail at national and cross-border level, which will be described in the final section.[36]

---

32 See EIOPA's Report on Best Practices by Insurance Undertakings in Handling Complaints, EIOPA-Bos-12/070, issued on 14 June 2012.

33 Erhard Blankenburg, 'The Infrastructure for Avoiding Civil Litigation: Comparing Cultures of Legal Behavior in The Netherlands and West Germany' (1994) 28 *Law & Society Review* 4, 789–808.

34 DG SANCO, *Study on the Use of Alternative Dispute Resolution in the European Union* (Berlin, Civil Consulting, 2009) at: http://ec.europa.eu/consumers/redress_cons/adr_study.pdf.

35 For more information see Christopher Hodges, Iris Benöhr and Naomi Creutzfeld-Banda (Hart, 2012).

36 A 2011 ADR consultation paper by the Commission highlighted that the existing ADR procedures do not cover all fields of consumer sectors and are often inconvenient in cross-border cases. See European Commission's Consultation Paper 'On the Use of Alternative Dispute Resolution as a Means to Resolve Disputes Related to Commercial Transactions and Practices in the European Union'.

1. Germany

Germany's civil litigation system is relatively inexpensive and efficient.[37] As a result, public out-of-court schemes for consumers have developed at a slower pace than for example in the UK. In the financial services sector, only a few public ADR facilities have been established,[38] as the majority of ADR schemes have been created by private business associations. A large number of financial services providers have voluntarily agreed to settle consumer disputes with the help of private conciliators or ombudsmen. These ADR units have been established as independent bodies within the industry associations of the respective companies. However, the ADR providers are fragmented, since they have arisen within the confines of the main historical sectors, notably private banks, co-operative banks and building societies.[39]

A major private consumer ADR scheme in Germany is the *Insurance Ombudsman*, which was established on 1 October 2001 on the initiative of the German Insurance Association (*Gesamtverband der Deutschen Versicherungswirtschaft*: GDV).[40] The scheme covers complaints that are brought by a consumer against an insurer if the latter is a member of the German Insurance Ombudsman Association.[41] Approximately 95 per cent of private insurance companies are members of the Insurance Ombudsman Association (*Versicherungsombudsman eV*). The objective of the founders was to promote out-of-court dispute resolution between insurance companies and consumers and to overcome 'structural asymmetry' between the parties.[42] Insurance contracts are often complex and

---

37 Burkhard Hess and Rudolf Hübner, 'Germany', in Christopher Hodges, Stefan Vogenauer and Magadalena Tulibacka (eds), *The Costs and Funding of Civil Litigation: A Comparative Perspective* (Hart 2010) 369.

38 ADR facilities were established by the German central bank (*Deutsche Bundesbank*) and only recently within the Federal Financial Supervisory Authority (*BaFin*), see more in Christopher Hodges, Iris Benöhr and Naomi Creutzfeldt-Banda (supra note 7) 90–4 and 100–108.

39 BaFin provides information about the ADR schemes at: www.bafin.de.

40 See also Jürgen Basedow, 'Small Claims Enforcement in a High Cost Country: The German Insurance Ombudsman' in Peter Wahlgren (ed), *What is Scandinavian Law? Social Private Law* (Stockholm Institute for Scandinavian Law 2007) 54.

41 A natural person who concludes an insurance contract for a purpose that is outside his or her trade, business or profession, may lodge a complaint. However, the Ombudsman is not competent, inter alia, in cases regarding healthcare insurance or if a case is already pending in a court or arbitration tribunal.

42 http://www.versicherungsombudsmann.de/Navigationsbaum/WirUeberUns/AufgabenUndZweck/index.html.

difficult to understand for consumers, and providers have more legal expertise and financial resources to enforce their rights. The Ombudsman procedure was specifically intended to demonstrate the commitment of insurance providers to taking consumer issues seriously, and hence support confidence in the sector. Insurers have an obligation to inform customers of the Ombudsman procedure in every contract and in any relevant discussion.

The Ombudsman scheme is funded by an annual contribution paid by the companies that are members of the Insurance Ombudsman Association, and by case fees.[43] For consumers the dispute resolution scheme is free of charge and they retain the option either to file a claim with a state court or with the Insurance Ombudsman. While this facilitates consumers' access to the dispute resolution scheme, the full funding of the scheme by insurance businesses might in principle jeopardize the neutrality of this institution. To address this issue, several safeguard measures have been put in place to foster the Ombudsman's independence and impartiality. First, candidates to the office have to demonstrate particular expertise in insurance matters and impartiality. In particular, they cannot hold assignments in the insurance sector that may cause conflict of interest with the Ombudsman function.[44] As a further guarantee of impartiality, the Ombudsman is appointed by the Advisory Council of the Ombudsman Association, where insurers and consumer organizations are represented equally. The duration of office is for a period of five years and dismissal is only possible for obvious gross misconduct of the Ombudsman's obligation.[45] Finally, the Ombudsman is free in his or her decision-making, provided that the law is observed.

The Ombudsman scheme offers a flexible dispute resolution mechanism limited to simple issues that can be decided expeditiously. Intervention of lawyers is not required and they are normally not involved by the parties. A complaint can be made orally, in writing or in other forms, and the respondent usually has to reply within a month.[46] Before lodging a complaint the consumer must have contacted the insurer providing at least a six weeks deadline for a reply. In exceptional circumstances, a complaint can be refused, if it would use excessive scheme resources. Furthermore, if a complaint deals with a question of 'legal principles' the case must be

---

43 The annual contribution by the companies varies depending on their gross premium income.

44 Jürgen Basedow (supra note 40) 55.

45 www.versicherungsombudsmann.de/Navigationsbaum/WirUeberUns/StellungUndKompetenz/index.html.

46 Jürgen Basedow (supra note 40) 56.

referred to the court, which would then decide on the case.[47] The Insurance Ombudsman investigates the facts of the cases *ex officio* and can take a legally binding decision up to a sum of €10,000.[48] Above that threshold he or she may pronounce non-binding recommendations in disputes about claims of up to €100,000.[49]

The Ombudsman usually adopts a conciliation function as a first step, prior to making a decision, and the former is often successful. If the Ombudsman is likely to decide against an enterprise, the company might be informed about the potential outcome to provide it with the option to settle the case directly with the customer in an amicable way. If the Ombudsman decides in favour of the insurer, he or she pays particular attention to providing the consumer with an explanation of the decision.

The majority of cases are decided within three months. The Ombudsman procedures have become more efficient with time and are shorter than the usual court procedures. The decision by the Ombudsman is legally binding for the insurance companies, while the recommendations are voluntary for both consumers and companies.[50] Even after the decision by the Insurance Ombudsman, the consumer can still lodge a claim with the ordinary court.[51]

To conclude, the Insurance Ombudsman has increasingly been recognized by both public bodies and private actors as an effective dispute resolution provider. This ADR model was copied by the German transport sector Ombudsman and may inspire wider areas of consumer dispute resolution.[52] Insurers have applied this dispute resolution mechanism as a marketing advantage. The costs are lower than court proceedings and involve less potential for adverse publicity. Consumers, in turn, have an additional option to file a complaint without the financial risks that a court procedure would entail.

2. France

In France, mediation plays a major role in consumer ADR. The French mediators function in similar fashion to what would be called an

---

47 Section 8 para 2 of the Ombudsman's procedural rules. See Jürgen Basedow (supra note 40) 58.

48 Jürgen Basedow (supra note 40) 58.

49 See section 2 of the Insurance Ombudsman procedural rules. Prior to November 2010 the limit was €80,000.

50 Section 11 para 1 of the Insurance Ombudsman procedural rules.

51 Section 11 para 1 of the Insurance Ombudsman procedural rules.

52 Jürgen Basedow (supra note 40) 61.

ombudsman in other Member States. There is also a strong system of local conciliation through a court-annexed justice conciliator, who is highly accessible to those involved in litigation.[53]

Implementation of the EU Mediation Directive in 2011 introduced a definition of mediation in French law, and some criteria of what constitutes a 'good' mediator, namely that the mediator must accomplish the mission with impartiality, competence and diligence.[54] It is debatable whether the omission of a requirement for independence is significant, given the number of in-house mediators in French companies.

In the insurance sector, several mediators exist to deal with insurance complaints. A majority of these schemes are not notified to the European Commission and have not become members of FIN-NET.[55] This makes it more difficult to identify competent ADR schemes in the insurance sector or to check their quality standards, in particular in cases of cross-border complaints.

The mediator of the French Federation of Insurance Companies (*Fédération Française des Sociétés d'Assurance,* FFSA)[56] is the only notified insurance mediator scheme in France; it complies with the Commission Recommendation 98/257 and is a member of the cross-border European network FIN-NET. Established in 1993 by the members of FFSA this mediator is a private and voluntary ADR scheme, which is able to rule on disputes involving FFSA members that have signed its Charter. This latter document is intended to provide a framework whereby policyholders and third parties can reach settlement of their disputes, without resorting to litigation. Under the Charter, the insurer and the insured can seek advice from the in-house mediator or refer the matter to the FFSA-appointed mediator.

The FFSA mediator is appointed unanimously, for a renewable two-year term, by a board comprising representatives from the National Consumer Institute (*Institut National de la Consommation*), the Advisory Committee of the National Insurance Council (*Commission Consultative du Conseil*

---

53 See also Christopher Hodges, Iris Benöhr and Naomi Creutzfeldt-Banda (supra note 7) 46–56.

54 www.legifrance.gouv.fr/affichTexte.do?cidTexte=JORFTEXT000025179010&fastPos=1&fastReqId=1554304886&categorieLien=id&oldAction=rechTexte.

55 See for instance: *médiateur du GEMA*, *médiateur du CTIP*; other insurance mediators are : *médiateur de la Chambre Syndicale des Courtiers d'Assurances* (CSCA), *médiateur de la Fédérale Mutualiste* (www.mutualite.fr); for more information regarding these schemes see: www.acam-france.fr/mediateurs.

56 www.ffsa.fr.

National des Assurances) and the FFSA. The mediator calculates his own budget and the funding for the scheme is provided by the insurance industry under the Mediation Charter. Consumers thus do not contribute to the cost, and can bring a complaint free of charge.

Insurers must specify in information documents made available to prospective policyholders the conditions in accordance with which complaints shall be processed. These documents should also inform the policyholder about dispute resolution mechanisms within the company and provide contact details of a mediator.

A request for mediation can only be accepted after all the internal, contractual or other means of redress made available by the insurance company in question have been exhausted. The FFSA mediator scheme should deliver its opinion within three months. In practice, the time taken to handle a complaint varies according to the individual files. Article 8 of the mediator's Charter provides that the mediator's opinion should take into account elements of law and equity. If mediation does not give rise to an agreement, the mediator issues a non-binding written opinion and the parties remain free to bring the matter before the courts.

3. United Kingdom

Out-of-court resolution mechanisms have flourished in the UK and are now generally highly developed, as they were recognized comparatively early on as an expeditious and necessary alternative to costly court litigation procedures.[57] Another characteristic of the UK schemes is that they operate on a sectoral basis and that they differ significantly in models and visibility across sectors.

In the UK, Ombudsmen have been established in an increasing number of sectors since the 1960s, often being designed as an integral part of a new regulatory structure, operating alongside public regulators of privatized or opened markets. The UK also has a strong national policy and culture of self-regulation, complementing a robust cadre of public regulatory authorities.[58] The Financial Ombudsman Service (FOS) was established in 2001 by Parliament under the Financial Services and Markets Act 2000 as an independent body to resolve disputes between consumers and financial

---

[57] See more on the litigation costs in John Peysner, 'England and Wales', in Christopher Hodges, Stefan Vogenauer and Magdalena Tulibacka (eds) (supra note 37) 289–302.

[58] See Christopher Hodges, Iris Benöhr and Naomi Creutzfeld-Banda (supra note 7) 272–83.

firms quickly and with minimum formality.[59] It incorporated the former Ombudsmen for banking, insurance, building societies and investment into a single body and was designed to function in close cooperation with two other key regulatory authorities: the Financial Conduct Authority (FCA) (previously the Financial Services Authority)[60] and the Office of Fair Trading (OFT).[61] The FOS was thus an integral part of a large project aimed at simplifying the regulatory landscape while embracing a self-regulatory philosophy.[62] One of the advantages of the new system was to create a single point of contact for consumers' enquiries and complaints, and to draw clear lines of accountability.[63]

Part of the function of the FOS is to balance the bargaining powers of consumers against companies.[64] Its recommendations are binding on providers, and the service is free to consumers. The FOS is funded by an annual levy paid by the financial businesses it covers, and by case fees that it charges businesses for settling disputes.[65] The budget is proposed by the chief Ombudsman and then adopted by the board of the FOS, which requires a final approval by the FCA. A significant difference between the FOS and other ADR schemes funded by private firms is that firms covered

---

59 The FOS also received further powers under the Consumer Credit Act 2006. See Rhoda James and Philip Morris, 'The New Financial Ombudsman Service in the United Kingdom: Has the Second Generation Got it Right?' in Charles Rickett and Thomas Telfer (eds), *International Perspectives on Consumers' Access to Justice* (Cambridge University Press, 2003) 167.

60 Following the merger of the FSA into the Bank of England in 2013, the consumer protection functions of the FSA have been subsumed by the newly established Financial Conduct Authority (FCA).

61 See Christopher Hodges, Iris Benöhr and Naomi Creutzfeldt-Banda (supra note 7) 272–83. See R James and P Morris, 'The New Financial Ombudsman Service in the United Kingdom: Has the Second Generation Got it Right?' in Charles Rickett and Thomas Telfer (eds), *International Perspectives on Consumers' Access to Justice* (Cambridge University Press, 2003) 167.

62 See HM Treasury, *Financial Services and Markets Bill: A Consultation Document. Part One: Overview of Financial Regulatory Reform* (London, HM Treasury, 1998), 8.

63 Andromachi Georgosouli, 'The FSA Regulatory Policy of Rule-Use: A Move Towards More Effective Regulation?' (London, WP University of London – Centre for Commercial Law Studies, 2006) 2.

64 Ian MacNeil, 'The Future for Financial Regulation: The Financial Services and Markets Bill' (1999) 62 *Mod L Rev* 725.

65 The FCA collects the levy for the FOS at the same time that it collects its own regulatory fees. See the information guide provided by FOS to funding and case fees, which can be accessed at: http://www.financial-ombudsman.org.uk/faq/answers/research_a5.html.

by the Ombudsman are obliged by law to contribute.[66] This strengthens the independence of the Ombudsmen.

The board members of the FOS are appointed by the FCA,[67] but they are independent from the FCA. The public interest board of the FOS in turn appoints the Ombudsmen. The FOS assists in the application of the law and rules and, despite not being a regulator itself, it can influence the regulatory process in an indirect way, through co-operation with the FCA. The FOS deals with complaints about most financial products and services (including banking and insurance services), the way firms make their business decisions, and investment performance evaluations. Although the FOS cannot give personal advice about financial matters or debt problems, it plays an important role in sharing knowledge and experience, helping consumers and businesses settle problems, and helping to eliminate the causes of complaints.

Consumers first have to complain to the financial service companies in order to give them a chance to evaluate the problem.[68] If the complaint handling by the firm is not satisfactory or no solution is found within eight weeks the complaint can be referred to the FOS. The consumer must do this within six months of the firm's final response letter. As a result, an adjudicator is assigned to each case. The adjudicator will contact both parties and attempt to mediate a solution. If the case is not settled, the adjudicator will make a finding. Either party may then appeal against this finding to one of around 90 Ombudsmen for a review and final determination.

The FOS has extensive discretion, as it is to base decisions on what is 'fair and reasonable' on a case-by-case basis. This has been criticized by firms since the FOS can, at least in theory, depart from the legal requirements, which may lead to confusion. The FCA Handbook, however, requires the Ombudsman, in considering what is fair and reasonable, to take into account relevant law and regulations, regulators' rules and codes of practice.[69] In practice, most cases revolve around factual situations only

---

66 See information provided by the FOS on funding and case fees at: http://www.financialombudsman.org.uk/.

67 See the website of the Ombudsman: http://www.financial-ombudsman.org.uk/default.htm.

68 www.financial-ombudsman.org.uk/consumer/complaints.htm#1; H Davies, 'Reforming Financial Regulation' in Ellis Ferran and CAE Goodhart (eds), *Regulating Financial Markets in the Twenty First Century* (Hart, 2001), 5 and 20.

69 FCA Handbook, Dispute Resolution: Complaint handling procedures of the Financial Ombudsman Service.

and are also of low value. The 'fair and reasonable' test is intended to avoid the disproportionate cost of a full judicial-style inquiry, in order to facilitate access to justice and an equalization of power between firms and consumers. The FOS has the power to dismiss a case if it would be better dealt with in court, for instance if there is an important question of law. The Ombudsman can award up to £150,000.[70]

If a consumer does not agree with the decision of the FOS he or she can file a civil legal action in court.[71] However, in practice, courts often agree with the FOS. If a consumer accepts an Ombudsman's decision, it is binding on both the consumer and the business. If a consumer rejects an Ombudsmans decision, neither party is bound. In addition to resolving individual complaints, an essential objective of the FOS is to inform firms how to improve handling of their complaints and promote market transparency. Under FCA rules, individual financial services firms are required to publish their own complaints data[72] and the FOS also publishes businesses complaints data on its website in order to help people see how individual firms handled their customer complaints.[73]

In conclusion, ADR mechanisms in the UK, France and Germany share a number of important characteristics; among these, their source of funding. However, they also differ in many other regards, as they vary in size, in nature (public versus private) and in coverage. The next section will extend the analysis from a country-specific to a cross-border perspective.

IV. NEW EU INITIATIVES

The EU recently commissioned a number of studies on the effectiveness of ADR mechanisms in the EU and in the Member States. These studies showed that while ADR has developed considerably, various shortcomings are still present; among them lack of information about available schemes, wide diversity across Member States and a lack of general coverage.[74]

---

[70] This was increased from £100,000 in 2011.

[71] Financial Services and Markets Act (FSMA).

[72] PS10/1: *Publication of complaints data including feedback to CP09/12*, January 2010.

[73] See the complaints data at: http://www.ombudsman-complaints-data.org.uk/ (accessed 29 November 2010).

[74] See the Study on the Use of Alternative Dispute Resolution in the European Union of 16 October 2009 and the Leuven Study on alternative means of consumer redress other than redress through ordinary judicial proceedings, 2007.

Furthermore, in the specific field of financial services, the European Commission issued a consultation document in 2008 on 'Alternative Dispute Resolution in the Area of Financial Services', which seeks to find new ways to improve consumer redress to overcome persistent gaps in coverage of ADR schemes in this sector.[75] The need to foster ADR mechanisms was also highlighted in a Green Paper on retail financial services in June 2008 where the European Parliament stressed that consumers should have easy access to ADR schemes requesting the Commission to promote best practices on ADR.[76]

As a result of the above ADR studies and consultations, on 29 November 2011, the European Commission issued two new legislative proposals to facilitate consumer ADR in general: a draft Directive on ADR[77] and a draft Regulation on ODR.[78]

1. The Proposed Directive on Consumer ADR

The Commission proposed a specific Directive on consumer ADR to ensure the quality and availability of such schemes for contractual disputes. According to Article 1, the objective of the Directive is:

> to contribute to the functioning of the internal market and to the achievement of a high level of consumer protection by ensuring that disputes between consumers and traders can be submitted to entities offering impartial, transparent, effective and fair alternative dispute resolution procedures.

The proposal applies to procedures for the out-of-court resolution of consumer-related disputes, also covering ADR in financial services. It regulates contractual disputes arising from the sale of goods or the provision of services by a trader established in the Union, to a consumer resident in the Union (Article 2). Hence, the draft Directive would cover both

---

[75] See the Consultation Document on *Alternative Dispute Resolution in the Area of Financial Services* (2008), issued by the European Commission, DG Internal Market and Services on 11.12.2008, MARKT/H3/JS D(2008).

[76] European Parliament resolution of 5 June 2008 on the Green Paper on the retail financial services in the single market (2007/2287(INI)).

[77] Commission (EC) 'Proposal for a Directive on alternative dispute resolution for consumer disputes and amending Regulation (EC) No 2006/2004 and Directive 2009/22/EC (Directive on consumer ADR)', COM (2011) 793/2, final, 29 November 2011.

[78] Commission (EC) 'Proposal for a Regulation on online dispute resolution for consumer disputes (Regulation on consumer ODR)', COM (2011) 794/2, final, 29 November 2011.

domestic and cross-border disputes whilst not applying to in-house dispute resolution services operated by traders, to direct negotiation, or judicial attempts at settlement.[79]

In particular, this Draft Directive tackles three key shortcomings[80] which impede the effectiveness of consumer ADR:

(a) Gaps in the coverage of ADR entities at both sector-specific and geographical levels;
(b) Lack of awareness and insufficient information preventing consumers and businesses from using ADR entities; and
(c) Variable quality of ADR, as a significant number of ADR entities are not in line with the core principles laid down by the two Commission Recommendations.[81]

Consequently, the four main elements of the legislative proposal are:

(1) *Ensuring that ADR procedures exist for all consumer disputes.* Member States under the proposed Directive have to ensure that disputes can be submitted to an ADR scheme for all consumer disputes. In addition, ADR schemes should provide the possibility to file a case online and exchange information via electronic means (Article 5 Draft Directive).[82]
(2) *Information on ADR and cooperation.* According to Article 10 of the Draft Directive, traders must inform consumers about the relevant ADR schemes and whether or not they commit to use ADR in relation to complaints lodged against them. Member States have to ensure that consumers can obtain help regarding their cross-border complaints – an obligation that Member States can delegate to their ECC-Net offices (Article 11 Draft Directive). Moreover, the

---

79 See also Iris Benöhr, 'Consumer Dispute Resolution after the Lisbon Treaty', (2013) 36 *Journal of Consumer Policy*, 1, 87–110 and Iris Benöhr, in Christopher Hodges, Iris Benöhr and Naomi Creutzfeldt-Banda (supra note 7) 22 et seq.

80 See Study on the use of Alternative Dispute Resolution in the European Union of 16 October 2009, http://ec.europa.eu/consumers/redress_cons/adr_study.pdf, 56-63; 112-115; 120-121.

81 Commission (EC) 'Communication by the European Commission on Alternative Dispute Resolution for consumer disputes in the Single Market', COM (2011) 791 final, 29 November 2011, 6.

82 Commission (EC) 'Proposal for a Directive of the European Parliament and of the Council on alternative dispute resolution for consumer disputes and amending Regulation (EC) No 2006/2004 and Directive 2009/22/EC (Directive on consumer ADR)', COM (2011) 793/2, final, 29 November 2011, 4.

proposal encourages cooperation between ADR entities and national authorities entrusted with the enforcement of consumer protection legislation.

(3) *Quality of ADR entities.* ADR schemes should respect the quality principles provided by the two Commission Recommendations. The Draft Directive also includes a number of quality requirements that an ADR scheme has to comply with: expertise, impartiality, transparency, effectiveness and fairness (Articles 6–9). In addition, the proposal states that disputes should be resolved within 90 days, and that ADR procedures should be free of charge or of moderate cost to consumers.

(4) *Monitoring.* In each Member State, a competent authority will be in charge of monitoring the work of ADR entities established on its territory (Article 15). The ADR bodies have to notify these national authorities with information including their contact details, the name of the persons responsible for the ADR scheme, funding and by whom they are employed, rules and length of procedures and fees (Article 16).

2. The ODR Regulation

The Draft Regulation on Consumer ODR, which aims at fostering the EU internal market, has a special focus on e-commerce. Recent data[83] showed that current ADR schemes for e-commerce are incomplete and only half of the existing schemes offer the possibility of submitting consumer complaints online while very few provide the option to deal with the entire process online.[84] Thus, a key element of the Draft Regulation addresses precisely this point, by proposing the establishment of a *European online dispute resolution platform* ('ODR platform').

The platform will consist of an interactive website offering a single point of entry to consumers and traders who seek to resolve disputes out-of-court. In the current proposal, this platform would apply to disputes

[83] The 2010 report of the European Consumer Centre's Network indicates that more than half of complaints (56.3 per cent) received by the ECC-Net were linked to e-commerce transactions. However, out of the 35,000 cross-border complaints received by the ECC network in 2010, 91 per cent could not be referred to an ADR scheme in another Member State as no suitable ADR scheme existed (http://ec.europa.eu/consumers/ecc/docs/2010_annual_report_ecc_en.pdf).

[84] Commission (EC) 'Proposal for a Regulation of the European Parliament and of the Council on online dispute resolution for consumer disputes (Regulation on consumer ODR)', COM (2011) 794/2, final.

arising from cross-border e-commerce transactions and would be free of charge.[85] Consumers and traders would be able to submit their complaints through an electronic form on the platform's website. The platform would then check if a complaint can be processed and seek the agreement of the parties to transmit it to the competent ADR scheme. The chosen ADR scheme would, in turn, try to resolve the dispute, in accordance with its own rules of procedure, within 30 days from the date of receipt of the complaint. It would notify the platform of relevant information regarding the development of the dispute.

Moreover, the draft regulation proposes to establish a network of online dispute resolution facilitators ('ODR facilitators' network'). Such a network will have one contact point in each Member State, and will provide support to the resolution of disputes submitted via the platform. Another important element of the proposal is that it requires EU traders engaged in cross-border e-commerce to inform consumers about the ODR platform. This information should be made easily, directly and permanently accessible on the traders' websites, and will be provided again when the consumer submits a complaint to the trader. The compliance by ADR schemes with the obligations set out in this Regulation will be monitored by the competent authorities to be established in the Member States, in accordance with the Directive on consumer ADR.

3. The New Legislation on ADR and ODR

In spring 2013 the Council of the European Union eventually adopted a final revised version of the proposed legislation on ADR and ODR. Subsequently, on 18 June 2013 both legislative acts were published in the Official Journal of the EU.[86] As a result, Member States will now have to implement the EU rules on consumer ADR and ODR by July 2015. The ODR platform will be established in January 2016.[87] Both legislative

---

85 ADR schemes established in Member States, notified to the Commission in accordance with the 'Directive on consumer ADR' would be automatically registered electronically with the ODR platform.

86 See OJ L 165 Volume 56, 18 June 2013: Regulation (EU) No 524/2013 of 21 May 2013 on online dispute resolution for consumer disputes and amending Regulation (EC) No 2006/2004 and Directive 2009/22/EC (Regulation on consumer ODR), Directive 2013/11/EU of 21 May 2013 on alternative dispute resolution for consumer disputes and amending Regulation (EC) No 2006/2004 and Directive 2009/22/EC (Directive on consumer ADR).

87 See the Commission's website at: http://ec.europa.eu/consumers/redress_cons/adr_policy_work_en.htm.

acts are ambitious and essential tools to strengthen consumer ADR in the EU. The combination of both the ODR regulation and the ADR framework Directive is a promising move towards a comprehensive solution for consumers to access out-of-court schemes. The ADR Directive will help to overcome existing gaps in the financial services dispute resolution landscape, raising protection standards in countries where some ADR mechanisms have important limitations in terms of transparency or independence. By setting quality requirements with respect, for example, to the impartiality and transparency of ADR schemes, the new legislation will strengthen the independence of ADR bodies, which is something especially needed for schemes funded and monitored by private associations.

However, it remains to be seen how the new ADR schemes will be funded. As all Member States now have to provide full coverage of consumer ADR, the establishment of such a system may turn out to be expensive and challenging. Nonetheless, the new legislation on consumer ADR and ODR is a welcome initiative that can help to overcome problems of lack of information and gaps in coverage which also afflict financial services ADR schemes. In particular, the ODR Regulation will facilitate processing consumer complaints in e-commerce matters.

V. CONCLUSIONS

This chapter has discussed recent trends, at the EU and Member State level, in the design and adoption of ADR schemes for consumers, focusing on financial services disputes. Out-of-court redress mechanisms are increasingly recognized as an important element in strengthening access to justice and protecting consumers effectively. Consequently, a growing number of EU measures and initiatives in Member States have adopted specialized financial services ADR schemes, which vary extensively across Europe.

In the last decade, the EU has become more active in the regulation of consumer ADR. While this has been done initially through soft law recommendations, the current trend is towards adopting binding measures for consumer ADR. At the same time, the recent reform of the financial services system, with the establishment of new supervisory authorities, has put a stronger focus on effective consumer protection, producing for example new Complaints-Handling Guidelines and Best Practices for insurance companies.

A comparison of consumer ADR schemes in the financial insurance sector across Germany, France and the UK reveals different out-of-court models.[88] While some financial services ADR schemes (such as the FOS in the UK) are established by law, others rely rather more on self-regulation (as in Germany). When it comes to the funding arrangements, all assessed ADR bodies are financed by the financial services providers, ensuring that the complaints procedure is free of charge for the consumer. Given this funding structure, several safeguarding measures have been put in place to strengthen the independence and impartiality of the ADR bodies. In France and Germany, representatives from both the business and the consumer side are involved in the process of selection of the Ombudsmen, aiming to ensure a balanced representation of interest. As for the UK, the Ombudsmen of the FOS are appointed by the public interest board of the organization. Furthermore, the impact of the decisions adopted by ADR schemes also differ: some are merely voluntary opinions (e.g. those of the insurance mediator in France), whereas others are binding on the parties, if the complainants accept the final decision taken by the ombudsman (in the case of the FOS).[89]

Another distinctive feature is that in some national systems, including those of France and Germany, a large number of ADR schemes exist for the financial services sector (e.g. investment, banking or insurance). In contrast, the FOS covers all major areas of financial services.

Recent developments show that services for insurance, investment or banking are becoming more interrelated.[90] This suggests that a single ADR body might help to prevent overlap or gaps in ADR schemes in financial services, ensuring potentially more efficient processing of cases. Moreover, a single point for financial services complaints could facilitate access to ADR for consumers, preventing confusion regarding competences.[91] As shown previously, while there has been an increase in financial services ADR schemes in Europe, the availability and quality of ADR schemes for consumers across the EU Member States differ considerably in this sector, leaving important gaps in coverage.[92] The recent ADR and ODR rules adopted by the EU will help to overcome some of these challenges.

---

88 Adrian S Zuckerman, *Civil Justice in Crisis: Comparative Perspectives of Civil Procedures* (Oxford University Press, 1999) 3 et seq.

89 http://ec.europa.eu/consumers/redress/out_of_court/index_en.htm.

90 See the Report by David Thomas and Francis Frizon, 'Resolving Disputes Between Consumers and Financial Businesses: Fundamentals for a Financial Ombudsman', *The World Bank*, January 2012.

91 See also the recommendations by David Thomas and Francis Frizon, 'Resolving Disputes Between Consumers and Financial Businesses: Fundamentals for a Financial Ombudsman. A Practical Guide Based on Experience in Western Europe', *The World Bank*, June 2011, 32.

92 See also the report at www.fin-net.eu.

Member States now have an obligation to ensure that ADR schemes are available for all consumer disputes, and that they respect certain quality principles. At the same time, the proposal builds on existing ADR schemes, leaving Member States free to decide how to transpose the obligations therein.

12. Public enforcement and A(O)DR as mechanisms for resolving mass problems: a Belgian perspective*

Stefaan Voet

I. INTRODUCTION

A debate about mass problems frequently gets bogged down in a discussion about class actions as a private litigation mechanism to achieve collective redress. This also seems to be the case in Belgium. Every media comment on a mass case provokes a clash between proponents and opponents of American-style class actions. What is often forgotten in these animated discussions is the existence of non-court mechanisms and their possible potential for achieving collective redress.

In his *New Framework for Collective Redress in Europe*, Hodges pleads for an integrated approach.[1] The voluntary and ADR approach, *ie* direct negotiation, mediation, arbitration, conciliation, and ombudsman systems, must be prioritized. Secondly, there is the (commonly overlooked) potential of public enforcement or regulatory oversight, where public bodies, sometimes merely because of their inherent authority coupled with the threat of damage to a trader's reputation after the announcement of the imposition of a public penalty, can force this trader to compensate. And finally, as a last resort, Hodges puts forward the private litigation model: resolving collective redress through private collective actions in the court.

* Some topics of this chapter were presented at conferences in Rotterdam ('Resolving Mass Disputes: ADR and Settlement of Mass Claims' on 27 June 2012), Moscow ('2012 International Association of Procedural Law Conference' on 21 September 2012) and Zürich ('Building Effective Markets – the Role of an Integrated Legal System' on 29 January 2013). I thank Professor Christopher Hodges for his insightful comments. The law is stated as at 8 July 2013.

1 Christopher Hodges, *The Reform of Class and Representative Actions in European Legal Systems: A New Framework for Collective Redress in Europe* (Hart 2008) 223–49. For a summary see Christopher Hodges, 'Collective Redress in Europe: The New Model' (2010) *Civil Justice Quarterly* 29(3), 370–95.

In this chapter I will describe these three pillars from a Belgian perspective, with a particular focus on the ADR and public enforcement model, including the *"partie civile"* technique for crime victims.

II. PRIVATE LITIGATION – BELGIAN CLASS ACTIONS?

Currently, class actions do not exist in Belgium.[2] In 2009 and 2010, three class action proposals were launched: one by the government copying the Dutch Collective Settlements Act and the class action system in Quebec,[3] one by the Green opposition parties,[4] and one by the Flemish Bar Council.[5]

---

2 Jean-Pierre Fierens and Bart Volders, 'Belgium' in Paul G Karlsgodt (ed), *World Class Actions. A Guide to Group and Representative Actions around the Globe* (Oxford University Press 2012) 271 (*"The starting point of this chapter is that full-fledged opt-out class actions (. . .) are not available before the Belgian courts. Even the more moderate opt-in class action proceedings (. . .) cannot be initiated in Belgium"*).

3 "Wetsontwerp betreffende de procedures tot collectieve schadeafwikkeling" (in Dutch) – "Projet de loi relative aux procédures de réparation collective" (in French). The proposal, that was drafted by two academics from the University of Brussels (ULB), is available at <http://www.tijd.be/massaschade> accessed 28 January 2013. For an analysis by its authors see Hakim Boularbah, 'Des "actions groupées" vers l' "action de groupe": quelle valeur ajoutée pour l'avocat?' in X., *La valeur ajoutée de l'avocat. Actes du Congrès de l'O.B.F.G. du 17 février 2011* (Anthemis 2011) 33–85 and Andrée Puttemans, 'L'introduction d'une forme d'action collective en droit belge' in Angélique Legendre (coord), *L'action collective ou action de groupe. Se preparer à son introduction en droit français et en droit belge* (Larcier 2010) 24–46.

4 "Wetsvoorstel tot wijziging van het Gerechtelijk Wetboek wat het instellen van een collectieve rechtszaak betreft" (in Dutch) – "Proposition de loi modifiant le Code judiciaire en ce qui concerne l'instauration d'une procédure collective" (in French) (proposal of 29 May 2009, Parliamentary Record of the Belgian Chamber of Representatives 2008–2009, No. 2019/001; available at <http://www.lachambre.be/kvvcr/showpage.cfm?section=flwb&language=fr&cfm=/site/wwwcfm/flwb/flwbn.cfm?dossierID=2019&legislat=52&inst=K> accessed 27 January 2013). The proposal was resubmitted on 6 February 2012 (Parliamentary Record of the Belgian Chamber of Representatives 2011–2012, No. 2035/001; available at <http://www.dekamer.be/kvvcr/showpage.cfm?section=flwb&language=nl&cfm=/site/wwwcfm/flwb/flwbn.cfm?dossierID=2035&legislat=53&inst=K> accessed 28 January 2013).

5 "Wetsvoorstel tot invoering van Titel XXVI over de collectieve vorderingen in Boek IV van het gerechtelijk wetboek" (in Dutch). Available at <http://www.advocaat.be/UserFiles/Positions/OVB-wetsvoorstel%20class%20actions%20website.pdf> accessed 27 January 2013. For an analysis by one of its authors see Patrick Hofströssler, 'Waarom een "class action" in België? Krijtlijnen van het voorstel van de Orde van Vlaamse Balies' (2011) *Orde van de Dag*, No 54, 95–103

All three proposals failed since a political consensus could not be reached.

In the 2011 coalition agreement, the government Di Rupo aimed to put in place a (non-defined) procedure of collective claim settlement for consumers.[6] In June 2013, the Minister of Consumer Affairs proposed his consumer class action.[7] The proposal is currently pending before the Council of State and will probably be submitted to Parliament in the fall of 2013. Based on what the Minister declared in the media, this class action will probably look like an exclusive consumer class action to be included in the new forthcoming Belgian Code of Economic Law. It will not be possible to use this class action in, for example, a securities case, although in the last of couple of years the Belgian judicial system has had to deal with multiple mass securities cases.[8] This exclusive field of application could be considered a constitutional discrimination by the Belgian Constitutional Court.[9] A key safeguard will be that only associations and organizations will have standing, which is to be applauded.[10] These associations and organizations representing a class of consumers will be forced to negotiate with the trader to try and settle the dispute before going to court. This is clearly influenced by the Dutch system.[11] Class action procedures will be treated on an opt-in or opt-out basis.

---

and Patrick Hofströssler, 'Een Belgische class action: de OVB schrijft' in X., *Liber amicorum Jo Stevens* (die Keure 2011) 353–83.

6 Available at <http://assets.rug.be/img_art/site/images/37343FEF-AE8C-4987-B0A4-6C330A31A8DB.pdf> accessed 27 January 2013.

7 'Consumenten kunnen samen naar de rechter', De Standaard 8 July 2013 and 'Le conseil des ministres donne son feu vert à la "class action"', La Libre Belgique 5 July 2013, <http://www.lalibre.be/actu/belgique/le-conseil-des-ministres-donne-son-feu-vert-a-la-class-action-51d729ca35708f47759f5dac> accessed 8 July 2013.

8 *Eg*, Lernout & Hauspie case, Spaarselect case, Fortis case, etc.

9 Ivan Verougstraete, 'Class Actions: les doutes et certitudes du magistrat' *Cahier du Juriste* 2012/4, 100 (*"Ce domaine a été limité dans la déclaration gouvernementale au domaine du droit de la consommation mais il serait parfaitement concevable de l'étendre au domaine financier qui a donné des beaux exemples pratiques ces dernières années. Une telle extension semble à l'heure actuelle peu probable en Belgique mais il est toujours fâcheux de créer un type de procédure et de juridiction par type de contentieux. Notre Cour constitutionnelle n'aime d'ailleurs pas les différenciations . . ."*).

10 For a thorough analysis see Stefaan Voet, 'Cultural Dimensions of Group Litigation: The Belgian Case' (2013) *Ga J Int'l & Comp L* (forthcoming).

11 Article 3:305a of the Dutch Civil Code contains a general statutory collective action. Paragraph 2 of this article stipulates that a legal person filing a collective action is inadmissible if he, in the given circumstances, has made insufficient attempts to reach a settlement over its claim through consultations with the defendant.

This is not the place to elaborate on the question what a Belgian class action should look like. I have tried to do this elsewhere.[12] In this context, it is important to underline that an integrated approach is required to tackle mass harms. It is unwise to put all the eggs in the private litigation basket. As long ago as 1975, Mauro Cappelletti wrote that optimal collective redress can only be achieved by a matrix of intertwined models.[13] Especially in the European orbit, the potential of A(O)DR and public redress mechanisms and models for small claims has to be underlined. In that sense, possible Belgian class actions should be viewed as *additional* legal protection tools. From a procedural point of view, this will emerge in the superiority inquiry. Contrary to his U.S. counterpart, a Belgian judge will more easily accept the existence of other available methods for adjudicating the controversy, such as ADR and public enforcement mechanisms.

Shaping class actions, as additional legal protection tools, comes down to a continuous quest for safeguards to level the playing field in order to restore the procedural imbalance that marks group conflicts.[14] On the one hand, the absent class members have to rely on the class representative to enforce their rights. On the other hand, the defendant has to be protected against the power of the group. Belgian class actions will be shaped differently from U.S.-style class actions, because they will be embedded in a different procedural culture, with different rules on standing, funding and financing litigation, and court involvement. Contrary to U.S.-style class actions, Belgian class actions must be initiated by an ideological plaintiff, cannot be funded on a contingency (or success) fee basis, and must be dealt with by one competent court.[15]

---

12 Stefaan Voet, supra note 10; Stefaan Voet, *Een Belgische vertegenwoordigende collectieve rechtsvordering* (Intersentia 2012) and Stefaan Voet, 'Massaschadeafwikkeling door een Belgische bril' (2012) *Tijdschrift voor Civiele Rechtspleging* 177–85.

13 Mauro Cappelletti, 'La protection d'intérêts collectifs et le groupe dans le procès civil – Métamorphoses de la procédure civile' (1975) 27 *Rev int dr comp* 571.

14 See Rebecca Money-Kyrle and Christopher Hodges, 'European Collective Action: Towards Coherence?' (2012) 19 *MJ* 4 (listing and discussing a series of safeguards against abusive collective litigation).

15 See extensively Stefaan Voet, supra note 10.

III. BELGIAN PUBLIC ENFORCERS WITHOUT RESTORATIVE POWERS

Belgium also has multiple public enforcers/regulators that can potentially play a key role in tackling mass cases. I will briefly describe below the most important ones in the fields of general consumer policy, medicine, financial services, telecommunication, and energy.

The main public enforcer in the field of general consumer policy is the Federal Public Service (FPS) Economy, Small and Medium Enterprises (SMEs), Self-Employed and Energy.[16] The most important directorate-general (DG) is the DG Enforcement and Mediation (DG-EM), which acts as a kind of "economic police".[17] It contributes to the proper functioning of the goods and services market through its inspections checking compliance with economic legislation. Under the supervision of the Office of the Public Prosecutor, DG-EM agents have wide-ranging investigative powers. They can conduct independent investigations and hear witnesses, draw up reports having probative force, monitor any form of transport, take samples in accordance with prescribed standards, seize goods and documents, affix seals, make requisition orders, request assistance from experts or law enforcement agencies, carry out home visits, and appear before courts as witnesses. DG-EM agents may also negotiate settlements of infringements. In principle, the judicial authorities are responsible for penalizing any infringement uncovered by the DG-EM. The Public Prosecutor has the right to institute legal proceedings before a criminal court; to offer the infringer an out-of-court settlement, payment of which rules out criminal proceedings; or to dismiss the case. Nonetheless, under certain laws, the DG-EM has the power to propose that the infringer pay a sum of money that rules out criminal proceedings. In the event of a refusal to pay, the case is transferred to the Public Prosecutor. If harm is caused to a third party, no settlement is proposed.

The Federal Agency for Medicines and Health Products (FAMHP) is the Belgian regulatory authority responsible for the quality, safety and efficacy of medicines and health products.[18] The FAMHP was established on

---

16 <http://economie.fgov.be/en/> accessed 1 February 2012. Royal Decree of 25 February 2002 on the creation of the Federal Public Service Economy, Small and Medium Enterprises, Self-Employed and Energy.

17 X., 'Belgium' (2011) <http://ec.europa.eu/consumers/overview/country_profile/BE_web_country_profile_en.pdf> accessed 1 February 2013.

18 <http://www.fagg-afmps.be/en/> accessed 27 January 2013. Act of 20 July 2006 on the creation and functioning of the Federal Agency for Medicines and Health Products.

1 January 2007 and consists of a team of 390 (mainly scientific) employees that work for the three DGs: the DG PRE manages all activities dealing with the first license for launching a medicine or health product on the market, the DG POST manages all activities after the first license has been granted, and the DG INSPECTION deals with inspection and control. With respect to active pharmacovigilance (PHV),[19] the FAMHP can undertake different actions in case of non-compliance with the PHV-system:[20] education and recommendations to the Market Authorization (MA) holder to improve its PHV-system, its practices or processes and introduction of an action plan; a formal warning reminder of the legal obligations of PHV; administrative fines; and urgent actions (suspension or cancellation of registration, withdrawal, suspension of the MA, recall, etc.).[21] Everyone can notify to the FAMHP adverse reactions or incidents relating to medicines for human use, medicines for veterinary use, medical devices and/or accessories, the administration of blood or a blood derivative, or human body material.[22] For PHV, there is an online system for health care practitioners. Since September 2012, patients have been offered a filing card and Q&A document.

Since 1 April 2011, the regulatory supervision of the various players in Belgian financial business have been organized according to the so-called "Twin Peaks" model, with two autonomous supervisors: the Financial Services and Markets Authority (FSMA),[23] and the National Bank of Belgium.[24] [25] The FSMA is competent in six domains: supervision of the

---

19 *Ie*, the science and activities relating to the detection, assessment, understanding and prevention of adverse reactions or other problems linked to medicinal products.

20 <http://www.fagg-afmps.be/en/human_use/medicines/medicines/pharmacovigilance/inspections_QPPV/> accessed 1 February 2013.

21 For an analysis of the investigative powers of the FAMHP see Annabelle Bruyndonckx, 'Pouvoirs d'investigation de l'AFMPS' in Olivier Mignolet (ed), *Traité de droit pharmaceutique. La commercialisation des médicaments à usage humain* (Kluwer 2011).

22 <http://www.fagg-afmps.be/en/notification_effets/> accessed 1 February 2013.

23 <http://www.fsma.be/en.aspx> accessed 27 January 2013. Chapter III of the Act of 2 August 2002 on the supervision of the financial sector and on financial services. For a brochure in English see <http://www.fsma.be/~/media/Files/fsmafiles/pub/en/FSMA_brochure_201201.ashx> accessed 1 February 2013.

24 <http://www.nbb.be/pub/home.htm?l=en> accessed 1 February 2013.

25 For an analysis of these new rules see Reinhard Steennot (ed), *Financiële regulering in de kering. IFR-dagen 2011* (Intersentia 2012). This book contains multiple contributions about regulation, enforcement, and legal protection. See also Eddy Wymeersch, 'The Structure of Financial Supervision in Europe: About

financial markets and listed companies, supervision of rules of conduct, product supervision, supervision of financial service providers and of supplementary pensions, and contribution to improving financial education. In carrying out its supervisory tasks, the FSMA can take a wide range of actions:[26]

1 The FSMA is first of all a contact point where companies, institutions and persons that come under its supervision can turn for information and explanations of the rules in force.
2 The FSMA can use circulars, communications, recommendations and moratoria to explain and interpret legislation. They enable the FSMA to indicate how it will apply the rules, so that the actors concerned know precisely how to implement the legislation.
3 The FSMA can impose a variety of corrective measures. For instance, where the FSMA determines that some information is missing, it can require the undertaking or issuer to publish a correction. If that is not done, the FSMA itself may publish the additional information. Advertising materials for various financial products may also be adjusted by the FSMA, if necessary.
4 The FSMA can ask the undertakings under its supervision to provide the necessary documentation and information, and can conduct on-site inspections in order to verify compliance with all the rules.
5 If financial services are offered without the necessary authorization, the FSMA publishes a warning advising the public not to do business with the provider in question. This information is also reported to the judicial authorities.
6 The FSMA ensures that price-sensitive information concerning listed companies is available to everyone at the same time. If this is not the case, then the FSMA may decide to suspend trading in the shares until the information has been made available to everyone.
7 If the FSMA determines that a financial service provider no longer fulfills the conditions for registration or authorization, it may take administrative measures. The most severe measure is striking the intermediary from the register or revoking its authorization. If that happens, the person may no longer carry out his or her activities.
8 The FSMA may impose fines or penalties for infringements of financial

---

single Financial Supervisors, Twin Peaks and Multiple Financial Supervisors' (2007) *EBOR* 8(2), 237–306.

[26] A sanctions committee is established to determine the imposition of administrative sanctions. It consists of ten members: six magistrates and four others.

> legislation. It is not only actors in the financial sector that fail to keep the rules that may be sanctioned. Companies or individuals who, for example, infringe the rules on market abuse may also be required to pay a fine. There is a specific procedure to follow for imposing administrative fines. This procedure can also lead to an agreed settlement.

If consumers have a complaint about a financial service, they can submit it at no cost to one of a number of specialized institutions, for example the Ombudsman in financial matters,[27] or the Insurance Ombudsman.[28] The FSMA itself handles complaints regarding mortgage loans and supplementary pensions. Complaints about other financial services may also be submitted to the FSMA. The FSMA will investigate the complaint in its capacity as supervisor, and will take action where necessary. However, the FSMA is not competent to mediate between a financial institution and a client.

The federal telecommunications regulator is the Belgian Institute for Postal Services and Telecommunications (BIPT).[29] On the one hand, the BIPT is the supreme authority in specific technical fields, for example sharing, regulating and monitoring the use of the electromagnetic spectrum.[30] On the other hand, the BIPT makes the necessary arrangements in order that the regulatory framework is observed, competition can develop fully and fairly, certain tasks of public interest are carried out and consumer interests are protected. In this context, the BIPT can for example organize investigations and public consultations, can ask anyone relevant information within a certain time span, can collaborate with and provide information to other national, European and international regulators, etc. With a view to guaranteeing the satisfactory operation of the postal and telecommunications sector, disputes between operators can be settled swiftly and effectively by filing a request for mediation with the BIPT.[31] The

---

27 <http://www.ombudsfin.be/> accessed 1 February 2013.

28 <http://www.ombudsman.as/> accessed 1 February 2013.

29 <http://www.bipt.be/Home.aspx?levelID=1&lang=nl> accessed 27 January 2013. Act of 17 January 2003 on the statute of the regulator of the Belgian postal and telecommunications sector. See David Stevens, 'Institutional Aspects of Electronic Communications Regulation' in Jos Dumortier et al (eds), *A Decade of Research @ the Crossroads of Law and ICT* (Larcier 2001) and David Stevens, *Toezicht in de elektronische communicatiesector. Constitutionele en institutionele aspecten van de wijzigende rol van de overheid* (Larcier 2010).

30 In the Belgian federal context, due to its cultural character (radio and television) broadcasting falls within the competence of the three communities: the French, Flemish, and German-speaking communities.

31 The procedures are laid down in a Royal Decree of 5 May 2006.

BIPT also has an eye for consumer protection, for example with respect to tariff transparency. However, if a consumer wants to make a complaint against an operator he or she has to do so with the Ombudsman for telecommunications,[32] who is a part of the BIPT.[33]

In the energy sector, there are four regulators in Belgium: a federal one, and three regional ones. I will only touch upon the federal and Flemish one.[34] The Commission for the Regulation of Energy and Gas (CREG) is the federal regulator and is entrusted with the supervision of the transparency and competition in the electricity and gas market.[35] The CREG inspectors have wide-ranging investigative powers with respect to interrogations and the submission of documents.[36] In Flanders, the Flemish Regulator of the Electricity and Gas Market is the VREG.[37] The VREG is responsible for the efficient organization and working of the deregulated Flemish electricity and gas market, by appointing the distribution network operators and granting delivery licenses to suppliers. The VREG also draws up technical regulations for access to the electricity and natural gas network and for the management and expansion thereof. It mediates and deals with disputes relating to access to the distribution network and the application of the code of good practice and the technical regulations. The VREG also has a control function. It carries out careful monitoring to ensure that the distribution network operators and suppliers comply with legal and statutory obligations. Examples of these are the public service obligations to which the various parties in the market are tied. Both the CREG and the VREG refer customers with complaints to the Energy Ombudsman.[38]

Although more empirical research has to be conducted to uncover if Belgian and regional public enforcers/regulators dispose of restorative

---

32 <http://www.ombudsmantelecom.be/en/home.html?IDC=101> accessed 1 February 2013.

33 Article 43bis of the Act of 21 March 1991 on the reform of some economic state enterprises.

34 The Walloon one is the Walloon Commission for Energy (CWaPE) (<http://www.cwape.be/> accessed 1 February 2013). The Brussels one is the Brussels Regulator for Energy (Brugel) (<http://www.brugel.be/> accessed 1 February 2013).

35 <http://www.creg.be/nl/index.html> accessed 1 February 2013. Act of 29 April 1999 on the organization of the electricity market.

36 Royal Decree of 13 December 2009 on the inspectors of the Commission for the Regulation of Energy and Gas.

37 <http://www.vreg.be/en> accessed 1 February 2013. Flemish Energy Decree of 8 May 2009.

38 <http://www.ombudsmanenergie.be/> accessed 1 February 2013.

powers, the bottom line seems to be their exclusive focus on deterrence and their limited powers and tools in offering restitution and imposing civil sanctions.[39] They have wide-ranging investigative powers (*eg*, conducting investigations, interrogating witnesses, ordering the submission of documents, etc.) and may also in some cases negotiate settlements of infringements, but once third parties (consumers) complain, they will refer them to ombudsman services, or, in case of law violations, transfer the case to the Public Prosecutor who eventually will initiate legal proceedings before a criminal court.

IV. *"PARTIE CIVILE"* TECHNIQUE FOR CRIME VICTIMS

1. European Background

In recent decades, both the Council of Europe[40] and the European Union have increasingly paid attention to the role of the victim in criminal cases, and more specifically the possibility for that victim to claim compensation from the defendant in a criminal procedure, or in some cases from the State.[41] On the EU level there is the 2004 Council Directive relating to compensation to crime victims focusing on access to compensation by the State in a cross-border context.[42] At the end of 2012, the European Parliament and the Council adopted a new Directive establishing minimum standards on the rights, support and protection of victims of crime.[43] This Directive replaces the Council Framework Decision of 15 March 2001 on

---

[39] See Richard B Macrory, *Regulatory Justice: Making Sanctions Effective. Final Report. November 2006* (HM Treasury 2006).

[40] See Recommendation R (85) 11 on the position of the victim in the framework of criminal law and procedure, Recommendation R (87) 21 on assistance to victims and the prevention of victimization, and Recommendation R (2000) 19 on the role of the public prosecution in the criminal justice system. See also the European Convention on the compensation of victims of violent crimes [1983] *ETS* 116.

[41] See on this topic Matthew Hall, *Victims and Policy Making. A Comparative Perspective* (Willan Publishing 2010).

[42] Council Directive 2004/80/EC of 29 April 2004 relating to compensation to crime victims [2004] OJ L261/15.

[43] European Parliament and Council Directive of 25 October 2012 establishing minimum standards on the rights, support and protection of victims of crime, and replacing Council Framework Decision 2001/220/JHA [2012] OJ L315/57.

the standing of victims in criminal proceedings.[44] Article 16 (of the new Directive) regarding the right to a decision on compensation from the offender in the course of criminal proceedings stipulates:

1. *Member States shall ensure that, in the course of criminal proceedings, victims are entitled to obtain a decision on compensation by the offender, within a reasonable time, except where national law provides for such a decision to be made in other legal proceedings.*
2. *Member States shall promote measures to encourage offenders to provide adequate compensation to victims.*

2. Belgium's Liberal "*Partie Civile*" Technique

How are these recommendations and directives currently implemented in the different Member States?[45] Belgium and France have the most liberal systems.[46] In most common law systems, the victim is absent in a criminal trial. He or she can, and in most cases will, be called as a witness, but is not a formal party to the criminal proceedings. The victim cannot claim his or her damages during the criminal trial, and may only do so in a separate civil case.[47] In Belgium, the victim is a formal party to the criminal proceedings, with the Public Prosecutor and the defendant. There is no jury. In most cases victims will formulate their civil claim before or during the criminal proceedings. This is the so-called *"partie civile"* tech-

---

[44] Framework Decision 2001/220 on the standing of victims in criminal proceedings [2001] OJ L82/1.

[45] I only focus on the possibility for a crime victim to claim compensation during the criminal proceedings. In this (limited) context I do not pay attention to the role of the victim during the criminal investigation.

[46] The Belgian rule is laid down in article 4 of the Preliminary Title of the Belgian Code of Criminal Procedure. For a brief introduction to Belgian criminal procedure see Brigitte Pesquié, 'The Belgian system' in Mireille Delmas-Marty and JR Spencer (eds), *European Criminal Procedures* (Cambridge University Press 2002). A lot of information can be found on the website of the European Judicial Network in civil and commercial matters. For information about compensation to crime victims in Belgium see <http://ec.europa.eu/civiljustice/comp_crime_victim/comp_crime_victim_bel_en.htm> accessed 2 February 2013. For France see <http://ec.europa.eu/civiljustice/comp_crime_victim/comp_crime_victim_fra_en.htm> accessed 2 February 2013.

[47] But in the United Kingdom a criminal court may make, and since 2012 must consider in every case making a compensation order in favour of the victim for any personal injury, loss or damage resulting from the offence: the Powers of Criminal Courts (Sentencing) Act 20000, s130 and the Legal Aid, Sentencing and Punishment of Offenders Act 2012, s63.

nique.[48] After the criminal judge has dealt with the criminal aspect of the case, and has convicted the defendant, he *must* rule upon the civil claims. He cannot refuse to do so. Where the judge acquits the defendant, he will logically not rule upon the civil claim, but the victim can initiate a follow-on civil case based on another cause of action, *eg* negligence if the defendant was acquitted of fraud. The gain for the victim in formulating his or her claim before or during the criminal proceedings is that he or she can "piggyback" the evidence brought forward by the Public Prosecutor. To establish civil liability, the victim has to demonstrate a fault (*ie*, a law violation), damages and causation.[49] A "piggybacking" civil claimant in a criminal procedure only has to prove damages and causation. It is up to the Public Prosecutor to demonstrate a law violation (*ergo*, a civil fault).

On the other hand, a victim can freely choose not to "piggyback" the criminal case, but to initiate a civil case. Where a concurrent criminal case against the same defendant is pending, the civil judge will have to suspend the civil case until the criminal judge has ruled on the criminal case. This principle is expressed in the French adage: *"le criminel tient le civil en état"* (the criminal case goes before the civil case). It is also possible for a victim to use both tracks: a *"partie civile"* during the criminal proceedings, and initiating a separate civil case. This is done frequently in complex criminal cases (including mass cases) where the statute of limitations in the criminal case could be tolled. As a precaution, victims initiate civil proceedings as a backup, in case the criminal case is dismissed. Because of the *"le criminel tient le civil en état"* rule, these civil proceeding are mostly suspended until the outcome of the criminal case.

The *"partie civile"* mechanism is highly relevant for mass cases since many, if not all, Belgian mass cases go through the criminal carousel. In most of these cases, victims have brought their civil claim before or during the criminal proceedings and "piggybacked" the Public Prosecutor.[50] In securities cases, most victims are represented by (consumer or shareholder)

---

[48] See Ugo A Mattei, Teemu Ruskola and Antonio Gidi, *Schlesinger's Comparative Law. Cases-Text-Materials. Seventh Edition* (Foundation Press 2009) 855–62 and Christopher Hodges, 'Multi-Party Actions: A European Approach' (2001) 11 *Duke J Comp & Int'l L* 321, 331.

[49] Article 1382 of the Belgian Civil Code. Note that the burden of proof for a victim in a criminal case is identical to the burden of proof in a civil case.

[50] For example in the Lernout & Hauspie case (securities) there were ± 19,000 civil claimants; in the Spaar Select case (securities) ± 350 civil claimants, and in the Gellingen case (mass disaster) ± 400 civil claimants. For a description of these cases see Stefaan Voet, supra note 10.

associations or organizations, through the technique of party representation, which makes it possible for a natural or legal person (the representative) to represent a group of individuals if he or she receives an explicit mandate from each individual member of the group.[51] In such cases, only the class members who gave a mandate will be represented in court, and will be considered as a party to the proceedings. From a procedural point of view, the technique implies that as a result of a dispute over a substantive right, the holder of that right grants another (natural or legal) person the power to initiate the action resulting from that substantive right.

The *"partie civile"* technique in mass cases has four major advantages. First of all, it is easily accessible. Victims can formulate their civil claim orally or in writing by depositing an informal note or brief.[52] Moreover, it is cheap, in the sense that no court fees have to be paid, and that the victim does not have to be represented by a lawyer, and can easily act *pro se*.[53] The technique also enables cheap and easy access to information and evidence from the criminal investigation. And finally, as already mentioned, the victim only has to prove damages and causation, and not fault.

In a mass context, the biggest drawback is the fact that it is an opt-in system.[54] *All* civil claimants individually have to come forward, even when using the technique of party representation. Moreover, once the criminal court has dealt with the criminal aspect of the case, it has to adjudicate *all* civil claims, which can lead to an overload of the criminal court.

---

[51] Articles 1984–2010 of the Belgian Civil Code. See Hubert Bocken and Bernadette Demeulenare, 'The Defence of Collective Interests in Belgian Civil Procedure' in X, *Effectiveness of Judicial Protection and the Constitutional Order. Belgian Report at the II International Congress of Procedural Law* (Kluwer 1983) 161.

[52] Article 67 of the Belgian Code of Criminal Procedure.

[53] For example, in the Lernout & Hauspie case there were 2,347 shareholders acting *pro se* for whom the Court set up stands outside the courtroom with ten to 15 clerks. The clerks had prepared completion forms that could be filled out. These forms contained this sentence: *"I claim . . . euros, and . . . euros interest"*. For most lawyers the addition of the interest phrase was improper because the Court could not suggest that civil claimants claim interest. The form also contained a list with all of the defendants. The civil claimants had to cross a box next to the name of the defendant from whom they wanted to claim money. It was noted that the clerks advised people to cross all of the boxes.

[54] Another obstacle is the duration of the criminal investigation. In both the Lernout & Hauspie case and the Gellingen case the criminal investigation took more than five years.

3. Outsourcing Civil Claims to Special Masters?

A possible solution for this problem could be the outsourcing of civil claims by the criminal court to special masters,[55] as the Gellingen case illustrates. In the summer of 2004, a car park was constructed on a building site in Gellingen (Ghislenghien in French). During these works a mechanical soil stabilizer probably drove over a gas pipeline. Two weeks after the completion of the car park, on 30 July 2004, gas pressure was increased in the pipeline, which ruptured, triggering a massive explosion in which 24 people died and more than 150 were injured. At the end of a criminal investigation 14 individuals and companies were indicted.[56] There were about 400 "piggybacking" civil claimants. In first instance, the (criminal) Court of First Instance of Tournai acquitted most defendants.[57] On appeal, they were convicted.[58]

At that point the Court of Appeal of Mons was confronted with the question of how to deal with all of the civil claims. As usual, the court first appointed a number of doctors as court-appointed experts to examine the victims and to advise the court about their physical and moral damages. In addition, and this was innovative, based on a very liberal and creative interpretation of the rules on expert witnesses,[59] the court appointed two coordinating experts or special masters[60] to manage the work of the doctors and to try and reach an overall settlement between the defendants and the victims. In the course of 2013, these special masters, together with the court, will probably achieve this.

---

55 Another solution could be a criminal class action with the Public Prosecutor or an association or organization acting as class representative. See Adam S Zimmerman and David M Jaros, 'The Criminal Class Action' (2011) 159 *U Pa L Rev* 1385.

56 The "deep-pocket" defendants were Fluxys, the natural gas operator, and the company of Husqvarna, the proprietor of the site where the explosion occurred.

57 Judgment of the Court of First Instance of Tournai of 22 February 2010.

58 Judgment of the Court of Appeal of Mons of 28 June 2011. Excerpts of this judgment were published in *Ius & Actores* 2012/1, 113.

59 Articles 962–991bis of the Belgian Judicial Code. The court particularly focused on article 977 stipulating that the court-appointed expert must try and reconcile the parties.

60 See Dominique Mougenot, 'Une expertise sur mesure pour Ghislenghien' (2012) *Ius & Actores* 121. One of the special masters is a professor of law (Guy Horsmans). The other one a professor of medicine (Jean-Paul Beauthier).

4. Netherlands and Germany

From a comparative law perspective, it is informative to examine if crime victims in other jurisdictions also can use the *"partie civile"* mechanism in criminal cases, and if so, whether this has any potential in mass cases. In the Netherlands, the "clear case" criterion prevailed before the act of 17 December 2009. This meant that the victim could only bring his or her civil claim before the criminal judge if the claim was simple and not complex. The adjudication of the civil claim could not be at the expense of a smooth adjudication of the criminal case. If so, the criminal judge could declare the civil claim inadmissible, in which case the victim had to start separate civil proceedings. In practice, civil claims were almost always refused because they were viewed as being too complex. Only civil claims that were clear from the beginning were accepted and dealt with by the criminal judge. This practice was considered to be dysfunctional and unjustified.[61] The Act of 17 December 2009 introduced a new criterion: the criminal judge can declare the civil claim inadmissible if the adjudication of this claim leads to a disproportionate burden of the criminal case.[62] In mass cases, this will probably always be the case. Hence, I do not see a lot of good in the *"partie civile"* technique in Dutch criminal mass cases.

The same conclusion can be made with respect to the German *Adhäsionsverfahren*: the victim may, in criminal proceedings, bring a property claim against the defendant arising out of the criminal offence if the claim falls under the jurisdiction of the ordinary courts and is not yet pending before another court.[63] When the civil claim is not inadmissible or unfounded, the court may reject the claim if it is not suitable to be dealt with in criminal proceedings, for example if its further examination would considerably protract the proceedings or if there are complex issues of civil law.[64] Once again, this will mostly be the case in mass cases.

---

[61] This was one of the conclusions of the research project 'Strafvordering 2001' and the subsequent legal reform (see Marc Groenhuijsen and Tijs Kooijmans, *The Reform of the Dutch Code of Criminal Procedure in Comparative Perspective* (Martinus Nijhoff Publishers 2012)).

[62] Article 361.3 of the Dutch Code of Criminal Procedure. The provision entered into force on 1 January 2011.

[63] § 403 of the German Code of Criminal Procedure (this code is available in English: see <http://www.gesetze-im-internet.de/englisch_stpo/englisch_stpo.html> accessed 2 February 2013).

[64] § 406(1) of the German Code of Criminal Procedure.

V. BELMED: BELGIUM'S A(O)DR MECHANISM[65]

1. Introduction

In 2002, the Ministry of Economic Affairs was to become the FPS Economy, SMEs, Self-Employed and Energy. As already mentioned, one of its key DGs is the DG Enforcement and Mediation (DG-EM). The content of the mediation aspect was left completely open, so the DG was given a free and broad discretion to interpret it. From the beginning, one thing was clear: besides ethical objections, the DG did not have the financial resources and infrastructure to intervene or mediate in individual (consumer) cases. The first thing the DG did, under the mediation umbrella, was sectoral mediation. They invited the market players (business and consumer associations) and tried to solve complaints on a sectoral basis. Because the DG is convinced that creating a favorable environment for consumer A(O)DR leads to a better functioning of the goods and services market,[66] it decided, still under the mediation umbrella, to promote A(O)DR. This led to the Belmed project.

Belmed was created in three phases. First, a feasibility study was ordered on the introduction of an online mediation tool. The research explored the legal, economical and technical (IT) possibilities of online mediation. One of the conclusions was to establish a private-public partnership to create an ODR (online dispute resolution) tool. In a second phase, and on the basis of this study, a stakeholder consultation was organized. Enthusiasm was great, except for the financial aspect. None of the stakeholders wanted to support the project financially. In a third and final phase, a European tender was launched to develop the software. Eight companies were interested, including IBM. In January 2010, the tender was assigned to IRIS Solutions & Experts, an IT company from Louvain-la-Neuve.

Belmed, which is an abbreviation for *Bel*gian *Med*iation, was presented in April 2011. It is a digital ADR and ODR portal, which is to be promoted and made more accessible. The website of Belmed is www.belmed.fgov.be, and is available in Dutch, French, German, and English.

As an aside, it has to be noted that it is not only the Belgian Government that prioritizes consumer ADR and ODR. On 21 May 2013, the European Parliament and Council adopted a Directive on consumer

---

[65] This part is based on Stefaan Voet, 'Belgium' in Christopher Hodges, Iris Benöhr and Naomi Creutzfeldt-Banda, *Consumer ADR in Europe. Civil Justice Systems* (Hart 2012).

[66] At the launch of Belmed, the Belgian Economy Minister expressed it like this: *"Belmed is a facilitating instrument for economic life, not a control instrument"*.

ADR,[67] and a Regulation on consumer ODR.[68] The purpose of the ADR Directive is to contribute to the proper functioning of the internal market by ensuring that consumers can, on a voluntary basis, submit complaints against traders to entities offering independent, impartial, transparent, effective, fast, and fair alternative dispute resolution procedures (Article 1). The purpose of the ODR Regulation is to provide a European ODR platform ('ODR platform') facilitating the independent, impartial, transparent, effective, fast, and fair out-of-court resolution of disputes between consumers and traders online (Article 1).

2. Information

The first Belmed pillar is information.[69] The information part contains a guide on how to settle a dispute in an amicable way.[70] It not only explains what a formal notice, a consumer dispute, a third party, and alternative dispute resolution are, but also offers concrete examples of a formal notice, a general purpose registered letter, a registered letter dealing with a product breaking down, and a registered letter to terminate a contract.

Furthermore, the information part offers a convenient outline of all existing Belgian ADR agencies.[71] It gives an overview of all Belgian arbitration,[72] conciliation,[73] mediation,[74] and ombudsman agencies.[75] All

---

[67] European Parliament and Council Directive 2013/11/EU of 21 May 2013 on alternative dispute resolution for consumer disputes and amending Regulation (EC) No 2006/2004 and Directive 2009/22/EC [2013] OJ L165/63.

[68] European Parliament and Council Regulation 524/2013 of 21 May 2013 on online dispute resolution for consumer disputes and amending Regulation (EC) No 2006/2004 and Directive 2009/22/EC [2013] OJ L165/1.

[69] <http://economie.fgov.be/en/disputes/consumer_disputes/Belmed/what/> accessed 2 February 2013.

[70] <http://economie.fgov.be/en/disputes/consumer_disputes/Belmed/what/guide/> accessed 2 February 2013.

[71] <http://economie.fgov.be/en/disputes/consumer_disputes/Belmed/what/alternative_settlement_options/> accessed 2 February 2013.

[72] Real Estate Conciliation, Arbitration and Mediation Board (<http://www.ccai.be/> accessed 2 February 2013); Arbitration Commission for Consumers and Textile Carers (<http://www.fbt-online.be/> accessed 2 February 2013); Travel Disputes Commission (<http://www.clv-gr.be/> accessed 2 February 2013); and Furniture Disputes Commission (<http://www.navem.be/> accessed 2 February 2013).

[73] Real Estate Conciliation, Arbitration and Mediation Board (see supra note 72); Travel Dispute Commission (see supra note 72); Second-hand Vehicle Reconciliation Commission (<http://www.federauto.be/> accessed 2 February 2013); and Construction Reconciliation Commission (<http://www.bouwverzoening.be/> accessed 2 February 2013).

[74] Real Estate Conciliation, Arbitration and Mediation Board (see supra note

this information is also offered for each sector: consumer goods, general consumer services, financial services, postal services and electronic communications, transport services, leisure services, energy and water, health, education, and cross-border disputes.[76] The information outline of each agency is similar. At a single glance, all relevant information can be consulted: the address, the website, for which problems the agency is competent, the prerequisites for access, how the process works, a complaint form, the rules, and the costs.

3. ODR

The second pillar is that Belmed offers the possibility of making an online application for arbitration, conciliation, or mediation. The idea is to create a single digital access point for the consumer and tradesman. If a consumer or tradesman wants to make an application, he or she has to click on the "make a request for mediation" link on the introductory webpage.[77]

The consumer or tradesman visiting the Belmed platform for the first time will be faced with two accessibility criteria. On the one hand, an application can only be made when one has already contacted the other party to report the problem and try to solve it. If not, the applicant will be referred to the aforementioned guide in the information part, which contains an example of a formal notice. On the other hand, an application can only be made if there is no court proceeding pending. If there is, the applicant will receive (very limited) information on how to mediate during a court proceeding.[78]

---

72); Federal mediation service 'Patient rights' (<http://www.health.belgium.be> accessed 2 February 2013); Bemiddelingsplatform (<http://bemiddelingsplatform.be/> accessed 2 February 2013); and the Belgian Conflict Management Centre (<http://www.cebegeco.be/nh>). A list of approved mediators is available at <http://www.juridat.be/mediation/> accessed 2 February 2013.

[75] The Mediator for rail passengers (<http://www.ombudsmanrail.be/nl/onthaal.html?IDC=6> accessed 2 February 2013); Ombudsman Service for the Postal Sector (<http://www.smspo.be/> accessed 2 February 2013); Telecom Mediation Service (<http://www.ombudsmantelecom.be/> accessed 2 February 2013); Ombudsman Service for Energy (<http://www.mediateurenergie.be/> accessed 2 February 2013); Ombudsman in financial matters (<http://www.ombudsfin.be/> accessed 2 February 2013); and Insurance Ombudsman (<http://www.ombudsman.as/> accessed 2 February 2013).

[76] <http://economie.fgov.be/en/disputes/consumer_disputes/Belmed/what/help/search_sector/> accessed 2 February 2013.

[77] <http://economie.fgov.be/en/disputes/consumer_disputes/Belmed/> accessed 2 February 2013.

[78] The applicant will see the text of article 1730, §1 of the Belgian Judicial Code: any party can propose to the other parties, independently of any judicial

If the applicant has contacted the other party to no avail, and there is no court proceeding pending, he or she can log in and register. There are two ways to register. First, every Belgian resident can use his or her electronic ID card or token with the federal authentication portal to register. Secondly, every Belgian and European private individual or tradesman can create a personal Belmed account. All European consumers can use the system. For the moment, they can only do so when they have a dispute with a company that is registered in the Belgian Register for Companies.[79]

An ODR request can be made in three capacities: as a private individual consumer, as an intermediary for a private individual consumer,[80] and as an intermediary for a company.[81] The structure of the ODR request is based on the 2010 Commission Recommendation on the use of a harmonized methodology for classifying and reporting consumer complaints and enquiries.[82]

First, the two admissibility questions are asked once again: "have you contacted the tradesman/consumer concerned to report your problem?" and "did you take the matter to court?". Then the applicant has to fill out information about the provider (there is a tool to search for the supplier's business number), or, if the application is done by a tradesman, information about the consumer who for example did not pay an invoice. The request information is vital, because based on this, the system will send the application to the competent agency. The applicant has to fill out:

- the sector (and subsector) where the problem has occurred (consumer goods, education, energy and water, financial services, general consumer services, health, leisure services, postal services and electronic communications, or other);
- the sales method (distance or face to face);

---

or arbitral procedure, before, during or after a judicial procedure, to resort to the mediation process.

[79] *Eg*, a German consumer living in Berlin who bought a second-hand vehicle in Antwerp, or an Englishman living in Brussels having a dispute with a real estate agency in Bruges.

[80] *Eg*, a son making an application for his 80-year-old grandmother who has a problem with her electricity supplier, or a father making an application for his 15-year-old son who has a problem with his new cell phone.

[81] *Eg*, a lawyer or accountant.

[82] Commission Recommendation 2010/304/EU of 12 May 2010 on the use of a harmonised methodology for classifying and reporting consumer complaints and enquiries [2010] OJ L136/1.

- the type of problem (contracts and sales, delivery of goods/provision of services, invoicing/billing and debt collection, price/tariff, privacy and data protection, provider change/switching, quality of goods and services, redress, safety (covers both goods (including food) and services), unfair commercial practices, warranty/statutory guarantee and commercial guarantees, or other issues);
- the value of the claim.

Finally, there is an unlimited empty field ("description") where the applicant can provide additional information. It is also possible to add scanned documents (*eg*, an invoice, pictures, a letter, etc.), which can also be sent by regular mail.

When the applicant clicks on "send", the application will be sent, through the Belmed system, to the competent ADR agency. From that moment on, this agency will deal with the case: they will contact the applicant, examine the admissibility of the application,[83] contact the opponent, explain the arbitration/conciliation/mediation process, etc. The entire process proceeds online.

Currently, seven ADR agencies have signed a protocol to work with the Belmed system: the European Consumer Centre, the Ombudsman Service for Energy, the Mediation Service for Banks–Credit–Investments, the Construction Reconciliation Commission, the Second-hand Vehicle Reconciliation Commission, the Furniture Disputes Commission, and the Travel Disputes Commission. In the long run, the FPS wants to capture *all* ADR agencies into the Belmed system. If two or more agencies are competent in one sector, the consumer will be able to choose based on specific parameters (*eg*, cost and speed). In other words, competition between the ADR agencies will be tolerated and even stimulated. All Belmed partners must comply with the minimum guarantees of the two EU Recommendations of 1998 and 2001 to promote consumer ADR.[84]

Attention is also paid to consumers who do not have computer

---

[83] If the agency is not competent (because the applicant chose the wrong sector), this will be communicated to the applicant, who will have to make a new application. In other words: the "incompetent agency" will not send the application directly to the "competent agency".

[84] Commission Recommendation 98/257/EC of 30 March 1998 on the principles applicable to the bodies responsible for out-of-court settlement [1998] OJ L115/31 (independence, transparency, adversarial principle, effectiveness, legality, liberty, and representation) and Commission Recommendation 2001/310/EC of 4 April 2001 on the principles for out-of-court bodies involved in the consensual resolution of consumer disputes [2001] OJ L109/56 (impartiality, transparency, effectiveness, and fairness).

access.[85] [86] A collaboration has been established with non-profit organizations helping poor and socially excluded people, and with Public Computer Spaces (*eg*, libraries and schools). In those Public Computer Spaces, and with the help of those organizations, consumers who do not have a computer, or do not have computer skills, also can make an application.

Finally, the Belmed site contains some success stories in the sectors of consumer goods,[87] general consumer services,[88] financial services, leisure services, energy,[89] and cross-border disputes.[90] Recently, a satisfaction survey on the use of Belmed has been added.

---

85 One of the frequently asked questions is: "If I do not have a computer, how can I contact 'Belmed'?". The answer is: "You can go to a public computer room (PCR) where someone will help you browse the Belmed website. Info: PPS Social Integration, anti-Poverty Policy, Social Economy and Federal Urban Policy: tel: +32 2 508 85 85 or +32 2 508 85 86."

86 For the visually impaired, it is possible to enlarge the screen.

87 An example about spots on sofas: "Mr and Mrs X fell in love with a two-seater and a three-seater couches in the exposition hall of a well-known furniture maker. Four months after the delivery, the customers noticed that some spots are appearing on the furniture. The tradesman picked up the couches, delivered a replacement of equal value and repaired (color touch up) the furniture in agreement with the supplier. A few days later, the couches were brought back to the customers, who refused them because they would have preferred to receive an entirely new set. The tradesman refused to provide new furniture and claimed that the discoloration was removed by professionals and was in itself an adequate solution. The Disputes Commission met with the customers and the tradesman and thoroughly analyzed the couches. The tradesman claimed he had done everything to satisfy the customers and demanded 250 euros in compensation for the prolonged use of the replacement couches. The Disputes Commission followed the reasoning of the tradesman and decided that the couches were repaired by professionals and no longer showed any sign of discoloration, but denied the tradesman's compensation request."

88 An example about a deficient vehicle: "A vehicle – still under guarantee – had a recurring problem. In the beginning, the garage supported the first repairs, but started sending invoices claiming it could no longer intervene for free in such a context. The customer had to contact the importer. As this did not solve the problem and the vehicle constantly broke down, the customer decided to try mediation. A settlement was reached [through the Belgian Conflict Management Centre] with the car dealer, and the vehicle was finally replaced."

89 An example about invoicing: "Mrs F. disputed her bill from 21 January 2010 because it covered her consumption in 2007 and 2008. According to her, this bill did not respect the supplier's general terms, which state that an invoice is sent every year. As the supplier did not send the annual bill to Mrs F. (while he did receive the indices from the network operator in 2007 and 2008), the bill was considered abusive as it did not respect the general terms (an invoice is sent as soon as the supplier receives the indices validated by the network operator). The bill was entirely cancelled and is no longer due for payment."

90 An example from the European Consumer Centre Belgium: "Mrs H. plans

4. Statistics

It has to be underlined that Belmed only serves as an administrator or "serving-hatch". The FPS does not see the identity of the applicant, nor does it read the application, nor does it interfere in the ADR process. This makes sense, because the FPS is the control agency of some of the ADR agencies. The FPS only collects statistical data (how many times the system is used, how many people clicked on the guide, how many people made an application for mediation with respect to a travel dispute, etc.).[91]

This data is vital for two reasons. First, if a lot of applications are made in a sector where there currently is no ADR agency (in which case the applicant receives general information on how to start an informal conciliation procedure with the Justice of the Peace), this is an objective policy argument for the FPS to persuade the sector to create such an agency. Secondly, a lot of similar applications (*eg*, with respect to a specific deficient product) can indicate a collective problem, which can be a trigger for a governmental regulatory (or other) body to act and seek collective redress.

Table 12.1 details the (general) statistics between April 2011 and June 2013.

VI. CONCLUSION

This chapter makes clear that an evolution is taking place in Belgium on the private enforcement and A(O)DR fronts with respect to collective redress. A possible consumer class action could see the light, hopefully

---

a trip to Morocco and is browsing various websites looking for the best value hotel room. Once she has made a decision she books via a French website. The website offers a 'lowest price guarantee', ie. if a customer finds a similar offer with better conditions on another website, he or she is entitled to ask for a refund of the price difference and will get an additional 10 per cent discount. Mrs H. finds a similar, but cheaper, offer for the same Moroccan hotel on an Italian website. She contacts the French website immediately in order to benefit from their lowest price guarantee. However, the site fails to uphold its promise because the name of the room on the Italian website differs from that on its own website. Mrs H. is convinced that she is right and contacts ECC Belgium. Notwithstanding the fact that the names differ on the two websites, they are referring to the same room. The conditions required to benefit from the lowest price guarantee have, therefore, been fulfilled. Following our intervention the French website decides to refund Mrs H. the price difference supplemented by an additional 10 per cent discount."

[91] This statistical data will be published.

Table 12.1 BELMED April 2011 and June 2013

Total number of cases[1]				638
	Non-covered sectors[2]			259
	Covered sectors			379
		Still pending		55
		Finished		324
			Rejected[3]	141
			Stopped[4]	131
			Settled	25
			Failed	12
			Advice	15

Notes:
1 Most of the applications deal with electricity and gas.
2 The ADR agencies in these sectors have not yet signed a Belmed protocol.
3 By the ADR agency because the rules were not respected, or because the ADR agency was not competent.
4 By the applicant.

with strong safeguards to protect the interests of class members and defendants against frivolous or meritless claims. With Belmed, Belgium is one of the European ODR frontrunners. The information and ODR pillars of this unique digital platform are well developed, although it will be vital to capture the other Belgian (and why not European) ADR agencies into the system. More awareness also seems to be key.

Public enforcement as a mechanism to resolve mass problems is still largely undiscovered. A particular form of public enforcement is the prosecution by the Public Prosecutor of wrongdoers before a criminal court, a constant practice in Belgian mass cases. Belgium's liberal *"partie civile"* system definitely has potential in tackling mass cases. The Gellingen disaster shows that criminal judges can outsource the bulk of civil claims to special masters. The role of public enforcers/regulators (*eg*, in the fields of consumer policy, medicine, financial services, telecommunication, and energy) in offering collective redress is virgin territory. More empirical research is crucial, in particular about offering strong(er) restorative powers to these agencies.

13. Online dispute resolution in the EU and beyond – keeping costs low or standards high?[1]

Julia Hörnle

I. INTRODUCTION

European consumer protection law is currently being widened to add Online Dispute Resolution (ODR) into the toolbox of European consumer redress. The European institutions are currently adopting a Directive on ADR[2] and a Regulation on ODR[3] based on Article 169 (1) and 169 (2) (a) of the TFEU. The proposed Directive on ADR is discussed further in Chapter 10.

Cross-border Online Dispute Resolution (ODR) has extensively been discussed since at least 2000 in *academic*, theoretical literature as a kind of magic bullet solution for redress in international e-commerce, particularly for consumer disputes at the lower value end.[4] Now, some 12 years later,

---

1 An edited version of this chapter has been published in (2013) 38 *European Law Review* 187–208.

2 Directive 2013/11/EU of the European Parliament and of the Council of 21 May 2013 on alternative dispute resolution for consumer diusputes and amending Regulation 2006/2004 and Directive 2009/22/EC (Directive on consumer ADR) OJ 2013 L165/63.

3 Regulation (EU) No 524/2013 of the European Parliament and of the Council of 21 May 2013 on alternative dispute resolution for consumer diusputes and amending Regulation 2006/2004 and Directive 2009/22/EC (Regulation on consumer ADR) OJ 2013 L165/1.

4 See Ethan Katsh and Janet Rifkin, *Online Dispute Resolution* (Jossey-Bass San Francisco 2001); Colin Rule, *Online Dispute Resolution for Business* (Jossey-Bass San Francisco 2002; Oliver Märker and Matthias Trenel, *Online Mediation* (Sigma 2003); Gabriele Kaufmann-Kohler and Thomas Schultz, *Online Dispute Resolution* (Kluwer Law International 2004); Lucille Ponte and Thomas Cavenagh (Pearson New Jersey 2005); Susan Schiavetta, *Electronic Alternative Dispute Resolution* (PhD Thesis, Faculty of Law, University of Oslo 2008); Julia Hörnle, *Cross-border Internet Dispute Resolution* (Cambridge University Press 2009); Pablo

ODR has been firmly entrenched on the agenda of policy makers: both the EU and UNCITRAL have recently issued proposals on creating ODR systems for solving e-commerce disputes.

The main focus of this chapter is to analyse the new proposed EU regime supporting and regulating ODR. However, this has to be placed in the context of the discussions of and proposals for ODR at UNCITRAL, which this chapter will discuss first. By comparing and contrasting the UNCITRAL proposals with those of the EU, the differences in approach will become evident. This is crucial for understanding how ODR may function in the EU in the future. Finally, this chapter will pinpoint where and how the EU Proposals should be improved, in particular as regards the potential for co-operation between public consumer protection authorities and private ADR bodies interacting through the ODR platform. However, such co-operation would raise serious data protection issues, which this chapter also analyses, suggesting appropriate safeguards. It concludes by evaluating the Proposals and assessing their real contribution to the EU *consumer acquis.*

II. DEFINITION OF ODR

Before doing so, and by way of background, it may be helpful to explain what ODR means. In a nutshell, ODR is dispute resolution outside the courts, based on information and communications technology and in particular, based on the power of computers to efficiently process enormous amounts of data, store and organise such data and communicate it across the internet on a global basis and with speed.[5] As a concept ODR arose from, and is based on Alternative Dispute Resolution (ADR) which refers to extra-judicial dispute resolution processes such as arbitration and mediation. However, in addition to processes such as online mediation and online arbitration, ODR has developed innovative online processes, such as mock trials[6] (where a 'jury' of online volunteers give a verdict based on a set of facts as a form of crowd sourcing[7]) or blind-bidding

---

Cortes, *Online Dispute Resolution for Consumers in the European Union* (Routledge 2011).

[5] Julia Hörnle (supra note 4) 75; Gabriele Kaufmann-Kohler and Thomas Schultz (supra note 4) 7.

[6] www.ejury.com and www.virtualjury.com.

[7] See further Jan van den Herik, 'Towards Crowd Sourced Online Dispute Resolution' (2012) 7(2) *Journal of International Commercial Law and Technology* 99–111, 101.

negotiation[8] techniques (where each party makes successive monetary settlement offers, which are not disclosed to the other party and lead to a settlement if and when the bids come within close reach of each other).[9]

UNCITRAL's draft Procedural Rules define ODR as follows: online dispute resolution is a mechanism for resolving disputes through an IT based platform and facilitated through the use of electronic communications and other information and communications technology.[10]

III. UNCITRAL'S PROPOSALS

This section will briefly analyse the UNCITRAL initiative for comparison purposes. The UNCITRAL draft Procedural Rules envisage a three-stage procedure: (i) automated/assisted negotiation between the parties without a human neutral, which may include blind-bidding techniques, (ii) mediation/conciliation, and (iii) arbitration leading to a decision which can be enforced.[11] If the dispute is not solved by negotiation within ten calendar days the procedure will automatically move on to the next stage, conciliation.[12]

The main thrust of the UNCITRAL initiative is to establish an internationally accepted and trusted, normative framework for ODR.[13] This is an ambitious and far-reaching project which will establish a new paradigm for dispute resolution for e-commerce, in a similar way that the Uniform Dispute Resolution Procedure adopted by ICANN has changed the paradigm for disputes arising out of the conflict between domain names and trademarks.

In establishing this normative framework, UNCITRAL is planning to draft the following six 'model' rules and guidelines: (1) Procedural

---

8 Called automated negotiation in the UNCITRAL terminology.

9 See further Julia Hörnle (supra note 4), Chapter 5; Gabriele Kaufmann-Kohler and Thomas Schultz (supra note 4) 10–21; Pablo Cortes (supra note 4) 52–4.

10 Draft Article 2 (6), UNCITRAL Working Group III (Online Dispute Resolution) Note by the Secretariat 28 February 2012.

11 A/CN9/WG III/WP112 UNCITRAL Working Group III (Online Dispute Resolution) Note by the Secretariat 28 February 2012, paras 5 and 46.

12 Article 5 (2) draft Procedural Rules A/CN9/WG III/WP112 UNCITRAL Working Group III (Online Dispute Resolution) Note by the Secretariat 28 February 2012.

13 As to the trust argument, see further the discussion in Mireze Philippe, 'Now Where do We Stand With Online Dispute Resolution (ODR)?' (2010) *International Business Law Journal* 563–76, 566.

Rules for ODR, (2) Guidelines for Neutrals,[14] (3) Minimum Standards for ODR Providers, (4) Supplementary Rules for ODR Providers, (5) Substantive Legal Principles for Resolving Disputes, and (6) Cross-border Enforcement Mechanisms.[15] To date UNCITRAL has commenced its work on the Procedural Rules for ODR but has not yet produced drafts of any of the other rules and guidelines. [16]

Of particular significance is the intention to draft Substantive Legal Principles and Cross-border Enforcement Mechanisms. Their significance is that these instruments address the three main challenges[17] for the success of ODR as a 'magic' bullet solution for providing redress in e-commerce disputes: (1) incentivising the parties to agree to participate in ODR, (2) according to which (national consumer protection?) law the dispute is evaluated, and (3) guaranteeing that the parties comply with a settlement or decision, or in other words, ensuring enforcement.

UNCITRAL's initiative attempts to move away from domestic consumer protection law and embraces a form of transnational consumer protection law (in the shape of the Substantive Legal Principles), yet to be developed. UNCITRAL's initiative also attempts to steer clear of private international law and using the courts for enforcing ODR, instead relying on private enforcement mechanisms as far as possible.[18] What shape these enforcement mechanisms will take is as yet unclear. However, payment providers such as credit card issuers, payment intermediaries such as Paypal and other internet intermediaries, such as online platforms and web 2.0 services hosting and organising content, domain name registrars and search engines may also have to play a role as the gate-keepers of the internet.[19]

UNCITRAL's proposals are informed by the assumption that ODR will provide more effective, efficient, speedy and low-cost dispute resolu-

---

[14] Ie, the person in charge of dispute resolution, mediators or arbitrators.

[15] Preamble 2 draft Procedural Rules and A/CN9/WG III/WP112 UNCITRAL Working Group III (Online Dispute Resolution) Note by the Secretariat 28 February 2012, para 3.

[16] But see the Canadian delegation's proposal of principles for neutrals A/CN9/WGIII/WP114 of 12 March 2012.

[17] Pablo Cortes (supra note 4) 72–85 and 204–5; Gabriele Kaufmann-Kohler and Thomas Schultz (supra note 4) 132 et seq; and Julia Hörnle (supra note 4) 220 et seq.

[18] See A/CN9/744 UNCITRAL Report of Working Group III (Online Dispute Resolution) Meeting May 2012, para 120.

[19] See further Jack Goldsmith and Tim Wu, *Who Controls the Internet?* (Oxford University Press 2008) 68–84; Julia Hörnle, *Cross-border Online Gambling: Law and Policy* (Edward Elgar 2010) 111–39.

tion in cross-border e-commerce than the courts can provide, but ODR has remained stilted in its growth because disputants are not aware of the concept nor of its benefits and do not use or trust ODR and therefore it has been difficult for ODR providers to build successful schemes.[20]

UNCITRAL's initiative is informed by the belief that a clear and authoritative legal framework in the form of rules promulgated by UNCITRAL will overcome this problem and hence kick start activity in the ODR field.

Another important aspect of the UNCITRAL proposals is that they are not primarily driven by consumer protection concerns. Naturally, UNICTRAL approaches the ODR framework from the perspective of its previous work on arbitration and conciliation. An example of this is draft Article 7 (4) which provides that each party shall have the burden of proving the facts he or she relies on as part of the claim or defence.[21] Such a provision may not be suitable in a B2C transaction, where the business frequently has more information and greater resources. Consumer protection law therefore, frequently reverses the burden of proof.[22] This was pointed out by members of the Working Group in May 2012.[23]

Given that UNCITRAL does not concentrate on consumers, the Procedural Rules do not make a distinction between B2B, B2C and C2C disputes and apply to all three types of disputes. The Procedural Rules will be model rules which the ODR providers and the parties may decide to use on a voluntary, contractual basis.[24] This, of course, again raises the question whether a pre-dispute arbitration agreement in a consumer contract is valid, a question to which different national laws provide different answers.[25]

---

[20] With the exception of ODR provided by some of the large online marketplaces such as Amazon and eBay.

[21] See A/CN9/WGIII/WP112/Add1 Addendum to the Note of the Secretariat of 28 February 2012.

[22] See for example Directive 1999/44/EC on the sale of consumer goods and associated guarantees of 25 May 1999 L171/12 of 7 July 1999 as amended by the Consumer Rights Directive 2011/83/EU, Article 5 (3) provides that any defect which becomes apparent within six months of the sale of the goods is presumed to have existed at the time of the sale.

[23] A/CN9/744 UNCITRAL Report of Working Group III (Online Dispute Resolution) Meeting May 2012, para 111.

[24] Article 1 of the draft Procedural Rules and also A/CN9/WG III/WP112 UNCITRAL Working Group III (Online Dispute Resolution) Note by the Secretariat 28 February 2012, para 5.

[25] A comparative analysis of the validity of consumer arbitration clauses is complex and merits a treatise on its own and is therefore outside the scope of this chapter, but see Julia Hörnle (supra note 4) 171–85 and Pablo Cortes, 'Building a Global Redress System for Low-Value Cross-Border Disputes: An (European)

Under one proposal, the UNCITRAL Working Group has also stated that its normative framework has no intention of superseding national mandatory laws. In other words, domestic laws invalidating pre-dispute arbitration clauses in consumer contracts used against a consumer would be applicable. The idea is that the UNCITRAL rules are applied to a dispute by contractual agreement of the parties only to the extent that the domestic law allows such rules to be enforced. The latest discussions proposed that the following article be included in the draft Procedural Rules:

> The Rules shall not apply where the law of the buyer's state of residence provides that agreement to submit disputes within the scope of the ODR Rules are binding on the buyer only if it was made after the dispute has arisen and the buyer has not given such agreement after the dispute has arisen or confirmed such agreement (. . .). [26]

Under an alternative proposal, the UNCITRAL discussions seem to suggest that as long as the consumer has given express and informed consent to a pre-dispute arbitration clause, it should be valid.[27] Which one of these two approaches is going to prevail remains to be seen as the Procedural Rules crystallise.

The Working Group has also stated that it is not the objective of the UNCITRAL initiative to lead to law harmonisation or law approximation or to change domestic laws on a global basis. Instead the purpose of the UNCITRAL instruments will be to provide practical avenues of redress for small-value disputes where currently none exists.[28]

It is also important to point out that the UNCITRAL initiative is designed for cross-border low-value, high-volume disputes, which are mass claims not involving complex factual or legal issues.[29] The Working Group has decided not to define the terms 'cross-border low value and high volume disputes' but intends to provide more guidance in a commentary.[30]

Therefore, the key question, as yet unanswered, is: what disputes are

---

Appraisal of the UNCITRAL Rules on Online Dispute Resolution' (forthcoming article) Section III 2.

[26] A/CN9/744 UNCITRAL Report of Working Group III (Online Dispute Resolution) Meeting May 2012, paras 16, 29.

[27] Ibid, paras 26–7.

[28] Ibid, para 15.

[29] Preamble 1 to the draft Procedural Rules and A/CN9/716 UNCITRAL Report of Working Group III (Online Dispute Resolution) December 2010, para 115.

[30] A/CN9/WG III/WP112 UNCITRAL Working Group III (Online Dispute Resolution) Note by the Secretariat 28 February 2012, para 9.

low value and high volume? The problem with the concept is that it is an entirely subjective assessment relative to the wealth and priorities of the claimant. One claimant's low-value claim may be another claimant's high-value claim, especially in cross-border disputes involving countries with varying living standards. This then raises the question of how does due process fare under the rules. Arguably given the focus on low-value, high-volume cases, due process (perhaps correctly) has a low priority.

A first example for the lack of focus on due process is the provisions on the notification of the respondent about the claim brought against him or her. It is clearly fundamental in any dispute resolution system that a respondent is notified of any claims, so that the respondent has an opportunity to defend himself or herself. A lack of diligence in notification may mean that a decision by default is reached, depriving a defendant of the opportunity to defend himself/herself. Therefore, most dispute resolution systems require the claimant to exercise a degree of due diligence in serving the claim and notifying the respondent. Clearly in e-commerce, in a transaction concluded online over the internet, it is even more tricky to track a respondent compared to the offline world. Therefore, the UNCITRAL Procedural Rules simply state that: 'the electronic addresse(s) for communication of the notice by the ODR provider to the respondent shall be the addresse(s) of the respondent which has [have] been provided by the claimant'.[31] This does not impose any obligation on the claimant or the ODR provider to ensure that he or she gives the correct email address or carries out due diligence by, for example, conducting a Who-is search.[32] This may not be an issue in the majority of the 'run of the mill' e-commerce type cases, which the ODR rules are designed to cater for, but illustrates the 'rough justice' nature of the proposal.[33]

A second example of the lack of focus on due process is the provision ensuring that the time limits under the draft Procedural Rules are squeezed

---

[31] Article 3 (3) of the draft Procedural Rules A/CN9/WG III/WP112 UNCITRAL Working Group III (Online Dispute Resolution) Note by the Secretariat 28 February 2012.

[32] This concern has also been raised in A/CN9/744 UNCITRAL Report of Working Group III (Online Dispute Resolution) Meeting May 2012 para 74 and is reflected in draft Article 7 (6) obliging the neutral to ensure that the notification has been received by the respondent, para 116.

[33] This was further discussed in the latest UNCITRAL meeting in May 2012 adding a proposal that the address for notification should be the address agreed at the time when the ODR agreement is made – this may be a more sensible approach, see A/CN9/744 UNCITRAL Report of Working Group III (Online Dispute Resolution) Meeting May 2012, para 68.

tight: the respondent has seven calendar days to respond to the claim.[34] Compare this, by way of example, to an existing, national, highly successful (consumer) ODR system, namely the Dutch Consumer Complaints Boards, where the respondent has four weeks to prepare a defence.[35]

While internet communications technology may only take minutes or seconds to travel around the globe, the human effort involved in preparing a response and gathering relevant evidence may take significantly longer, particularly where the respondent is temporarily unavailable or needs to obtain information from a third party. Such short deadlines are therefore likely to lead to unfairness. The Working Group itself pointed this out and recommended that the deadlines be handled liberally to prevent unfairness to the respondent.[36]

The other side of the coin is, if payment intermediaries are used to enforce claims and therefore payments (for goods or services) have to be held in escrow during dispute resolution, then timeframes have to be quick in order to enable payment flows with which sellers can cope. This can be illustrated by a case where a buyer unjustly claims that goods are defective, if the seller does not receive payment until the dispute has been solved, and if the dispute resolution takes three months to complete, this may cause problems to the seller's cash-flow.

A third example of the lack of focus on due process in the draft Procedural Rules are the provisions on the language in which the dispute resolution is conducted. The rules currently provide that both the claimant and the respondent may select their preferred language, but crucially they do not provide what would happen if these choices do not match.[37] However, in practice this may not be an issue for the types of disputes envisaged, as the claim form and the response should be multilingual and automated.

---

34 Draft Procedural Rules Article 4 (3) A/CN9/WG III/WP112 UNCITRAL Working Group III (Online Dispute Resolution) Note by the Secretariat 28 February 2012.

35 Christopher Hodges, Iris Benöhr and Naomi Creutzfeldt-Banda (eds), *Consumer ADR in Europe* (Hart 2012) 142; likewise in the recent English case on the disclosure of the addresses of internet subscribers who are accused of copyright infringement by peer-to-peer file sharing to copyright owners the court held that to give the consumer respondent 14 days to respond to an allegation of copyright infringement is not sufficient and a breach of the principles of fair justice – Mr Justice Arnold suggested that a deadline for response of 28 days is more suitable, see para 29 of *Golden Eye International Ltd v Telefonica* [2012] EWHC 723 (Ch).

36 A/CN9/WG III/WP112 UNCITRAL Working Group III (Online Dispute Resolution) Note by the Secretariat 28 February 2012, para 31.

37 Ibid, para 38.

The UNCITRAL initiatives took as the starting point for their deliberations, eBay's dispute resolution procedure and the procedures developed by the major credit cards for Chargeback.[38] The Chargeback procedures of the major credit card providers rely on sets of automated, standardised and coded electronic messages between the credit card issuer and the merchant's bank, involving Chargeback reason codes such as 'merchandise defective', 'merchandise not as described', 'cardholder cancelled recurring transaction', 'goods or services not provided or not delivered'.[39]

For this reason the Working Group is considering whether to limit the grounds on which claims can be brought to certain typical heads such as those described in the previous paragraph and to limit the remedies available. It considered whether:

> Annex A should enumerate the grounds on which claims can be made and the available remedies. In a global cross-border environment for resolving low-value high-volume cases it may be necessary to limit the type of cases to simple fact-based claims and basic remedies, to avoid the risk of overloading the system with complex cases (. . .).[40]

The idea behind the proposals is that the resolution of such 'simple', run-of-the-mill disputes can be achieved with a high degree of automation, quickly, in an efficient manner and cost-effectively, using automated forms and responses for communicating the claim, the defence and related evidence. Over time, as the system learns from the experience of a large volume of cases, more complex situations can be built into the communication and dispute resolution patterns. However, this rough-justice approach is only justified in low-value, high-volume cases, hence it is all the more important that (i) the application of the rules is clearly defined, and (ii) redress to the courts for consumers is still possible (including collective action, where available), unless the consumer has agreed to arbitration *after* the dispute has arisen. In low-value, high-volume claims it is unlikely that consumers will regularly resort to litigation in any event.

UNCITRAL therefore takes a pragmatic approach to dispute resolution,

---

[38] S Co A/CN9/WG III/WP112 UNCITRAL Working Group III (Online Dispute Resolution) Note by the Secretariat 28 February 2012, para oper; Colin Rule and L Del Duca, 'From Lex Mercatoria to Online Dispute Resolution: Lessons From History in Building Cross-Border Redress Systems' (2011) 43 (3) *UCC Law Journal* 1–15, 13.

[39] See for example, MasterCard, Chargeback Guide 29 June 2012, para 3.6 available from http://www.mastercard.com/us/merchant/pdf/TB_CB_Manual.pdf.

[40] A/CN9/WG III/WP112 UNCITRAL Working Group III (Online Dispute Resolution) Note by the Secretariat 28 February 2012, para 36.

moving away from law harmonisation or approximation, and focusing on a cost-effective procedure for high-volume, low value disputes. It considers consumer protection and private international law of secondary importance, justifying this approach with the nature of disputes covered by the Proposal. Its weakness however is that its scope (high-volume, low value disputes) is ill defined and this raises the question whether the initiative will receive the trust of the parties. This can be contrasted with the approach in the EU, which will be discussed next.

IV. THE EUROPEAN UNION PROPOSALS

As part of the Digital Agenda announced in 2010[41] and the Single Market Act communicated in 2011[42] the Commission has taken action in this field, promulgating the twinned Proposals[43] for a Directive on ADR[44] and for a Regulation on ODR.[45]

The main thrust of the EU Proposals is twofold: (1) they aim to ensure that there is an ADR scheme, complying with certain minimum standards, for *each type* of B2C dispute in the EU regardless of the sector in which the business operates, and (2) they create an ODR platform for cross-border B2C e-commerce disputes to ensure that such disputes can be solved efficiently.

While the EU institutions (like UNCITRAL) regard ODR as an important mechanism for solving cross-border e-commerce disputes, the EU proposals have as their central focus and aim the improvement of consumer protection (unlike UNCITRAL). In fact, as will be seen from the following discussion, it can be argued that the EU Proposals have three main goals: (i) integrating the ADR mechanisms already existing in various Member States and making them function more effectively across

---

41 European Commission, 'A Digital Agenda for Europe' COM (2010) 245, 13.

42 European Commission, Commission Communication 'Single Market Act' COM (2011) 206, 9.

43 http://ec.europa.eu/consumers/redress_cons/adr_en.htm.

44 Directive 2013/11/EU of the European Parliament and of the Council of 21 May 2013 on alternative dispute resolution for consumer disputes and amending Regulation 2006/2004 and Directive 2009/22/EC (Directive on consumer ADR) OJ 2013 L165/63.

45 Regulation (EU) No 524/2013 of the European Parliament and of the Council of 21 May 2013 on alternative dispute resolution for consumer diusputes and amending Regulation 2006/2004 and Directive 2009/22/EC (Regulation on consumer ADR) OJ 2013 L165/1.

a border; (ii) strengthening the existing *consumer acquis* (ie, the harmonised EU consumer protection rules); and (iii) bolstering due process standards in consumer ODR. The idea is that increased consumer protection, effectiveness of ODR and high standards will increase trust in ODR (and ultimately e-commerce in the Internal Market).

The remainder of this chapter will focus solely on ODR and the new Regulation on ODR, as the ADR Proposal is discussed in detail in Chapter 10.

1. The ODR Platform and its Functions

The Regulation on ODR creates a pan-EU online platform for ODR.[46] Its main purpose is to allow a consumer in Member State A to file a dispute against an e-commerce business in Member State B, thus facilitating and automating the work currently carried out by the European Consumer Centres (ECCs). The network of ECCs enables a consumer to contact the ECC in his or her own Member State of residence in a complaint against a business established in another Member State. The consumer's local ECC then contacts the ECC in the business's Member State. The ECC in the business's Member State informs the consumer's ECC about ADR available and assists in negotiating a solution or bringing a claim. This process is labour intensive and will be greatly assisted by the ODR platform which will provide a gateway to all compliant ADR mechanisms in all Member States.

Thus the ODR Platform links the compliant ADR schemes in the EU through one single 'ADR hub' or single point of entry.[47] The online platform essentially will be a website and gateway to ADR in the Member States allowing consumers to file a claim through a multi-lingual complaint form and it will operate in all official languages. The platform will be operated by the European Commission at an implementation cost of Euro 4.586 million.[48]

In order to assist consumers with their claims, the ODR Regulation also establishes a network of 'ODR facilitators' in each Member State whose function is to facilitate communication and assist with the filing of claims, similar to the existing ECC-net and, in fact, the ODR Regulation envisages that this function may be carried out by the ECCs.[49] Furthermore, traders

---

46 Supra note 44.
47 Draft Article 5 (2).
48 COM (2011) 794 final, 5, see also Recital 14 and Draft Article 5(5).
49 Draft Article 6.

will be obliged to inform consumers about the ODR platform, in order to encourage its use.[50]

This platform will be designed for ADR (extra-judicial dispute resolution) for *contractual* B2C disputes arising from *cross-border* online transactions for the sale of goods or the provision of services.[51] Therefore the scope of the ODR Regulation is narrower than the ADR Directive in two respects: it only applies to e-commerce disputes and it is restricted to cross-border disputes, ie, it does not apply to domestic disputes. The term 'cross-border' is defined as meaning that the trader is established in one Member State and the consumer is resident in another at the time of the online order.[52] In other words the platform cannot be used if either the trader or the consumer are outside the EU. The Regulation provides in Article 9 (b) that the procedure should completed within 30 days from the start of the proceedings. It should be pointed out here that this is a completely unrealistic time limit.

The functioning of the ODR platform can be best understood by conceptualising its activities into five functions: (i) Clearing House Function, (ii) Referral Function, (iii) Transparency Function, (iv) Transfer Function, and (v) Enforcement Function.[53]

Before describing these functions it should be pointed out that one function which such a platform should fulfil is completely missing from the draft ODR Regulation. The ODR platform should provide a set of negotiation tools, enabling the parties to engage in negotiation without the intervention of a third party. While this may not be ADR (under the definition in the draft Directive) it would help the parties to settle early. Other authors have criticised the proposals for the omission of direct negotiation from the toolkit.[54] ADR (and ODR) works most efficiently as a tiered procedure, starting with negotiation, moving to conciliation and using arbitration/adjudication only in a minority of cases.[55]

The first function of the platform is the Clearing House Function,[56] which ensures that only ADR mechanisms which comply with the quality

---

[50] Draft Article 13 (1).

[51] Draft Article 2.

[52] Draft Article 4 (e).

[53] My terminology.

[54] David Thompson, 'Online Dispute Resolution Expansion in the EU' (2012) 22 (6) *Computers & Law* 31–4, 32; Pablo Cortes, 'Improving the EU's Proposals for Extra-judicial Consumer Redress' (2012) 23 (2) *Computers & Law* 26–9, 27–8.

[55] For example Pablo Cortes (supra note 54) 26–9, 28–9 and Mireze Philippe (supra note 13), 568.

[56] Draft Articles 2, 4 (h), 5 (3) (g), 5 (4).

and due process standards set out in the draft ADR Directive[57] are admitted to the ODR platform. In other words this function effectively sets minimum standards for ODR providers by only admitting those which comply.[58]

The Referral Function[59] means that the ODR platform provides a search engine enabling complainants to find a competent ADR/ODR provider which can deal with the dispute. Hence the ODR platform signposts the complainant to a competent ADR/ODR provider.

The Transparency Function[60] ensures that the complainant party is given all the information he or she needs in order to make an informed choice whether to use a particular ADR/ODR provider. This includes statistics on the outcome of complaints handled by the ADR/ODR provider in draft Article 5 (3) (i). As was discussed above, transparency about outcomes is important to encourage settlement and while statistics in themselves are not sufficient to achieve this, it is a step in the right direction.

The Transfer Function[61] means that the complainant can directly and conveniently file his or her claim (argument and evidence) online via the ODR platform which transfers the case to the chosen ADR/ODR provider. Draft Article 5 (3) (a) provides that the electronic complaint form can be completed online by the consumer on the ODR platform and draft Article 5 (3) (c) expressly provides that the ODR platform transfers the case to the ADR/ODR provider which the parties have agreed to use. Thus it is envisaged that the ODR platform be used for transmitting the complaint to the relevant ADR/ODR provider. As the Explanatory Memorandum to the ODR Regulation points out, this would encourage consumers to conduct the whole procedure online.[62]

What is at odds with common ADR practice is how the procedure is set out in the draft Regulation. It requires the consent of *both* parties before a case can be submitted to an ADR entity.[63] More usual is a procedure

---

57 Discussed above.

58 This has been proposed for a long time as an effective regulation of ODR; see for example Mireze Philippe, 'Where is Everyone Going with Online Dispute Resolution?' (2002) *International Business Law Journal* 167–210; Thomas Schultz, 'Does Online Dispute Resolution Need Governmental Intervention?' (2004) 6 *North Carolina Journal of Law & Technology* 71–106, 94–100; Julia Hörnle, 'Online Dispute Resolution in Business to Consumer E-commerce Transactions' (2002) 2 *JILT* http://www2.warwick.ac.uk/fac/soc/law/elj/jilt/2002_2/hornle.

59 Draft Articles 5 (3) (b) and 7 (3).

60 Draft Articles 5 (3) (b) (g) (h) and (i), 7(3) and 8 (3).

61 Articles 5 (3) (a), 5 (3) (c), 5 (3) (e), 7(1) and 8(1).

62 COM (2011) 749 final at 2.

63 Articles 5 (3) (c), 7 (3), 8 (2) (a)–(f).

whereby the claimant chooses the ADR provider and submits a claim and if the process is voluntary and the respondent is not obliged to take part because he or she is obliged to do so on the basis of a contractual agreement, the respondent will then decide whether to participate and file a response or not. The disadvantage of the procedure in draft Article 8 is that the disputant parties are unlikely to agree to use the same ADR provider, particularly if they are in different Member States. It is also at odds with existing ADR schemes.[64]

Finally, the Enforcement Function is the most difficult to delineate. My idea behind this function is that complaints data should be used not only for the purpose of *private* dispute resolution, but also for *public* law enforcement. As has already been pointed out, the draft ADR Directive in Article 14 provides for co-operation, and in particular mutual information exchange between ADR bodies and law enforcement authorities.[65] This is important, as systemic problems, such as widespread consumer scams or unfair commercial business practices, may need a response by public law enforcement authorities in addition to, or instead of, dispute resolution in individual cases. However, as has been pointed out above, if consumers' complaints do not reach beyond the ADR provider, law enforcement authorities do not find out about such systemic problems in time to deal with the problem, as the scammer may have taken his or her profits and disappeared. This information flow problem is worse in the international (and intra-European) cross-border context, where direct communication links only exist between the ECCs and between the ECC and *its national* consumer enforcement authority, but no direct communication link exists between an ECC and a foreign enforcement authority.

Therefore the information flow could be speeded up considerably if the consumer protection law enforcement authority in Member State B had direct access to consumer complaints originating from consumers in Member State A (against traders in Member State B). In my view therefore, the consumer protection law enforcement agencies of the Member States should have access to (some of) the complaints data on the ODR platform.

This chimes with the current tendency by scholars and regulators to regard consumer protection law enforcement as a graduated mix of public *and* private law instruments and mechanisms, including ADR and

---

64 See also Pablo Cortes (supra note 54) 26–9, 28.

65 Although it is questionable whether this provision will survive the negotiations in the European Council.

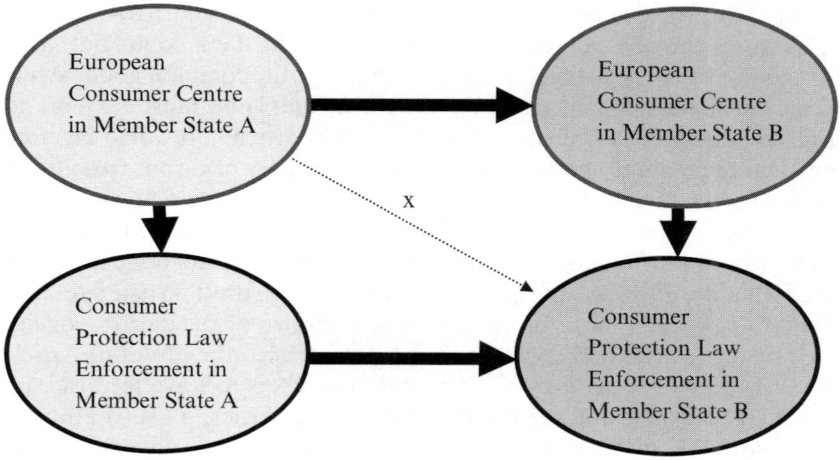

Figure 13.1 The ECC in Member State A cannot directly communicate with the consumer protection law enforcement authorities in Member State B

collective mechanisms.[66] If this perspective is correct (and in my opinion it is), this would mean that private and public law mechanisms need to be integrated more closely, certainly on the level of information exchange.

A precedent for such a platform/database can be found on an international basis in the shape of an initiative of the International Consumer Protection Enforcement Network (ICPEN). ICPEN is a co-operation network of consumer protection authorities of 42 member states, formed by the OECD (but not limited to OECD members) in 1992.[67] ICPEN encourages consumers to file complaints at econsumer.gov, which is the gateway to the Consumer Sentinel database operated by the US Federal Trade Commission (FTC). This database is made available to participating consumer protection authorities in order to detect large-scale scams and consumer fraud. However, the econsumer.gov initiative is limited in that

---

[66] See for example Willem van Boom and Marcus Loos, 'Effective Enforcement of Consumer Law in Europe' in Willem van Boom and Marcus Loos (eds) *Collective Enforcement of Consumer Law* (Europa Law Publishing 2007) 231–54, 250–1 and Christopher Hodges, 'Developing Approaches to Public and Private Enforcement in England and Wales' in Fabrizzio Cafaggi and Hans-W Micklitz, *New Frontiers of Consumer Protection* (Intersentia 2009) 151–69, 157; Chris Marsden *Internet Co-Regulation* (Cambridge University Press 2011) 221 et seq.

[67] http://icpen.org/for-consumer-experts/who-we-are/participants.

it *does not* provide consumer redress in the form of dispute resolution.[68] This raises the question of why consumers would file a complaint, as it would not be to their direct benefit, but only for the common good. While some consumers may be altruistic and file a complaint, most are not and as a consequence the facility is not very well known and it would be more efficient to combine complaints data for the purpose of dispute resolution *and* public enforcement.

Having discussed what the ODR platform *ought to* provide in terms of the enforcement function (normative assessment), it should be next considered what it *will provide* (positive law). According to draft Article 9 (c) (iii), the ADR provider must inform the ODR platform of the date of conclusion of the process and its result. Furthermore, according to draft Article 5 (3) (f) the ODR platform must enable consumers to leave feedback on the ADR provider and the ODR platform, and Article 5 (3) (i) provides that the ODR platform must provide statistics on the outcomes of the dispute resolution processes of each ADR provider. Therefore, the ODR platform must collect data on the outcomes of the ADR processes and consumer feedback and make statistics publicly available. This provides a degree of transparency on the kind of processes dealt with by each ADR provider and its effectiveness. However there is no provision whatsoever for complaints data being made available to consumer protection authorities for enforcement purposes and Article 11 of the Regulation limits this availability.

One argument *against* the making available of complaints data to the national consumer protection authorities of the Member States is that data protection law may impose restrictions on such disclosure. For this reason this chapter will analyse data protection law in this respect.

2. Integration of Private and Public Law Enforcement vs Data Protection Law

The Article 29 Working Party has examined[69] the operation of the Consumer Protection Cooperation System, which creates an information and data sharing system among national consumer protection enforcement authorities in the EU and was established by Regulation EC/2006/2004. In its Opinion it points to the risks created by a centralised database of consumer enforcement data: (i) that more data is shared than is strictly necessary for enforcement purposes, (ii) that data may remain longer in

[68] http://www.econsumer.gov/english/report/overview.shtm.

[69] WP 139 Opinion 6/2007 of 21 September 2007.

the database than is necessary, and (iii) that security may be an issue; as in any computer network, overall security is determined by the weakest link in the network.[70]

The European Charter of Human Rights has elevated data protection as a human right in Article 8 (1): 'Everyone has the right to the protection of personal data concerning him or her'. Article 8(2) stipulates that 'such data must be processed fairly for specified purposes and on the basis of consent of the person concerned or some other legitimate basis laid down by law.'[71] These principles are further fleshed out in the Data Protection Directive 1995/46/EC,[72] which sets out an administrative regime and places obligations on data controllers to comply with eight data protection principles.[73]

A data controller is the person who determines the purposes and means of processing.[74] The Directive only applies to the processing of personal data, which is data relating to an identified or identifiable natural person. An individual is identifiable if he or she can be identified, directly or indirectly, in particular by reference to an identification number or to one or more factors specific to his (or her) physical, physiological, mental, economic, cultural or social identity.[75]

The concept of personal data is complex and multi-faceted and hence cannot be discussed conclusively in the framework of this chapter. However, it should be pointed out that the influential Article 29 Working Party has interpreted the concept widely[76] and it includes, for example,

---

70 Ibid, at 4.

71 OJ 2007 C 303, at 1.

72 OJ No 281/31 of 23 November 1995.

73 This will be replaced by a Regulation and Directive in the future, see draft Regulation COM(2012) 11 final of 25 January 2012, http://ec.europa.eu/justice/data-protection/document/review2012/com_2012_11_en.pdf. The final shape of the outcome of data protection law is not yet clear, therefore this chapter will focus exclusively on the 1995 regime. For lack of space this discussion will not cover all eight principles, sensitive data or security issues, but will instead focus on the principles most relevant to this analysis. For a more detailed discussion of data protection law the reader is referred to Pablo Carey, *Data Protection: A Practical Guide to UK and EU Law* (3rd Edition, Oxford University Press 2009) and for the new Regulation see Ashley Winton and Neil Cohen, 'The General Data Protection Regulation' (2012) 18 (4) *Computer and Telecommunications Law Review* 97–101.

74 Art 2 (d) Directive 1995/46/EC.

75 Art 2 (a) of Directive 95/46/EC and Regulation 45/2001/EC.

76 See for example Article 29 Working Party Opinion WP 148 of 4 April 2008 (Search Engines) stating that log files of a person's search terms and IP addresses may constitute personal data, p 6 and WP 136 of 20 June 2005 (Concept of Personal Data), which mentions such examples as house prices or car service records when linked to an individual.

complaints data such as names and addresses, email addresses, photographs of persons, billing information and other data linked to an individual. The case law of the Court of Justice of the European Union also shows a similarly wide interpretation.

While it has been clear for a while that a person's name combined with other information such as their earnings[77] or their working conditions and hobbies[78] or their telephone number[79] counts as personal data, it is also clear that even without mentioning personal details such as names, information can count as personal data:

In *Case T-300/10 Internationaler Hilfsfond*, the Court held:

> Thus, in addition to names, it must be held that information concerning the professional or occupational activities of a person can also be regarded as personal data where, first, the information relates to the working conditions of the said persons and, second, the information is capable of indirectly identifying, where it can be related to a date or a precise calendar period, a physical person.[80]

So, if complaints data is capable of indirectly identifying an individual, it will be personal data.

Focusing on the disclosure of personal data to national consumer protection authorities, potential data controllers are: (i) the ODR platform provider making the data available (which is likely to be the European Commission[81]), (ii) the national Consumer Protection Authorities accessing and processing the data, (iii) the complainants when notifying the claim against the respondent, and (iv) the ADR provider feeding back data to the ODR platform.

The first principle is that personal data must be processed fairly and lawfully[82] and this means that one of the grounds of justification for processing listed in Article 7 of Directive 1996/46/EC must be applicable to the data controller's processing.[83] The ADR provider feeding the data back to the

---

[77] C-139/01 *Österreichischer Rundfunk and Others* [2003] ECR I-4989, para 64; Case C-73/07 *Markkinapörssi* [2008] ECR I-9831, para 35.

[78] Case C-101/01 *Bodil Lindqvist* [2003] ECR I-12971, para 24.

[79] Ibid.

[80] Available on Westlaw, para 117.

[81] The European Commission will be responsible for the ODR Platform, see draft Article 5 (1) of the ODR Regulation; the European Commission's data processing will be governed by Regulation EC/45/2001.

[82] Art 6 (1) Directive 1995/46/EC and Art 4 (1) (a) of Regulation 45/2001/EC.

[83] Member States may provide for exceptions to this principle when necessary to safeguard the prevention, detection, investigation and prosecution of criminal offences, Article 13 (d) of the Data Protection Directive 1995/46/EC, and Member

ODR platform would be covered by Article 7 (c), which is in compliance with a legal obligation imposed on the controller, here the obligations imposed by the ODR Regulation.[84] The complainant when notifying the claim and the respondent's contact details would be justified by Article 7 (f), which covers processing necessary for protecting the legitimate interests of the data controller (here the complainant) balanced against the data protection rights of the respondent (unless the claim against the respondent is vexatious, malicious or trivial). Article 7 (f) requires a proportionality analysis balancing the rights of the respondent with that of the complainant.[85] Weighing in favour of the complainant is his or her quest for justice, but to the extent that complaints data is irrelevant or excessive this would have to be anonymised and a complaint would also not be justified if it is an abuse of process.[86]

The national consumer protection authority would be justified by Article 7 (e), which states that processing is necessary for a task carried out in the public interest or in the exercise of official authority. Finally the ODR platform provider would have to rely on the complainant's consent under Article 7 (a)[87] and in respect of the respondent on Article 7 (e).[88]

The processing under Article 7 (e) would have to be necessary for the public interest, which involves weighing up the public interest with the data subject's interest. In this case it is justified as it is in the interest of justice that a complainant can file his or her claim and it is in the public interest to have effective enforcement of consumer protection law, provided that there is a presumption of innocence of the respondent (in relation to public law enforcement) and the data collected is not excessive.[89]

One of the most relevant principles here is the purpose limitation principle.[90] This means that if the processing of personal data is justified for

---

States have provided for such exceptions in their implementation legislation. To the extent that national consumer protection authorities have powers in respect of fraud and consumer scams this may mean that they do not need any further justification for processing the complaints data; see also Article 5 of Regulation EC/45/2000.

[84] See for example draft Art 9 (c); see also note 105 p 16.

[85] Case C-468/10 *ASNEF* of 24 November 2011, Westlaw para 40.

[86] See also Article 29 Working Party Opinion WP 158 of 11 February 2009, p 10.

[87] Art 5 (d) of Regulation EC/45/2001.

[88] Art 5 (a) or (b), see Article 29 Working Party Opinion WP 139 Opinion 6/2007 of 21 September 2007, 16.

[89] See also Case C-524/06 *Heinz Huber* [2008] ECR I-9705, para 66.

[90] In respect of the EU Commission Article 6 of Regulation EC/45/2001 allows for limited change of purpose.

a particular purpose (such as dispute resolution or consumer protection law enforcement[91]) it must not be used for another purpose (such as marketing). Furthermore, data subjects must be informed of the purposes of processing and again, personal data must not be processed for any other purpose. Hence it is important that both the complainant and the respondent are informed about all the recipients of the complaints data (including law enforcement authorities) and the purposes and extent of processing (dispute resolution *and* consumer protection enforcement).[92] The data controller must inform the data subject of his or her own accord.[93] If the ODR platform collects personal data about the respondent from the complainant in the claim, the ODR platform must inform the respondent about the processing in an individual notice (unless this defeats law enforcement), or through a privacy policy on the website.[94]

The data minimisation principle,[95] ie, the principle that a data controller must not process excessive data, ie, personal data which is not necessary for the purpose of processing, means that national consumer protection authorities should only have access to complaints data to the extent that this is necessary for their enforcement function.[96] In other words, access should be on a strict 'need to know' basis.[97] This could mean for example that they should only have access to complaints data if it relates to repeated complaints against the same supplier or complaints showing a similar pattern of infringement or complaints data which indicates fraud. Safeguards must be built into the system so that companies against whom consumers have complained are not automatically blacklisted as companies who are suspected of fraud and who are not to be trusted.[98]

Furthermore personal data must not be stored any longer than is needed for the purpose of processing[99] and data must be accurate and kept up to

---

[91] This would have to be specifically defined, see Article 29 Working Party Opinion WP 139 Opinion 6/2007 of 21 September 2007, 17.

[92] Arts 10 and 11 Directive 1995/46/EC.

[93] Case C-553/07 *Rijkeboer* [2009] ECR I-3889, para 68.

[94] See Art 11 and fn 122 and Recital 21 of the draft ODR Regulation.

[95] Art 6 (1) (c) Directive 1995/46/EC: 'data must be adequate, relevant and not excessive', for the purposes for which it is collected, Article 4 (c) Regulation EC/45/2001.

[96] In relation to the function of dispute resolution, see draft ODR Regulation Art 7 (6).

[97] Art 29 Working Party Opinion WP 139 Opinion 6/2007 of 21 September 2007, 20.

[98] Art 29 Working Party Opinion WP 139 Opinion 6/2007 of 21 September 2007, p 20.

[99] Art 6 (1) (e).

date.[100] Therefore, it is important to ensure that complaints data is deleted when no longer needed and after a certain time limit or immediately, when it becomes clear that a complaint is unfounded.[101]

In conclusion, therefore, the ODR platform could be opened up for data sharing with CPC consumer protection enforcement authorities, provided certain safeguards are built into the system, in order to ensure compliance with data protection law.

V. CONCLUSION

The EU Proposals on ADR and ODR are a great opportunity to provide improved redress for consumers in intra-EU, cross-border e-commerce disputes. As has been pointed out above, ODR has been discussed as a magic bullet for increasing cross-border redress in e-commerce for a long time and the EU Proposals will help to kick-start ODR in the EU. They are, therefore, of enormous significance to the EU *consumer acquis*, as theoretical rights under consumer protection laws which cannot be enforced before the courts because of the cost of (cross-border) litigation do little to enhance consumer protection by themselves.

The focus on consumer protection and minimum due process standards will mean that consumers trust ODR procedures and procedures are fair. However, it is far from clear yet how Member States eventually tasked with the implementation of the Proposals will deal with the costs of ODR. Since the procedures must be free or low cost for consumers this raises the question who will have to pay for the process? In times of recession, businesses and in particular small- and medium-sized businesses are unlikely to be willing or able to foot the bill and since the use of ODR under the Proposals is not binding on businesses they are unlikely to adopt it, unless there are clear commercial advantages for doing so. The EU Proposals are providing some incentives for businesses (such as having to inform consumers whether the business commits to ADR), but whether these are sufficient remains to be seen.

The main criticism of the ODR system envisaged in the EU Proposal relates to its effectiveness: co-operation with consumer protection law enforcement authorities is necessary to ensure effectiveness in the case of large-scale, low-value consumer scams. This would require disclosure of complaints data to law enforcement authorities and, given the data

---

100 Art 6 (1) (d).
101 See fn 105.

protection concerns, the Proposal has refrained from giving the consumer protection law enforcement authorities access to the ODR platform. This chapter has shown that such data protection compliant access can be achieved subject to appropriate safeguards.

The consumer protection focused approach of the EU can be contrasted with the UNCITRAL Proposals, which focus on encouraging ODR but impose fewer quality standards as their stated ambit is narrowed to run-of-the-mill, low-cost, high-volume cases. This may be more realistic and pragmatic, but may mean that consumers do not trust such procedures. This is even more pronounced by the fact that their scope is not clearly defined. This lack of definition is highly regrettable as this concept of low-cost, high-volume disputes is central to UNCITRAL's pragmatic approach. The draft Procedural Rules move away from due process, as was shown in the discussion above, and justify this with the argument that cross-border low-value and high-volume disputes cannot be solved other than through very efficient, highly automated, and hence, cost-effective procedures. It remains to be seem which of the two approaches, that of the EU or that of UNCITRAL will be more successful in encouraging ODR.

Index